RICHARD A. FREUND is Maurice Greenberg Professor of Jewish History and director of the Maurice Greenberg Center for Judaic Studies at the University of Hartford. He is the author of several books on biblical archaeology and has been featured on *Nova*, CNN, the History Channel, and the Discovery Channel.

DIGGING THROUGH
THE BIBLE

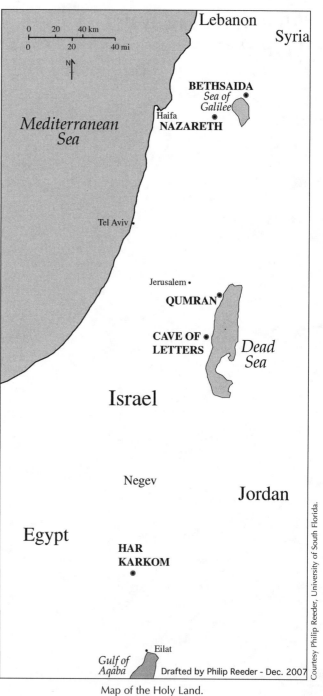

Map of the Holy Land.

DIGGING THROUGH THE BIBLE

Understanding Biblical People, Places, and Controversies through Archaeology

RICHARD A. FREUND

ROWMAN & LITTLEFIELD PUBLISHERS, INC

Lanham • Boulder • New York • Toronto • Plymouth, UK

JKM Library
1100 East 55th Street
Chicago, IL 60615

ROWMAN & LITTLEFIELD PUBLISHERS, INC.

Published in the United States of America
by Rowman & Littlefield Publishers, Inc.
A wholly owned subsidiary of The Rowman & Littlefield Publishing Group, Inc.
4501 Forbes Boulevard, Suite 200, Lanham, Maryland 20706
www.rowmanlittlefield.com

Estover Road
Plymouth PL6 7PY
United Kingdom

British Library Cataloguing in Publication Information Available

Library of Congress Cataloging-in-Publication Data

Freund, Richard A.
  Digging through the Bible : understanding biblical people, places, and controversies
through archaeology / Richard A. Freund.
      p. cm.
  Includes bibliographical references and index.
  ISBN-13: 978-0-7425-4644-8 (cloth : alk. paper)
  ISBN-10: 0-7425-4644-6 (cloth : alk. paper)
  eISBN-13: 978-0-7425-6349-0
  eISBN-10: 0-7425-6349-9
  1. Bible—Antiquities. 2. Bible—Evidences, authority, etc. 3. Bible—History of Biblical
events. 4. Palestine—History—To 70 A.D. I. Title.
  BS621.F736 2009
  220.9'3—dc22   2008018594

Printed in the United States of America

∞™ The paper used in this publication meets the minimum requirements of American
National Standard for Information Sciences—Permanence of Paper for Printed Library
Materials, ANSI/NISO Z39.48-1992.

contents

Chronology of Events   vii

Introduction   A CRASH COURSE IN BIBLICAL ARCHAEOLOGY   1

CHAPTER 1

The Search for Sinai: Archaeological Reflections on Moses,
the Exodus, and the Revelation at Mount Sinai   47

CHAPTER 2

Searching for King David and King Solomon and the
Ancient City of Jerusalem   107

CHAPTER 3

Searching for Jesus in Galilee and Babylonia   147

CHAPTER 4

Searching Her Stories: Women in Ancient Israel   183

CHAPTER 5

Searching for Synagogues: A Lost Synagogue Ritual
Recovered by Archaeology   225

CHAPTER 6

Searching for the Teacher of Righteousness at Qumran
and in the Dead Sea Scrolls   247

CHAPTER 7

Seeking Mary, Mother of Jesus; Miriam, Sister of Moses;
and the Well and Bathhouse of Nazareth   295

CHAPTER 8

The Search for Bar Kokhba: One "Biblical" Character
Who Was Found   323

Appendix   EXPLORING AN ARCHAEOLOGICAL SITE   337

Acknowledgments   341

Bibliography   349

Index   365

Chronology of Events

5500–4500 BCE	Neolithic (Stone) Age. Pottery was introduced
4500–3200 BCE	1. Chalcolithic (Copper) Age. Copper and flint used
	2. Writing developed in Mesopotamia
3000–2700 BCE	3. First and Second Dynasties of the Egyptian Kingdom
3200–1200 BCE	4. Bronze Age (Early, Middle and Late)
1200–586 BCE	5. Iron Age (From the Exodus from Egypt until the destruction of the First Temple by the Babylonians in 586 BCE)
586–539 BCE	Babylonian Exile
546–333 BCE	Persian Period
332–63 BCE	Greek Period
63 BCE–325 CE	Roman Period
325–638 CE	Byzantine Period
638–1096 CE	Early Muslim Period
1100–1200 CE	Crusader Period
1200–1517 CE	Later Muslim Period (Mamluke)
1517–1917 CE	Ottoman Empire Period
1917–1948 CE	British Mandate Period
1948–Present	Modern Israel Period

The History of Ancient, Medieval, and Modern Israel

1800–1500 BCE:	1. Matriarchs and Patriarchs
	2. Abraham in Mesopotamia
	3. 1648–1540 BCE Hyksos rule Egypt

1300–1200 BCE:	1. Traditional date of the Exodus from Egypt, Moses, Conquest of Canaan
	2. 1020–1000 BCE Saul, First King of Israel
1000–922 BCE:	1. United Monarchy of David and Solomon- Building of the First Temple by Solomon. After the death of Solomon, Israel is divided into two parts; Northern Kingdom of 10 tribes and 2.5 tribes in the Southern Kingdom (including Jerusalem).
	2. Rehoboam, King of Judah (Southern Kingdom) and Jeroboam I, King of Israel (Northern Kingdom)
600–500 BCE:	1. Fall of Jerusalem, Destruction of First (Solomonic) Temple by Babylonian King Nebuchadnezzar and Babylonian Exile of the Judeans to Babylon (587/6 BCE)
	2. Cyrus the Great's Persian Conquest of Babylon (539 BCE) and return of some exiles from Babylon
500–400 BCE:	1. Editing of Hebrew Bible
	2. Rebuilding of Temple completed 515 BCE
	3. Ezra arrives 445 CE
400–300 BCE:	1. Alexander the Great's (Greek) Conquests (333–323 BCE)
	2. After Alexander the Great's Death, divided Greek kingdom: Ptolemy I, Greek King of South (Egypt and Judea) and Seleucus, Greek King of North and Eastern (Babylon) part of the kingdom
300 BCE–70 CE:	1. Hellenistic/Greco-Roman Period
	2. Septuagint-Greek translation of the Hebrew Bible (250 BCE)
	3. Jerusalem becomes a Greek Seleucid city and renamed Antiochia (172 BCE)
	4. The Maccabean Revolt Against the Seleucid Greek King, Antiochus Epiphanes IV (164 BCE)
	5. Hasmonean Jewish Rulers: Judah Maccabee (166–160 BCE)
	6. John Hyrcanus I (135–104 BCE)

7. Alexandra Salome, Queen of Judea (76–67 BCE). In 63 BCE, Pompey, a general of the Roman army, marches into Jerusalem and establishes Roman hegemony in Judea

8. Herod the Great (37–4 BCE). The four sects of the Jews: Pharisees, Sadducees, Essenes, and Zealots contend for authority in Judaism. Essenes are associated with the site of Qumran on the Dead Sea. Zealots later become the nationalist, military party that urges freedom from the Romans

9. Jesus of Nazareth (6 BCE–30 CE?) and his movement of Apostles

10. Herod's Kingdom divided among his sons, Archeleus in Judea (4 BCE–6 CE), Antipas in Galilee (4 BCE–39 CE), and Philip in Ituraea and Golan 4 BCE–34 CE)

11. Roman Empire. Emperors of Rome: August Caesar (27 BCE–14 CE), Tiberius (14–37 CE) Nero (54–68 CE), Vespasian (69–79 CE), and Titus (79–81 CE)
Procurators ruling Judea, 6–41 CE: Pontius Pilate (26–36 CE)

12. Paul's travels and death (50–early 60s CE)

13. The First Jewish Revolt against Rome begins in Galilee (66–73 CE). The last battle is traditionally seen as the capture of Masada in 73 CE

14. Qumran is destroyed by Romans as they proceed to Jerusalem (68 CE). The Dead Sea Scrolls are placed in the caves around Qumran

15. Destruction of Second Temple of Jerusalem (70 CE). Rabbi Yohanan Ben Zakkai begins a new movement of Rabbis at Yavne

16. Written accounts of Jesus' life and teachings and the Writing of the New Testament (Gospels according to Mark–John: 70–100 CE?)

17. Rise of Rabbinic Judaism

18. Writings of Philo of Alexander (Egypt) and Josephus Flavius (Rome)

100–200 CE: 1. Rise of Christianity

2. The Sanhedrin and the Rabbinic academy meets in Yavne (70 CE), later moves to Lod, Usha, Shefaram, Bet Shearim, Sepphoris, and finally to Tiberias in Galilee after the Second Revolt against Rome, the Bar Kokhba Revolt. The Mishnah, the earliest Rabbinic corpus, is edited by Rabbi Judah HaNasi (the Prince) at Sepphoris

3. Trajan, Emperor of Rome (98–117 CE), conquers the Nabateans. Jewish Revolt in Babylon and Judea put down by Trajan's General Lucius Quietus (115 CE)

4. Hadrian, Emperor of Rome (117–138 CE)

5. The Second Revolt against Rome: The Bar Kokhba Rebellion (132–135 CE)

6. Beruriah, famous Rabbinic wife of Rabbi Meir

7. Babatha's documents in the Cave of Letters

8. The Temple of Jerusalem is converted into a Roman Temple, and the name of Jerusalem is changed by the Romans to *Aelia Capitolina*; the name of Judea and Israel, in general, is changed by the Romans to Palestine

200–300 CE:

1. Rav and Shemuel establish Babylonian Rabbinic academies

2. Political status given to Jews and Christians in parts of Roman Empire (212 CE: Edict of Caracalla, Emperor of Rome)

3. Rabbinic texts continue to be written/discussed: Midrash Aggadah (Rabbinic interpretations on the Bible) and Midrash Halachah (Rabbinic interpretations of legal sections of the first five books of the Bible), Tosefta, (Tannaim)

4. Palestinian Talmud: Beginning of commentary on the Mishnah

300–400 CE:

1. Roman Emperor, Constantine, becomes Christian

2. Church Council of Nicaea

3. Earliest documentation of settlements of Jews in Europe

	4. Palestine: The Sanhedrin and Rabbinic Academy is moved to Tiberias. In Babylon, Rabbinical Academies flourish (or are built) in Nehardea, Sura, Pumbedita, Netzivim, (Amoraim)
400–500 CE:	1. Jerusalem (sometimes called: Palestinian Talmud or PT) Talmud is completed in Tiberias 2. The Sack of Rome by the Visigoths (410) and the Vandals (455)
500–600 CE:	1. Babylonian Talmud (BT) is completed in Babylonia 2. The birth of Muhammad (570 CE)
638–1096:	1. Spread of Islam to Syria, Palestine, Egypt, Persia, North Africa, Asia Minor, and Spain. Koran is completed 2. Jewish Academies and synagogues in Babylon and North Africa and Western and Eastern Europe. The rise of the Geonim, name for Jewish Diaspora leadership 3. The Jerusalem Temple area is converted into two Mosques: The Dome of the Rock and the Al-Aqsa Mosque
1096–1200 CE:	1. The European Crusades (11th–12th century) Godfrey de Bouillon conquered Jerusalem in 1099; Latin Kingdom of Jerusalem established 2. The Jerusalem Temple Mount was converted into *Templum Domini* and the Dome of the Rock converted into a church with a cross on the Dome 3. 1187, Saladin (Salah al-Din) conquers Jerusalem, and Islamic rule in Israel continues
1250–1517 CE	1. Mamluke Muslims rule Egypt, Libya, Syria, Israel, and western Arabia 2. The reconquest of Spain by Christianity results in the "Expulsion" from Spain of hundreds of thousands of Muslims and Jews (1492)
1517–1917 CE:	Ottoman Muslims rule the region from Constantinople 1. Jerusalem was rewalled. It had been unwalled since 1219 2. Suleiman I (the Magnificent) built the present walls of the city (1537–1541 CE)

xii   CHRONOLOGY OF EVENTS

1900–2008 CE:
1. 1917: Establishment of British Mandate in Middle East and Israel
2. 1947: Discovery of the first Dead Sea Scrolls near Qumran
3. 1948: Establishment of the State of Israel
4. The five Qumran excavations conducted by Fr. Roland DeVaux (1951–1956)
5. 1960–1961: Cave of Letters is excavated by Yigael Yadin
6. Masada is excavated 1964–65 by Yigael Yadin
7. 1967: Six Day War-Israel takes the Golan, West Bank of Jordan River, Sinai, and East Jerusalem
8. 1987–Present: Bethsaida Excavations Project
9. 1999–2001: John and Carol Merrill Cave of Letters Project
10. 2001–2002: John and Carol Merrill Qumran excavations Project
11. Announcement of the final publication of the Dead Sea Scrolls (2002)
12. 2002–Present Mary's Well and Nazareth Excavations
13. 2003–Present Yavne Excavations Project
14. 1982–Present Har Karkom Excavations Project
15. 2005–2006 Burgos, Spain Excavations Project

Introduction: A Crash Course in Biblical Archaeology

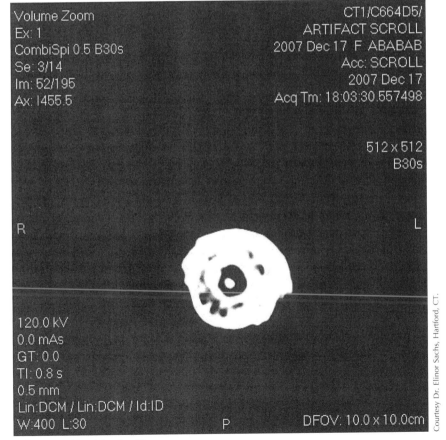

Volume Zoom
Ex: 1
CombiSpi 0.5 B30s
Se: 3/14
Im: 52/195
Ax: I455.5

CT1/C664D5/
ARTIFACT SCROLL
2007 Dec 17 F ABABAB
Acc: SCROLL
2007 Dec 17
Acq Tm: 18:03:30.557498

512 x 512
B30s

R

L

120.0 kV
0.0 mAs
GT: 0.0
TI: 0.8 s
0.5 mm
Lin:DCM / Lin:DCM / Id:ID
W:400 L:30

P

DFOV: 10.0 x 10.0cm

Is this a new Dead Sea Scroll?

Almost everyone has questions about the truth behind their religious beliefs at some point in their lives. Most of the time beliefs have to be taken on faith alone, but science and the scientific method have been used over the past few hundred years to understand traditionally held beliefs. One area of science, archaeology, offers us the rare chance to assess traditionally held views on the Bible. In *Digging through the Bible* I will explore what archaeological evidence proves (and doesn't prove) about some of the Bible's most intriguing people, places, and controversies. Drawing on my work at numerous excavations in the Holy Land, as well as my experience as both a rabbi and university professor, we will see how the coincidence of artifacts and literature enlighten us to the Bible and archaeology. Some of what I have to say is found in other books, but some of what I write here is not found in any other book; it is information that I have come to understand only from my experience in the field.

I have always been interested in answering questions with evidence. When I was a child, perhaps eight years old, I vividly remember an experience in Sunday School that caused me to embark on a lifelong search for physical evidence of the Exodus and its meaning. I was fascinated with the Tabernacle that the Israelites built in the desert after their Exodus from Egypt. This Tabernacle, or movable tent shrine, was unusual because of all of the materials necessary for its creation. I remember reading the section on the creation of the Tabernacle in the Book of Exodus 25, right after the story of the Exodus and was intrigued by one detail. In most translations of the story, it says that they decorated the Tabernacle with a covering of *dolphin skins*. I asked my teacher: "Mr. Stanger, where did these former slaves from Egypt in the middle of the Sinai desert get the dolphin skins from?" It was a moment that forever changed my thought process. The teacher turned to me with a look that reminded me of a deer caught in the headlights and did not know what to respond. He understood that the dolphin skins were an exotic item for former Egyptian slaves to have had with them as they left Egypt, and he realized that there were no *Wal-Marts* in the middle of the Sinai Desert, but he also understood a child's need for a practical and reasonable solution to a simple question. His answer came after a short silence. He replied: "God can provide anything, even in the desert. Why not dolphin skins?" For some of the children in the Hebrew School it was a reasonable answer. But I was not satisfied with the answer. It put me on a lifelong search for more evidence. Archaeology has provided some of that evidence, offered a method for study, and given me a respect for what material culture can and cannot do in understanding an ancient literature like the Bible.

I am interested as a professor of ancient history in a college devoted to arts and sciences to know how we know what we think we know about the Bible and the world. I think knowing how we know what we know (and what we do not know) is one of those fundamental questions of the university that I have had to deal with in working in biblical archaeology. Before the present period, we knew what we knew from traditional sources of wisdom that did not have to be challenged. Traditional wisdom about the world had to be accepted by people because it was a part of their religious and often national identity. With the rise of the modern nation-state and academic disciplines in unaffiliated universities that were unfettered by the confines of ancient traditional wisdom, many of the dogmas that were a part of religion and science were questioned. The modern study of archaeology and the Bible has been rocked by questions that challenge generations of traditional knowledge. What was it that made the *Da Vinci Code* so provocative? Even as fiction it was supposedly based upon information that had been discovered in the past sixty years and which challenged traditional wisdom about the nature of Jesus and Mary Magdalene. The recent publication and fascination with the nearly eighteen-hundred-year-old Gnostic *Judas Gospel,* which was revealed to the public in the same year as the *Da Vinci Code* movie, raises a similar question. What if Judas as depicted in the canonical gospels was different from the historical Judas? A spectacular archaeological discovery at Nag Hammadi in the desert of Egypt just over sixty years ago brought these "alternative" gospels to light, and they continue to challenge our traditional understandings of the canonical biblical accounts. In many ways, the *Da Vinci Code* controversy and the Judas Gospel and many other issues that I will be presenting in this book are asking the same question. What if all of the major assumptions about the people and places of the Bible are just elaborate deceptions that have gained credibility with time but they were not true even in the period in which they were written down? Would it make a difference? I think so.

What Is the Bible?

It was with these provocative questions in mind that *Digging Through The Bible* was born. This book is about the people, places, and controversies from the Hebrew Bible (Old Testament), New Testament, and even books that did not make it into the canon of the Bible but were clearly intended to be considered holy in antiquity, and how archaeology has helped us better understand these people, places, and controversies. The idea of biblical figures and their continuation throughout and beyond the scope of the

Bible is also a major focus in the book. A biblical figure has a trajectory that goes beyond the scope of just the Bible. Unlike many of my colleagues, I value biblical commentaries and their interpretations as providing an insight into the text. Sometimes the insight is far afield from the ancient "original" meaning of the text, but sometimes it contains the seed of an ancient tradition that we could not recover but for this medieval kernel of information. When compared with archaeological and other ancient comparative materials, the biblical commentators often seem out of place and clearly off the mark, but sometimes they preserve an understanding of the text that explains the archaeology and comparative materials better than the ancient materials explain themselves.

I discovered just how important traditional common wisdom about an individual can be when I excavated a site that has become associated with John the Baptist. I became known for a time as the person who "discovered" the site of the burial of John the Baptist, and although I never said that I had discovered John the Baptist (as you will read in this book, it was the result of a well-intentioned press release by my university that just got out of control), it was interesting just how important it was to people on the street. To this day I meet people and they say: "Oh, yeah, I know you, you are the person who discovered John the Baptist!" The next question they asked was: "Did you discover his head with the body?" This is not a simple question and answer as you shall see. I began investigating the traditions surrounding John the Baptist and discovered that John the Baptist's head and body are located by many postbiblical traditions in many different locations around the world, and so we had become (not intentionally!) another one of these postbiblical traditions.

When speaking in front of teachers, students, and community people at universities, churches, synagogues, and civic organizations, I have heard an increasing number of questions about what evidence (outside of the Bible) exists to authenticate the stories of the Bible. Often what this question misses is just how much more we know today about how and why the Bible was written that affects our understanding of biblical traditions. I have noticed that people's general knowledge about the Bible has decreased in the past generation, but their curiosity about the biblical places and people has grown in this same period. I have found that people really want to know what can be proven about those places and people. So I set out to see for myself what could be discovered using archaeology and a variety of other techniques that historians use to evaluate traditional, as well as conventional wisdom. Since I have been working in the discovery of sites that are mentioned in the New Testament, I found that people wanted to know what the evidence suggests about Jesus, Joseph, Mary, Mary Magdalene, John the Baptist, Paul, the Apostles, Herod the Great, and a host of others. Mary, Mother of Jesus, for example, appears in so many places throughout the world, I started to track her throughout these different places from Israel, Europe, and Latin and North America. In addition, I have found that interest in biblical figures such as Abraham, Moses, King David, Solomon, and others was so intense that a book that tracked what we know from archaeology and comparative literature would be valued by the public. Also, many other significant people (both men and women) appear in the Bible, about whom we do have real historical information. Some of these people are perhaps not as famous as Abraham, Moses, King David, Jesus, and John the Baptist, but what we know about them tells us something about the ancient period and how people wrote about people in the ancient period. Some of the people included in this book will be individuals that you will recognize; others you will not. All of these figures contribute to what we know about people, places, and events in the Bible.

What I mean by the Bible is slightly different than what is common wisdom. I include in my definition of the "Bible" six very different parts:

1. *The Hebrew Bible:* including the thirty-nine books that Jews call the *Tanach* and Christians call the "Old Testament."
2. *The Apocrypha and Pseudepigrapha of the Hebrew Bible:* depending on the different collections, could include as many as thirty to forty more books that were written down in the Hellenistic-Roman periods.
3. *The New Testament (or Greek/Christian Bible):* including the twenty-seven canonized books that Christians call the New Testament.
4. *The New Testament Apocrypha and early Christian traditions* in the forms of commentaries: including what is commonly called the Gnostic Gospels and as many as thirty different works that were written down from the third century CE through the early Middle Ages but which preserve early Church traditions about biblical figures and places.
5. *The Rabbinic and Jewish (pre-Rabbinic) writings:* including the writings of Josephus, Philo, Mishnah, the Talmudim, Midrash, and even early medieval Rabbinic Bible commentaries that preserve information about biblical figures and places.
6. *The Koranic and Islamic "versions" of biblical stories:* In the Koran and the Hadith (and even Islamic commentators and historians such as Muhammad ibn Jarir al-Tabari in the ninth and tenth century CE,

for example) traditions are found that preserve ancient knowledge about people and places in the Bible.

The Critical Study of the Hebrew Bible

The Bible is greater than the sum total of the individuals and places mentioned in it. There was a sense up until the Middle Ages that ongoing revelation empowered writers even in the medieval period to continue to "write" about biblical figures as if these writings were original to the Bible. Our knowledge of these places and people is also greater than the sum total of the parts of the Bible that mention these places and people. Also, the Bible is not a book of literature, poetry, liturgy, theology, history, religion, science, or even a book in the conventional sense of the word. It is an *anthology* that was written down over a long period of time by multiple authors and edited together as if it were a single book. Anyone can instinctively see that the composition contains many books that say they were written by different people. A part is called the *Book of Isaiah* because it is seen to be the writing of a prophet Isaiah, but not the prophet Jeremiah. The *Book of Jeremiah* was not written by Ezekiel, but by Jeremiah (or better by his scribe, Baruch ben Neriah), etc.

But Bible scholars for the past couple of hundred years have also come to another, broader conclusion about the writing of the Bible. They have unraveled a secret of ancient writing that is demonstrated throughout the Bible. Multiple authors wrote down diverse oral traditions even from the most ancient period of the Bible, and those multiple traditions and writings were edited into what we today call the Bible. Scholars generally call this the "documentary hypothesis" because it assumes that ancient documents were edited together into what we call the Bible. That is one of the reasons why one cannot easily read the Bible from Genesis to Deuteronomy. It jumps around because different traditions were edited together not so much for easy reading but to provide different traditions the opportunity to be presented.

This edited Bible finally reached a form of completion in the Persian period (fifth to fourth century BCE). Professor Richard E. Friedman, the author of *Who Wrote the Bible?*, and other source critics have demonstrated that the Bible is a complex document constructed from different and ancient oral and/or short, written versions or accounts that were edited/redacted together following major historical events, such as wars or changes in leadership, in the biblical period. Historians in many fields have recognized this simple rule of thumb for written documents from the ancient through the premodern periods. Writing was not the preferred mode of communication of the traditions and ideas for ancient peoples. For the vast majority of ancient peoples, oral transmission was the preferred mode of communication and writing was used to preserve unique customs and ideas of a people at crucial moments in the history of a people. Writing required specialized talents and materials and until the advent of the printing press, was so unusual that often only a few exemplars of a written work would circulate at any given moment. In short, the creation of what we know as a written Bible would have required an impetus to take the oral tradition and commit it to writing. The impetus that most literary historians have identified was the preservation of a unique event or to save the tradition from extinction. The biblical writing process is linked to the most significant events in the history of the Israelites and the Judeans.

These historical events were so significant that the leaders entrusted with the oral traditions decided to write them down. Following cataclysmic episodes in the biblical period (the schism between the Ten Northern Tribes and the Southern Tribes, the conquest of the ten northern tribes, the destruction of Judea and the Temple of Jerusalem, etc.), many of these leaders were convinced that if the oral traditions were not written down in their own time periods, the entire history might be forgotten. This process of moving the oral biblical traditions to a written form parallels the later but similar process for the redaction/editing of Rabbinic texts. We are lucky that the Rabbis actually relate the reasons why they wrote down their oral traditions. The Rabbis feared that the Jewish people (and the oral traditions that they possessed) would not survive and decided to write down the oral traditions rather than having them be forgotten. The moving of oral Rabbinic traditions to a written form took place in the third century CE, and we can extrapolate from the experience of the Rabbis that a similar fear may have motivated the Gospel writers in the first century CE and even earlier the writers of the Hebrew Bible. Modern New Testament scholars think that all of the canonical Gospels (Matthew, Mark, Luke, and John) were written down in the late first century CE, following the destruction of the Temple (in 70 CE) and following the dispersion of the Jewish people from Jerusalem and Judea. In the third century CE, following two devastating wars of the Jews against the Romans (First Revolt against Rome 66–73 CE and the Second Revolt against Rome 132–135 CE), the Rabbis concluded that the earliest oral parts of the Jewish tradition (the Mishnah) needed to be written down and properly arranged so that the story of the Jewish people and their laws would not be forgotten.

We know who did this Rabbinic redaction because the process is written about by the Rabbis themselves. Rabbi Yehudah HaNasi finished the first redaction of the earliest group of traditions, the Mishnah, in the third century. But it is clear from the Rabbinic process that many other periods of redaction and editing of these traditions followed for the next three hundred years. New and old traditions continued to be fused into the literature that became the Talmud. This is very similar to the pattern of editing and redaction that the Bible followed. Many modern biblical scholars determined that the Bible was written down over a long stretch of time in critical periods of Israelite/Jewish history, and these critical periods also correspond to archaeological information that excavators have been digging up for more than a century in the Land of Israel. Since I will be relying on the reader to know these events and periods I have summarized them here.

I. The First Period of Biblical Writing
The United Kingdom: 1000 BCE–922 BCE

Since we know from archaeology that the earliest of the few discoveries containing ancient Hebrew writing only date from around the year 1000 BCE, this must be considered the first period of Israelite writing activity that corresponds to the new situation that emerged in the period of the United Kingdom of David. For the first time in the ancient history of the people of Israel, under King David and later his son, Solomon, the United Kingdom of Israel afforded the people the opportunity to have a level of security and stability that invited this writing down of the national epic in their own language. Understanding that the writing was done in this period is important. This United Kingdom was certainly a significant event for the Israelite nation and would have emboldened Israelite writers to see their story, the story of the people of Israel, as unique and worthy of writing down in their own language. Unfortunately, the wealth and optimism of the period of David and Solomon in the southern region of Judea and its capital, Jerusalem, also caused the northern tribes to want their own capital and Temples. This new development prompted the second period of biblical writing, the Great Schism.

II. The Second Period of Biblical Writing
The Great Schism: 922 BCE–722 BCE

The first period of biblical writing was very short and probably produced a small selection of the major biblical accounts we recognize today. The second period of biblical writing was longer and was ushered in by an event that pitted the northern tribes against the southern tribes of Israel in a "competition" for the loyalty of the followers of the God of Israel. The

Ten Northern Tribes of Ancient Israel "split" from the United Kingdom of King David after the death of Solomon. They built their own capital and Temples to suit the northern population and ultimately created and wrote down traditions that related to their own developing views of the Israelite God. This was similar to the great schism that gripped the Roman Catholic Church in the early Middle Ages when Eastern Orthodoxy emerged in the East leaving Roman Catholicism in the West and the American Civil War in which the United States were divided into the Union in the North and the Confederacy of States in the South. The Ten Northern Tribes seceded from their union with the Southern Tribes of the United Kingdom of David after Solomon's death and his son Rehoboam's succession in approximately 922 BCE, forming their own separate nation in northern Israel. The northern tribes had their own capital, kings, prophets and priests, and even their own holy Temples and shrines that were different from the Southern tribes that remained with Jerusalem and the Aaronid priesthood. Bible scholars assume that the Northern and Southern Kingdoms ("Israel" and "Judah," respectively) had their own separate versions of the original written documents as their own "Torah." It is not clear if this was a written document or still maintained in oral fashion, but in this model, both Judah and Israel each had a Torah they venerated. Similar to the Confederacy that had the Constitution and Declaration of Independence and the Roman Catholic Church and Eastern Orthodox Church that shared the New Testament and early Church documents, the Northern and Southern Tribes shared the earliest versions of the Bible, but they had different traditions about people and places in the Land of Israel. The new country of "Israel" that emerged in 922 BCE (sometimes called the Northern Kingdom of Israel), is distinguished from the earlier "Israel" that lasted from the time the Israelites came into the Land of Israel from the "Exodus" from Egypt (in the time of Joshua, thirteenth century BCE) until the dissolution of the Kingdom of David and Solomon in approximately 922 BCE.

In dividing the House of David (or the United Kingdom of David) into two parts, the Northern Kingdom (of ten tribes) retained the title: "Israel" and the Southern Kingdom was designated by the largest tribe of the region, "Judah." Scholars hypothesize that if this division had continued throughout time without further changes, there would be today two very different groups of people that would have had two different versions of the Pentateuch (called by Jews the Torah or the first five books of the Bible): one group would have been Israelites and the other called Judeans. During this entire two-hundred-year period of separation, they both developed laws, stories, and traditions that they closely related to the same nucleus of patriarch and matriarch traditions that the Northern Tribes shared with the Southern Tribes. Similar to the schism that produced Eastern Orthodoxy and Roman Catholicism, two forms of Christianity that both claimed access to the same ancient origins and preserved separate but equally important traditions, the Northern and Southern Kingdoms represent separate but equally authentic brands of ancient Israelite faith and life. Most people have never conceived of the Bible as a "compromise" document, a book that preserves the traditions of the Israelites and the Judeans with substantially more material from the Judeans because they survived the turmoil of antiquity, while the Northern Tribes did not. For those who know United States history, it is comparable to how the traditions of the Union in the North and the Confederacy in the South were somehow merged in the Reconstruction process following the Civil War. The leaders, ideas, and traditions of the South played a minority role in the history of the United States as it was written after the Civil War.

After the death of King Solomon, his son, Rehoboam, was unable to keep the United Kingdom together. In approximately 922 BCE, the two kingdoms became separate kingdoms. Some two hundred years later, in approximately 722 BCE, the Northern Kingdom was destroyed by the Assyrian Empire and the Israelites exiled from their land. The exiles were either forcibly moved to Assyria in what is modern-day Iraq or some drifted southward to merge with the Judeans and relatives who may have still lived in the south. In the period following the Assyrian Exile, the two main versions of the Bible, one that had developed in the north and one that had developed in the south, were merged into one text. The original writers and the texts they represented were designated by scholars as "J" (southern) and "E" (northern). The southern writer was called "J" for convenience sake by scholars because this writer predominantly used the title of the Divine in his writing as "Jehohvah," while the northern writer was called "E" because this writer predominantly used the title of the Divine in his writing as "Elohim."

III. The Third Period of Biblical Writing: 722 BCE–586 BCE

Although 922 BCE, the time of the *Great Schism* is very important, the period following the destruction of the Northern Kingdom, 722–721 BCE is a critical date for the redaction/editing of the text. It was a cataclysmic event that must have left many people living in the south with the feeling that the end of all Israelite/Judean religion was at hand. The refugees from the north who made it to the south brought with them their most precious legacy—the Torah of the north. This is the period of the "Assyrian Exile" of the northern Ten Tribes of Israel and the "survivors" who made it to the south who were a small minority among the southerners. The vast majority of northern tribes were sent into the vast parts of the Assyrian Empire, and there are peoples as far away as China, India, and Afghanistan who claim to be from one of the lost Ten Tribes of Ancient Israel. The northern tribe survivors ("E") brought their "Bible" with them from the north, and all of their traditions were merged with the traditions of the south ("J") into one text that became a Bible. But during this period, a third layer of literary activity began and complemented the recombination with these J/E traditions. This third layer of literary activity is from a group that heretofore had closely guarded their own traditions. Their view of what was now "Judahism" focused on the religious ideas that they, the priests, had carefully maintained.

It is possible to see differences between the J and the E designated texts, not only on the basis of the Divine names but also on issues related to religion and politics. Naturally, E focused primarily on the life of northern Israel and J focused on in events in southern Israel. J and E were probably religious and political leaders, but they were not the most elite group of Judea. The most elite group who carefully guarded their traditions and were responsible for the third literary wave of biblical writing were the Priests in Jerusalem.

The Priests in Jerusalem, starting from the time of King Solomon, were a special and influential group of families that closely guarded their dynastic rule. It is not surprising, therefore, that Bible scholars have found within the text of the Bible a very clear literary stratum that was written by the Priests. The priestly writer (*Kohanim*-Aaronids) designated by scholars as "P" wrote after 722 BCE, when a written, combined J/E text may have begun circulating, and before 586 BCE, the date of the destruction of the Temple of Jerusalem, when the central bastions of the power of the priesthood were suddenly removed. P appeared not long after the composition of the combined J/E text as a counterbalance to the stories being told by the J and E traditions that they did not control. P's version is an alternative view of the Bible to that of J and E, and one can easily see that the P writer is a different type of writer than the J and E writers. He uses lots of numbers, dates, and ages and has fewer puns and literary devices, such as irony, that appear in J and E texts. P is primarily interested in items related to priesthood, rituals, and promoting *only* priestly issues of sacrifices and priestly authority sometimes at the expense of other authority figures of the Bible from the Patriarchs and even before the time of the Patriarchs, such as Cain and Abel and Noah. Sacrifices in the Bible done by anyone other than the Aaronid priesthood were seen as invalid, and therefore the P text does not contain these narratives. The P writer probably felt that anyone else described as performing ritual sacrifices in the Bible undermined the priestly authority.

So when we read about the sacrifices of Cain, Abel, Noah, Abraham, Isaac, and Jacob, for example, even before there was a priesthood according to the final story line of the Bible, you can tell immediately that these are narratives that have been preserved by non-priests (J/E texts). But P also had a variety of theological differences with the rest of the people. In P's text the priest was the ultimate intermediary before God through the sacrificial ritual. It was probably hard for P to even hear the episodes about so many non-priests who had conversations with God. P's text does not have conversations between humans, and P's image of the Divine reveals a very impersonal and cosmic ruler in comparison with the writing of J/E. P's writings do not generally contain the concept of "mercy" for example, but "justice" appears many times, meted out by God's official representatives, the priests. No miraculous (breaking of Divine "nature") events occur that involve *talking animals* in the texts of P (J and E have talking snakes and donkeys), no angels (Divine messengers), no dream accounts (Divine dreams such as in the Joseph story), no prophets (except Aaron, of course). The holy four letter (tetragrammaton) name of the ancient God of Israel, YHVH is not the name of choice in the writings of P; Elohim is used because YHVH was seen as a "semi-secret" name used only by the High Priest on Yom Kippur (the holiest day of the year) in the Temple in the Holy of Holies to maintain its holy status.

IV. The Fourth Period of Biblical Writing: 640 BCE–586 BCE

The next major period of Biblical writing occurred in the period beginning with the rule of King Josiah in Jerusalem in 640–609 BCE and continuing up until the destruction of Jerusalem and the Babylonian Exile in 586 BCE. During this period many reforms took place, most of which were motivated by King Josiah in Jerusalem, probably through the intervention of a major literary prophet like Jeremiah. In this period, we have the writing of another version of the national epic, this time by a writer who has the advantage of knowledge of many more traditions, knows the traditions of J/E and P but has a history of events that were different from the other writers. This document became known by scholars as "D" because it starts in **D**euteronomy with a total recapitulation of all of the major ancient history from Egypt back to Israel. D is a self-contained literary unit that continues to include all of the events from the entrance into the Land of Israel at the end of the Exodus, the history of the Judges, the early Prophets and the beginnings of the kingship narratives. This was a totally different corpus of information probably maintained by the royal court scribes and the scribes used by the official prophetic groups that the court would consult. While the Priests would have their own scribes, the Court of the king would have its own scribes as well.

The court history came to a halting stop at the end of this period with the most cataclysmic event of biblical times—the destruction of Jerusalem in 586 BCE. The Babylonian Empire, which destroyed not only the Temple and the priesthood and exiled the people of Judah to Babylonia, but also destroyed the tradition of kingship among the Jews. The reforms of King Josiah may have spawned the court history version of ancient history of Israel to be written down for the first time just before the impending Babylonian Exile (ten years before the Exile—597 BCE—the Babylonians had already made their direction known). The Babylonian Exile lasted only about fifty years, but it sparked a new final editorial process that brought all of the disparate traditions together into a literary work that became something that was much closer to what we call today the Torah.

V. The Fifth and Final Period of Biblical Writing: 536–519 BCE and into the Fifth Century BCE

With the rise of the Persian Empire, especially Cyrus the Great, who basically liberated the exiles according to the Bible, the Judean exiles could choose to stay in Babylonia and throughout the Persian Empire or return to Israel. Many stayed in Persia, recorded in books such as Daniel and Esther, which are set in the Persian Empire, while others returned to their home country. The "Return to Zion" is the time beginning under the leadership of the Aaronids, who took remnants of the Judeans back to Jerusalem, reestablished the Temple, and then ritualized the reading of the Bible that they finished redacting during this period. Many scholars consider Ezra the Priest, also called "the Scribe" for his literary activity, in the fifth century BCE as the final **R**edactor or Editor, but he is referred to by modern Bible scholars who refer to him as "R."

The Maximalist-Minimalist Debate

As a result of serious biblical scholarship as well as archaeological discoveries made over the past 150 years, a new brand of skepticism has swept the world of both Bible scholars and archaeologists, especially in the past two decades. It is usually referred to as the "Maximalist-Minimalist" Debate.

It is hard to pinpoint when it began. It is my opinion that a new form of archaeological research in the 1960s and 1970s, which became known as the "New Archaeology," revisited old archaeological suppositions, and as a result of this "revisit," a new form of skepticism was born just as critically trained Bible scholars began to use these new archaeological conclusions in their own studies. The "New Archaeology" separated archaeology almost entirely from texts of any kind and tried to answer small and detailed questions without any need to solve biblical questions. Academic training of archaeologists changed as well with few archaeologists being trained in the scientific study of the Bible. This led to new and very significant conclusions about major archaeological questions all over the world, but most profoundly in Israel and Egypt.

Suddenly major sections of the Torah, the first five books of the Bible, came under assault. The Patriarchal traditions as well as the Exodus account in the first two books of the Bible were rendered invalid questions for archaeology. At the same time that the archaeology of Israel and Egypt were disconnected from the Bible, archaeological work in the 1970s and 1980s, for example, in Sinai and Egypt made many new discoveries but little that confirmed the biblical story. In this same period, scientific questions arose about material culture in ancient cities in Israel and whether any of these finds could demonstrate a major influx of immigrants in the Iron Age (as the Bible states). The "New Archaeology" while attempting to remove itself from any textual questions, brought into question the entire written record from the books of Joshua, Judges, and I and II Samuel. This fed the biblical scholarship of the 1980s and 1990s that raised questions about the entire Hebrew Bible. These questions led both archaeologists and Bible scholars to square off into two major camps by the 1990s. Groups of Maximalists and Minimalists developed as these issues were discussed in both popular and academic publications. *Fundamentalist Maximalists* held that every single word in the Bible was true and used archaeological discoveries only when it bolstered their case. The *Non-Fundamentalist Maximalists* extrapolated from every single archaeological discovery an argument in favor of the authenticity of larger and larger parts of the Bible and used some of the critical Bible study information. On the other side, the Minimalists insisted that every single archaeological discovery could and should be evaluated only as providing information about itself and that these discoveries could not solve any real larger, biblical questions.

In the archaeological camp are some extreme revisionists with an anti-Zionist agenda who questioned the actual collection of archaeological data by Israeli archaeologists and extreme revisionists among biblical scholars who

have used Minimalist assumptions being propagated by some archaeologists to build theories for a very late date for the Bible's composition. The
patriarchs and matriarchs, the Egyptian captivity and Exodus, the Judges
and early prophets, the kings and queens are all the result of a late Persian-
Hellenistic period of creativity and have little or no ancient antecedent.

The divide between these two camps, Maximalists and Minimalists,
began to manifest itself in articles, professional meetings, television documentaries, and then in books. Stances varied from scholars of the "New
Archaeology" and the new critical Bible scholars who staked claims to the
Maximalist and Minimalist positions. One of the most venerated scholars
of the "New Archaeology," William Dever, who was one of the first to
begin the early reexamination of the biblical claims, has himself come
under fire as he has staked out a more moderate Minimalist-Maximalist
stance. I define myself as a Minimalist-Maximalist. I really do see each
discovery as giving us only information about itself, but because extrapolation is a part of the modern scientific method we must see how every
archaeological discovery affects the whole study of the Bible. My study of
the Bible includes critical Bible studies, but it does not end with them. I
have colleagues who work with archaeology derived from the Americas
and have texts written in various time periods that are critically studied
and constantly used to inform the archaeologists' understanding of Mayan,
Aztec, and Incan discoveries. Similarly, all discoveries in Egypt are read in
light of Egyptian texts that are critical studies and date from different time
periods, so you can see that this kind of Maximalist-Minimalist debate is
not unique to the field of Biblical archaeology, but a common source of
conflict across areas of study.

So Where Do We Go from Here?

I will not enter into the discussion of whether the Bible is divinely in-
spired, revealed, or directly dictated to humans. Much the same way that
the theory of evolution can only begin from the most ancient forms of life
and trace it from there to higher forms of life without really speculating on
what came before these forms of life, so too the biblical text can be traced
back to its textual antecedents and I will not speculate on how these traditions were transmitted to human beings. *It is as it is*; a text that grew and
continued to be orally passed on creating more and more interpretations
of the revelations given to individuals over more than a thousand years.
These traditions that were written down by a variety of authors and edited
together in the Bible do not always agree because people had oral traditions

that were passed down to them, and their writing down of this tradition reflected their own human personality and interests on individual characters. These writers sometimes show us varying portraits of the patriarchs, matriarchs, kings, prophets, priests, and almost everyone mentioned in the Bible not only because the authors had different information but also because they had their own views of the world, power, and religion. The writers did not live in the same areas or even in the same time period, so these discrepancies are to be expected. This process sometimes reminds me of the way that an opposition Democratic legislator might describe a Republican administration and a Republican legislator would describe a Democratic administration. The same events would be seen through the lens of their own ideological beliefs. So too, it appears that the biblical writers wrote about the figures of Abraham, Sarah, the patriarchs, Joseph, Moses, Joshua, Saul, Solomon, and probably every individual in antiquity. Simple parts of the biography of each one of these individuals can be pieced together only by looking critically at the text of the Bible.

Looking "critically" at the Bible means that you read it and use different forms of analysis to understand what it is saying in the original context that it was written in. In the Book of Genesis, for example, we are told that "Abram" is from *Ur of the Chaldeans* and that he leaves there with his father at the end of chapter 11 in Genesis, verse 31. In the same book, chapter 12, verses 1–5, Haran appears to be the birthplace and land of departure of Abram. They are really not the same tradition. We are looking at different traditions that have been collapsed together into one running account of Abraham. What is interesting to me is that after a hundred years of excavating in the area that is today Iraq, we know a lot about the names and peoples that inhabited the area and when they were there. *Ur* is the name of an ancient city of the second millennium BCE, but the *Chaldeans* only arrived there about a thousand years later in the period of the ninth century BCE! This would be as if I were reading a supposed discussion about the island of Manhattan in the seventeenth century. If the writer used the term "New York" instead of "New Amsterdam," I would suspect that the article had been reworked by someone later than the seventeenth century and that they decided to use terminology that would be understood by the reader so they just said "New York" even though it was an anachronism. The "*Ur of the Chaldeans*" is an anachronism and shows us when the tradition was written down, after 1000 BCE, but it does not explain how two different places for Abram's hometown could have grown up. Of course, Bible commentators solved this problem by explaining that he went in stages from Ur, to Haran, and then on to Canaan, but using modern, critical literary theory we can explain the anachronistic reference to the Chaldeans in another way. E. A. Speiser in his critical *Bible Commentary of the Anchor Bible Series* (New York: Doubleday, 1985) on Genesis explains it thus: "Ur and Haran were centers of moon worship unrivaled in this respect by any other Mesopotamian city. It is remotely possible, therefore, that this religious distinction, which was peculiar to Ur and Haran, caused the two cities to be bracketed together, and then to be telescoped in later versions, at a time when the Chaldeans had already gained prominence" (p. 81). He is saying that the ancient tradition about Abraham put him in a moon worship center of Mesopotamia. Both Ur and Haran are ancient moon worship centers. The later writer (almost a thousand years later when the Chaldeans were located at Ur!) may have had both cities in the oral tradition before him and simply "collapsed" the traditions into one and added the detail of *Ur of the Chaldeans* because that designation would have made sense to the readers in the time he was writing. In addition, it is possible that there were two traditions about Abraham's hometown, Ur and Haran, and the two traditions were both incorporated into the written Bible. As we will discover when we get to the New Testament, this was a common type of editing done by ancient writers. We have two hometowns for Jesus, Bethlehem and Nazareth, and the two traditions were both incorporated into the written New Testament.

Varied sources and time periods, often formulated and passed down orally, led to changing and diverse formulations. These formulations had to be intelligible for the public in the time period when the writer was writing—such is the nature of the biblical text. The writer was not looking to be historically accurate for the period of the original event as much as he was trying to have the reader or listener better understand the tradition. Also, the final editing included the technique of "telescoping" or "collapsing" different traditions into a running story because it just seemed like the easiest way to incorporate two holy traditions together. Collapsing similar traditions into one another is very common editing technique in ancient texts. All of this collapsing and telescoping has engaged generations of later biblical commentators in the act of finding meaning in these new combinations.

What Is Collapsing and Telescoping?

I use these terms, "collapsing" and "telescoping" as if they are very well-known techniques. For most of us this technique seems odd and unusual, but in antiquity it was the easiest way to preserve elements of an oral tradition that may have not been intact when the writer received it. If we examine carefully the Book of Genesis, two different images of "Abraham" emerge from the sources that were edited together. One view of Abraham is strong and courageous, another view of Abraham is a more malleable figure who is easily manipulated by his wives, Sarah and Hagar and others. The text of the Bible that we read has both of these parallel traditions about Abraham "collapsed" and edited together, one after the other, with little attempt to explain why. Medieval commentators puzzled over unlocking the meaning behind these two different "collapsed" traditions. The Patriarch Jacob has two distinctive traditions about his life that have been collapsed into one another giving us two images of Jacob.

There are so many of these doublets and sometimes triplet literary traditions that portray the same event, person, or place in different ways that it would take a whole book to demonstrate how they line up. One tradition of Jacob portrays Jacob as an inveterate liar and trickster who gains all of his opportunities by deception. Another tradition of Jacob extols him as a virtuous man forced to make the most difficult moral decisions because the deck is always stacked against him. Traditional commentaries have found ways to harmonize these two views into some of the most creative story lines one could imagine. In most of these traditional commentaries, Jacob is a single "flawed" individual that combined the best and the worst of human beings. Because traditional commentators did not understand the process of ancient editing, they had to try to reconcile and harmonize the most outrageously diverse traditions. While I understand their need to make sense of a running text, none of these commentaries can account for the entire diversity of actions without creating characters that are difficult or nearly impossible to understand. But if you divide the traditions up stylistically, these different traditions line up as favoring (and denigrating) areas of the country as well as individual characters.

One example is the story of Jacob's acquisition of the famous northern Israelite city of Shechem. In one instance, some of the sons of Jacob massacre the men of Shechem and acquire the city after the rape of their sister (Genesis 34). This tradition is hardly a testament to the peaceful nature of the Israelites and at the same time casts dispersions upon the origins of the Israelite city of Shechem that later was to become the capital city of the northern kingdom. Now I could understand this tradition as a southern version of the founding of an important northern city. It simultaneously denigrates the northern capital city and many of the northern tribes located in the northern kingdom. It would be how a New Yorker might speak about the city of Atlanta, Georgia, in the period after the Civil War. He does not write favorably about the city, but rather casts dispersions upon its founding and its citizens. In the other version of the founding of Shechem in the book of

Genesis, Jacob acquires the city through lawful payment (Genesis 33:18–20) and no negativity is attached to its origins as an Israelite city. It is clear that someone, probably from the north, has preserved this tradition and while it is a beautiful tradition, it is totally at odds with the Genesis 34 tradition. When we read it today, the two traditions appear one after another in the text of Genesis 33–34. The two traditions were "collapsed" into one another, and they cannot easily be reconciled.

Who wrote these varied traditions? Bible scholars assume that someone from the north of Israel (maybe from near Schechem) wrote the positive tradition, but someone from the south of Israel (Judea) circulated the more sordid tale and preserved it until finally they both were included in the Bible. It is possible that the northerner knew the negative story (we all reveal and hide elements when relating an experience) but decided not to include it, while the southerner wanted to present it because he did not personally feel affected by its inclusion and because he wanted to make a point. The southerner's point was that Shechem was a sinful city to begin with, foreshadowing the northern kingdom's downfall. The northern tradition records the acquisition of Shechem the same way that many other cities and locations in Israel were acquired. Both can be equally ancient and true.

Another example that shows us the full effect these combined traditions have on the history of not only the text of the Bible but upon Judaism, Christianity, and Islam has to do with the Genesis 22 tradition. Genesis 22 contains perhaps one of the most important texts for theologians in the three monotheistic religions. It is used in countless sermons and theological tractates and has been the subject of countless artistic renderings and became so important to Judaism that it is the text that is read on the holiday of Rosh Hashanah, the New Year celebration. It is used in the modern period to show how Abraham is an obedient follower of God and yet a thinking individual. In Genesis 22, God asks Abraham to sacrifice his son. This chapter follows a series of difficulties that the Patriarch and Matriarch have in conceiving a child and is therefore all the more poignant. The child is the long awaited successor to Abraham. In the Islamic tradition, the son who faces this fate is Ishmael. In the text of the Hebrew Bible, the son is Isaac. In the Christian metaphoric interpretation of this section, the "son" is none other than Jesus.

To begin with, most scholars see this as a very ancient tradition. Child sacrifice was known in the ancient Near East for thousands of years. It would not be so unusual for the deity to ask for the full measure of the faithful's obedience. In the Hebrew Bible, Bible scholars trace the first part of the near sacrifice of Isaac to the northern tribes (E). It refers to the deity using the name, Elohim, in chapter 22, verses 1, 3, 8, and 9. As he is about to sacrifice Isaac, suddenly "the Angel of the Lord" stops him. This interruption by the "Angel of the Lord" has been attributed to another source (J) who used the tetragrammaton (translated as "Lord"), and it is J who utilizes "angels" in the book of Genesis. Some Bible scholars contend that two very different scenarios were preserved here that were collapsed or redacted together. In one version, Abraham did actually sacrifice his son (E) without the mediation of an Angel of the Lord, and in another tradition the sacrifice was suddenly stopped by the Angel of the Lord (J). Both traditions represent the ancient view that child sacrifice was a permitted action for the father. Without this premise, the entire story loses its drama. The J tradition shows how human sacrifice was no longer the desire of the deity, while the original story may have had no interruption.

If you read the story carefully, there is also a question about the age of Isaac during this event. Is Isaac a child or an adult? One tradition seems to hold that this is an adult "Isaac" going with his aged father, and the other tradition seems to indicate that "Isaac" is a young child obediently following his father up the mountain. Scholars think that these two different traditions were combined together in the period after the refugees came from the north to the south in the wake of the 722 BCE expulsion. In the E text, for example, "Isaac" does not seem to continue as a character after this event, which is placed at a different point in his life. While for some this may seem impossible, the changing plot lines for the rest of the book do allow for what seem like alternative plot lines for the Bible. Some modern writers and filmmakers have used this technique of parallel plot lines in modern cinema and books with great effectiveness. In antiquity this technique was a product of the conditions of the oral traditions.

While Genesis 22 is uniquely important because the story line is mentioned in other sections of the Hebrew Bible and in postbiblical Rabbinic Judaism, Christianity, and Islam, its use in the New Testament and in early Christianity reveals the complex nature of ancient oral traditions and how they seem to have a life of their own even after they are written down. When the New Testament and early Christian texts compare Isaac in Genesis 22 to the "sacrifice" of Jesus on the Cross, it seems to imply that there were Christians that understood Genesis 22 as a precursor to the death and resurrection of Jesus. They imply that Abraham may have actually gone through with the sacrifice of his son Isaac on the altar just as God allowed the sacrifice of Jesus on the Cross. So the New Testament states: "God so loved the world that he gave his only son, [Jesus]" (John 3:16) as if it is a direct parallel to Genesis 22:2: "Take your son, your only son Isaac . . . and offer him there as a burnt offering. . . ." One wonders whether both of the original oral traditions of the Genesis 22 text may have survived into the first century CE given the fact that Jesus is, in the end, crucified. No Angel of the Lord appears to stay the execution of Jesus. Rabbinic tradition from the second and third centuries CE contains a Midrash in which Isaac is indeed sacrificed and immediately resurrected just like Jesus. Both the early Christian and Rabbinic tradition seem to recognize that there existed a parallel version of the text in which Isaac indeed was sacrificed.

This "collapsing" or "telescoping" together of two very different texts, with two very different moral perspectives, yielded a third, very different literary tradition adopted by the final redactor, whose job it was to bridge the distinctive traditions. In this case the redactor created a *tension* that reveals a very complex Abraham figure. One Abraham who is an obedient Abraham and an independent Abraham who ultimately does not sacrifice his son. The complex Abraham figure of the Hebrew Bible is greater than the sum of its ancient literary parts. God demands ultimate attention even to ask the unaskable. It is interesting to note that this collapsing together of different views from sometimes very different time periods to create a third view is a regular feature of the text of the Bible.

In the case of Abraham, Jacob, and Moses, we think that the differences can be chalked up to the different writers who wrote down the traditions that they heard but were not happy with the veneration that the people had for the patriarchs, especially Moses, and wanted to make sure that their ancestor, Aaron, would become really the image of the leader of the people. I make this point so that you will understand that the traditions of the Bible are themselves in need of clarification, even as I present the archaeology that will illuminate the Bible. For if we rely only upon a harmonized view of the text and usually an interpreted commentary upon this harmonized view, we miss the ancient threads of story lines that are really biblical history. More important, if we want to compare the archaeological record to the Bible, it is better to have all of the different story lines available for examination.

The way that historians of religion understand the development of religion can differ from the way that individual religions present themselves. Biblical religion is no longer practiced. The sacrifices, priesthood, institutions and most of the rituals of biblical religion ended with the destruction of the Temple in Jerusalem and the subsequent exiles and developments in the Roman period. Judaism, Christianity, and Islam are religions that are all based upon the Bible, but they are not really performing the rituals of biblical religion. These religions developed into different religions, but they use the biblical stories to derive their religious authority and often develop the ideas of biblical religions in ways that would be hardly understood by most of the biblical characters. Most of the time these religions represent traditions that have developed in many new and unrelated social, political, and economic contexts, and the text of the Bible has become only a pretext for their own innovations. That is what makes these faiths dynamic and living faiths, but it is also confusing because they seem to imply that they are the legitimate heirs to the legacy of biblical religion.

Judaism, Christianity, and Islam

Postbiblical, Rabbinic Judaism is a religion based on more than just the Hebrew Bible and Torah (the first five books of the Hebrew Bible, sometimes called the Pentateuch). Judaism radically changed from a temple-priest-biblical text-land-oriented religion with the destruction of the Temple in Jerusalem and the dispersion of many Jews to the Diaspora (the Diaspora/Dispersion of the Jews happened many times but the first time in 586 BCE under the Babylonians so the experience was not entirely new) in the year 70 CE by the Romans into a synagogue-Rabbi-interpretative-Diaspora-oriented religion that was fundamentally different. Judaism for the past 2000 years is a religion that has moved beyond biblical stories to an understanding of how later Rabbinic commentators and decisors understand the import of biblical values and ideas. Judaism is the sum total of nearly three thousand years of divine revelation and interpretation. Often I find that the voluminous Rabbinic, and especially Babylonian (Talmudic) Rabbinic interpretation is as important as anything that one finds in the cryptic and abbreviated traditions of the Bible. While archaeology can add to an understanding of a biblical text, this added interpretation is just one in the pantheon of ancient understandings of the text.

Christianity, which uses the biblical texts I listed earlier, also engages in an intergenerational interpretation of these texts. Although Christianity as a distinct religion from Judaism did not fully emerge as such until the mid-second century CE, the process of differentiation began even earlier. Christianity emerged from Judaism at precisely the moment that Judaism changed into its new Rabbinic manifestation. The new church-Jesus-New Testament-Diaspora orientation made it a different manifestation of the same phenomenon that gave birth to Rabbinic Judaism. Archaeology plays the same role for Christians as it does for Jews—it is another interpretation in the pantheon of Christian understandings of the text. And with the traditions of the Christians now spread throughout Europe, these traditions resemble less and less the ancient Near Eastern traditions that gave birth to them.

Islam emerged in the seventh century CE, some five centuries after Judaism and Christianity had taken root as postbiblical, Rabbinic, and Church-based faiths, not as biblically oriented faiths. I include the Koran and Islamic traditions as my sixth category of biblical tradition. The initial thrust of Islam is that it is the continuation of the biblical tradition from the Hebrew Bible and the New Testament, and the holy book of Islam, the Koran, has parallel understandings of Abraham, Sarah, the patriarchs, Moses, Aaron, King David, Jesus, and Mary that are similar to but not the same as the biblical texts of the Hebrew Bible and the New Testament. I do not think it is an accident or a mistake that in Islam the son who is almost sacrificed by Abraham in Genesis 22 is Ishmael, not Isaac. This may indeed be an oral tradition that paralleled the ones that the biblical writers had available to them. It certainly would explain other aspects of the biblical tradition. Even more important, Islam continues to add to these biblical traditions not only in the Koran but in an oral tradition, called the Hadith, which is seen as authoritative as the Rabbinic traditions are for Judaism and church traditions are for Christianity. Islam's understanding of the biblical text, therefore, is another ancient source of divine revelation. When archaeology is added to this mix, we have a variety of competing interpretations of the reality of the Bible's rich past with the interplay of different literary sources that all have something to contribute. Although it is hard to imagine, Judaism, Christianity, and Islam all hold that they possess literary traditions that are the direct and authentic continuation of the biblical tradition, and so they are not really "new" traditions but new-old traditions and interpretations that Judaism, Christianity, and Islam have preserved.

In order to understand how archaeology fits into this mix, one has to first accept the fact that literary traditions were written down by different groups of people in different periods and that to compare and contrast biblical traditions with archaeological data, you must be able to use literatures from different periods that purport to tell you something about a very ancient period, which may in fact be written down hundreds (and often thousands) of years after those events. This book also deals with the controversial elements in archaeology and the use of archaeology to understand the nature of the Bible. Archaeology data are not self-explanatory alone, just as the Bible is not self-explanatory but rather mediated by different religious understandings of these texts. The interpretation of the archaeological data alongside the biblical materials is therefore a two-step difficulty that requires not only expertise of both, but also a recognition of a variety of religious ideas that accompanied their interpretations. This process is often fraught with controversy. But it is a controversy that is worthy of our exploration.

Searching for People and Places

The search for specific historical figures and places through the use of archaeology is generally a frustrating and often fruitless endeavor. Most people cannot accept that trying to find a single individual or place in ancient history, even a person or place of great importance, can be a complex and often counterproductive process. It is like looking for a proverbial "needle in a haystack." The search is complicated by the fact that the Bible contains information that cannot be fully verified by the scientific method, yet continues to have enormous impact even in modern society.

It is clear why we want to see artifacts associated with people and places mentioned in religious texts. It seemingly proves that these religious texts are true when one person or place is found to exist in an identifiable location. Endless debates about the truth of the Bible are predicated upon the verifiability of individual items in the Bible. Often, the argument goes as such: if one claim in a religious text is true or verified by modern scientific method, then by extrapolation all claims in that text are true. The obverse is rarely considered—that if one claim is shown to be incorrect, the entire text is untrue. Jews, in particular, are stymied by the fact that the theological premise of a God with no physical manifestation precludes finding any archaeological data about God's presence in the world, while the physical presence of major figures and places from religious texts might be known. Christians, on the other hand, have the physical presence of a historical Jesus and Mary as humans who lived among other humans and yet are also divine in their relationship to the world. Muslims, who accept many of the basic Christian and Jewish figures and places (albeit with their own understandings of the meanings) also have a stake in the evidence advanced for this truth. Thus, the archaeology associated with the places and people from Judaism, Christianity, and Islam and their followers' direct connection to God and the Bible holds great appeal for the modern reader. Finding artifacts associated with these Jewish, Christian, and Muslim figures and places, therefore, proves for some people that both God and the Bible are true and verifiable, making religion a "legitimate" modern pursuit. Even if you see the logical problems of this argument, you can understand why so many people are so interested in finding this documentation.

The modern skepticism of traditional religious texts that developed since the end of the Renaissance and became enshrined through the Enlightenment, contributed to the need for "factual" evidence of a specific person or event rather than textually transmitted religious traditions. One could only ask if the Exodus really happened and look to archaeology to prove or disprove it in the modern period. One would only ask if the Israelites were really enslaved in Egypt after the rise of modern Egyptian archaeology. Only in the modern period do people ask if the miracles mentioned in the Bible are provable through archaeology. Modern Bible commentaries of the Book of Exodus try to explain each individual plague that was exacted against Pharaoh and the Egyptian people in light of known events in Egyptian history discovered through the unraveling of Egyptian archaeology. Jesus' life and miracles are similarly viewed and explained by meteorologists, geologists, biologists, and medical doctors.

Unlike biblical archaeology which is obsessed with questions about figures, such as Moses and Jesus, Islamic archaeologists have little scientific obsession with the figure of Muhammad. Although there is interest in the material culture and places specifically associated with Muhammad in Mecca, Medina, and Jerusalem and even the traditions associated with the "beard" of Muhammad. Islamic archaeology centers upon post-Muhammad history. Islamic archaeologists will research questions associated with the early Caliphate, the post-Caliphate, and medieval Islam, but little or no effort is expended on the author(s) of the Koran, and the family of Muhammad. Little controversy exists among Muslim textual scholars and archaeologists about the physical existence of the Islamic foundational people, places, and events as one finds in Jewish and Christian archaeology. While Islam's events are relatively "newer" in history than the events of the New Testament or Hebrew Bible, this does not mean that they are more easily subjected to scrutiny. In Islam, traditional people, places, and events of the Koran and early Hadith are not investigated in the same way that Christianity and Judaism investigate their own major figures, places, and events. Islam has carefully separated the science of archaeology and literary criticism from the investigation of the textual information of the Koran and Hadith. Some say that this noninterest derives mostly from the absence of anything like the European Renaissance and Enlightenment in countries where Islam grew up. What's more is that Islamic sites that might hold archaeological interest have been continuously occupied by Islamic authorities from the inception of Islam to the present period, making archaeology very difficult. Muslims have carefully guarded the data of places such as Mecca, Medina, and Jerusalem, and so you have traditional sources and interpretations as the official source for most of the information that we possess of these people, places, and events. This is not the case in Christian and Jewish archaeology. Islam and early Hadith as well as Islamic archaeology do help us understand some of the biblical, Christian and Jewish archaeological people, places, and events, so despite its limitations, Islam is still another source to be reckoned with in our study of biblical archaeology.

"Proving" That They're Real
Relics, Forgeries, and the Accidental Tourist

One of the biggest problems in biblical archaeology is whether an object or place is really from the ancient biblical period or was created by later religious leaders to fit the sensibilities of pilgrims or their followers. I am not only talking about people who create objects to deceive people, I am also talking about the attempt by historical religious figures to associate an artifact with an ancient figure or place because of their religious intuition or their personal revelation. This is common not only to Judaism, Christianity, and Islam. It is common in almost every religion on the planet. A "relic" site is established to enable the faithful to have a place to concentrate on the message of the religious figure and the religion.

One of the most famous examples that I have come across was a site in Turkey that was on top of a mountain called Ararat that was thought to be Noah's Ark. The Ark or boat that was discovered there in the 1970s above the tree line was amazingly similar in size and dimensions to the one mentioned in the Book of Genesis. Ararat, an unknown location where the Ark rested at the end of the primordial flood, was in fact the same name as the mountain. It all seemed to fit. Even scientists in the 1970s were stunned to find, using good scientific equipment and methods, that the remains of what appeared to be an ancient wooden boat matching Noah's Ark was right below the surface. What looked like petrified wood was found all around the site. Most people were mystified by the appearance of such a large boat so high up on the mountain. The wooden planks were glued together with a special laminate that appeared to be only one thousand years old. But why was it there on top of this solitary mountain? Who had put it there? Scholars today now think that Byzantine monks in the area actually built the ark on top of the mountain because they had an oral tradition that this was the resting place of the original Noah's Ark and that they were just restoring what they "knew" had been there before. For most of us it is difficult to understand how industrious and well-meaning these monks in this area were. But this is a classic example of how a relic develops. Usually there is an oral tradition that becomes associated with a person, place, or event, and it is translated into an object that is either created a long time after the event or is a reconstruction of an article that did exist but has been recreated after the original is no more. A well-known relic is the *Shroud of Turin* in Italy, a textile that is said to be the burial shroud of Jesus. More than being just a simple white burial textile, people can see on the shroud the contours of the face and body of a man with a beard. Unfortunately, when the Shroud of Turin was carbon 14 tested it was only about eight hundred years old while the burial shroud of Jesus would have had to have been almost two thousand years old. Both of these cases, in Turkey and Italy, involve relics, items that religiously purport to be one thing while "science" proves that they are something else.

I have asked religious people what they make of this scientific faith, and some say that the miraculous nature of the Shrine is that it is intended to test one's faith. Others tell me that they think that the original shroud was lost and that this shroud was created eight hundred years ago to continue the faithful history, even though this is not the original. In both of these cases I distinguish relics from deceptions and fakes. In the case of the Ark of Ararat, the monks did not intend to deceive people. We assume they believed that this was the place and that they must have had a tradition that led them to this conclusion. It is even possible that they did have part of the original Ark when they began their work. We just do not know. We only know that this Ark is not the original Ark. So too, the Shroud was probably created not to deceive but to be an object of devotion to inspire others to understand the meaning of the life and death of Jesus and yes, the people who created the twelfth-century Shroud may have had an original that they were copying. But science needs to prove whether these objects of devotion meet standards of authenticity. When they do prove to meet standards of authenticity using whatever scientific technique is current, they will be acknowledged as "real." Until then I use the designation: relic.

Relics and relic sites are not unique to Christianity although there are considerably more relics and relic sites in Christianity than there are in Judaism. For some reason, most of the relic sites in Judaism are burials, but they all have a rich and sometimes unexpected history. The famous tomb of Samson in Gaza as well as its counterpart, Joseph's tomb in Nablus, are more likely medieval holy sites/burials that were turned into Jewish sites of veneration. Most medieval Jewish travelers were shown these tombs by local tour guides in the area so their origins are shrouded in mystery. Samson's tomb in particular is a rather problematic Jewish character because of his behavior in the Bible and even Rabbinic commentators were not able to restore him. It is therefore odd that Samson's tomb was venerated by Rabbinic Jews. According to the Bible, Samson intermarried with a Philistine woman and socialized with the local Philistine population. In the Midrash, although he pulls down the Temple of Dagon on himself and the Philistines, his body is taken from the Temple and put in the family tomb. The relic tomb is located in what is today the Gaza Strip. Nearby stands his father Manoach and Manoach's altar (Judges 13:19–24). The site is questionable because these burials appear to be inground burials with a building built above them to protect them, when it is much more likely that in this period the burials would be in local caves. So why, you might ask did his burial site become a relic? I think that medieval Jews who suffered at the hands of both Christians and Muslims in Europe and in many Muslim countries were particularly in need of a symbol of power against foreign religion. Samson's Tomb was a powerful symbol of hope and it may indeed have been the burial place of a "Samson."

Joseph's tomb is more complicated. Joseph the Patriarch makes the Israelites promise that they will bring his bones from Egypt to the Land of Israel. According to the Bible, Nablus/Shechem (Samaria) is the place of his burial, but no specific place is mentioned in Joshua 24:3. Shechem is an odd choice by Rabbinic standards, and other Jewish sources place the burial of Joseph near the graves of the other Patriarchs in Hebron while another tradition has him buried in Safed in Galilee. The sons of Joseph, Ephraim, and Manasseh are placed at the tomb of Joseph in Nablus as well. Nevertheless, some Muslims, who also venerate Joseph because he appears in the Koran, have identified the tomb of Joseph in Nablus by the tenth century CE. But the identification is problematic because it is called by some, not the tomb of the Patriarch Joseph, but the tomb of a medieval local sheikh, Yusef Al-Dwaik. The doubling up of identifications is quite common. Often it is not clear which of the individuals with the same name were actually buried in the tomb. This is usually a good indicator of a relic tomb built to accommodate a venerable figure. But Joseph, unlike Samson, was a very important figure for the Bible, Jews, and Muslims, so it is a little confusing why there is any question about the identification of his tomb. I think that the site became more important to Jews and Muslims who came to visit this region of the country precisely because there was another tomb of Joseph that had been established at Hebron to the south. This is usually another indicator of a relic tomb that regions vied for the privilege of hosting the tomb of a revered leader. Relics associated with John the Baptist are found in a dozen different locations. Medieval travelers to the north of the country were shown the tomb of Joseph in Nablus, and many Muslims and Jews assumed that this was the original Joseph. The importance for modern readers is that because both the tomb of Samson and Joseph are located in what is today the "West Bank and Gaza," the tombs and damage to the tombs in recent years has made them the source of tension between Jews and Palestinians. The problem is that no archaeological evidence specifically makes them historical, so we refer to them as "relic" sites.

There are, of course, deceptions, frauds, fakes, and forgers in all periods, who do create objects to deceive people (and earn high commissions for artifacts that are not what they purport to be), and I want to differentiate relics from forgeries. The most recent controversies over forgeries involve real ancient objects that have been tampered with to increase their value. Three involve inscriptions. The discovery in a dump site from the Temple Mount Al Aqsa Mosque enlargements, which are controversial because they are not being carried out by archaeologists, revealed an inscribed stone with an inscription from the ninth-century-BCE King Jehoash, King of Judah. The inscription writes about the repair of the Temple of Solomon. This inscription has been declared by the Antiquities Authority of Israel to be the work of a forger who created enormous ill will among Jews and Muslims by creating a forgery simply to mislead researchers. Another recent controversy involved the so-called "James" ossuary, a limestone bone box with the inscription, "James, son of Joseph, brother of Jesus." It went from being just a first-century-limestone bone box to being one of the most important pieces of evidence for the existence of Jesus of Nazareth. Was this the ossuary of the brother of the famous Jesus, the son of the famous Joseph (father of Jesus)? Committees from the Antiquities Authority of Israel declared that while the artifact is ancient, the inscription was a forgery. This entire atmosphere of suspicion of forgeries has created an opportunity for a reassessment of artifacts that were thought genuine and now are suspected of being forgeries. The most recent controversy involves what was thought to be the only surviving artifact from the Temple of Solomon. The "pomegranate" artifact has been on display at the Israel Museum for a long while, and only recently, because of the increased interest in forgeries it too began to be suspected. The controversy over the authenticity of the pomegranate involves the inscription on the side of the artifact that reads: " ...to the House of Yahweh, Holy to the Priests." Controversy stirred not over whether the pomegranate artifact was ancient and belonging to the right period of the Temple of Solomon, but rather whether the inscription (which essentially places the artifact in the Temple of Solomon) was put on the artifact after the fact by a forger to increase the artifact's value. The suspicion that had been created by the Jehoash inscription and the James ossuary inscription has had a "ripple effect" on unprovenanced artifacts that have been purchased from collectors. A similar atmosphere of suspicion occurred at the end of the nineteenth century when a Jewish antiquities dealer, Moses Shapira, came forward with what he claimed were the oldest versions of the book of Deuteronomy on leather strips that he said had come from Palestine. He tried to sell them to the British Museum, and it is thought that because he already had a record of selling forgeries, this too was declared a forgery by a well-known scholar of the period. The text was sold to a collector and lost in a fire in the 1930s. The discovery of the Dead Sea Scrolls in 1947 ironically made many scholars reassess the case of Moses Shapira and his leather "strips" of Bible.

There is a third category of artifacts that are neither relics nor forgeries. They are objects that are brought forward, often by what I call the "accidental tourist." Over the centuries, travelers and explorers happen upon an artifact in the course of their travels, pick it up, and assume that it is one thing or another. The object is thought by the accidental tourist to be a rare and important find, but after testing, it turns out to be something totally different. I was presented with such an "artifact" in 2002 by someone who had visited Israel in the 1970s and just picked up what they thought was an artifact and brought it home. When it was presented to me it looked exactly like one of the Dead Sea Scrolls that I had seen in photographs. A woman from Connecticut called me at the University of Hartford after she had seen my documentary on the Cave of Letters and said that she had a Dead Sea Scroll in her sock drawer and would I want it for the University's collection! I receive calls like this from time to time, and I try to honor each serious inquiry. I check out each one of these serious inquiries in the off chance that it is true. Many of the stories of the original discoveries of the Dead Sea Scrolls are as amazing as this story, so I began with a personal history and then attempted to verify her story with a scientific inquiry.

Having consulted people throughout the world I began with a non-invasive CT Scan at a local hospital. The figure on page 1 is the CT Scan we did of the "scroll" which was sent around the world for analysis. I asked her about the circumstances of its discovery and told her that if it was indeed a real Dead Sea Scroll that it would have to be brought back to Israel. When this woman brought the "scroll" to our Sherman Museum on the campus of the University of Hartford with her photos documenting where it had been discovered in the early 1970s, it reinforced my own curiosity. The "scroll" had been discovered near the caves where the other Dead Sea Scrolls had been found.

The CT Scan was the easiest way to "see" inside the scroll without unwrapping it. You cannot imagine the excitement of the radiologists at the hospital in Hartford, who gathered that evening to test the "scroll" and then read the CT scan for me. There was no doubt in their minds as they stood looking at the computer screen that it was indeed a "scroll," a rolled organic creation and among these specialists were those who were even able to identify what they thought was latent ink lettering on the inside of the scroll. I do not want to minimize the level of excitement that it stirred in the hearts of those scholars who were involved in the identification. But each one of the noninvasive tests that we performed was inconclusive. We ended up cutting a tiny section of the scroll and sent it for analysis. After six months, it was determined that it was not an ancient "scroll," but rather an ancient "rolled" up plant that had been repeatedly rolled in the unique Dead Sea mud during the infrequent rain storms around the Dead Sea. Science was able to prove something to be something other than what it appeared to be at first "scientific" glance. It was not a forgery; it was not a relic. It was a naturally occurring phenomenon that created an artifact that was found by an "accidental tourist" that looked like something that it was not.

Today we have a whole series of different sciences that can help determine the dating and identification of a site or other artifacts that are found nearby. The science of numismatics, for example, allows us to scientifically evaluate coins and most of the time determine whether other artifacts found with the coins are forgeries. Numismatics can detect coin forgeries as well. Coins are easily datable and identifiable so they are important to dating a site. Linguistic and various forms of language analysis is a science when done by anthropologists and linguists. The science of paleography dates inscriptions or manuscripts using paleographic comparative studies (studies of the development of handwriting and scripts) or carbon-14 dating (chemical analysis of amount of the carbon present in an organic artifact). Pollen, chemical signatures of soils, DNA evaluation, and many other chemical and biological sciences help us understand if an artifact is what people say it is.

Buildings and some archaeological objects may become associated with a single event in the Bible and Jewish history and end up as relics, objects, or places that have symbolic meaning but are not really datable to the time period they should be from. A relic site can be a religious location that is identified as the place where an ancient literary text says something happened and yet may not be exactly at the location where the religious site is located today. Jericho is an excellent example of how difficult the question of a relic or an original site is. Jericho has been inhabited almost continuously for over seven thousand years. The Bible mentions Jericho, so we expect to find corroboration of what the Bible says when we arrive there. Because we can date approximately backward from other more datable events of the Bible to the time of Joshua (the Babylonian Exile in 586 BCE and the Assyrian Conquest in 722 BCE, for example), the thirteenth century BCE was the assumed time period for the conquest of the Land of

Israel by Joshua by early twentieth-century archaeologists. So what should archaeologists find when they investigate the present archaeological mount site of Jericho at the archaeological stratum of the thirteenth century BCE? Well, a destruction of a city wall with pieces strewn about would be nice. Unfortunately, Kathleen Kenyon's investigations show that in the thirteenth century there was no destruction in the mound of Jericho, no indication whatsoever of a large-scale settlement. How do we then understand the Bible? Is the Bible wrong? Are the archaeologists wrong? Are they both wrong? Or, should we reconsider a number of the givens about the site? Is the thirteenth century BCE walled city located someplace else, is the text speaking of a destruction in this period or of a retrojected experience from the time of David when the Bible was begun to be written down, or is the Bible providing an inspirational story of courage rather than a lesson in history? It is difficult to know. But it is clear that the biblical text and archaeological evidence are not easily reconciled.

"Tradition" is a major source of identification of modern archaeological sites. Many people say that tradition is how we know that the churches of Bethlehem and Nazareth commemorate what they say they do, or that the site designated as Capernaum is the location of the synagogue in which Jesus preached during the first century as mentioned in the New Testament. Traditions within Judaism and Christianity are important, but they often go back a couple of thousand years at best and usually cannot be exactly traced any further. Relying on tradition is less problematic when we have an almost uninterrupted occupation of a site, such as Jerusalem, Bethlehem, or Nazareth, but often the exact location of certain events is disputed. These disputed locations became, in the case of Christianity, for example, a basis for doctrinal and theological sectarian questions.

Another source of information is modern Arabic or Semitic linguistic traditions that preserve elements of a named area. For example, an archaeological mound in Israel called by locals *el-Jib* in modern Arabic tradition was eventually identified as biblical Gibeon. One can see that the original sound of the ancient Hebrew name of the site was preserved over thousands of years. Some names preserved in Arabic preserve medieval or Byzantine traditions and can be documented only that far. Sometimes the modern Arabic names preserve ancient traditions about a location that have not been scientifically tested. At Capernaum, for example, many tourists (both medieval and modern) have been told a large synagogue structure at the site is the first century structure in which Jesus preached. Unfortunately numismatic evidence and other information point to the fourth or fifth century. Many Christian pilgrimage sites, such as in Nazareth, Jerusalem, and Capernaum, are more the product of the fourth and fifth century's spiritual journeys of informed Christian leaders searching for sites that represented the life and times of Jesus than authentic historical sites. They are old sites; just not old enough.

Even traditional sites associated with the major figures of Judaism and Christianity in Israel, Mesopotamia, Egypt, and Asia Minor, as well as in the Mediterranean and Europe are challenged unless they have been occupied continuously and verified by a chain of uninterrupted evidence. In most cases, the history in these places, unlike the early history of Islam, has been interrupted by a variety of wars and changes in ruling authorities. A classic illustration of this problem is tracing any person or place in Jerusalem. Although Jerusalem has been an uninterrupted settlement in recorded history, modern revisionist Palestinian and Arab historians have used some of the ambiguity created by modern Enlightenment challenges to traditional arguments to negate the historical veracity of the Roman Jewish Temple on top of the Temple Mount by the Western Wall. This is possible because of the shift in ruling authorities from the Byzantines, early Muslims, Crusaders, Mamlukes, and Ottomans to finally the British and Israelis who modified architectural features and constructed new buildings in Israel. Each evaluation has a "ripple effect" upon the entire discipline and is an attempt to prove that the Bible is true or untrue, the place as true or not, and the events as true or not.

The absence of specific archeological evidence for a person's life in history is not proof that the person did not exist. To illustrate, consider the first president of the United States, George Washington. To corroborate his existence we need physical evidence beyond the stories about George Washington. A burial place is not enough. Physical evidence could include houses, letters signed by Washington, and personal items. George Washington lived fewer than three hundred years ago, and most literary references to his exploits cannot be fully confirmed with physical evidence, although his existence can be documented. Tracking the existence of well-known religious figures is a little more difficult. In Jewish history, Israel Baal Shem Tov, the founder of the popular religious movement Hasidism, for example, who lived just over three hundred years ago in Poland, is difficult to track. Everyone writes about him, but physical evidence of his existence is almost nonexistent. Likewise, there is little or no physical evidence for the existence of most of the main figures of biblical and religious history. Bar Kokhba was an ancient religious figure who lived in the second century CE and, according to some of the Rabbis, was declared to be the much awaited "Messiah." Bar Kokhba appeared in religious literary texts from the Talmud to church documents to

Roman history and was regarded as any of the other great biblical heroes. His exploits are as legendary as the prophets of ancient biblical prophets and similar to the miracles and stories of the New Testament. The question is, did Bar Kokhba really exist as the ancient literary texts suggest? In the course of the Cave of Letters excavations, letters signed by Bar Kosiba (his real name according to the Talmud) were found that roughly approximated the type of person described in the Talmud and church and Roman histories. He wasn't exactly the same as the literary texts describe him, but extrapolating from the physical evidence of his existence, the type of character reflected in the letters matched the events found in the religious texts. That is pretty good and extremely rare in archaeology.

There is one example between archaeology and literary texts that seems to match even better. At Masada, a mountain top refuge in the Judean desert, just under a thousand refugees from the First Revolt against the Romans gathered after the destruction of Jerusalem. They thought they were safe from the Romans, but they were not. According to the Jewish historian, Josephus Flavius, in 73 CE, these refugees were hunted down by the Romans and on the eve of their being taken captive, they all allowed themselves to be martyred by their compatriots rather than be taken captive by the Romans. This massive "suicide" is so dissimilar to the Jewish values of the period that some modern historians have always suspected that it was fiction. The story is also unique because Josephus has such unusual details about how the killings were carried out in his book *The Jewish War*. Josephus states that the leader of the refugees, Elazar Ben Yair, gathered ten men who were chosen by lots to kill the people. Then the ten chosen men were instructed to kill each other and finally the last one would kill himself, so that it was not mass suicide but it was one person who performed this final act of personal martyrdom. During the archaeological excavations at Masada in the 1960s, Professor Yigael Yadin discovered in a small room eleven small pottery shards with names on the shards that he thought probably were the very lots that the group used on that fateful evening. One name on the pottery shards was Ben Yair. Although some have challenged whether these were in fact the pottery shards used for this selection, it is an extremely compelling example of how archaeology and ancient literary accounts could confirm one another. Minimalists ridicule the example of the shards by raising arguments like: how do we know that this is the same Elazar Ben Yair in the Josephus text? Others say that even if it is the Ben Yair, how do we know these are the lots used in the famous selection? They could just be food allocation or other coupons being used by the refugees. Unfortunately, we cannot know with 100 percent certainty how these shards were used, but the comparisons are striking and the hypothesis of Yadin is reasonable, but because of revisionism, many have come to doubt the conclusions.

The Revisionist Debate: Back to the Minimalists Versus the Maximalists

Biblical archaeology is said to be a discipline born in sin. In many senses this is true. In the nineteenth and early twentieth century, biblical archaeology was basically top heavy with theologians who saw each rock and pot as verification and authentication of everything. Students and faculty that I guided around Israel would tell me stories about other guides who had brought them to the same places and showed them amazing artifacts through inferences to biblical stories: "This rock may have been used by David against Goliath," ". . . this pot was just like the one used by Elisha in the oil miracles," "this is a tree limb that is like the staff of Moses." In a way, they are right. This rock, pot, and tree limb do resemble, in general, ones associated with biblical tales. It helps to connect people with artifacts in biblical stories that they are familiar with. But the theological approach goes further. Instead of just saying that these artifacts are like those mentioned in the Bible, artifacts that were excavated were designated as the artifacts themselves from the story. Biblical archaeology at its inception began with the Bible and ended with the artifacts. To be fair, most people took this same approach at the beginnings of Greek archaeology, Native American archaeology, Chinese archaeology, etc. The text helped initiate discussion about the artifacts. There was always a need to immediately connect the religious stories to a place and an artifact found there informed their discussion.

In most of these disciplines a correction or revisionism began a generation or two after the founders of these disciplines were no longer alive. In fact, the theological side of archaeology that had sparked its birth in the period before World War II caused a backlash of "new" (less theologically motivated) biblical archaeology, which started from the artifacts and began to ignore the text. Because of the "new" archaeology, we began to learn a lot about ceramics, metals, glass, and architecture and knew little about the potential connections to the social history of these artifacts. This attitude has wrought a totally new manifestation today. Minimalists are those who minimize the importance of textual connections and artifacts and Maximalists maximize every connection possible to the text. Extreme Maximalists hold that from a single artifact one can legitimate many different and unrelated textual references. Maximalist-Minimalists think that the extrapolation process should be restricted to learning as much as possible about a possible connection between material culture and the text.

Minimalists and Maximalists view the same artifact and make different connections. Among the city ruins of Tel Dan, a piece of evidence connected to a specific event was found in front of the City Gate. One of the remnants of a large basalt stele, thirteen lines of Aramaic script are partially preserved. The inscription was created by King Hazael of Aram-Damascus in about 825 BCE, and it relates to his father, Hadad II, being victorious in battle against King Jehosaphat of Judah (c. 860 BCE), a lineal descendent of David. The most important aspect of the text is that it specifically mentions defeating the "foot soldiers, charioteers and horsemen of the King of the *House of David.*" The much-prized Tel Dan inscription resides now in Jerusalem and is seen by many Minimalists and Maximalists as the Holy Grail of discoveries. In the inscription is mentioned the *House of [King] David.* What more evidence do you need to prove the reliability of King David as a real figure in biblical times than an inscription that mentions King David in precisely the same way that the Bible does?

Extreme Minimalists look at the inscription, *Bet David* (the House of David), and ask: which house of which David? They even question whether or not it really says *House of David* since the text has no vowels and can be read with different vowels. In this case, using different Hebrew vowels, the phrase can also be read as *Bet Dod* (the House of a "Beloved" or "the House of the Uncle") if you wish to make a case against the reading of the House of David. Extreme Minimalists say little could be learned from even a very specific reference like this. But unfortunately, extreme Maximalists create more from the discovery than the scientific method can accommodate. The extreme Maximalist sees an inscription like the House of David inscription and declares that since this confirms the existence of King David, it confirms every detail about King David in the Bible. This is where even the best archaeological evidence falls short. A Minimalist-Maximalist accepts that there was a House of David, just like the biblical expression, and learns that King David existed but cannot confirm all of the details about him in the Bible.

If this was the only reference to King David, I probably would remain skeptical. However, the Moabite Stone from about 860 BCE is another kingly stele that boasts of conflict with the ongoing Kings of Israel in a fashion that is very similar to the text of the Bible. This black basalt monument called the Moabite Stone was discovered in 1868 at Dhiban, 20 miles east of the Dead Sea (across from En-Gedi) and is now housed in the Louvre Museum in Paris. It contains thirty-six lines of Phoenician script that relate to the rebellion of King Mesha of Moab against King Jehoram of Israel and

King Jehosaphat of Judah. This battle is recounted in the Hebrew Bible's 2 Kings 3:5–27, but the Moabite Stone gives us a totally different version of the events of 2 Kings. The Moabite Stele is the exact mirror image of the events of the Bible. It is a perspective of Mesha, king of Moab, while the Bible has the perspective of the Israelites and Judeans. When I read it, it demonstrates to me how archaeology confirms the accuracy of what is in the Bible. Archaeology can confirm that indeed there was an event, a person, a place, but it does not confirm how it was written about in the Bible.

In the grand scope of biblical archaeology, the Moabite Stone is one more piece of evidence that shows the accuracy of historical information in the Bible. It does not prove that everything written in the Bible is true, but it does show that the writers were intimately aware of real "historically-verifiable" events that are recorded in the Bible. Together with many other elements, it shows a cumulative argument of how historically accurate the Bible is and in what sections of the Bible these historically verifiable elements fall. Because I take the Bible seriously but do not extrapolate beyond the issues that have logical conclusions, I have become known as a Maximalist-Minimalist. I think that the Bible is as venerable and as important as any pot, metal, glass, stone, or architecture. To me, everything in the Bible must be taken seriously as evidence of ancient traditions equal to if not greater than any piece of archaeological data. The biblical text and the archeological data must always be considered in tandem.

The Minimalists say a direct connection must exist between every piece of evidence to link it to a specific text, which does not leave much room for extrapolation. The Maximalists link every piece of evidence to every text, allowing extrapolation to easily flow from text to evidence. I return to our discussion about the James ossuary because it is emblematic of the differences between Maximalists and Minimalists. The ancient ossuary is indeed ancient; it is the inscription that is the problem. "*James, son of Joseph, brother of Jesus*" is the inscription on the side of the limestone bone box. The debate, which has many twists and turns, is important *because this bone box is the only specific physical evidence that mentions the key figure of the first century, Jesus.* Yes, this is the only specific physical evidence of Jesus. As I have been indicating, one should not be so surprised to hear this since it is so difficult to find specific archaeological data about a specific person from antiquity, even people who became important soon after their death, since it is "like looking for a needle in a haystack." Can we ever be 100 percent sure that the name matches the person in history (with that name) that we are looking for? The ossuary story, which is still unfolding since it was first brought to light some five years ago, has been questioned on many different technical archaeological grounds but is still a matter of debate among Minimalists and Maximalists. This is because some Maximalists, who accept the inscription as authentic, question whether James was indeed a "blood brother" of Jesus of Nazareth or someone else (a cousin, for example). Other Maximalists are willing to acknowledge that Joseph was indeed the "father" of James but are confused by the reference to Jesus on the ancient burial inscription. Why was the "brother of Jesus" even mentioned there? Minimalists, however, question the importance of the entire inscription, even if it is ancient. They ask, so what? What does this inscription really tell us. How do we know it is *the* James, who is the son of *the* Joseph, who is the brother of *the* Jesus (of Nazareth)? Minimalists hold that it could be any James, of any Joseph, of any Jesus, because these are common names in Jerusalem (and elsewhere) in this period. Some Maximalists-Minimalists (who basically accept the antiquity of the entire inscription) say that finding three (even common) names together in this type of formulation would be a huge coincidence if it were not related to the Holy Family. More serious Minimalists-Maximalists (myself included), however, can acknowledge that the inscription may be a hybrid: that is, an ancient inscription with added information (information that may have been added in antiquity and not necessarily in the modern period by a forger). In my estimation, even this hybrid approach would confirm information that is in the New Testament and confirm the existence in history of these three characters. It cannot corroborate everything in the New Testament, but it would at least confirm the accuracy of this information in the New Testament.

And therein lies a central question in *Digging through the Bible*. How much can we extrapolate even when the interpretation of archaeological information is deemed to be incontrovertible? There are three different ways of using archaeology in comparison with ancient texts. This book uses all three. They are: illumination, background, and comparative correlation.

The Three Roles of Archaeology in the Study of the Bible

Ilumination: The Most Common Use of Archaeology in Biblical Archaeology

"Illumination" occurs when the material culture "illuminates" or helps reveal elements in the text which would otherwise be missed. This does not mean that there is a direct correlation between the material culture evidence and the textual information, but if the evidence of the material culture is from the same area, time period, and fits the description of the text, "illumination" can be a meaningful comparison between text and artifact. One example of illumination, which is found in the next chapter, involves Moses and the Exodus. The book of Exodus, chapter 2, verse 3, states that the baby Moses was put in the Nile River in a basket made of bulrushes after the decree of Pharaoh to kill all of the Israelite male babies. When I saw a basket of this type in the Cairo Museum I realized how a good illuminating artifact helps us to understand the text. When I showed students the basket, they understood more about the custom (many of these baskets were commonly used as burial "coffins" for dead babies in Egypt) and why the mention in the Bible shows an understanding of ancient Egyptian life and culture. I would never say that this particular one or another is the baby Moses' basket of bulrushes, but the fact that I can point out one that is similar demonstrates how archaeological evidence can be used to illuminate the text of the Bible. There is a measure of authenticity to the story when I read about a basket of bulrushes and seeing an example from the Bronze Age of a basket of bulrushes. It is not the same basket that Moses was put in, but it is the same type of basket from the right region and time period. The story of Moses being placed in the basket of bulrushes also has an antecedent in Mesopotamian literature as well. This is the ancient story of Sargon of Akkad from Mesopotamia, which was itself preserved on an archaeological artifact that "illuminates" the Moses story. It would be circumstantial evidence in a court of law, but it does serve to establish the general, historical nature of an event, a person, and a place in Egypt in the right time period. Usually this relationship is twofold. The archaeological artifact illuminates the biblical event, but the biblical text also adds detail to an archaeological discovery. Without the story of baby Moses in a basket of bulrushes in the book of Exodus, the basket would just be a basket. With the story, every Bronze Age basket of bulrushes discovery in Egypt becomes more significant.

Background: A Common Form of Archaeological Comparison

The use of material culture to provide a general background for the text is the most common role of archaeology. Again, it does not mean that an artifact is a direct match between the biblical custom person or event, but it implies that the archaeology provides a close match with a text. There is one example of how archaeology can provide both illumination and background from our excavations at Bethsaida. Bethsaida (which means *the House of the Fisherman* in Hebrew) in the New Testament is a fishing village on the Sea of Galilee. The ancient mound we began excavating in 1987 was nearly two miles from the present day coastline of the Sea of Galilee. Our hypothesis was that the Sea of Galilee coastline had changed over the past two thousand years. We called in a geological team from the University of Nebraska at Omaha to test our hypothesis. They did a three-year detailed geophysical survey of the present-day dry Bethsaida plain from the Sea of Galilee coast to the back of the mound. They proved beyond a shadow of a doubt that two thousand years ago, the present-day dry Bethsaida plain was low lying, swampy water that was excellent for fishermen to go out on flat boats to the much deeper Sea of Galilee.

I remember presenting this geological information about Bethsaida in the early 1990s for the first time in Rome, Italy, at a Bible conference that took place near the Vatican. I presented slides of bore holes we dug in the presently dry plain of Bethsaida and described how the Bethsaida plain had changed over time due to sedimentation and earthquakes in the area. In a few of the slides, I showed how some two thousand years ago at Bethsaida there were areas of low lying, swampy water with depths differing from three to eight feet depending on the uneven sedimentation that had taken place over centuries. At the end of what I thought was a very nonbibli- cal presentation involving geology and archaeological analysis of types of Roman period flat (hippos) boats and nets that would have been used, I concluded that the Bethsaida plain was a low-lying, swampy area that would have been ideal for fishing in the first century CE. I finished and we went to questions and answers. One Bible scholar asked me a question that was both totally unexpected and enlightening about how archaeology can both illuminate and give background to the text of the Bible. He told me that this geology lesson I had given had solved a major biblical question he had always had about the New Testament story of Jesus' having been seen walking on the water. According to one account in Mark 6, verses 45–52, the "walking on the water" story happens at Bethsaida. The miracle is a turning point in the text of the Gospel, and yet it had always appeared to this Bible scholar to be totally lacking in any possible physical evidence. I listened to him explain how the geological and archaeological informa- tion we had unearthed had given him a new understanding of the text. "Of course," he said, "they saw Jesus walking on the water at Bethsaida, he must have been walking on a sandbar." He then showed me how archaeol- ogy can provide unexpected but meaningful detail to a story. He said: "Dr. Freund, according to your team, the only place on the entire Sea of Galilee where a person could be seen walking on the water would be at Bethsaida where the sedimentation patterns would allow someone to be seen walking on the water while they were walking on a sandbar. More important, if someone did not get out of the boat when Jesus told him to, that person might end up in the deeper water where one could not be seen 'walking on the water!' This solved a great biblical mystery, thank you!" I knew what he meant. It was the background for not only this Gospel account but the other versions in the New Testament as well.

Another version of the story in the Gospel of Matthew chapter 14 has the Apostle Peter, who hesitates when Jesus asked him to get out of the boat and walk with him on the water. Peter was fearful of drowning and did not get out of the boat when Jesus told him to and by the time he did get out, he immediately sank. The background of the story of Jesus having been seen walking on the water made a lot more sense since our excavations at Bethsaida. It did not tell me exactly where the event took place, but it did inform me about what type of conditions would have made the sighting possible. Of course the story was written down by people of faith who viewed these events with the eyes of the faithful and saw in it the theological idea of faith in the mission of Jesus. But behind the written text was a background that only archaeology could have captured. I was surprised by the observation, but it has since given me an understanding of the way that many pieces of archaeological data allow us to unlock one of the secrets for appreciating the "truths" imbedded in the biblical texts.

Direct Correlation: A Rare Archaeological Moment

A direct correlation between an event, artifact, or figure in an ancient literary account and archaeology is the rarest example of the use of archaeology in understanding the text. Besides the examples of Masada and the signed Bar Kokhba letters, one of the best examples is the famous Siloam inscription from Jerusalem. We have a copy of the inscription in our Sherman Museum at the University of Hartford, and it is usually the one example of the direct correlation between an artifact and a text that I show students when I teach about biblical archaeology. King Hezekiah of Judah, anticipating the conquest of the Assyrian King Sennacherib, commissioned a 533-meter-long water tunnel to be built from a nearby spring under the walls of ancient Jerusalem. The event, which is mentioned in the book of 2 Kings 18:13–16, can be dated to the fourth year of Sennacherib or 701 BCE. This inscription tells us that the event of 2 Kings and this one artifact testify to the same event. In a similar vein, another example of this phenomenon is the text of 2 Kings and the archaeological discovery of the so-called Prism text. It is different than the Siloam inscription because the Siloam inscription (a Hebrew inscription) directly correlates to the information in the Hebrew Bible, while the Prism text (cuneiform) demonstrates the opposite phenomenon. How archaeological finds from totally different areas, from Assyria and from the enemy of Hezekiah, and a text from the Bible directly correlate to corroborate a single event is beyond illumination and background. These parallels provide us with an insight into the problem of perspective of the ancient writers and the dilemma they faced when recording their own version of an event.

How an ancient event might be understood by an ancient reader/writer from different sides of the same event is rare. We know, for example, that the story of the near capture of Jerusalem by the eighth-century-BCE Assyrian King Sennacherib is recorded in both 2 Kings 18 as well as in the so-called Assyrian clay Prism text of Sennacherib's victories. Two versions of the same event told from opposing sides about the same event. We learn from this exercise that someone writing in ancient Israel may write about the same event with a totally different emphasis than an Assyrian writing about the same event in the same time period for an Assyrian audience. In both the Bible and the Assyrian Prism, the Assyrian King Sennacherib does not succeed in taking Jerusalem. In both, King Sennacherib exacts an enormous price from the Jerusalemites after capturing the surrounding towns. According to both accounts, the King of Jerusalem himself became a prisoner in his own city during the siege, and both use the phrase: "bird in a cage," to describe the King of Jerusalem. The accounts diverge from one another in a few points. In the Prism text, the courageous Assyrians have mercy upon the trapped King and his people and decided, after receiving the tribute that it was time to go home to Assyria, and they leave with their dignity intact. In 2 Kings 18 the facts appear to be the same but have been "spun" in a totally different direction. Yes, Jerusalem is besieged and yes, a tribute is paid to the Assyrians, but the Assyrians leave after suffering a humiliating defeat. It is interesting that even the Bible has three versions of the same basic story. In addition to 2 Kings 19, there are versions of these events in Isaiah 37 and 2 Chronicles 32. In them an angel stops the mighty warriors and commanders of the Assyrians, and then they leave with shame (after collecting the tribute that the king of a country would deserve during a state visit!) and even including a story about the killing of the King at the end of the expedition. 2 Kings 19 tells a similar story, but this time with details of a massive defeat of the Assyrians—again by an angel—(185,000 soldiers) and then the killing of King Sennacherib by his own named sons!

I present this story to show how even direct correlation of a single event in the Bible and archaeology can yield many different literary versions that are all describing the same event in different ways. Two different peoples,

Israelites and Assyrians, produced four surviving versions of the same event. This example shows us how it is possible to see how different writers, from the same country, will reflect upon the same event and write about it in different ways. What this means for assessing archaeology and the Bible is you must also beware of what survives. If we read only the biblical account, the Assyrian siege of Jerusalem looks like a huge defeat for the Assyrians. If we only had the Assyrian Prism account, we would think that the event was a huge defeat for the Judeans. The 2 Chronicles version is similar to but more devastating (and longer) than the Isaiah and 2 Kings version. Just because something survives does not make it the last word on a biblical event.

Drawing parallels between biblical texts and archaeology has been done in a variety of ways over the past century. Most people could point out parallels between the archaeological finds in Babylonia and Egypt in the past century and then find a biblical parallel. I think that what they are speaking of is a "background" to a biblical text. As we shall see, the background of a biblical story may indeed involve a very ancient "backstory." But the biblical writer, writing centuries after the event, may not have had all of the details of an ancient story and filled out the account with details that would have made sense to his reading public. Sometimes this "backstory" is one full running account that is ancient. Sometimes a few versions will be stitched together into what seems to be a full running account. The Book of Exodus provides examples of illumination and background that tell a totally different story than any of the individual writers of the Bible could ever have known. The background of a biblical account can involve a very well-known ancient Near Eastern story (such as the story of placing a baby in a basket on a river) or just a very good understanding of the topography, geography, architecture, weights, measures, and daily life.

Another form of background involves the "backstory" of a text that often is almost unknown to the modern reader but is very important to the writers and probably was still known to the ancient readers of the Bible. This backstory/backdrop involves a writer who is writing down his ancient narrative in the context of events of his own time. Often the writer cannot or will not set the entire tale in his own time period because the writer is afraid that it will lack authority or he recognizes that writing about a certain contemporary issue may put him in a precarious position.

The *Zohar*, the Jewish mystical "Book of Splendor," is an example of a book that was in need of just the right authority behind it in order to have people recognize its importance. The *Zohar* has come down to us in a version that is attributed to the ancient second century CE Rabbinic scholar from Galilee, Rabbi Shimon Bar Yohai. Modern scholars who have worked on the *Zohar* have shown that the book could not have been written any earlier than the twelfth century CE (one thousand years later than Rabbi Shimon Bar Yohai) and that the book is not from Palestine but rather from a European source. How could something like this happen? It is possible that parts of the work are older, but it is clear that the majority of the book represents theological musings that had begun to take shape among people with a mystical bent. The *Zohar* probably would not have been recognized as authoritative if the general public had known that it was written in the Middle Ages. So the author, Moses de Leon of Spain, attributed it to an ancient and venerable source, Rabbi Shimon Bar Yohai, who lived in the second century CE, because he apparently thought that the *Zohar* needed an ancient lineage in order to be accepted by the public.

The writer who sets his story in a different time period than his own does so to insure that the text is preserved by not only his own reading public but also by future readers. It is quite a different atmosphere for writing in antiquity. This is a very complex literary situation but is found in biblical writing all of the time. First, whole biblical books are attributed to a certain biblical figure. Even though the Bible does not literally say that the whole book Psalms was written by King David, it is traditionally attributed to King David. Although many Psalms contain information from various time periods before and way after King David lived, it seemed convenient to later Jewish and Christian tradition to attribute the whole collection to King David. Many books, such as *Song of Songs, Proverbs*, and *Ecclesiastes*, for example, are traditionally attributed to King Solomon while literary analysis shows that pieces of these books were written down in varying periods of time and represent theological ideas that were current one thousand years after Solomon's death. So why would someone attribute a book to King David and Solomon? Probably to make it more acceptable to the readers but also because the original authors did not think it was prudent to reveal their own identities. They may have seen themselves only as a conduit for this Divine information. The books were probably being read by the ancient reading public, and so they were recopied and preserved, but as the canonization process began (in the Greco-Roman period) the leadership looked for religious reasons for including all of the books that were accepted by the people.

Other "biblical" books in other eras show us that this technique was so popular that many works, in the pseudepigrapha and apocrypha, that did not make it into the Hebrew canonized Bible but were popular enough to survive in the larger Greek and other translations of the Bible, used it. Books called unabashedly "The Wisdom of Solomon," "The Book of Adam and Eve," "The Books of Enoch," "The Prayer of Manassas," "The Testament of Abraham," "The Assumption of Moses," and "The Martyrdom of Isaiah" were all written in the Hellenistic period but are attributed to a person and a period about a thousand years before they were written. They are all writing about ideas and reflect values from the Hellenistic world, and they are all attempting to retroject these values into the ancient narratives and figures of the Iron Age and even into the Bronze Age. Some of these works show a backdrop that is difficult to set in their own periods. In the book of *Judith*, for example, the writer sets the book in the time of the sixth-century-BCE conquest of Jerusalem by King Nebuchadnezzar even though it is clear that the whole book is about the second-century-BCE conquest of Jerusalem by the Seleucid King Antiochus Epiphanes. The writer may have felt constrained by writing so zealously against the Greek king in his own period, and so he set the work in the more ancient context of the King of Babylonia.

In order for a technique like this to work, the readers need to have some cue to know what "really" the text is about. Usually this cue by a writer will be something that only the readers of his time period will understand but will not tip off the outsiders to his real purpose. This technique was a "subversive" way to use ancient texts to mean different things in different periods. Did biblical writers use a cue in the text to show readers what they were really writing about? Although scholars acknowledge that the biblical writers in the Hellenistic period retrojected their writing into a more ancient period to allow them the freedom to criticize elements in their own time, scholars speculate whether this same technique was employed by the most ancient writers of the Hebrew Bible in all periods. I assume that the biblical writers used the same techniques in the classical Hebrew Bible as these other Jewish writers did in this later period. They were following in the footsteps of a common ancient writing practice. This means that you must "dig" below the apparent façade of a text to understand its original status. It is a form of what I call literary archaeology. Looking for when a text was written and why it was written in that time period is as important as what the text says. Only when we really know why and when a text was written can we make a comparison with material culture. Inevitably when a text was written down is going to be after the event actually happened. But to know when a biblical text was written down often means that you must "dig" much deeper than the time period the text is reporting about and you need to know a lot more history than you might think.

Although I have tried not to use too much jargon, I do move back and forth through a number of historical periods and locations in *Digging through the Bible.* I also assume basic knowledge about how an archaeological site works. The Appendix on "Exploring an Archaeological Site" introduces you to the details of an excavation. The chronology and map at the beginning of the text can serve as a useful reference as we embark on this tour through the mysteries of the Bible.

1

The Search for Sinai: Archaeological Reflections on Moses, the Exodus, and the Revelation at Mount Sinai

Figure 1.1.　Is this Mount Sinai?

Courtesy Gary Hochman, Har Karkom Project.

I BEGIN WITH AN ANCIENT and foundational question: the search for a historical Moses, Aaron, and Miriam, the Exodus of the Israelites from Egypt, and the revelation of the Law on Mount Sinai. Did these people, events, and places really exist in a verifiable historical context, or are they the invention of creative writers in some late and unknown period? These are some of the most controversial topics that we encounter when trying to use archaeology and biblical criticism scholarship. These are also examples that prove the rule of biblical and archaeological information: that it is not so easy to say that people, events, and places like those mentioned in the Bible didn't exist or happen just because we have not found conclusive evidence to authenticate them. Some of my answers to these questions come from my own excavations and study, and other answers come from the work of my colleagues. Some of our collaborations occurred in academic settings, but often the most productive discussions take place at the expedition dinner table or around the campfire at night.

My Passover at Mount Sinai

According to the Bible, Mount Sinai was the destination of the Israelites as they left Egypt after celebrating the first Passover, but many today question where Mount Sinai was located, if it even existed at all. The Passover and Mount Sinai are intertwined in the story of the Exodus. Fifty days after the Passover, the Israelites arrived at Mount Sinai. So it seemed to me very ironic that a few days before we began our work at what was being reported to be the new "Mount Sinai," an isolated mountain in what is today the southern Negev—on today's border with Egypt, I took our staff to a Passover Seder in northern Israel. Our staff includes some of the finest scientists from around the world, and we all had been intrigued by the possibility that, for the first time, a mountain that could be Mount Sinai was available for our research. Our geophysical group included this time, Paul Bauman from WorleyParsons Komex in Canada and his associate Chris Pooley, Harry Jol from the University of Wisconsin, Eau Claire, and Phil Reeder from the University of South Florida. We have worked together over the past decade on about twenty different archaeological excavations all around Israel and Spain, and we all know each other's specialties (and families) very well. One key to our success is that we have worked together so long that we can actually look at each other's data and help one another interpret the data as they are being collected. We have learned to ask each other questions that serve the research goals of our different disciplines. The other members of our team usually included

Christine Dalenta, our chief photographer, and our resident archaeologist, Maha Darawsha of the University of Hartford. Having a research team like ours who have worked together on so many different projects in caves, deserts, wetlands, cemeteries, shorelines, and mountains, to name just a few contexts, has taught us something about the value of research collaboration. Any one of us could go out and excavate alone, but together we have the opportunity to use our collective wisdom to solve a problem. We all work on these projects during the summer, winter, and sometimes in spring when our other faculty commitments permit. As I looked around the table at that Passover Seder, I realized how lucky we all were to have found each other from so many different disciplines and backgrounds, and how we needed each other in order to solve mysteries together that we could never solve alone.

This new site for Mount Sinai in the Negev provided evidence of massive and long-term settlement in the Bronze Age by a variety of different tribes and groups. I had heard about this "new" Mount Sinai that had been rediscovered by Professor Emmanuel Anati of Italy over the past decade. His 1986 book, *The Mountain of God: Har Karkom* (Rizzoli International Publications, New York) was a stunning and revolutionary attempt to up-end the traditional locations for Mount Sinai that had been produced over the past fifteen hundred years. He did what no other researcher was willing to do: propose a new hypothesis not only based on the archaeology present at the mountain, but also linked directly with the biblical Exodus story.

This new site is massive by any definition of an archaeological site. Anati's Har Karkom site is one of the largest archaeological concessions in the Middle East. At over 200+ square kilometers of territory surrounding the mountain, it is difficult to imagine how any archaeological team could ever complete such a large undertaking in one lifetime. To give you an understanding of how massive Anati's undertaking is, I will compare it to one of our excavation sites. We have been excavating for twenty years at an archaeological site in northern Israel (Bethsaida) that is in a beautiful, pristine location by the north shore of the Sea of Galilee with roads, lights, water, and bathrooms and accessible all throughout the year. We have worked every year for twenty years with thousands of volunteers for two to three months at a time, and the site is only twenty acres. In twenty years we have fully excavated about three acres! The idea of trying to make sense out of a site that is over ten times the size of Bethsaida in the middle of the Negev desert with no roads, lights, water, bathrooms and accessible only at limited times (one to two weeks a year) is mind-boggling. In the over twenty-five years of excavations that Anati has directed at Har Karkom, however, he has focused on the distinctive features of the mountain and its environs, including a collection of over forty thousand pieces of ancient rock art that ring the mountain and the surrounding valleys for miles around. We felt that we could do what no other research group could do: help design a subsurface map of what should be excavated using our high tech equipment and indicate what potential sites for excavations should be pursued.

The mountain is in a desolate area of the Israeli Negev and in a sensitive political area on an Israeli military base on the border with present-day Egypt. According to Anati's license, we would be permitted to work at the site only when the majority of soldiers were on leave, during the holiday of Passover! The irony of going to search out the major symbol of the Exodus, Mount Sinai, during the holiday remembering the Exodus from Egypt, Passover, was not lost on these scientists. I brought our staff to a large Kibbutz-style Passover Seder at Kibbutz Ginosar on the Sea of Galilee in northern Israel to celebrate the first part of the holiday and discuss our research goals.

Many of our staff had never been to a Passover Seder. Throughout the evening they were surprised by the intense interest that young and old had in the story of the Exodus from Egypt. Our Passover Haggadah with a translation into English gave our scientific staff access to the meaning behind every word and gesture of the officiating Rabbi. By the third cup of wine my curiosity got the better of me, and I simply asked the question that had been on my mind since we started investigating this mystery mountain in the southern Negev. "What," I asked "would happen to all these people and their interest in the Exodus from Egypt if we found out that it did not happen at all?" They all looked at me incredulous, as if I had asked the unaskable: "Look at all of these people praying and studying about the Exodus from Egypt, what do you think they would say if they knew that there was a possibility that the event, the Exodus from Egypt, never really happened in history but rather was just a symbolic or mythological story created by ancient writers to motivate ancient readers to live a better or more meaningful life?"

One of the geophysicists on our team answered the question the way that I have become accustomed to answering all of the excavation issues that we have faced over the past twenty years. He looked at me and simply answered: "What makes you think it is so easy to decide anything so decisively with science?" "But," he quickly added, "it does give you a sense of the enormity of the enterprise." Thus we began our own work on the search for Mount Sinai as a part of our own contribution to the understanding of the story of the Exodus.

Questions About the Exodus

My questions about the Exodus from Egypt and the Sinai event are different now than they were in the past. They are more mindful of the complexities of science and the varying shades of modern religious identity. Simply put, whenever I find that science is trying to solve an ancient mystery such as the origins of the universe, the meaning of the miracles depicted in the Bible, and a question such as the Exodus from Egypt and the revelation of the Torah/Law at Mount Sinai, I immediately recognize that science will be able to solve only part of a question. From that point onward, people extrapolate to find out the rest of the story. I am interested in why scientific answers have been given greater emphasis in the modern period over traditional answers, even when the traditional answers do not really challenge the scientific answers. Modern Jews, Christians, and Muslims, who all use the Bible in varying measures in their religious life, have accepted science as a determining factor for key religious questions, but differing denominations within these religions have accepted varying scientific answers to religious questions.

The enslavement of the Israelites, the Exodus from Egypt, and the revelation of the Law on Mount Sinai are major topics that unite Jews, Christians, and Muslims. These events are crucial in every major part of the entire Hebrew Bible—most of the thirty-nine books attest to the importance of the Exodus and it is mentioned in every division of the Hebrew Bible. Later Rabbinic texts and liturgy, Jewish daily rituals, and almost all Jewish holidays during the Jewish calendar year demonstrate the recognition of the Exodus from Egypt as a justification for the practice. One holiday, Passover, has an entire set of biblical and Rabbinic readings, the Passover Haggadah, devoted to it. Christians have used the enslavement of the Hebrews in Egypt and the Exodus from Egypt as one of the enduring themes of the earliest Gospel accounts and the New Testament, and it is a central pillar of the early Church Fathers. The Exodus fueled the creation of Christian hymns and liturgy throughout the past one thousand years. I remember singing the spiritual "Go Down Moses" in an elementary school concert—a sign of just how accepted the idea of the Exodus is in Western civilization.

For Muslims, the Exodus tradition is equally venerated. In Islam, the story of Moses, the enslavement of the Israelites and the Exodus take up major Surahs (chapters) in the Koran. These three religions have embraced the themes of Exodus as basic to the theological truths that these religions teach. I realize that just because it has been venerated by three thousand years of tradition, and all three of these major religions, it does not mean that it actually happened. But it does mean that it requires an enormous amount of evidence to overturn three thousand years of preserved literary and religious tradition. With little conclusive evidence, however, the idea that the Exodus did not happen has spread quickly from the halls of academe to the pews of churches and synagogues in the past decade. I decided I needed to reresearch the whole question the day after I read that a Rabbi received enormous media attention when he proclaimed in a published interview: "The truth is that virtually every modern archaeologist who has investigated the story of the Exodus, with very few exceptions, agrees that the way the Bible describes the Exodus is not the way it happened, if it happened at all." (*Los Angeles Times*, April 13, 2001). It all had gone too far, too fast, without a real attempt to test all of the theories.

Bad Science and Bad Religion

The problem of identifying biblical people and places is complicated by the way that modern archaeology and science in general is set up to answer questions. The scientific method that is at work in archaeology, like all other sciences, often leads to what we call scientific reductionism. It is a wonderful way to know more and more about less and less. The problem with reducing complex questions to their most basic parts is that it can lead to myopia that ignores the complexity of issues that are present in a problem. When scientists look at the complexity of the human body, for example, they end up breaking down the human body into component parts, studying an individual building block of our genetic makeup or individual chemicals in food and individual problems in the environment. In the end we know an enormous amount about how these individual processes work, but very little about how they function together in the human body. So too, the use of archaeology and the scientific method add to the meaning of the Bible. The Bible, like the human body is a complex creation. It is not like investigating the telephone book. Although most archaeologists know this, they tend to forget it the moment they reach the part where they have to compare their scientific conclusions to the Bible. The scientific method that directs one in archaeology is the same scientific method that directs one in the reading of the Bible. As we shall see, the interplay between small scientific details and the larger history has wide-ranging implications for the investigation of the Exodus and the search for Mount Sinai.

My questions are simple: Why are people in such a rush to dismiss an event that has been taken for granted for such a long time by three major religions? What is the improbable part of the Exodus? Is it the enslavement of an entire people by the Egyptians? Is it the saving of the infant Moses? Moses' going out and return from exile? Are the famous plagues that afflicted Egypt and the Egyptians so improbable? Is it that the people crossed the Red Sea on dry land? Is it that they arrived at Mount Sinai in forty-five days? Is it that the people had the Law revealed to them at the foot of a mountain in the desert? In this chapter I will grapple with what I believe to be the most contentious parts of the debate.

One of the most difficult points about the entire story of the Exodus from Egypt for most people to believe is the sheer numbers of refugees. If we accept at face value the *prima facie* reading of the Bible, 603,550 men plus their wives and children left Egypt in what is described in the Bible as a single event, it seems fantastic to the point of impossibility. The deserts of what is today Israel and Egypt could never have supported so many people for even a short period of time. If we uncritically look at the sheer numbers, 603,550 men plus their wives and children, this would be millions of people leaving in a single event. What makes it so difficult for scholars and casual readers is the fact that this number of exiles would represent a large percentage of the entire Egyptian population of the time. It just seems to be too large to be possible. Of course, today we look at the nearly twelve million Mexicans who have come in small bands and waves over the border of the United States, many illegally, and see that the number while large is not unprecedented. In the most recent conflicts in the Middle East in the past half century, millions of refugees moved from one part of the Middle East to another in waves. In the 1980s to 1990s millions of Russian Jews left the former Soviet Union in what was described then as an 'Exodus.' Yet even in modern Egyptian history, it is now accepted that the Hyksos, the rulers of Egypt for almost two centuries in antiquity, made a mass Exodus from Egypt, although there is little scientific evidence to support this Exodus. So why is the Hyksos Exodus more palatable than the Israelite Exodus? I think it is because there are no Hyksos to use this event in the modern period but the Israelite event may be viewed as having modern implications.

My archaeological inquiry into evidence about the historical possibility of the Biblical Exodus focused on three areas:

1. *The large numbers of people involved in the Exodus.* Why such large numbers of people did not leave us more physical evidence in the deserts of Sinai if the events recorded in the Bible occurred the way the Bible records them;
2. *The time period of the Exodus.* (Also the resulting reentry into the Land of Israel); and
3. *The background of the Exodus* or the evidence of the Israelites and whether they were in Egypt at all.

The story of the Exodus and the receiving of the Law at Mount Sinai are short in comparison with the great ancient national narratives in the Near East. The Exodus is presented in the fifteen opening chapters of the book of Exodus, the second book of the Bible. The continuing journey through the desert and the encounter with Mount Sinai is chronicled in the third book of the Bible, Leviticus, the fourth book of the Bible, Numbers, and again in the fifth book of the Bible, Deuteronomy. Even those people who reject the entire story of the Exodus and Mount Sinai as historical events start from the same basic assumptions. They assume that the events that are described in the end of the Book of Genesis and the beginning of the Book of the Exodus, from the Hebrew descent into Egypt, their enslavement, their Exodus and journey to the Promised Land, all happened in what archaeologists refer to as the Bronze Age (twentieth century BCE–1200 BCE). Most Bible scholars, archaeologists, and even learned members of the general public accept that if the events happened, they would have happened in this single historical period (the Bronze Age). After reviewing the evidence, my theory is that the events happened, but not in the way we traditionally expect. What if the Exodus was not one single event, but rather a series of events that began in one period and ended in another? Biblical writers were known for collapsing or telescoping materials together in their time period and as we have seen, the Redactor exercised a hand in piecing together disparate versions together into one account. Perhaps that is what happened in the story of the Exodus?

I begin with the time designations and the problems of definitions that often do not easily fit the evidence and why. If you are unfamiliar with the terminology, please refer back to the chronology that I have created for quick reference. Although most scholars think that the events of the Exodus occurred during the late Bronze Age (1900–1200 BCE), it is assumed that the Bible was finally written down in a form similar to the one we have today during the Iron Age and through the Persian period (539–332 BCE). If so, the biblical writers were writing about events that had happened over a thousand years before. By the twelfth century BCE, we have some evidence of a very diverse settlement pattern that continues to develop during the Iron Age of what scholars are willing to call the "Israelites" in the Land of Israel, and it fits into a chronological context of a more defined history of the Israelites in Egypt and Israel. Some basic facts are agreed to by most scholars, but most of the details of the Exodus, the events of Mount Sinai, and even the entrance of the Israelites into the Land of Israel are disputed, and the confusion about whether these events happened at all has developed over the past thirty years.

The story of the Exodus and the subsequent event at Mount Sinai are only found in the Bible and in the writings of the ancient Jewish historian, Josephus Flavius, who died at the end of the first century CE, but he quoted an even earlier Egyptian source, Manetho. In the first book of the Bible, Genesis, the sons of the Patriarch Jacob and their families come down to Egypt from the land of Canaan where they were residing after a terrible famine in their land. Joseph, Jacob's son, has assumed a leadership role under an unnamed Pharaoh and the brothers and then the Patriarch Jacob all take up residence in Egypt. The group, known as the "Hebrews" come to Egypt and live for a long period of time until the political fortunes of the group changes. A new Pharaoh emerges who decides to enslave the Hebrews (now called in the book of Exodus: *The Children of Israel*), forcing them to build the cities of Pithom and Rameses. This Pharaoh, according to the Book of Exodus, decides not only to enslave the people but to limit the number of Hebrews by instituting a national policy of infanticide for male children of the Hebrews. He tells the midwives of the Hebrews to cast the children "into the Nile."

Moses, a son of a Hebrew from the tribe of Levi, should have been cast into the river but is saved through a deception by his mother and sister. They place the baby Moses in a "basket of bulrushes caulked with bitumen and pitch" and placed it in the Nile. The daughter of the Pharaoh is bathing in the river, sees the basket, hears the crying of the child, and takes the baby into the royal family. Moses grows up as an Egyptian "prince" scarcely aware of the plight of the Israelites but is introduced into the dilemma and takes action that leads to his killing an Egyptian and his self-imposed exile. He is drawn back to Egypt from his exile in Midian by his encounter with a "burning bush" where the God of the Hebrews speaks to him and tells him to return to Egypt to ask for the release of the Hebrew slaves. He returns to Egypt, encounters the new Pharaoh, and together with his brother Aaron continues to demand the release of his fellow Hebrews throughout a sequence of ten environmental disasters that befall Egypt. After the tenth and final "plague" that results in the killing of all first-born children of Egypt, the Pharaoh releases the Israelites, who leave amidst a "mixed multitude" into the desert for their encounter with the God of Israel.

In the meantime, the Pharaoh decides that his decision to allow them to leave was premature and brings the Egyptian army to chase them into the desert. As they reach the Red Sea, a dry path in the seabed allows the Israelites to pass through on dry land, but when the Egyptians reach the same path they are drowned under a returning deluge of water. The Israelites continue for forty-five days, finally reaching the foot of Mount Sinai where they encounter the God of Israel for one brief moment and then receive the Divine Law through Moses. From this encounter, Judaism, Christianity, and Islam derive their concepts of power and ongoing authority. A God who speaks to a people through a prophet gives them a testament to follow and sends them on a mission that is intended to extend far into their future. In short, this is the basic story of the Exodus and the Sinai event as recorded in the book of Exodus.

It is not the story itself that raises the rankles of controversy for biblical archaeologists. It is that we do not have a comparative body of archaeological evidence to discuss the historical accuracy of this story. When I was a student some thirty years ago, the questions about Exodus began. I remember hearing Egyptologists say that from Egyptian records, it is clear that the Egyptians never enslaved anyone in antiquity, so the biblical account must be wrong. I often thought about that as axiomatic of the whole question of the Exodus. If you were the leader of a nation that enslaved another people, would you laud it in your own literature or not? I answered my own question by the negative. I later studied ancient Egyptians in great detail and have become convinced that they, like the Stalinist regime of the former Soviet Union, were concerned with controlling the information flow, had an overarching perspective on their cumulative history, and were indeed experts in public relations. I cannot imagine that they would have advertised in their written or pictorial history their need to enslave anyone to create the marvelous institutions of Egypt. In addition, as with many other peoples in antiquity, the recorded history of the Egyptians was *the history of elite indigenous Egyptians*, excluding any "foreigners/peoples" that may have populated Egypt in any particular period. So, in fact, I learned the first lesson of looking for historical evidence in Egyptian history. Beware of what you find and what you do not find.

Searching for Biblical Figures: Moses, Miriam, and All of the Other Named and Unnamed Men and Women of the Bible

The idea of an "historical Moses" is problematic for a number of reasons. Trying to authenticate the existence of a single person, such as Moses, through archaeology is much the same as looking for a single needle in a haystack. Even with historical figures about whom we have plenty of contemporary information, such as George Washington, it is difficult to weed through the literary accounts and material culture (the "George Washington slept here" traditions, for example) to fully validate the near mythological stories of his life. Much less can be said for Moses because there is no other contemporary source for his existence outside of the Bible. Even the name of Moses is a mystery. The name "Moshe" in biblical Hebrew is given a nice etymology in the book of Exodus as being derived from the word for "to be drawn from" (Exodus 2:10): ". . . because I (Pharaoh's daughter) drew him out of the water." This final comment is clearly a writer's attempt to give meaning to what was otherwise a good Egyptian designation. Although the name is fitting (he was *drawn out of the water*) because of the play on words, this meaning makes sense only to the reader in later biblical Hebrew. The name, "Moses," can more easily be derived as a shortened Egyptian name, "*Mses*" or "son," which would have made more sense because it is the daughter of Pharaoh that is giving him this name. On the other hand, it is possible that the original name of Moses is unknown, and this is just a "placeholder" name that was given by the writer as he completed writing down the oral traditions that he had in his possession. The Bible is replete with names that are not really names, but rather "placeholders" that the writers of the biblical text used because either they did not know the name or this was the oral tradition that had been passed down to them.

But surnames in the Bible were important for providing another aspect to the story. A name allowed the writer to develop drama, foreshadowing, and character. The names of the first children in the Bible, Cain and Abel, are a good example. Abel (*Hevel* in Hebrew), is the first murder victim in the Bible and has an unusual name that may have been a literary signal to his fate. Abel (*Hevel*) means "nothingness" in Hebrew. Cain (*Qayin* in Hebrew) is thought to mean something like "acquired" in Hebrew. The biblical writer may not have known their real names but had the oral version of the story and realized that the names could provide important opportunities for foreshadowing of their fates and providing the reader with their character traits. Would you really name a child "nothingness"? Was it his real name or is this just a symbolic placeholder that the Bible writer used to foreshadow his fate—death at the hand of his brother? The case of Moses is similar. It is probably not a Hebrew name since Hebrew probably did not exist as a language yet, and it is a well-documented Egyptian royal designation. Rameses, Ra-M[e]ses, the son of Ra (or born of Ra) and Tuthmosis, the son of Tuth (or born of Tuth) show us this form. The commonality of the Egyptian naming system and the absence of another character named Moses in the Bible implies that the name was probably an Egyptian loan name. Was Moses just called "a son" (of the Pharaoh)? If so, Moses was, like many others in the Bible, given a name that was a description of his status.

It is hard to know why it was not more common in the Hebrew Bible, but clearly the name Moses is not unique for Egyptian literature. There are two references to a "Mose" in documents dating to the time of Rameses. The existence of a name like that in documents suggests that it was possible that real people had just the "Mses" denomination, but even knowing that the name exists still does not tell us that a particular person in the court of Pharaoh did what the Bible says he did. Names are particularly difficult elements to track within the text of the Bible.

But aspects of Moses' life are illuminated by ancient archaeological discoveries. The main story of Moses' birth and journey in a "basket" on the Nile is interesting in the context of ancient Near East history. A similar story is told in Mesopotamian texts of the birth and journey in a "basket caulked with bitumen and pitch" on a different river for the leader Sargon of Akkad. Is it a coincidence that such a story appears in antiquity about two very different leaders, or is it just another example about how the biblical writing is demonstrating a familiarity with these stories by including them? Walking through the Cairo Museum on my last trip to Egypt, I noticed on display small baskets for infants that were generally thought of as "burial baskets." Perhaps we can learn from this that the Bible is recording a real event. The mother of Moses placed him in a burial basket and then placed the basket in the Nile as a cheap and meaningful burial for a child that Pharaoh had ordered to be "cast into the Nile." The most important part of these burial baskets is that they are indeed Bronze-Age-period burial devices that survived the millennia and illuminate an aspect of Moses' enigmatic life.

The fourth and fifth century CE traditions in the Babylonian Talmud (Tractate Megillah 13a), as well as various Midrashim, tell us that Moses had a total of seven different names. The Rabbis are attempting to harmonize the very different biblical traditions about Moses with their own more detailed view of the narrative. In addition to the name "Moshe," Rabbinic tradition relates that he had many other names, including *Yered, Avigdor, Chever, Avi-socho, Yekutiel, and Avi-Zanoach*. All of these names are interpreted from incidents in the text of the Bible that seem to be talking about Moses, yet in each case another name is mentioned. The Rabbinic conclusion was that these were all references to Moses, even though another name is mentioned in each instance. In addition, since Moses is not a king, nor is he a judge (he is, however, called a prophet) and definitely not an Aaronid priest/Kohen (although he is seems to be from the same Levite tribe as his brother Aaron), it is hard to establish what his base of authority is in the Bible. He is primarily a "prophet," a person through whom the will of God is communicated to others. This is the primary definition of a prophet in the Hebrew Bible. He does not predict the future, he does not relate his own thoughts, but he is a messenger of God's will. Although Moses is the one who basically initiates the conditions for Aaron to officiate in the Tabernacle, Moses is called in two places, "a man of God (Elohim)" and "a servant (*eved*) of the Lord." These are probably synonyms for his status as prophet in the book of Deuteronomy, which has a different vocabulary with regards to the Exodus, the journey in the desert and the revelation at Mount Sinai. The issue of who Moses is (or was) cannot be resolved without a totally independent piece of literature or artifact in which he is mentioned. To date, we do not have such an artifact or piece of literature, so Moses remains a mystery man with enormous importance for Jews, Christians, and Muslims since he appears in Jewish, Christian, and Muslim literature from the Hebrew Bible onward. He is seen as a man of mystery, wrapped in the shroud of a conundrum, but a very well documented conundrum.

The Documentary Hypothesis and Moses

The "Documentary Hypothesis" is a modern literary method that plays a key role in understanding why the Bible is written the way it is and can be used to unravel the literary pieces that have been "sewn" together in antiquity. The documentary hypothesis was developed over the past 150 years by literary scholars of the Bible who felt that there was no reigning hypothesis to guide modern research of the Bible. It is similar to Darwin's *Origin of the Species* hypothesis for the development of human beings in that it divides the Bible up into different developmental documents and stages of writing that were added to over the centuries to create what we refer to as the Bible. Archaeologists today rarely use the results of the documentary hypothesis and are simultaneously reading the Bible in a nonscientific, almost literalist, way and then complain that the stories do not match scientific data they have discovered. All scientists who use different disciplines in their work should begin their studies using the scientific method used in that discipline. The documentary hypothesis is the best scientific theory for reading the Bible that we currently have. It systematically analyzes the language, context, style, and vocabulary of the different literary parts of the Bible and then reconstructs from this analysis a hypothesis that divides the Bible into different documents that were edited together. To read a text using the documentary hypothesis takes some training and practice. The documentary hypothesis recognizes that there was an ancient oral tradition of the Hebrews and the later Israelites that was only written down once they were settled in their land and had a chance to develop a written language. That written language, Hebrew, which is contained in the Hebrew Bible is a rather late innovation in human history, perhaps dating to the tenth century BCE. So the events that were from the period before the advent of Hebrew writing were preserved as oral traditions and then were set down in writing many centuries after the events that had happened. The Priests (Aaronid/Kohanim) of ancient Israel who were involved in writing down the Bible in the earliest period of Israelite (Hebrew) writing were probably the most educated class of Israelites and perhaps the most knowledgeable about the oral traditions of the ancient Israelites from a Priestly perspective. The Aaronid priests were human beings who, like all human beings, beyond just telling the traditional oral histories that were passed down to them also had a clear theological agenda based upon their experience in the priesthood. Biblical scholars have found, for example, that the priests did not like miracle stories and did not like to emphasize non-Aaronid (Priestly) figures in their stories. Moses' role in this whole adventure is complicated by the Priestly writers who have a need to present Aaron as the "true" leader of the Israelites. Moses is at once a Levite and member of Aaron's immediate family, but he is also a competitor for Aaron in his leadership of the Israelites in the desert. Two different traditions about Moses emerge in the Bible. There are, in fact, two separate views of leadership at play in the book of Exodus—one that diminishes Moses' stature and another that presents him as the most courageous and daring leader of the Israelites, unparalleled in this period. Scholars who carefully looked at the text found that the diminishing of Moses appeared only in certain sections of the book of Exodus. In one tradition, Moses alone is nearly infallible and is the originator of miracles and strategies. In the other tradition, Moses is always portrayed alongside Aaron who is needed to perform each miracle and to make each strategic move. In what may seem as the ultimate irony, the latter tradition has a story of Moses encountering God on top of Mount Sinai and then coming down from this encounter with some type of facial disfigurement that forces him to wear a veil on his face. According to this tradition, Moses' face was apparently scarred by his encounter with God to the point that he is forced to wear a veil for the rest of his life (Exodus 34:29–35). Who wrote this last tradition that diminishes Moses' importance and contact with the Israelites in the Bible? It is thought that Aaronid (the descendents of Aaron) priests (Kohanim) preserved this oral tradition about Moses' disfigurement while the non-Aaronids preserved a totally different tradition about Moses. It is not that one or the other writer "made things up," rather that one tradition preserved a view that negatively impacted the influence of Moses while the other oral tradition did not preserve this view or decided to ignore it. The combined final edited version gives us very different views of Moses.

From Moses to Aaron

When Moses appears in his role of challenging Pharaoh, Aaron stands often in the Priestly versions of these tales as Moses' coequal in the pronouncement of the punishment to the Egyptians. Aaron's "staff" is used by Moses while in other parts of the story, Moses' staff is used to exact punishment upon the Egyptians. When I was a child and read these sections one after another I always asked myself: Why does Moses suddenly use Aaron's staff? What happened to Moses' staff? Scholars began to hypothesize that there were two separate traditions intertwined here: one in which Moses' staff was used and another view that had the miracles and punishments exacted through the use of Aaron's staff. In general, scholars also distinguished a very specific attitude towards miracles. Whenever a section of Bible dealt with miracles, it was either done through Aaron or there was no miracle. Bible scholars noted that the Priestly writers generally did not include in their versions of some stories characters or events that suspended the natural laws. They eschewed the talking animals, angels, and traditions in the Bible. When we find that a snake or a donkey talks, we know that these were not traditions preserved by Priestly writers. They apparently felt that the intervention of God in daily life would undermine the authority of the earthbound servant of God, the Aaronid Priest. Others obviously delighted in preserving these "miracle" traditions. In non-Priestly traditions, Moses stands alone. In the Priestly tradition, whenever God's will is done, Moses and Aaron are in the tradition together. It is a hallmark of Priestly writing to place Aaron at the center of most of the major episodes of Exodus, most of the time alongside Moses. It is Moses and Aaron who are condemned for their anger with the people (Exodus 17 and Numbers 20), so much so that they are *both* not allowed into the Promised Land. This is odd because it is clear from the traditions in the Bible that only Moses should be condemned for his anger with the people. In the Priestly tradition, if an interaction with the Divine happened, it happened to Moses and Aaron.

The accounts of Moses encountering God without Aaron are not found in the Aaronid versions of these Bibles. One account is of Moses at the "burning bush" talking directly with God and being summoned to Mount Sinai to encounter God alone. It is clearly not a Priestly account because the Priests would have carefully guarded their exclusive rights to encountering God. Contrasting this with the Priestly accounts of Moses, he is invariably paired with Aaron (his spokesman) each time there is a miracle to be wrought. In this Priestly tradition, Moses uses *the staff of Aaron* to act, and finally it is Moses who cannot face the people after his encounter with God on the Mount, and thus uses Aaron as his surrogate. The Tabernacle,

God's dwelling place in the desert, is the domain exclusively of the Aaronids and the only place and way to really communicate with God. To communicate with God, one must do it through the Priests and the sacrifices in the Tabernacle. The documentary hypothesis gives us a totally different text to consider when we read the Bible. It sets the traditions into different contexts and can make the reading more meaningful but vastly more complex in comparison with medieval commentators. Judaism, Christianity, and Islam employed commentaries written in the Byzantine period and into the Middle Ages to make sense out of many of the problems that documentary hypothesis scholars have explained in different ways. A scientific reading of the text of the book of Exodus reveals many parallel story lines going on simultaneously in the Exodus account(s) in chapters 1–15 and in the Exodus to Sinai (chapters 15–20). These parallel story lines show that there are different accounts that have been put together here by the person that Bible scholars call "the Redactor." The Redactor is the person, who lived in the Persian period, when most of what we call the Hebrew Bible was edited together. He had to find ways to "transition" from one literary block (or oral tradition) that he was preserving to another. He lived after the most traumatic time of Israelite history, the destruction of the First Temple, in 586 BCE and the Exile of the Judeans from their land to Babylonia. He probably began his task because of these great tragedies, but he may have finished his work as a way of reorienting the returning Exiles to their ancient heritage. Whatever his motivation, Bible scholars assume that the Redactor wanted to make sure that most of the surviving biblical accounts, (which were probably still circulating in both oral and written fashion among certain groups) were formalized or finalized into the religious history of the people of Israel. He was faced with many choices of editing and transitioning between the traditions that had been transmitted from generation to generation in his own day. He followed a famous editing technique of antiquity found throughout many other religious texts. He decided to "collapse" the parallel accounts of people, places, and events that had been passed down to him into a woven tapestry of a text. It is not known if he was trying to create a unified, continuous, chronological text, but he clearly chose the technique of weaving rather than the other ancient alternative of parallel, distinct accounts. Some of you might ask how I can be so sure that this was the method of editing that was done? The answer is because we have many other ancient examples that we can compare the Bible to.

In some ancient religious texts, parallel versions of people, places, and events were kept separate. This is what we have, for example, in the case of the parallel versions of Alexander the Great's "lives" or the four canonized versions of the Gospels of Jesus in the New Testament. The four parallel canonized Gospels contain contradictions, inconsistencies, and redundant accounts, but since they were separated out into four distinct Gospels that developed in different places and championed by different writers in the first century, they were not originally read together. They were read (or probably heard) by distinct audiences who came to venerate each particular version. In the fourth century CE a Redactor attempted to weave all four of the accounts together into one unified account (similar to the Hebrew Bible's Redactor) and the result, the *Diatessaron*, is a unique example of how an ancient editor worked. Unfortunately, by the time he did this editorial work, all of the canonized Gospels had become too well known and venerated to allow the *Diatessaron* to become the only text of the Church. The Redactor of the Hebrew Bible, on the other hand, either because of the time period in which he did his editing (writing and copying were still very unique and difficult), the lack of circulating exemplars as competition, or perhaps because of the stature the Redactor enjoyed in the community, was able to weave his tapestry. The Redactor chose the more complex, weaving edit that allowed all the traditions that he had to flow into one another, even with all of the problems of redundancy, contradictions, and inconsistencies remaining. He included two versions of a creation of the world and human beings in the opening chapters of Genesis even though they disagree on fundamental issues. He included two versions of an antediluvian flood that differs on fundamental issues such as the duration of the flood and what was brought on the ark. Most Bible scholars reason that two versions of important accounts were circulating in antiquity. The Redactor of the Bible made an editorial decision to "collapse" the two versions into one continuous story even though by doing so he was actually creating a third, new hybrid account.

Such hybrid accounts have implications for our understanding of Moses and Aaron. Examples of this phenomenon abound in the Hebrew Bible, but especially in the first five books of Moses. In the book of Numbers, chapter 16, a relative of Moses and Aaron, Korah, rebels against Aaron and relatives of the tribe of Reuben, and the tribe of the first born of the Patriarch Jacob, Dathan and Abiram, rebel against the leadership of Moses. As we read in the book of Numbers, it appears as if there is one big rebellion against Moses and Aaron. But in the conclusion to the story there is a revealing glitch. In the end of the rebellion, the book of Numbers chapter 16, verse 31ff, states that "the earth opened its mouth and swallowed them [the rebels] up . . . So they and all that belonged to them went down alive into Sheol and the earth closed over them, and they perished from the midst of the assembly." According to the book of Numbers this includes everyone, Korah and his followers and Dathan and Abiram and his followers. But in the rest of the Bible, Korah and his family have survived and continued to live on amongst the priestly tribes. This "contradiction" allowed biblical commentators to create some of the most elaborate literary superstructures to accommodate what they saw as a unified story line. Modern Bible scholars think that the Redactor collapsed the two rebellions into one rebellion here, even though the results were very different. The rebellion against Moses ended in the earthquake swallowing up the rebels. The Korah and his priestly followers who rebelled against Aaron probably faced a different punishment. But since collapsing and weaving traditions together was apparently a well-respected form of editing among the Jews, the story remains a biblical commentator's opportunity to add all manner of interpretation to harmonize the "contradictions." This editing technique continued for the next two thousand years. A couple of examples from different periods of biblical and Jewish history will suffice.

The most famous example of editing and weaving texts from different, parallel sources is found in the Talmudim. There are two Talmuds, the so-called Jerusalem or Palestinian Talmud (PT) composed in Israel and the Babylonian Talmud compiled in Babylonia. The Talmudim show us how historical events and periods were often collapsed into one another in order to make sense of events that occurred in periods about which they had little or no systematic information. In the Talmudim, Rabbis living in the first and second centuries CE in Israel are having discussions with Rabbis living in Babylonia centuries later. Although one might argue that they are in a literary discussion, it appears from the text that they are actually in a discussion, since a second or third century CE (Tana) will actually answer a question from a fourth or fifth century (Amora) in both the Palestinian and the later Babylonian Talmud. It is not surprising that the final version of Rabbinic liturgy (which is edited in the early Middle Ages) also used this method of editing. Rabbinically sanctioned liturgical compilations began to become canonized in the seventh and eighth century CE, and they employed this Rabbinic editing technique of collapsing events into one another for brevity and for dramatic effect.

The most famous example of this is the weaving and editing technique found in Jewish liturgy. Ancient Jewish (nonbiblical) prayers and biblical texts are often woven together in a patchwork that mixes elements from many different centuries. One example is the famous so-called "Martyrology" which is recited on Yom Kippur, the Day of Atonement. This "martyrology" is a "collapsed" version of the Rabbinic martyrdom accounts recorded in many different periods, but when you read the prayer it appears as if all of the martyrs died one after the other in one massive and horrible event. The Rabbis who redacted the prayer book used biblical tales, Midrashim, and the Talmudim that represented the work of many different hands from a few hundred years. This net effect of having all of these martyrdoms occurring one after the other is both dramatic and gives them all a greater signficance. The liturgy "collapses" the historical events into a single event. This process tells us more about the way that ancient writers wrote than it does about history. For the most part writers in ancient times were more concerned with presenting the material they had than whether it fit what we today refer to as "history." No one has ever suggested that since they are all "collapsed" into one event that they are therefore not accurate or "true." It is just understood as the way that the liturgical editing put the events together. So too the Bible.

Finding the Redactor's Moses and Comparing Him to the Archaeological Record

Archaeology does not provide us with any information of this specific man Moses, although it does provide us with insights into the accuracy of the information in the book of Exodus and thereby gives us some idea as to the accuracy of the text in general. It provides another view of these events, but archaeology also shows us just how important it is to read the Bible critically and recognize that these multiple views of the Moses and Exodus suggest that more than one version of the Exodus and Moses is being described by different authors in different time periods. Sometimes these versions suggest varying traditions about the same person, place, or event, and sometimes the versions preserve different events, people, and places that have been collapsed into one continuous account.

One of the biggest differences that I have found between the Redactor's Moses and Aaron is a theological gap between the different writers. The Priestly writer seems to transform God into a transcendent, cosmic God that can only be worshipped by way of the Priestly rituals. The Priestly writer does not seem to allow anyone but the Aaronid priest to perform anything extraordinary. In the Priestly account of Exodus, Moses is a man who is in need of Aaron, his older brother and confidante, and cannot really perform any of the "wonders" without Aaron and his staff. But in other parts of the book of Exodus, it is Moses alone who stands before God on top of Mount Sinai, speaks to God at the Burning Bush, and has a face-to-face encounter with God. It is as if there are two Moses being presented: one who is the Man of God and the other who is the assistant to Aaron. An example of this editing technique of the Redactor is evident throughout the text. So one finds Moses (alone) at the center of the miracle which turns the River Nile to "blood" in Exodus chapter 7, verse 14: "Then the Lord said to Moses: 'Pharaoh's heart is hardened, he refuses to let the people go. Go to Pharaoh in the morning as he is going out to the water; wait for him by the river's brink, and take in your hand the rod which was turned into a serpent. . . . by this you shall know that I am the Lord: behold, I will strike the water that is in the Nile with the rod that is in my hand and it shall be turned to blood.'"

But right after this statement, another statement appears that seems to direct the attention to Aaron for this miracle. In Exodus chapter 7, verse 19: "And the Lord said to Moses, 'Say to Aaron, "Take your rod and stretch out your hand over the waters of Egypt, over their rivers, their canals, and their ponds, and all of their pools of water, that they may become blood and there shall be blood throughout all the land of Egypt, both in vessels of wood and in vessels of stone."'"

Just as there were multiple versions of Moses and Aaron, there are multiple versions of the Exodus, but I suspect that the reason for the multiple versions of the Exodus is not only to preserve different versions of the same event but to preserve different versions of different events. In Exodus, chapter 13, verses 17–18, the language of a non-Priestly text includes a long and protracted southern Exodus: "When Pharaoh let the people go, God did not lead them by way of the land of the Philistines [to the north], although that was near, for God said: lest the people repent when they see war, and return to Egypt. But God led the people round by the way of the wilderness [to the south] toward the Red Sea." Modern Bible scholars who have carefully studied the Priestly account recognize that this writer was concerned with moving as quickly as possible through the entire prehistory of the Israelites from the Patriarchal period through the Exodus. Among many differences, the Priestly account skips the entire Golden Calf incident (for obvious reasons—Aaron is at the center of the pagan creation!), the visits to different places, and escapades in the desert of Sinai, either because he did not think it was important or because these events were not preserved among his traditions. Most important, the Priestly writer preserves a tradition of a very direct, northern route that gets the Israelites immediately to Mount Sinai. In the book of Exodus, chapters 16–19, the Priestly Exodus gets the Israelites to Mount Sinai in a short space of forty-five days. The Priestly version of the Torah traditions is very concerned with specific details, dates, names, and places for other Bible stories, but in his version of the Exodus there are not as many names and places as in the J/E accounts, suggesting that perhaps he is describing a totally different Exodus from Egypt.

If one follows the route described in the Priestly account of the Exodus, Mount Sinai is a major goal and is a short trip from the crossing of the Red Sea to the mountain. For this and many other reasons, it seems as if the only explanation is that there were multiple *Exoduses* written down by different authors of the Bible. The Priestly version takes the Israelites to the north along a coastal route to *Migdol* and *Baal Zephon* in Exodus, chapter 14:1–4 and then continues in chapter 14:8–9, (again to the north) wandering in what is today the southern Negev. In short, the Priestly account puts the Israelites stay in the desert of the northern Sinai not in southern Sinai. The Priestly account places Mount Sinai in what is Israel's Negev, not the Sinai desert where it is placed in the non-Priestly account.

At first, I was shocked by these totally different versions of the Exodus—one has the Israelites going to the north and another that appears to have them going to the south. I am not the first person to notice what seems to be two clearly different directions for the Exodus. Bible commentators were amazed by the conflicts in direction and were forced to come up with enormously complex literary superstructures to support the contradictions. What I can see are at least two different routes of at least two different Exoduses that were collapsed into one another, woven together, probably by the Redactor, and it is one of the reasons why the account is so difficult to follow in the text and nearly impossible to document in archaeology. In fact, after much research I have come to the conclusion that there were probably three ancient versions of the Exodus that were circulating among writers of the Bible, and with these three Exoduses there is a body of archaeological data to support the historicity of the Exodus.

Three Exoduses, Two Moseses, Two Mount Sinais, and One Account

In addition to three different Exoduses, it also appears that at least two different Mount Sinais are alluded to in the texts of the Bible. After tracking these traditions I have come to the conclusion that the three Exoduses preserved in the Bible can be placed in the following time periods:

1. sixteenth century BCE
2. fifteenth century BCE
3. thirteenth century BCE

These three time periods are not only suggested by internal biblical analysis but also by the archaeological and nonbiblical evidence found in these periods. I am not surprised that the Exodus was presented by different sources of the Bible, written down at different times and different authors under varying conditions and that the information they present may not totally agree with one another. I also was not surprised that the writers were preserving different events and not the same event. What this new understanding allows me to do is incorporate archaeological and nonbiblical data in understanding what happened in each one of these Exoduses. This understanding allows me to consider all of the evidence and not eliminate evidence that does not fit one time period or another. In addition, since we know that many of these Exoduses were written down a hundred and up to a thousand years after the event itself, I am not surprised that they contain discrepancies. With this in mind, we must consider what the biblical writers knew and when they knew it. While they would have had oral traditions that were from a very ancient period, the written formulations were cast in the image of the time in which they were written down.

I have been asked many times whether the biblical account of the Exodus is true. My answer to this question is "yes," the Exodus is true, but it is how it is true that is important. The Exodus account is as true and correct as any other ancient tradition written down hundreds and often thousands of years after the event occurred. It is as true as anything else that is recorded in the Bible and as true as any other ancient text preserved in the way the Hebrew Bible was preserved. It is just as likely logically, archaeologically, and scientifically that the Exodus from Egypt occurred than not, and that it occurred the way the Bible describes it. But how the Bible describes events is the caveat. The Bible often describes events recorded by multiple witnesses as a single, continuous account. It is not a history book or a modern novel. I admit that all of the details of the Exodus account cannot be confirmed by archaeology. For that matter little in antiquity can be held to this exacting modern standard. But reading the Bible as a history book or a modern novel has led some to make a series of different mistakes that ultimately lead to the false conclusion that an Exodus of Israelites from Egypt never happened. I will point out the mistakes and some corrections that illustrate why the Exodus(es) happened and suggest how to interpret the archaeological and non-biblical data that document it (them).

The First Mistake: Rameses II has to be "the" Pharaoh of "the" Exodus

My most recent trip to Egypt with students gave me a clue to the controversy about the Exodus. While traveling around the country, our Egyptian guide pointed out the many statues and sites that have been discovered in the past one hundred years. He began with a replica of a famous Rameses II statue on the way from the airport to our hotel. The tour continued in and around Cairo, at the Cairo Museum, at the visits to the Ramesseum, the Valley of the Kings, and at the Temple of Karnak in Luxor. The guide emphasized that the long and prosperous rule of Rameses II (66+ years! 1279–1213 BCE—sometimes called Rameses the Great) gave rise to the unprecedented building projects he sponsored. It prompted one of the students to comment: "Boy, Rameses II, was the Pharaoh's Pharaoh!" That one moment summarized the problem of identifying Rameses II as "the" Pharaoh of the Exodus. I often play a game with the students in my Biblical Archaeology course involving the names of the Pharaohs as a pedagogic tool. I ask them to name one famous Pharaoh that they know; inevitably it is Rameses. Now it is true that the name "Rameses" is the only Pharaoh name that is actually used in the first five books of the Bible, but the question is whether the name is really the name of the Pharaoh Rameses or just a placeholder by the later biblical writer for the name of an unknown Pharaoh.

When I ask individuals in foreign countries to name a famous historical American president, they usually name Washington and Lincoln. This I think is a clue to the identification of the Pharaoh of the Exodus as Rameses II. Rameses was probably the name that most people in the Fertile Crescent in antiquity knew as the name of a famous Pharaoh, and when the book of Exodus was written down from the oral traditions that were circulating hundreds of years after the events of the Exodus, the name Rameses became enshrined as the Pharaoh of the Exodus perhaps because this was the only Pharaoh that these writers knew. Many things point to this process of transcribing the oral traditions of the Exodus into written form that may have involved serious editing questions as we mentioned before. In the book of Genesis, chapter 47, the Bible states how the aged Patriarch Jacob came down to Egypt from Canaan at the request of his son, Joseph. He and his family were authorized by an unnamed Pharaoh in Genesis 47:11 to live in the land of Rameses: "Then Joseph settled his fathers and his brothers, and gave them a possession in the land of Egypt, in the best of the land, in the *land of Rameses,* as Pharaoh had commanded." A few chapters later in the opening of the book of Exodus, an unnamed Pharaoh "who did not know Joseph" suddenly comes along, some ten generations later, after the settlement of the Israelites in the land of Egypt and enslaves the children of Israel. Exodus 1:11 states: "And they set taskmasters over them to afflict them with heavy burdens; and they built for Pharaoh store-cities, Pithom and Rameses." The problem is pretty obvious: the use of the name "Rameses" in Genesis 47:11 is what has been identified by nearly every biblical commentator as an anachronism. An anachronism is something that is out of place, often chronologically, for a running, chronological narrative. The two passages from the book of Genesis and Exodus are supposed to be separated by hundreds of years and yet they both are taking place in the time and place of Rameses! Nowhere in the Bible does it say that the Pharaoh of the Exodus was the "Pharaoh Rameses." The name of the location in northern Egypt (Goshen) had become linked with the name Rameses and so it appears in the earlier narrative about the arrival of the Israelites and in the story of their departure. Although there were many Pharaohs named Rameses in Egypt, it is clear that the writers of the Bible, writing hundreds of years after the events, were referring to the area using a name that had become synonymous for them and their readers with the title of the monarch's property in Egypt: "Rameses." The name had become a general locator for the place for biblical writers who were not concerned with whether it was anachronistic or not. It may have been the only name they knew for the area. There are many anachronisms in the Bible. In fact, anachronisms prove the rule about why we must not read the Bible like a history textbook or modern literature. These anachronisms show us when the Bible was written down and why archaeologists need to be careful in comparing archaeological data with the Bible. When we find in the Book of Genesis that Abraham comes from "Ur of the Chaldeans" we see a similar problem. By placing Abraham in "Ur of the Chaldeans," the Bible is trying to give Abraham's background in Mesopotamia a specific known location. Unfortunately the "Chaldeans" arrived in Mesopotamia almost a thousand years after Abraham was there. The writer who used this designation wanted his readers to know that he was referring to the Ur that was located in Mesopotamia, not elsewhere.

Now almost every biblical commentator has noticed all of these anachronisms in the Bible. They even devised a stock phrase to explain how anachronisms could happen in a continuous, ancient and Divinely revealed text. They simply answered: "there is no chronological order in the Bible," and left it at that. I do not think this answer addresses the whole problem. My explanation of this anachronism ("Rameses" in the book of Genesis, for example) is that the writer added a famous Pharaoh name that would be recognized by his readers. Notice that it never says that the Pharaoh is Rameses, it just says in the *Land of Rameses*. It is an attempt to place the Israelites in the Delta region of Egypt and not in some other location in southern Egypt. Unfortunately, some archae-ologists, ministers, and not a few Rabbis and Bible scholars have been misled by this name. Without this mistake, we can see that according to the Bible the Israelites resided in this particular place in Egypt and that the Exodus started off from there, but not necessarily in the time of the Pharaoh Rameses.

THE SCIENTIFIC METHOD AND THE INVESTIGATION OF THE EXODUS

I have frequently referred to the scientific method because it raises a methodological problem in the field of Biblical Archaeology. If people today are going to seriously hold that the events in Exodus actually happened, the story has to have some authoritative scientific proof behind it, not just "religious tradition" saying it is so. I will outline a series of well-known arguments that can apply the principles of the scientific method to our study of the truth behind Exodus. I start with the literary argument because it is usually not raised by archaeologists or Bible scholars.

A literary argument has to do with the way that a text functions. It is important to note that different texts function differently in different periods, but rules exist for the way that a writer will write and for whom the writer will write. These rules conform to certain criteria that can be researched and understood. Because the text of the Bible is a literary text, it can be compared with other literary texts from the same period (that it was written in) and distinguish unique elements of style, form, voice, language, and audience. These arguments, by the way, do not resolve the problem of whether the text was written under Divine inspiration or dictated by the Divine to a human scribe. It assumes that the text, once it was written down, is like all other texts and conforms to rules that can be analyzed and understood. An example of a literary argument would be assessing the idea that Shakespeare wrote all the works associated with his name. A question, such as whether or not a person, William Shakespeare, actually wrote all of the works ascribed to him would be analyzed using literary arguments but would be assisted by historical arguments. In the case of the Exodus, the literary arguments reveal just how important it is to know how the Bible, as a literary exemplar, presents its information.

Most people like to think that they understand historical argumentation, but in the case of the Bible one needs to understand how history, as a discipline, has evolved. The historical argument has to do with the way that people understand the historical time lines, chronologies, development, and flow of information/data from any historical period. It assumes that it is possible to analyze patterns of historical information in any given period and assess the historical trends by comparing and contrasting historical information gained from other historical traditions of the same time period. History relies upon literary analyses but also upon other data for its assessments. An example of a historical argument would be whether or not World War I began with the shooting of the Archduke Ferdinand. Historical arguments would be brought to assess the validity of this statement and literary evidence from many European sources will be evaluated. In the case of the Exodus, the historical arguments and the comparative literary analysis actually bolster the contention of the historicity of the event.

The archaeological argument brings many different fields of study to understand a person, place, or event. If I wanted to assess the validity of any historical "fact" using archaeology, I would have to consider issues relating to a variety of subdisciplines and sciences that are used by archaeology. If, for example, I was interested in archaeologically evaluating the claim of some Byzantine literary texts that there had been an earthquake that destroyed many cities in the Middle East in 363 CE, I would begin by evaluating a specific place mentioned in the diverse literary texts and then scientifically analyze all of the possible archaeological data from the different subspecialties that can be dated to this period to see if there is enough archaeological data to support the claim of the texts. I would have geophysicists assess the geological history of the place, pottery specialists evaluate the pottery, carbon 14 studies to assess the organic matter, numismatists to evaluate coin finds, architectural specialists to assess the buildings, glass experts to evaluate the glass finds, art historians to assess the adornment on the buildings, etc. It is a cumulative argument that establishes whether or not this is a valid "historical" fact, despite the ample literature about the event in Byzantine literature. Usually the archaeological argument will be both problematic and insightful for those that have never seen how archaeological information is used. In the case of every assessment, the archaeological record is both fragmentary and cumulative. Each piece contributes towards a hypothesis. In the case of the Exodus, the archaeological argument is not as simple as the experts have made it out to be.

I want to distinguish between the archaeological argument and what I call the monumental artifactual argument. A monumental or artifactual "smoking gun" is a major artifactual piece that is so specific that it really shifts the other archaeological data to meet it. It is rare to find one major artifact that shifts the entire archaeological paradigm, but it happens. This is pretty much what happened when Yigael Yadin discovered in the Cave of Letters a series of dated and signed letters from Simon Bar Kokhba. Yadin simply assigned most everything in the cave to be from the Bar Kokhba Revolt because of this discovery. Roland De Vaux decided that the proximity of the caves where the Dead Sea Scrolls were found were so close to the village of Qumran that they must have been connected. For better or for worst, the monumental or artifactual argument is very persuasive and shifts the archaeology from being random points on a line to being a very specific point. In the case of the Exodus, there are some "smoking guns" and several specific monumental artifacts that I feel give us some very specific periods for the Exodus

Finally, one of my favorite arguments for exploring the relationship between ancient texts and their historical reality is the geographical argument. The geographical argument is a very powerful argument because it raises scientific parameters that are corroborated by simple rules of motion and mechanics. This is the one that every crime scene investigation story has as a basic twist. If one were confronted with evidence that a crime took place on a certain date at 3 p.m. in Los Angeles and the presumed perpetrator was in New York on that date at 3 p.m. (EST), it would be hard to argue that the presumed perpetrator could have been in Los Angeles at 3 p.m. given our present means of transportation. It is just not feasible for a person to have "geographically" been in these two places at the same time. Often the crime scene investigator will have to go back and assess all of the details of the crime scene and reevaluate the movements of the main suspects to see if it is physically possible for one or an other to have been at the scene when the event happened. Geography (and the related science, geology) is always something I consider when I begin an investigation. When we started to investigate whether et-Tell, a solitary mound by the Sea of Galilee was in fact an ancient fishing village that had somehow become distanced from the Sea, we called upon geographers and geologists to help us solve the mystery. One of my most respected colleagues, Father Bargil Pixner, told me that for him, after the first four canonical Gospels the geography and topography of the Land of Israel are the "Fifth Gospel." It is the one element that can reveal much about the text. In the case of the Exodus, we are forced to look carefully at what the text really says about the Exodus and their journey in the desert to Mount Sinai.

The Second Mistake: What Ancient Literature Can and Cannot Tell Us

Literary historians have come up with a variety of different literary arguments that help them assess the historicity of literary texts in all periods. One literary principle in particular is an unusual but powerful principle for the study of ancient texts. It is called the principle of dissimilarity. If an ancient story line contains information that is dissimilar to other contemporaneous story lines and also disagrees with many of the doctrines of the tradition that preserves the text, it is thought that the ancient story line is probably more historically accurate than story lines that agree with the ongoing tradition. In other words, if an ancient text contains something so "dissimilar" to the prevailing or later views of the ongoing tradition that preserves the text or is "embarrassing" to the entire later tradition (that preserves the text), that literary account is seen by literary critics to be more authentic than other traditions that generally agree with the later tradition. The most famous contemporary example of dissimilarity is found in the recent Albert Einstein biographies that all preserve a very curious story from Einstein's youth. The story goes that when Albert Einstein, the single, greatest scientist of the twentieth century, was a youth, many people thought he was mentally challenged. Although it is anecdotal, this story is a classic case of dissimilarity. Why would anyone make up a story like this? Because it is so alarmingly different than anything we know about the later Einstein, most biographers assume that the story is authentic.

So too, the Exodus is clearly the foundational epic for the creation of the Israelite nation, yet the story is so dissimilar to every other foundational epic in antiquity and so different from the values of later Judaism, Christianity, and Islam that preserved it that it is probably more authentic than not. Simply put: why would anyone make up a story that disagrees with the fundamental views of most religions of the period and those that preserve it unless it is historically accurate? The story of the Exodus, the enslavement of the people in a foreign nation, the enigmatic disputes of the people with their God and their leader Moses, and the unexplained wanderings in the desert (yet led by the Divine) for forty years is the foundational account of the creation of the Israelite nation, and it is so antithetical to what other people might say about themselves in a foundational document that it must preserve an authentic tradition. The great and heroic stories of the *Iliad* and the *Odyssey*, the *Osiris, Isis and Horus Epics of Egypt*, the Sumerian *Gilgamesh and the Land of the Living*, among many others show us ancient literary traditions that are so unlike the rather ignoble tale of the Exodus as to be humorous. The literary problem of the story of the Exodus is that it is so unlike anything else that was produced in antiquity that it stands out as an example of what must have been an authentic experience of the ancient Israelites. Although it was humiliating, it was what had happened and therefore needed to be reported. It is not a story of courage and heroism. It is the story of the enslavement of an entire people for a very long time, their life in continuing degradation and their subsequent Exodus (and according to the Bible with many other peoples) and wandering for a long time in the desert, complaining and rebelling at every stage, worshipping foreign gods even as God is revealing the Divine message to Moses, and being too fearful to even directly encounter Him. It is just so improbable and antiheroic to make it both embarrassing and dissimilar to the ancient reader and also gives it the power of authenticity. Its unusual literary nature is what makes the Exodus story so authentic. One or two other examples of how the biblical text preserves accounts that I think are more authentic than not are important to point out. It is not just the Exodus account, it shows us how to identify authentic ancient traditions.

We have already encountered a great account that fits the description of "dissimilarity" in the "wife-sister" stories of the Patriarch (Abraham/ Isaac) and their wives in Genesis 12, 20, and 26. It is such an embarrassing message for later generations that it is probably an authentic memory of the Patriarchs than other stories about them that are purely praiseworthy. We see a truly human Patriarch who is forced into a difficult situation and demonstrates his cunning by employing a Mesopotamian custom to save his life. The fact that this tale is told three different ways in the Bible indicates another principle of biblical research, multiple attestation. The fact that it is told three different ways does not diminish its importance; it actually enhances its authenticity. Multiple attestation or the telling of the same story multiple times suggests that it was a very well-known account despite how poorly it reflects upon the Patriarch.

An example of the principle of dissimilarity (and multiple attestation) from another ancient text will show that this principle can be used to understand the literary traditions of other time periods, not just the Hebrew Bible. In the New Testament's Gospel of Mark 8:22–26, Jesus is asked to heal a blind man. The healing of a blind man account is told in Mark 8, Mark 10, and in John 9 and is a key to establishing Jesus' authority. Blindness was a very common affliction in the ancient Near East, so common that almost anyone in the period would understand its meaning. In the Gospel of Mark 8 there is a strange but revealing difference between the other healings of Jesus. Jesus is forced to attempt to heal the man multiple times. He tries using very unmiraculous items like spit and dust instead of the really miraculous form of healing he employs elsewhere of just touching the man (or his garment) and healing him (as other miracles suggest he did for men and women). What makes this section so important is that it is so dissimilar to the Jesus that the Church would come to venerate. In this text Jesus is so very human rather than Divine. His method and attempts suggest the antithesis of what Jesus, the Son of God, became. If Jesus is the Son of God (and empowered as the terminology might suggest in Greek and Roman literature of the period), he should have been able to immediately cure the blind man without resorting to multiple attempts and a use of unconventional items. The fact that he was unable to do this miracle the first time and had to do it a second time shows that this was part of a story about a historic (and more human) Jesus. It also makes it more probable than not as an authentic, ancient, historical event.

I have found that ancient history (and ancient life in general) is not half as neat as most historians or textual scholars think. In fact, the neater that a historical tradition is, the more I suspect that it has been seriously altered to make it agree with later traditions. Mostly, history does not always fit the beautiful categories that historians set for it. But when you encounter a literary tradition that is so "dissimilar" to most other national epic or expected values of that genre in the ancient world, one has to suspect that the tradition is a reflection of what really happened. For this reason, this modern literary tradition defends the authenticity of the Exodus account and has led me to take a second look at the way that history and archaeology have treated the account.

The Third Mistake: What History Can and Cannot Tell Us

The modern discipline of history is very different than the way history was understood in the ancient period. Today, we think that history works in very specific, systematic, and progressive ways and then are surprised that it does work in that way when we see it mapped out by historians. The historical argument says that if an historically accurate event was written down at a later time period, the writers from the later period will try to make the historical account intelligible to the later reader. The writer may not be able to write his account for the period in which the event originally occurred, but often he is presented with accurate pieces of information that are so specific and exact that he must include them. So any historically accurate element in the story validates, in part, the historicity of the account. If I were writing, for example, today about the history of automobiles and wanted my audience to understand the significance of the cost of the automobile in the 1930s, I would say that the cost of a Ford Model T represented half a year's salary of a general laborer of the time. It would signal the importance of the auto. If I said the cost was $300, it would be accurate but almost meaningless to a contemporary reader, but its presence in my history is important because it corresponds to the period. Does this mean that I wrote the account in the 1930s? No, but it means that I had access to true and accurate information from that period. The Exodus account was written down centuries after it occurred, yet it contains historically accurate details of Egypt from the time that it purports to be writing about. So, to "prove" the account is true, we need to find out if details in the story that are presented in the Exodus account are historically accurate. The answer is: they are.

Most of the references to names, weights, measures, and customs are historically accurate for Egypt in the Bronze Age, the time period that the Exodus is supposed to occur. The cost of a slave in the Bronze Age (20 shekels) is accurate to the shekel in comparisons with the Egyptian texts from this period (Bronze Age). Although the text may have been written down in the Iron Age, it contains so many details that are accurate from the earlier period that it implies that these are authentic oral traditions that have been faithfully preserved throughout the ages. This implies that the text was intimately aware of basic Egyptian issues in the Bronze Age even when the text was finally written down at a much later period. The writer did not totally create new standards from the period in which he was writing, but rather used the accurate standards from the period that he was writing about. Whoever was writing this down had details that were very accurate from Egypt in a certain, very ancient and specific period. The earliest Hebrew writing we have is from the eleventh century BCE. The Bronze Age is some two to three hundred years before this period. The fact that these standards are historically accurate to the earlier period is important because it implies that the tradition, probably an oral tradition, was transmitted accurately down to the time period in which it was written.

WHY DONKEYS ARE GOOD AND CAMELS ARE BAD

I use one archaeological example to demonstrate just how careful we must be in using the text as a historical document. From what we know about the text of the Bible, some of the ideas of the text may have been formulated four thousand years ago but were written down only about three thousand years ago. After this delay, the original meanings were edited and sometimes reinterpreted to meet the sensibilities of the readers of the day. One example involves donkeys and camels in the most ancient literary strata of the Hebrew Bible. We know from archaeology, for example, that the camel was domesticated in the Middle East only about three thousand years ago in the Iron Age. There is no mention of camels in Ancient Egypt until the Persian period. Although there was a type of camel in Mesopotamia, these were apparently not domesticated in Canaan/Israel until the eighth century BCE. This is important because the earliest historical (in the time of Abraham and Sarah) texts of the Bible purport to be about events that occurred nearly four thousand years ago in the Bronze Age, but some of the Patriarchs and Matriarchs in the text of Genesis are sitting and traveling on camels. They were riding on camels because the writers writing in their own periods when camels had become common felt that this was more intelligible to the reader of the day than it may have originally been. It is clear that some of the writers of these sections were not concerned with what today we call "the historical accuracy" but were sometimes concerned with the sensibilities of the readers. In this period, some four thousand years ago, small donkeys were the beasts of burden, and their bones have been found in archaeological excavations throughout the Middle East. The very famous Beni Hassan tomb paintings that I mentioned earlier show these Semites in their striped tunics coming down with their donkeys by their side. These donkeys were so beloved that many were buried with the families in their homes. Why did the ancient writer change this in the text as these oral traditions were written down three thousand years ago? I think because this writer thought that it would be more dignified for a Patriarch and Matriarch to be riding on a camel than on a little donkey. So historical standards that are accurate are significant signs of the authenticity of an account. When I read a story about Bronze Age characters riding on donkeys in the Bible, it indicates a "higher" level of authenticity than accounts that have camels. When I read the Genesis 22 story of the "binding of Isaac" and Abraham, Isaac and his servants are riding on donkeys (despite the long distance that they were traveling). Or when I read the Joseph story in Genesis 38 of Jacobs's brothers coming down to Egypt and they are riding upon donkeys or carrying the grain and all of their possessions, I know that I am reading a very ancient story that has been carefully preserved by the writer, even though he is writing the story down almost a thousand years after the event occurred. While donkeys and camels were well-known ancient words with relatively clear designations often an ancient word's meaning will change. Historical standards aside, often it is our interpretation of the actual Hebrew words used in the text of Exodus that have caused a large amount of confusion about whether the Exodus happened or not.

The Fourth Mistake: What Numbers Can and Cannot Tell Us

According to the text of the Book of Exodus, chapter 12, verse, 37, "And the people of Israel journeyed from Rameses to Succoth, about six hundred thousand (*elef*) men on foot besides women and children." 600 *elef* men were in the desert. The word *elef* is usually translated as 1000 by modern Hebraists. So, by this counting, six hundred thousand men wandered in the desert for forty years. When you add their children and wives, the number easily equals nearly two and a half million people. Linguists have studied this word and have decided that the word *elef* may have only meant in its original, historical usage, "a legion," "a clan," or "a group." As noted above, it is important to know the original historical meaning of a text. A Priestly tradition, for example, in the book of Numbers, chapter 1, verse 16 states: "These were the ones chosen from the congregation, the leaders of their ancestral tribes, the heads of the clans (*elfei*) of Israel." It is clear that the Priestly writer here was using the word *elef* as a parallel for the word "tribes," and most translators agree that it probably means "clans." In each of the subsequent uses of the term *elef* in the counting of the Isra-elites in the book of Numbers, it appears that we should translate it not as a "thousand" but rather simply as a "clan." It is not only in the book of Numbers. In the book of Judges 6:15, the Judge Gideon complains: "How can I rescue Israel? See my *elef* (my clan) is the weakest in Manasseh." Here it clearly means an extended family or clan. So, if the word *elef* just meant a clan or group and not a thousand men, it means that the translation of the number of people who went out of Egypt should be changed from six hundred thousand plus wives and children to six hundred clans and their wives and children. Does this make a difference in how we perceive the story and the kind of evidence that archaeology would need to look for to verify the Exodus? Of course. A clan can be as many as ten people. So instead of looking for millions of people in the desert, we are looking for thousands of people. Maybe eight thousand people in the vast deserts of Sinai. Demographers have always been amazed by the number 2.5 million people (six hundred thousand men plus their wives and children). It is just such an overwhelming number given the entire population of Egypt in the Bronze Age. This represents almost half of the entire population. But 8,000 people was the size of a minority in ancient Egypt.

Demographers of the ancient period have also pointed out another is-sue. According to the book of Exodus, the children of Israel were chased down by the army of Egypt at the Reed Sea. Most battles that are won in antiquity used "overwhelming" forces over smaller opponents. In the book of Exodus it states that when Pharaoh decided to go out after the Israelites he brought six hundred of his best charioteers to face them. Six hundred good chariots against 2.5 million people would be a bad imbalance, and any military leader would have seen the problem. In a similar military epi-sode related by the Bible from the period after the Exodus in the book of Judges, Deborah the Israelite judge and her general, Barak, mass ten thou-sand troops, and the enemy brought nine hundred chariots to fight them. If nine hundred chariots were used against ten thousand troops, it makes sense that the Bible is saying that six hundred chariots faced off with about eight thousand troops. Militarily, it appears, that the Egyptians thought they were going to engage a force of perhaps eight thousand people in the Exodus account, not more than 2.5 million people. If there were six hundred clan leaders and their families that left in the Exodus, we have a demographically, militarily, and historically more accurate account to compare with the archaeological data from various periods of Egyptian history.

The Fifth Mistake: No One Has Ever Found Artifacts Associated with the Exodus

Monumental artifacts are not rare but they are extremely significant. Steles, standing stones that are put up to commemorate victories, establish regional or city rights, or to designate the influence of king or god are found throughout the Near East. Steles are unusual but very prevalent artifacts used by Egyptians and most everyone in the ancient Near East to celebrate major events. They are artifacts that are indicators of the significance and permanence of something that someone important wanted to preserve for posterity. There are many steles in Egypt, but two steles that give us the historical framework for all of the Exoduses. They are the "smoking guns" for the beginning and the ending of different Exoduses. I think that the Redactor of the Bible not only combined the different versions of the Exodus but also the different time periods when they happened. The first stele is the so-called *Tempest Stele* of Ahmosis I who lived in the sixteenth century BCE. It is now located somewhere in the bowels of the Cairo Museum, but it is significant because it establishes a time period when an Exodus from Egypt did happen. While the stele itself does not suggest that there was an Exodus, it does suggest that a number of terrible plagues afflicted Egypt that were extremely similar to the ones that are mentioned in the Bible. The information is a list of some of the worst types of disasters that afflicted Egypt in any period: *". . . now then . . . the gods declared their discontent. The gods [caused] the sky to come in a tempest of r[ain], with darkness in the western region and the sky being unleashed without [cessation, louder than] the cries of the masses, more powerful than [. . .], [while the rain raged] on the mountains louder than the noise of the cataract which is at Elephantine."*

The sixteenth century BCE is one of the time periods for the Exodus, but as we shall see, it is possibly the earliest time of the first Exodus that became fixed in the memory of the Israelites and in fact was a time when perhaps a group of Israelites left Egypt for the Land of Israel for the first time.

The second monumental piece is a stele from the thirteenth century BCE, and it too commemorates an important event. Archaeologists and historians agree that the famous Israel stele (also in the Cairo Museum) was created by King Merneptah (1213–1203) after his successful battles in the East: probably in 1206–1207. When Merneptah writes of his conquest he boasts of his conquests in what was the Land of Israel: "Carried off is Ashkelon; seized upon is Gezer; Yanoam is made as that which does not exist; [the people of] Israel is laid waste, its seed is not; Syria has become a widow of Egypt." The stele states: the "people of Israel," not a city or region, but a people that was located in direct proximity to the cities where the Egyptian armies had done great damage. This boast is a piece of ancient propaganda, typical of the hubris of the Egyptians but is unusual because it recognizes that a people, called Israel, was living in the land in the thirteenth century BCE. The archaeology from this time period reveals the existence of the places and cities in this time period in this region, the late Bronze Age to the early Iron Age. What we learn is that even if Merneptah only defeated these places and took tribute (the Egyptians traditionally did not establish their own settlements outside of Egypt), it signals that the people of Israel were already living in the land when he arrived there in the thirteenth century BCE. So from these two steles we learn what I think was the starting point of the Exoduses and the terminus of the Exodus. If there was an Exodus it may have begun in the sixteenth century BCE, and by the thirteenth century the Israelites were already in the Land of Israel.

It is possible that an Exodus happened under Rameses II. Rameses II ruled for a very long time. Dates differ on the exact beginning and end of his rule, but almost everyone assumes that it continued for over sixty-six years, and I will use the dates 1279–1213 BCE. In the twenty-first year of his reign after many years of battles with Canaan, he suddenly stops his foreign conquests—around 1258 BCE, and suddenly he engages in no more battles outside of the country. Something happened to cause him to stop going out of Egypt to do battle and begin taking care of business only in Egypt. According to Egyptian records, he did not venture out of Egypt again for the better part of forty-five years. We also have documentary information that major building projects were being done in Egypt in this period. During his long rule, he built and battled and then suddenly stopped. If Rameses II was the Pharaoh of an Exodus, an Exodus could have occurred in the period before 1258 BCE. Curiously, we note that Rameses lost his first-born son under suspicious conditions in this period and never again left on missions of foreign conquest as he had earlier done. If we combine the information from both of these steles we have some of the major components of the Exodus accounts in the book of Exodus. But one other artifact confirms part of the story as well.

One of the most unusual discoveries of the past 150 years of archaeology in the Middle East has been the recovery of written materials on parchment and papyrus. The climate in many areas of the region is desert-like with little humidity, and many intact documents have been discovered that preserve traditions that might not otherwise be known. The *Ipuwer Papyrus* simultaneously attests to the same incident as the *Tempest Stele* and to additional information that parallels the plagues mentioned in the book of Exodus. The *Ipuwer Papyrus* (Leiden 344) was discovered in the nineteenth century CE and dated to the sixteenth century BCE and mentions the disasters that plagued Egypt in the sixteenth centuries BCE. The *Ipuwer Papyrus* 2:5–6 states, "Plague is throughout the land. Blood is everywhere," which correlates to the book of Exodus 7:21 ". . . there was blood throughout all the land of Egypt." Again the *Ipuwer Papyrus* states in 5:5 "All animals, their hearts weep. Cattle moan. . . ." Likewise, Exodus 9:3 reads, ". . . the hand of the Lord is upon the cattle which is in the field . . . there shall be a very grievous disease." One might ask the same question about the *Ipuwer Papyrus* that one asks about the account in the book of Exodus. Did all of these events really happen or not? But since the *Ipuwer Papyrus* is a document that is definitely describing an event in history and was written down in that time period, it is just assumed that it is true. Recently, a new theory from the field of geophysics that bolsters our understanding of both the *Ipuwer Papyrus* and the *Tempest Stele* has emerged. Geophysicists think that the volcanic eruption on the island of Santorini, (ancient Thera) Crete in the seventeenth or sixteenth century BCE (and perhaps the eruption of Mount Vesuvius in the same general time frame) may have been at the root of both accounts. Most scholars now date the Santorini event in the sixteenth century. If these eruptions took place within a short period of time of one another the devastation and repercussions for many places on the Mediterranean would be evident. Geophysicists draw their conclusions by comparing the devastation caused by the eruption of a smaller volcano on the island of Krakatoa, near Java, in the nineteenth century CE, that included daylong episodes of darkness and disasters some 250 miles from the epicenter. The eruptions of Santorini and Vesuvius would have given rise to the plagues tradition found in the *Ipuwer Papyrus,* the *Tempest Stele,* and probably formed the basis for the first account of an Exodus from Egypt. It is well known that after such disasters, large numbers of people flee as a result of the economic, social, and political upheavals that follow.

Another piece in this puzzle is that there is a recorded Exodus in the sixteenth century CE that was indeed connected with the Exodus of the Israelites by a nonbiblical source. In the writings of two ancient Greco-

Roman authors, Hecataeus of Abdera and Josephus Flavius, a tradition of an Exodus is preserved. Hecataeus, who lived in the third century BCE and traveled in Egypt and gathered material in his *Aegyptiaca* is not a historian by modern standards, but he is preserving oral and written traditions that no one else in his time period seems to be interested in collecting. This account, the fullest and oldest account of the history of the Jews by a non-Jew preserves a curious piece of information that confirms the idea of multiple Exoduses. He writes:

"When in ancient times a pestilence arose in Egypt, the common people ascribed their troubles to the workings of a divine agency; for indeed with many strangers of all sorts dwelling in their midst and practicing different rites of religion and sacrifice, their own traditional observances in honor of the gods had fallen into disuse. Hence natives of the land surmised that unless they removed the foreigners, their troubles would never be resolved. At once, therefore, the aliens were driven from the country, and the most outstanding and active among them banded together and, as some say, were cast ashore in Greece and certain other regions. . . . But the greater number were driven into what is now called Judea, which is not a far distance from Egypt and was at that time utterly uninhabited. The colony was headed by a man called Moses, outstanding both for his wisdom and for his courage."

While this account is not contemporary with the Exodus, it has one group of leaders being driven out in what vaguely sounds like the post-Santorini time period and then another group that leaves in a desert journey and apparently led by Moses. Josephus Flavius, a Jewish historian and military leader from the Galilee of the first century CE, wrote a multivolume book on the *Ancient History of the Jews* (*Antiquities*) and other books chronicling the history of the Jews from biblical times until his own. In one of these books he countered charges about the Jews in Egypt and quotes an even earlier source, a man named Manetho, who Josephus says was an ancient Egyptian priest. Josephus' book, *Against Apion*, held that the Israelites had left in the time of the Ahmose I at the same time as the Exodus of the Hyksos from Egypt in the sixteenth century. Josephus and other writers and travelers in the Greco-Roman period such as Africanus, Clement, Tatian, and Theophilus believed that at this time Pharaoh Ahmose I drove out the Hyksos. Josephus identified them with the Israelite "forefathers (who) were delivered out of Egypt, and came thence and inhabited this country (Judea) 393 years before Danaus came to Argos." [Josephus, *Against Apion* 1:16]. The Hyksos are one of the most significant little-known episodes in the history of ancient Egypt. From approximately the seventeenth to the sixteenth century, northern Egypt was conquered by a group from Asia that is known by the name Hyksos. As far as we can tell, Ahmose I was able to defeat the Hyksos leaders and exiled them from the country. As I related above official Egyptian history that was preserved does not even mention the Hyksos invasion and residence. Apparently Egyptian court historians, in order to preserve the integrity of the Pharaoh's rule, erased the entire episode. But Manetho preserves an oral tradition that thankfully is included in Josephus' writings that come down to us in many ancient manuscripts. Manetho, the Egyptian Priestly source quoted by Josephus, connects the events of the Hyksos arrival with the Israelite Exodus. He writes in *Against Apion* 1:86: "The kings of Thebes rose in revolt against the Hyksos and a great war broke out, which was of long duration. Under a king named Mishphragmouthosis, the Hyksos were defeated and driven out of the rest of Egypt and confined to a place called Avaris . . . (the king) beseiged the walls with 480,000 men and endeavored to reduce (the Hyksos) to submission by siege. Despairing to achieve the goal, he concluded a treaty under which they were all to evacuate Egypt and go wherever they wanted unmolested. *Upon these terms no fewer than 240,000 households left Egypt and traversed the desert to Syria.* Then terrified by the might of the Assyrians who were at the time masters of Asia, they built a city in the country now called Judea . . . and they gave it the name of Jerusalem."

It is clear that Manetho and apparently Josephus in the first century CE understood that hundreds of thousands of people left in this Exodus. Similar to the biblical texts, Manetho has collapsed the history of the Jews and the ancient Israelites into one Exodus that ends with the Jews in Jerusalem. It is clear from this account that neither Josephus nor Manetho connects the Exodus with the Pharaoh Rameses. The area of the major battle is placed at Avaris, the Egyptian town of *Het-Uar,* which in ancient Egyptian means: "the Temple of Babylonia." This is fascinating because the name may preserve the ethnic origin of the people that settled there as being originally from Mesopotamia. Egyptians were very sensitive to ethnic origins, and this would have been extremely meaningful to designate the people as being from a major center like Mesopotamia. The city, Avaris, has been excavated at modern Tell el-Dab'a, and it is clear that it was indeed destroyed in approximately the first third of the sixteenth century BCE. What is important about the Tell el-Dab'a excavations is that although it was destroyed in the sixteenth century BCE, much the way Manetho describes, it was rebuilt in the time of the thirteenth century BCE rule of Rameses II and was probably the ancient city of Rameses mentioned in the book of Exodus 1.11. If so, the book of Exodus preserves an accurate and historically verifiable fact:that the sixteenth century BCE Exodus began from Avaris, which was indeed, at a later time, a city of Rameses. What has also been discovered in recent excavations of the area of northern Sinai from the time of Rameses (thirteenth century BCE) is that the entire northeastern front of Egypt had been reinforced in the time of Rameses II with fortresses making a northern route out of Egypt very difficult. But excavations also reveal that in the earlier period, the sixteenth century BCE, these fortresses did not exist along the northern border and would have made an easy exit and egress place for anyone fleeing or attacking Egypt.

Josephus is an important, nonbiblical, source of the Exodus and ancient history. His literary tradition agrees, for the most part, with the Priestly version of the Exodus. He tells us that he is from a Priestly background in his other writings, but it shows us that writing traditions persisted amongst groups of Jews well into the first century. What is in Josephus' writings is just as significant as what is not in his writings. According to Josephus, the Israelites are not necessarily building the cities of Rameses, there is no southern route, there is only an Exodus through the northern route and he, like the Priestly sources in the book of Exodus, brings the Israelites directly to Mount Sinai. In addition, Josephus places the events of the Exodus at Avaris. He writes in his *Antiquities* 2:15: "So the Hebrews went out of Egypt, while the Egyptians wept, and repented that they had treated them so harshly. Now they took their journey by Letopolis, a place at that time deserted, but where "Babylon"[Avaris] was built afterwards, when Cambyses laid Egypt waste; but as they went out hastily, on the third day they came to a place called Baal Zephon, on the Red Sea."

If we understand Josephus' use of this text in his own version of the *Antiquities of the Jews,* he too connects the event with the Exodus along the northern route as in the Priestly account, leaving out many of the details that the Priestly account deletes. He leaves out, for example, the rather seminal piece about the creation of the Golden Calf and Aaron's role in the making of the Golden Calf, just as the Priestly account did. It is also interesting to note that Josephus, who tells us in his autobiography that he is a Priest, (and a rather well-connected Priest at that), preserves this particular tradition despite the fact that he does it at the expense of the final redacted text of Exodus that he without doubt possessed. Many people today might not be familiar with the history of Egypt, but the history of Egypt was a very well-preserved tradition in Egypt in the first century CE and the exploits of Ahmose I in the sixteenth century BCE against the Hyksos would easily have been distinguished from the exploits of Rameses II in antiquity. But what we now know is that the entire history of the Hyksos was almost entirely erased from Egyptian history in antiquity because it was so degrading for the ancient Egyptians to acknowledge. It is therefore plausible why the biblical author did not immediately connect the Exodus to Ahmose. He may not even have known about it living a thousand years after the event. But the Josephus/Manetho tradition preserves what must have been a very painful oral tradition for Egyptians. The Hyksos and the Israelites had left the country in droves after the defeat of the Hyksos and a national, natural disaster from the Santorini event.

The big question is why the sixteenth century BCE event, a massive Exodus that happened in the wake of the eruptions of Santorini and Vesuvius, and accompanying the Hyksos Exodus, is associated with Rameses II at all. Professor William Dever, one of the foremost archaeologists of Israel in this period, in his article "Is There Any Archaeological Evidence for the Exodus," (in *Exodus: The Egyptian Evidence*, 1997, 71) writes:

> Is it merely fortuitous that these delta sites, some known to the biblical writers, had a substantial Canaanite or Asiatic presence in the so-called patriarchal period, and that the two were rebuilt (Tell el-Dab'a and Tell el-Mashkhuta) under Egyptian aegis in Ramesside times, which is when an Israelite sojourn in Egypt would have to be placed archaeologically?

The answer is that it is not merely fortuitous, it is precisely why different accounts were collapsed into one another by the Redactor of the Bible. The writers are recounting two or three different Exoduses that were redacted into one flowing account by the later Redactor, creating a third version of the Exodus going north and south at the same time that is impossible to track in any age, let alone in the period of Rameses II. The connection for the Redactor appears to be the location. The Avaris/Rameses area was the area of the Israelites and the place from which at least two and perhaps all three of the Exoduses originated. If there were two or three different Exoduses, in two or three different periods, which left from virtually the same place but ended up going in totally different directions because of the changing defense systems of the ancient Egyptians, then this might be the reason why they were all edited together into one Exodus account! The Priestly account in Exodus 14 has the Israelites leaving from *Avaris* going up the northern route towards Israel in what I think better suits the sixteenth century BCE defenses, and the non-Priestly account has the Israelites leaving from *Avaris* (by now called Rameses) but going to the south in what better suits the situation in the thirteenth century

THE SEARCH FOR SINAI 87

BCE when the northern route *was too fortified* for easy access into ancient Israel. The two accounts were "collapsed" into one account, but the seams of the two Exoduses are still very much present when the text is critically examined. If we follow the Redactor's final editing, we see that he follows a very specific northern route and even transitions the literary pieces that he is combining with key locations. One example is in the book of Numbers, chapter 33. Biblical scholars believe this chapter to be the work of the Redactor because it intrudes in the middle of a unified account about the future allocations of the tribes of Israel when they reach the Promised Land in chapter 32. The Redactor, who lived in the sixth or fifth century BCE and is assumed to have been an Aaronid, seems to have made opportunities to summarize his own understanding of the text and add his own details. So the Redactor in chapter 33 of the book of Numbers tells us key information that is not duplicated elsewhere but which can only be gleaned by following the Priestly account:

> These are the stages of the people of Israel when they went forth out of the land of Egypt by their hosts under the leadership of Moses and Aaron. Moses wrote down their starting places, stage by stage by command of the Lord. . . . They set out from Rameses in the first month, on the fifteenth day of the first month. . . . So the people of Israel set out from Rameses, and encamped at Succoth, and encamped at Etham, which is on the edge of the wilderness. And they set out from Etham and turned back to Pihahirot, which is east of Baal Zephon and they encamped before Migdol, and passed through the midst of the sea into the wilderness and they went three days journey into the wilderness of Etham.

The Redactor accepts the northern route as the basis for "the" Exodus and moves them from the city of Rameses through the Reed Sea to a few locations. He then takes them through a very short trip that includes Marah and another location, Elim, and then "they encamped at the Red Sea." In all of the Redactor's view of the Exodus, it is all taking place by the north. They then arrive at Rephidim, which is located directly adjacent to the wilderness of Sinai. Rephidim is mentioned only five times in the Bible, most of them as additions by the Redactor in the midst of an otherwise flowing narrative. But Rephidim is reached according to the Redactor in 19:1–2a " . . . on the third new month after the people of Israel had gone out of the land of Egypt . . . and there Israel encamped before the mountain." So at least according to the Redactor and the Priestly account, the Divine mountain was located within a short range of the Red Sea and the original Exodus site of the city of Rameses.

The Sixth Mistake: "The Absence of Evidence is Evidence of Absence"

I am going to use the phrase that summarizes what I think represents the sixth and most illogical mistake made by those who claim that the Exodus of the Israelites from Egypt never happened. It is usually not phrased like this, but it is essentially the way that these scholars present their information. There are several versions of the same argument, but it is all based upon the absence of archaeological data from the appropriate period to confirm the Exodus. For many of these scholars the absence of archaeological evidence is evidence of the absence of the Exodus, Mount Sinai, and in fact the entire reconquest mentioned in the Hebrew Bible. I will return to the phrase and the negative evidence they refer to a number of times, but the use of the argument that if you do not find it, it does not exist is one of the most illogical arguments in all science and needs to be challenged. First, one cannot scientifically draw any conclusions from the absence of evidence. Second, as we shall see, if you are looking in the wrong time period even at the right place, you won't find what you are looking for.

The main archaeological argument relating to the Exodus is now much easier to clarify. Most archaeologists have not uncovered any direct evidence in the Sinai Desert from the thirteenth century BCE for an Exodus. Although archaeologists have found what we might call slave "camps" or mining enterprises that were using slaves to mine precious stones in the Bronze Age, most of these camps were not in operation in the thirteenth century BCE. Further and probably the most problematic archaeological argument comes from what is not found in thirteenth century BCE Israel. In the period of the late Bronze Age, the thirteenth century BCE, the cities that are mentioned as having been conquered in the Land of Israel, Ai and Jericho for example, were not even inhabited in this period. But what if the most ancient Exodus took place in the Middle Bronze Age (sixteenth century BCE) when indeed the cities of Jericho and Ai were functioning cities? Instead of looking at the Merneptah Stele as the beginning of the Israelite period in Canaan (as most archaeologists and biblical scholars do), what if it was confirming the end of the reconquest period? What if we have been simultaneously looking in the wrong time period and the right places? When the famous archaeologist, Kathleen Kenyon, excavated the city of Jericho in the 1950s, for example, she presented a tremendous challenge to the theories of biblical scholars from the early twentieth century who thought that the Exodus had happened in the thirteenth century BCE. She wrote that the city of Jericho in the thirteenth century was uninhabited and so the entrance into the Land of Israel by Joshua and the Israelites could not have happened, and it immediately had the ripple effect of challenging the entire story of the biblical Exodus as understood by modern scholarship. But Kathleen Kenyon did confirm that at the end of the Middle Bronze Age, in the sixteenth century BCE, the walls of Jericho were violently destroyed and that after the battle, it was abandoned. What if there was more archaeology from the sixteenth century BCE that confirmed the influx of a people from the Delta region of Egypt to the cities of Jericho, Hazor, and Ai from the Middle Bronze Age, and no one noticed because they were not looking for it? This would tell us that the two accounts, the Exodus and the reentry of the Israelites did happen in a historical context.

The Seventh Mistake: The Byzantine Mount Sinai is "the" Mount Sinai

Another part of the absence of evidence argument is related to the location of Mount Sinai. One of the most troubling aspects of all Exodus research is the question of Mount Sinai. How did the people know where the mountain of God was? If they did know where it was, how could its location not have been carefully preserved by the generations of ancient Israelites? If you combine all of the texts (Priestly and non-Priestly traditions), it is clear that the mountain of God was located close to the border of Egypt because Moses visits the site and experiences the "Burning Bush" there. The mountain is outside the border of ancient Egypt but close enough for Moses to tell Pharaoh that the people just want to go there to sacrifice and return and seems to have been well known enough for Moses to tell Pharaoh where he was going and have the location of this mountain be meaningful to both Moses and Pharaoh. This is not the question that has occupied the research of archaeologists in the past half century. They are wondering why, if the mountain is so well known, why material culture has not been found at the site of what people have been calling "Mount Sinai." Archaeologists have searched in vain for evidence of a mass immigration of 2.5 million people into the Land of Israel, of the existence of 2.5 million people in the Sinai desert, and for a Mount Sinai that also has this evidence to support 2.5 million people in the thirteenth century BCE and have yet to find anything approaching evidence supporting these claims. But what if the entire period, number of people, and locations of Mount Sinai were wrong? What if they should be looking for thousands of people in the sixteenth century BCE and not in southern Sinai, where the traditional site of Mount Sinai is located, but in the southern Negev? Most of these questions are well known to archaeologists. In this case, I think that the traditional identification of Mount Sinai has misled most scholars and archaeologists and created another negative piece of evidence for claiming that later writers invented the entire Exodus.

The traditional site of Mount Sinai is called in Arabic *Jebel Musa*, (Mount Moses) and is a mighty red granite mountain in the Sinai Desert in modern Egypt. Byzantine Christians established this location in the fifth century CE when Christianity was establishing holy sites all around the Mediterranean associated with Jesus, the Holy Family, the Apostles, and biblical sites that figure in the New Testament and the Hebrew Bible. Saint Catherine's Monastery, located at the base of the mount, is named after an Egyptian Christian martyred in Alexandria in the fourth century. Legend has it that Catherine's bones were carried by angels to this spot after her martyrdom. While it is a very impressive mountain, it probably became famous as a holy site because of its location. It is located on a very well-trod point on a Byzantine trade route going east and west and north and south. The caravans which used domesticated camels starting in the Persian period would have found it a welcome spot to stop on their way to Cairo or Baghdad for about the past 2,500 years, but it is probably not the site of Mount Sinai in the middle Bronze Age when donkeys were the main mode of transportation.

Relic sites like this is are common in this period as Byzantine monks attempted to place all of the events of the Hebrew Bible and New Testament into the locations that they knew best and which allowed them to direct the new pilgrims from the Roman Empire to places that bolstered their religious identities. They relied upon oral traditions that were circulating in their own period and in some cases manufactured not a few of these places from their own inspiration. A dozen Greek monks still live at Saint Catherine's monastery and an eleventh century CE mosque at the top of Jebel Musa testifies to the importance that even local Muslims attached to the site. The monastery's original foundations are from the Byzantine monks, funded by the mother of Constantine the Great, who after becoming a Christian and perhaps convincing her son also to adopt Christianity, funded the identification of holy sites throughout the region. The Monastery even has one of the world's oldest libraries in the world, with one of the oldest Greek manuscript translations of the Bible (third century CE). The site established by the early Byzantine Church soon became the goal of many Christian pilgrims from all over the world. Travelers described the mountain, their personal experience on the mountain, and the traditions of the monks, and, as time passed, the location became unquestioned. But, argue archaeologist and biblical scholars alike, if so many people (2.5 million) were in this desert and at the mountain for so long, then where is all of the physical evidence? Where is all of the pottery, combs, personal items, and so forth, which archaeologists have not found here or in the rest of Sinai? So what makes this Mount Sinai? Not the Bible and not the archaeology. Just a religious tradition dating from the Byzantine period. Of course, the lack of any evidence there makes it much easier for people to dismiss the entire Exodus and Sinai experience. But there are other contenders for the title of Mount Sinai. There are many different mountains in the Sinai and Paran deserts. It is possible that there were different mountains of God that the people exiting in different time periods and areas went to in different areas of these deserts. The mountains that we know are not Mount Sinai are the ones without archaeological evidence, the ones with material culture from the Bronze Age that are possible contenders for the title of "Mount Sinai."

If one can say that there are different versions of the traditions of the Patriarchs and Matriarchs, the Exodus, and the Ten Commandments, there are also different versions of the Mount Sinai story that have different names for the mountain where the giving of the law took place. Mount Sinai is only one of the names for the place where the Israelites met God. Others include "the mountain of God," "the mountain in Horeb," "the mountain of God in Horeb," "Mount Horeb," "Mount Paran," and even just "the mountain." The differing literary traditions throughout the Bible all agree on the importance of the location, but it seems that even by the time these traditions were written down in the Iron Age and finally redacted in the Persian period, the original location of the mountain may not have been clear to the writers, or competing mountains were part of the oral and then written traditions. Not only does the book of Deuteronomy almost systematically rename the mountain as Mount Horeb, it relocates it in relation to the main oasis site of Kadesh Barnea and other sites along the itinerary. In Deuteronomy (chapter 1, verse 2 states that it is a journey of eleven days from Mount Horeb/Sinai to Kadesh Barnea) and in other non-Priestly stories in general, Mount Sinai is much further from Egypt than in the Priestly story line. I am not going to elaborate on the modern speculations that the different literary traditions suggest a southern route of an Exodus, a central route of an Exodus, and a northern route of an Exodus. I actually agree that there may have been three different Exoduses leading around to different regions of the Sinai and the Negev. I have become increasingly convinced that the literary tradition of the Priestly author that suggests a northern route and a mountain both closer to the ancient Egyptian border (and in the historic Land of Israel) may not only be the most detailed of the literary traditions that emerged among the writers in the Iron Age, but may also be the most authentic of all of the traditions of Mount Sinai.

Jebel Musa, the traditional Byzantine site of Mt. Sinai, is very far from the borders of Egypt and has always provided archaeologists with enormous problems. One of the largest problems is the lack of material culture from the Bronze Age at the traditional site of Jebel Musa. *Jebel Musa* geographically does not fit the Priestly literary account, but when we remove the mistaken time period for the thirteenth century BCE and the need to accept the Byzantine location in southern Sinai, Mount Sinai could be almost anywhere from the present day Suez Canal to the Gulf of Aqaba. Many different mountains have actually been suggested with more evidence than *Jebel Musa*. *Jebel Musa*, (literally Mount Moses), a mountain called Mount Catherine and even a mountain called Mount Serbal, all fit the possible location of Mount Sinai once the impediments of the mistaken time period are removed. Another site in Saudi Arabia, at *Jebel El Lawz*, has also been suggested, but part of the problem is just how far all of these mountains are from the ancient border of Egypt. The distance from the ancient border of Egypt is a real question when you look carefully at the text. In the book of Exodus, chapter 16, verse 1, the Israelites arrive at the foot of Mount Sinai in the fifteenth day of the second month after leaving Egypt. This is a very specific tradition. The writer does not employ the system of religious numbers (as symbols) which one finds throughout the Bible. In this system of religious and symbolic numbers, multiples of 7, 10, 12, and 40 (including multiples of 10 and numbers such as 70, 120 or 400) are what I call symbols rather than real numbers. It is the equivalent of being asked today how far one city is from another and just stating "far," "very far," or even "not very far." For the ancient reader these round numbers indicated a general category of information, not a specific number. But what is different in the Exodus 16 tradition is that it is so specific. Forty-five days from the border of Egypt, Mount Sinai is located. Whether there were 2.5 million men, women, and children and their flocks or eight thousand people and their flocks, it is difficult to imagine that they could have moved more than five to six miles per day. Anthropologists have tracked tribal movements in the present period, and they have come to the conclusion that five to six miles per day is a reasonable distance for people to travel with their old, young, and flocks to feed. Meaning that if this tradition is correct, Mount Sinai could only be some 250 miles (45 days x 5 miles = 225 miles) from the border of Egypt. This would rule out most of the candidates for the title of Mount Sinai in southern Sinai and Saudi Arabia.

The most reasonable locations that have been proposed for Mount Sinai are in what is today called the Negev, the southern desert of present-day

Israel. Most of these sites are not on the medieval or Byzantine caravan routes, but it is for this reason that they probably were not even considered. The geographical references that follow the Priestly account of the Exodus, place the northern route as the place where the Israelites crossed over and left the last *Migdol*, a tower fortress used to mark the boundary of Egypt into the Negev. In the Negev we have a number of mountains with archaeological credentials that date to the Bronze Age and are within 250 miles of the ancient border of Egypt. Mount Helal, Mount Yaalak, Mount Maghara, Mount Yeroham, and Mount Karkom are located in the vicinity of what we could call "the northern route" in what is today called the northern Sinai of Egypt and the southern Negev of Israel. Our own work took us to Mount Karkom in 2007 because of the excavations that had been done for over the past twenty-five years by Professor Emmanuel Anati.

IS MOUNT KARKOM MOUNT SINAI?

Dr. Anati is unique because not only has he been publishing archaeological finds at the mountain for over twenty-five years, but also because he has tirelessly tried to combine the location of Mount Karkom, the findings of his excavations, with citations and events in the Bible associated with the Exodus in his writings. First, the location of Mount Karkom is approximately 250 miles from the ancient border of Egypt. Mount Karkom is near a major water source, and it has a variety of different archaeological features that no other mountain in the Sinai or Negev has. It has the best chance of being the solution to all of the archaeological and geographical problems not only because of the location, the water, and the material culture, but because Dr. Anati has also created a literary theory that takes into consideration many of the text critical ideas that we have mentioned in the introduction of this book. An Italian archaeologist who was trained in Israel, Professor Anati has been working at this site for over twenty-five years in the limited periods of time each year when the site is accessible to him. At 2,778 feet and near the Sinai Peninsula, Mount Karkom has both unique rock art, scores of altars, and common ware finds from thousands of people who visited the place in the Middle Bronze Age. When the University of Hartford Geophysical Survey Project went to visit the site during Passover 2007, we were shown hundreds of examples of the rock art that are unlike anything that exists in the rest of the Sinai and Negev. According to Anati, the over forty thousand rock art examples include traditional pictures of the menorah, the rod of Moses turning into a serpent, a carving that resembles the Ten Commandments, a map that shows the mountain and encampments around the mountain, thousands of hunting scenes, and figures in prayer. The many altars and cult sites that Anati has excavated around the mountain are unparalleled elsewhere in the region. Anati's finds indicate that the mountain was a cult site up until the Middle Bronze Age and then again in the ninth century BCE (Iron Age) onward, with an intriguing gap of almost one thousand years in between. Why would an important mountain that had been in use for a very long time (Neolithic times–Middle Bronze Age) as a famous cult site suddenly be abandoned for one thousand years?

It is interesting that that the site was abandoned in the ninth century BCE—precisely when camels were domesticated in the Middle East and changed caravan routes throughout the entire region nearly overnight. Old sites were abandoned in favor of new caravan routes that were newly possible with animals that could travel for long stretches of time without water. If Mount Karkom was Mount Sinai, it is understandable that it was abandoned. It no longer was on the new caravan routes and like the towns that were located on old wagon train routes in the Southwest before the coming of the railroads and similar to the towns that were located next to old route 66 across the United States before the coming of the interstate system, many of these towns were abandoned and became "ghost towns." People abandoned the town and before long, no one could even remember that there had been a town there. Mount Karkom may have been the original Bronze Age site of Mount Sinai, abandoned after the new caravan routes and forgotten within a few generations.

The ninth century BCE date for the abandonment of Mount Karkom is also important for another reason. This is the period when the earliest oral traditions of the Israelites were committed to writing, including the earliest Biblical writings by J and E. It is not, I think, an accident that the ninth century BCE Hebrew prophet of Elijah is the only other person to speak about Mount Horeb (Sinai) in 1 Kings. In it he takes his journey from Beersheva to Mount Horeb where he too has his own revelation. These Elijah stories are the only prophet writings to allude to the story of Moses and the Exodus. Elijah seems to be living in the middle of this epic story and still knows where Mount Horeb is located.

THE BACKGROUND THEORY AND PROFESSOR EMMANUEL ANATI

I have heard Professor Anati present his theory about Har Karkom as Mount Sinai multiple times while I was on expedition with him. He would sit in front of Israelis and other other groups who now make their own pilgrimage to the area when he is excavating (and when tourists are allowed onto the military base), and each time I heard it I became more and more convinced that his view explains many of the problems of the Exodus and the location of Mount Sinai. He asks a simple question to his audience. How is it possible the site of the mountain where the Israelites met their God could so easily be forgotten? How could this knowledge have been lost? He does not claim that he has found "the" Mount Sinai where Moses and the Israelites met God. He suggests that the writers of the Bible used Har Karkom and its general setting as the model for what they were writing down for the first time in the their sacred scriptures. The location of many different holy sites from the Bible were purposely disguised in order to not have them known to the general populus. The location of Moses' burial site, for example, is not known, and the Bible goes out of its way to say that the location is a mystery. It is possible that the locations of many sites where the experiences of the Patriarchs and Matriarchs occurred were disguised so that they would not become the site of continued Israelite and Judean worship. By the time the Bible was being written down, Jerusalem had emerged as the main place for pilgrimage and to create the possibility that other sites might compete with it for attention, and pilgrimage would probably have been seen by all writers of the Bible as counterproductive. Mount Moriah, for example, a mountain where the near sacrifice of Isaac had taken place, is clearly not in Jerusalem if you follow the story line. Rabbinic tradition made Mount Moriah into the Temple Mount. In particular, I think, the Priestly writer was using the Mount Karkom area as his backdrop for the Exodus and Mount Sinai even as Jerusalem became the holy mount.

According to Professor Anati, Mount Karkom was first populated in the Stone Age and has considerable activity in the Bronze Age. The remains include numerous circles of boulders and what he calls "*matzebot*" (standing stones that were used for cultic rites and burials). Several other ruined architecture structures appear to have been small temples from different time periods. One unique structure is located on the mountain, where it commands a beautiful view of the area. It includes a number of "*matzebot*" beside an altar platform. Many campsites from this period were found along the trail to the mountain. Apparently, a large number of people once lived there until the Middle Bronze era, and then it was abandoned until the Iron Age II period. From the ninth century BCE through the Roman period, the mountain was again a place of reduced activity and then slightly inhabited during the Byzantine period and then completely abandoned. During the 1980s, as the expeditions of Professor Anati began, some of his discoveries suggested more than just a place where some general cultic activity took place. It suggested specific comparisons with the biblical text. At the foot of Mount Karkom, Anati discovered a group of twelve standing stones, as seen early in this chapter in figure 1.1. Next to these "*matzebot*" were the remains of a platform and a courtyard. This site resembles the passage ". . . and Moses built an altar under the hill, and 12 pillars, according to the 12 tribes of Israel" (Exodus 24:4). A small cleft found on top of the mountain suggested to Anati that it was the place where Moses stayed in his personal encounter with God. To find such a rock shelter on the very summit of a mountain is geologically scarce and again, this is where archaeology can contribute significantly by meticulously examining the area. It bears a striking correspondence to the described cleft on Mount Sinai: "And the Lord said . . . that I will put you in the cleft of the rock, and will cover you with my hand while I pass by" (Exodus 33: 21–22). Another item of interest is the small Bronze Age temple at the center of the plateau on the mountain. The Bible makes clear that Moses saw an old temple on top of the mountain, which he later used as a model. As Anati discovered more and more striking parallels between the biblical descriptions and the discoveries at Mount Karkom, he came to the conclusion that this was the best contender for the title of Mount Sinai among the less than ten mountains that also fit the geographical context.

So why is this mountain, Mount Karkom, virtually ignored by many scholars when they write about the Exodus? First, I think it is because the knowledge of any new archaeological discovery that challenges what has become the status quo needs many years of vetting before becoming widely accepted. It took us twenty years of discoveries, hundreds of thousands of finds, and many books, papers, documentaries, and supporters to convince the academic community that we had discovered the site of Bethsaida. The fact that our site was so close to other archaeological sites associated with early Christianity and because it was more easily accessed than Mount Karkom made our efforts much easier. Simply put, I think that because Mount Karkom is so inaccessible to the general public and most scholars, it is just not very well known despite over twenty-five years of excavation and the publications Professor Anati has produced. Given what I know about the writing of the Bible and how much evidence is found at Mount Karkom, I think that it is clearly the best option for understanding a historical Exodus and Mount Sinai.

The Eighth Mistake: What Does and What Does Not Constitute Evidence

One of the strongest arguments against an Israelite Exodus in any period is the lack of evidence for the existence of Israelites in Egyptian literature from the time. This is a continuation of the "Absence of Evidence is Evidence for Absence" argument mentioned above. It is important to distinguish what does and does not constitute evidence. No mention of the Israelites having been in Egypt or served as slaves appears in any ancient Egyptian source. There is no Egyptian archaeological evidence of Israelites in Egypt from the Bronze Age, Iron Age, or Persian period, despite hundreds of thousands of discoveries in Egypt over the past 150 years of serious archaeological research. The first mention of the Exodus outside of the Bible is in the writing of Josephus Flavius, which we looked at earlier. Flavius places the Exodus in the Hellenistic period, some three hundred years earlier.

One piece of indirect archaeological evidence was rediscovered only recently in Egypt. Frank J. Yurco, a brilliant Egyptologist, reassessed the meaning of a 3,200-year-old Karnak relief and concluded that the people in the relief were probably Israelites in an article in *Biblical Archaeology Review* (16.5) in 1990. He and others have speculated that the Israelites were depicted on the walls of Karnak in a relief, from the thirteenth century but again, there is no specific reference to the Israelites. This negative evidence doesn't negate the Exodus, it just does not prove it. When there is such a disparity between the evidence that something happened from one source and no evidence from another source, it raises the suspicion that the evidence of one or the other has been seriously tampered with. As we have seen, the ancient Egyptians were extremely conservative about what made it into their history. For example, very few women in the ancient world wielded any real political power. The greatest woman of ancient Egypt was Hatshepsut, who ruled for more than two decades in the fifteenth century BCE. Later rulers did not see Pharoah Hatshepsut's reign in Egypt as fitting into the developing concept of Egyptian history, and they attempted to edit out every reference to her. Egypt was the most powerful land in the eastern Mediterranean during the early part of the New Kingdom. Hatshepsut was the daughter of Tuthmosis I, the third pharaoh of the eighteenth Dynasty and she married her half-brother, Tuthmosis II. After her husband's early death, she became regent to Tuthmosis III, the son of Tuthmosis II by another wife. In the midst of this period, Hatshepsut took the extraordinary step of proclaiming herself king. After her death, her nephew made a systematic effort to erase every mention of her name and destroyed or disfigured her statues in an attempt to keep her legacy out of the "official story." Later Egyptian rulers also eliminated every mention of male Pharoahs they found objectionable. Akhenaton, for example, the religious reformer of the fourteenth century BCE (who advocated a form of henotheism, or monotheism associated with Aton), was summarily omitted from the official lists of kings of Egypt because his reforms did not meet their standards of the "normative" history of Egypt. His capital city was destroyed but thanks to careful archaeology the entire episode has been reconstructed.

Egyptian history is replete with examples of a very selective version of the actual events of ancient Egypt. If we assume that the Exodus, even with a reduced number of Israelites exiting in different periods, represented a small number of people, it is not surprising that they are not mentioned in Egyptian texts. Most people do not realize that despite the fact that much has been discovered in Egypt only a small percentage of the vast amount of ancient texts and material culture has been excavated and researched. If the Israelites represented a significant part of the Egyptian populace that just got up and left, it is clear that Egyptian rulers would have made every effort to exorcise the memory of this event from Egyptian history. As I have mentioned a few different times in this chapter, the example of the Hyksos is so unusual as to make it the norm. The Hyksos, or shepherd kings of Asia whose rule of Egypt spanned nearly 150 years in the eighteenth and seventeenth centuries BCE, were neatly exorcised from the official ancient Egyptian history record. It is thanks mostly to careful archaeology from other areas of the Middle East that had contact with the Egyptians in this ancient period that we know anything about them. The absence of evidence may just be in the end the *planned* absence of evidence. One just cannot use the negative evidence to prove anything but that more needs to be excavated to confirm the truth.

The Ninth Mistake: Are We Looking at the Right Places?

We do not know exactly where the Israelites crossed over the Re(e)d Sea, and we do not know exactly where Mount Sinai is because the Bible is not a text of geography although it does give some geographical references. The Exodus happened in a place where the natural forces of an east wind, a small tsunami forced out the water (the Sea, not always the Reed Sea) and later the water came back, according to Exodus Chapter 14, verse 21–23. If there is a miracle here, it is the timing of the event that coincided with the Israelites' Exodus from Egypt. No hand of the Divine is described as just grabbing the Israelites (*Deus Ex Machina*) and transporting them to the other side. In fact, it is difficult to know where exactly the Israelites crossed over. Lake Balah, Lake Sirbonis, north of Lake Balah, and the Bitter Lakes, south of Lake Balah all have been suggested as the spot where the crossing took place. Most of these places around Lake Balah have been suggested since the ancient Reed Sea (not the present-day Red Sea) simply makes more sense when synchronized with the biblical account. The ancient coastline of Egypt has changed dramatically in the past 3,000 years. All of these locations are much different today than they were in antiquity, but the changing size and configuration of lakes is a very well-known factor in geology and archaeology. We will see that the same phenomenon occurred on the Sea of Galilee later in this book when I write more about our discovery of Bethsaida, a fisherman's village that at present is two miles away from the shore.

It is hard to look at a map today and know what it looked like in antiquity, but this is especially true when assessing bodies of water that are on active fault lines and subject to silting and earthquake sedimentation. Again, looking for the crossing of the Red Sea, a wide and deep body of water, makes archaeologists skeptical about the entire event. The eastern delta of north Sinai near the isthmus of Suez has a series of silted-in areas that in antiquity were covered with a low-lying swampy area (thus the Reed Sea) that are much closer to Egypt and the northern location alluded to in Exodus 14. The famous exit area for Egypt for thousands of years was the "Highway of Horus." It was always the place that kings and invaders would use in and out of the country, but recent archaeology has revealed that it was more and then less accessible as the Egyptians built fortresses and towers to guard the borders of Egypt. I learned all this from an archaeologist who has spent his life working on Egyptian sites. The most recent excavations of Professor James Hoffmeier, working at a site in the Delta region of Egypt called *El Borg* ("The Tower" in Arabic) may provide some new information about these fortresses and the geomorphology of the Delta region and especially where the Mediterranean Sea and the Reed Sea were originally located. Professor Hoffmeier has tracked the fortresses of the Delta region that were built in different time periods and also the existence of lakes surrounded by reeds in antiquity. He has written numerous scholarly works and articles dealing with early Israel, including *Israel in Egypt: Evidence for the Authenticity of the Exodus Tradition* (1997 and 1999) and *Ancient Israel in Sinai: The Evidence for the Authenticity of the Wilderness Tradition* (2005). His work suggests that there were periods when the Egyptians feared that their northern borders needed more protection and built defensive walls and towers to keep out the foreigners from Asia. The Arabic "El Borg" site name may preserve the tradition of fortresses as the word means "Tower." It may preserve the idea that there were towers and fortresses in the area that were known in the sands of the Delta right up until the modern period. But when were these defensive fortresses and towers built? It would probably be after the Hyksos were finally ejected in the sixteenth century BCE, and they were there in the period of Rameses II. Professor Hoffmeier's work suggests that the period before and after the radical reforms of Pharaoh Akhenaton (fourteenth century BCE) is when fortresses and towers were built and then reinforced in later periods. It seems to suggest that there were northern routes of exit that were known and used, but the fortresses were built in order to keep the outsiders from coming back in to conquer Egypt. What these defensive towers do not tell us is whether they could or would be used to keep the insiders, the Egyptians, from leaving? Probably not. They would be able to inhibit the movements of people from Egypt to the north, but they were primarily of use for stopping invasions.

If we combine studies about the geography of Mount Sinai, the Sea of Reeds (which was probably in the Delta region and other geographical issues), one has to wonder whether archaeologists have been looking in the right places for the evidence of the Exodus. If the Israelites were leaving the country through the northern route, the location of Mount Sinai according to this tradition would be in the southern Negev, not in the southern part of the Sinai peninsula. The tradition of escaping through the northern route, even after the construction of the fortresses and towers along the northern border, is corroborated by *Papyrus Anastasi V*, the document from the reign of Pharaoh Seti II in the thirteenth and early twelfth century BCE, which demonstrates that despite these fortresses, escaping slaves chose this northern route because it was the closest. The *Papyrus* reads:

> I was sent forth from the broad-halls of the palace—life, prosperity, health—in the 3rd month of the third season, day 9, at the time of evening, *following after these two slaves. . . .* [Now] when [I] reached the fortress, they told me that the scout had come from the desert [saying that] *they had passed the walled place north of the Migdol of Seti Mer-ne-Ptah—life, prosperity,~health!—Beloved like Seth. When my letter reaches you, write to me about all that has happened to [them].* Who found their tracks? Which watch found their tracks? What people are after them? Write to me about all that has happened to them and how many people you send out after them. [May your health] be good!
>
> (Cited from *Ancient Near Eastern Texts Relating to the old Testament,* edits by James Prichard [Princeton: University Press, 1969], p. 259)

Were people still escaping through the northern protected border even into the thirteenth century? I think so, but it probably was easier to escape to the south or the middle of the country where there were less fortresses but much more desert.

The Deuteronomistic Tradition: The Exodus in Deuteronomy to the Books of Kings

The third Exodus is one that is created in the literary tradition of the Deuteronomist in the Torah. The Deuteronomist was the written tradition that emerged in the period of King Josiah and remained a predominant force through another series of books, including Joshua, Judges, 1 and 2 Samuel, 1 and 2 Kings, and the book of Jeremiah. It is clear that the Dueteronomistic tradition sees that Mount Horeb is Mount Sinai, in close proximity to the historical land of Israel and not in the Sinai desert. I mentioned above that according to the book of Kings, Elijah living in the ninth century still knew the location of Mount Sinai. Elijah, who during most of the book of 1 Kings resides in the northern part of Israel near today's Haifa, goes to Beer Sheva in the beginning of chapter 19 and, is fed by an "angel" to give him enough substance for the journey to Horeb. He travels for the requisite "forty days and forty nights" and reaches the mountain. The number of days is very symbolic. This is the same number of days that Moses passed in the period of the receiving of the Ten Commandments, and again it is probably the same type of symbolic number that forty is elsewhere in the Bible. It means that he spent a long time getting there. This name of the mountain, "Horeb," is significant because it figures in the books of Exodus and Deuteronomy, but it is especially significant because it is the name of the mountain of God in the book of 2 Chronicles 5:10, a different tradition. The Deuteronomistic and the Chronicles traditions, written later than the Priestly tradition of the eighth and seventh centuries, indicate that the mountain's name was seen as Horeb for most of the period when the text was being written down. The Chronicles traditions are different than the Deuteronomistic history and are later than the Deuteronomistic traditions. In the book of 1 Kings 19, in the episode of Elijah at Horeb, there is also a parallel to Moses' other encounter with God in Exodus 33:22. Elijah's encounter with God occurs close to the historic land of Israel and is associated with a cave, while Moses' encounter takes place by the cleft of a rock by Mount Sinai. Elijah is told to leave the cave and "stand before God."

The encounter, perhaps one of the most poignant and poetic in the entire Hebrew Bible is also a description of geological forces present near the mountain. There was a wind, "but God is not in the wind," an earthquake, "but God is not in the earthquake," a fire "but God is not in the fire," then "a still small voice" comes to Elijah, and this is his encounter with the Divine, outside of a cave, associated with Mount Horeb. According to some Christian traditions, it is at Horeb that Moses and Elijah appear with

Jesus at the moment of Jesus' "transfiguration" (found in all three Synoptic Gospels, the "transfiguration" refers to the radiance of Jesus' face when he comes down the mountain) to express the same type of transfiguration that happened to Moses in Exodus 34:29 after his own encounter with the Divine. It is the traditions of Moses, Elijah, and Jesus they are all encountering the Divine at a Mount Sinai that later pushed the early Byzantine monks to look for a pilgrimage site for Mount Sinai in the first place.

The Deuteronomistic historical tradition was, according to most Bible scholars, written down in the period seventh century BCE before the Babylonian Exile and includes the books of Joshua, Judges, 1 and 2 Samuel, and the two books of Kings. The separations of books 1 and 1 were not original divisions of the texts. The Deuteronomistic history is therefore not only a record of the events of the Bible and the desert wanderings, it includes the entire core history of the people of Israel from a different perspective than the other writers of the early books of the Bible. The Deuteronomist's vantage point afforded him an opportunity to locate the Exodus in a specific historical context in the entire history of ancient Israel—something that none of the other writers of the Bible could have done. It is not surprising therefore that the Deuteronomist gives a very specific date which can be corroborated with the biblical Exodus. The Deuteronomist is the only one who could have done this. In the book of 1 Kings, chapter 6, verse 1 we find: "In the 480th year after the people of Israel came out of the land of Egypt, in the fourth year of Solomon's reign over Israel, in the month of Ziv, which is the second month, he began to build the house of the Lord." It is possible that this is a symbolic number (multiples of forty are religiously symbolic in the entire Bible), but he is placing the Exodus in a history that is more easily calculated from the Deuteronomist's perspective than by any other writer. If we use the numbers as "real" and not just symbolic, Solomon's reign began in the early tenth century BCE, then the Deuteronomist saw the Exodus as an event in the fifteenth century BCE. Why am I so sure that the fifteenth century BCE is the time period in the book of Kings? Because the story of King Solomon and the Temple in Jerusalem in the tenth century BCE is one of the few pieces of biblical history that can be corroborated by Egyptian history. Egyptian records indicate that in approximately the last quarter of the tenth century, the Pharaoh Sheshonk came to Jerusalem and despoiled the Temple of Jerusalem. If Sheshonk came to Jerusalem in the tenth century and despoiled the Temple (Egyptian records have been carefully coordinated with our present chronologies) then the Temple was standing in the middle of the tenth century BCE. If the Temple was standing in the middle of the tenth century BCE, then the biblical citation of the book of Kings that says that the Israelites left Egypt 480 years before the Temple's founding would put the Exodus squarely in the fifteenth century. The Deuteronomist placed the Exodus into one of the few ancient historical contexts that can be cross-checked with Egyptian history.

Another detail in this Deuteronomistic tradition seems to support this view as well. In the book of Judges, chapter 11, verse 26 speaks of Israel having possessed the land "for three hundred years" by Jephthah the Judge's time. Since Jephthah was the eighth Judge of Israel according to the Book of Judges, it would bring us to an Exodus in the fifteenth century BCE. The court history that continues from Joshua–Kings is very detailed, and this correlates well with the citation in the book of Kings. From Jephthah to Solomon was another 180 years of history. The Deuteronomist does not tell us which Pharaoh was the Pharaoh of the Exodus, nor does he tell us how he knew his information, but he does place it in what is the Middle Bronze Age. Thus the Deuteronomist gives us the third "literary" Exodus time period as the fifteenth century BCE.

Summary: Let's Start with Fewer Assumptions

Based on the documentary hypothesis of the modern study of the Bible and the available archaeological data, I hold that there were three literary versions of Exoduses that can be documented. It is hard to know if they are truly three distinct Exoduses, three different versions of one Exodus, or a combination of many different Exoduses that were collapsed together. It is clear that the Redactor has tried (as he did elsewhere) to recombine contradictory accounts. It is also clear that three different versions emerged in three different time periods of biblical writing and that they did not agree as to when the Exodus(es) happened. The Exodus of J/E, written down in the ninth to eighth centuries BCE, is the only one that consistently includes a reference to the city of *Rameses* from Genesis–Exodus onward. I think that these writers may have believed that the Exodus occurred in the period of Rameses, but it is possible that the name "Rameses" was used in the account because this was the only Pharaoh that they knew. The J/E version of the Exodus also includes the *"mixed multitude"* reference in the story of the Exodus. Unlike the other Exoduses that make the Exodus a purely Israelite event, J/E makes the event an Exodus with other peoples. J/E has no reference point for the date of the Exodus, although Genesis 15:13 states that the Israelites were in Egypt for four hundred years of servitude in Egypt. Yet the J/E tradition also recorded another shorter period of servitude as well—80 to160 years of servitude in Egypt in Genesis 15:16.

Four generations or 160 years eerily parallels the period of the Hyksos so-journ in Egypt, so it is possible that even J was preserving a tradition of an Exodus in the early Bronze Age with the Hyksos. This has led me to the conclusion that perhaps the J author is reporting on an Exodus tradition of Israelites in the period of the Hyksos Exodus in the sixteenth century BCE, and this may very well parallel the one by the Priestly tradition. The biggest difference between the J/E presentation of the Exodus and the Priestly presentation of the Exodus is the route for the Exodus. J/E places the Exodus to the south and P to the north. If so, it is possible that the J/E author only could imagine a southern route because of the well-known obstacles that had been built in the north.

The Priestly tradition does not have the anachronistic references about the store-cities of Rameses as the building of the Israelites' servitude. In addition, the biggest difference in the Priestly tradition in comparison with the J/E version of the Exodus is that he recounts a smaller Exodus with more named characters. He also records the Israelites alone, without the mixed multitude, and they take a northern route that leads through Migdol into northern Sinai, directly to Mount Sinai.

The Deuteronomistic history has the Exodus taking place along the northern route into the southern Negev and an unusual circuitous route that takes them back and forth from the Reed Sea. Again there is no "mixed multitude," but only a group of Israelites heading for a Mount Horeb (not Mount Sinai) with a number of stops along the way, but not nearly as many stops as in the J/E's traditions. There is no date in the book of Deuteronomy for the reckoning of the Exodus, but there are specific historical contexts for the Exodus in the books of Judges and Kings. They both point to an Exodus in the fifteeenth century BCE.

In short, the steps followed the normal sequence of J/E, P, and Deuter-onomistic historian parallel traditions in other sections of the Pentateuch. The J/E traditions were written down first, probably in the ninth to eighth centuries BCE. I think J/E knew about the very ancient Hyksos Exodus of the sixteenth century BCE and added elements from the period of the thirteenth century BCE Pharaoh Rameses either because Rameses was the most famous Pharaoh of Egyptian history or because he may have had information that actually connected the Hyksos with Rameses. Why did the J/E writers have this tradition? I think the Egyptian ruler Rameses II was connected to the Hyksos story. Egyptian records point to the fact that Rameses II celebrated during his reign, the four-hundredth anniversary of the defeat and exile of the Hyksos and the celebration of the Storm god Seth's rule at Tanis. The city is rebuilt and renamed Pi-Rameses. If Rameses

II was celebrating this event, he was doing so either because he felt some affinity for the Hyksos or to celebrate his own victories over the Asiatics. This would have been an indication that the Asiatics may have been linked to a similar four-hundred-year celebration that the Bible associates with the Exodus of the Israelites from Egypt.

I close this chapter with one of the most asked questions about the Exodus. If Mount Sinai is so important to Judaism, Christianity, and Islam, why was the knowledge of the location of the site of Mount Sinai lost? I think it has everything to do with the two main issues of *Digging Through the Bible*: editing techniques and archaeology. Originally, I think that the Negev site of Mount Sinai made more sense in a world in which donkeys were the main mode of transportation. I could imagine the Israelites coming out of Egypt on their small donkeys and their possessions. The Israelites I imagine moved from one well/oasis site with their livestock, and the short travel distance was crucial to the movement of ancient peoples. In the Bronze Age, Mount Sinai in the Negev may have better fit the donkey caravan routes that depended on short travel from oasis to oasis. In the time period in which the Exodus accounts were being written down, however, (almost a thousand years later than the events that they portray) a major change in modes of travel was also taking place in the Middle East. When the camel was domesticated in the Middle East in the ninth and eighth century BCE, the caravan routes could now be changed to move people and goods farther distances in the desert without resorting to the short distance travel of the Bronze Age. The Sinai desert became more accessible and travel through the Negev desert less necessary. With the change in caravan travel, a Mount Sinai of the Negev became a casualty of history. Forgotten, except for small indicators in an ancient text that pointed to an original story line with different characters and locales. Also as the holy mountain of Jerusalem became more important, the holy mountain of Sinai had to become less important.

But the final combination of the Redactor is the real story. He preserved details and combined all of these different versions of the Exodus and Mount Sinai and wove them into a rich, complex and multilayered text that gave infinite possibilities for biblical commentators and created havoc for future archaeologists.

2

Searching for King David and King Solomon and the Ancient City of Jerusalem

Figure 2.1.   Early twentieth century, the Wailing Wall.

Courtesy Hazza Abu Rabia Collection, University of Hartford.

The past twenty years of excavation at our Bethsaida site in Galilee have revealed more about King David, King Solomon, and ancient Jerusalem than many other sites around Israel, including Jerusalem itself! Bethsaida is one of the largest unexcavated sites of ancient Israel, and it is far from Jerusalem on the Sea of Galilee in northern Israel. How is it that a city so far from Jerusalem reveals more about Jerusalem than Jerusalem itself? It is because archaeology at places that have been continuously occupied like Jerusalem are difficult excavation projects to begin with, Jerusalem has been in a continuous flux of building, rebuilding, and destruction by three religions, many sects, and over three thousand years of wars and conflicts, it is nearly impossible to put all of the pieces neatly together. It is difficult to pinpoint a time period for an artifact or excavate a clean and untouched area in the Old City, and the new city and suburbs are an unknown archaeological mystery. Bethsaida, on the other hand, was abandoned some eighteen years ago on the Sea of Galilee, and because of unusual geological circumstances including earthquakes and flooding, was never rebuilt or inhabited. It is a pristine archaeological site and most important, it was connected in the Bible with the Davidic families in a very intimate way.

The Bethsaida excavations have revealed a walled city on the northeast shore of the Sea of Galilee that includes two prominent layers of occupation, one from the Greco-Roman period and the other, much more ancient, from the Iron Age. Bethsaida has revealed many things about the city in the time of the Romans but has revealed even more from the earlier time of Kings David and Solomon. This has fueled a counterargument to what has become a regular trend in archaeology over the past ten years. During the past decade many of the traditional assumptions about the existence of a Davidic dynasty in the tenth-century-BCE unified kingdom of David have been challenged by Bible scholars and archaeologists. Our work at Bethsaida has given a fresh and unique counterargument to the skepticism about the time of King David and Solomon. At Bethsaida, one can see undisturbed evidence of the tenth century BCE because the site was abandoned in the third century CE and remained virtually untouched until our arrival in 1987. This is not the case in Jerusalem, which was continuously settled and renovated many times. In addition, the city of Bethsaida was the capital city of biblical Geshur, a city that was interwoven with the history of King David and the Davidic dynasty. As such, the city provides one of the best chances for reconstructing the historicity of this dynasty and gives us an insight into what tenth century Jerusalem and the palaces, city wall, and gates in the time of King David and King Solomon might have looked like.

The Geshurite connection with King David is not very well known, but it was central to the Davidic dynasty. As King David expanded his united kingdom north and south, he made treaties with small and large empires that surrounded him to insure his own kingdom's security. Today we would call them peace treaties. In antiquity leaders simply married into the families of the kingdoms they wished to secure a peace treaty with, and it made it more difficult for a foreign leader to attack his own flesh and blood. In 2 Samuel 3:3 we learn that King David married Maachah, the daughter of the King of Geshur, Talmai. In antiquity, there were two levels of importance placed upon the peace treaty. Usually a king would give his son or daughter to the daughter or son of a foreign king. This signaled the balance of power between them. In the case of Geshur, King David himself married the daughter of the King of Geshur to insure the stability of the nation and perhaps because he felt a deep kinship for Talmai and Maachah. Whatever it is, Geshur was a kingdom that apparently spanned the area of the Golan and went north in the direction of today's Damascus and would have been politically necessary for the long-term security interests of the entire Kingdom of David. We now know that the capital city of Geshur must also have been a very important city for David. Not only does the son of Maachah and David, Absalom, become the primary son for succeeding David, but the name of the Queen, Maachah, appears repeatedly in the Davidic history as a well-known queen name. I am not even surprised to find the name "Maachah" in the book of Genesis or the "Maachites" in Deuteronomy, given the importance of this name precisely in the period when the Bible was being written down. Maachah must have been perceived by most in this period as a "Martha Washington" of sorts, and the name would have been a show of the writer's recognition of this fact. According to what we know from excavations in Jerusalem and Bethsaida, the capital city of Geshur in the tenth century would have been bigger in size than Jerusalem of the same time period. The capital city of Geshur—its walls, palaces, altars, and gate(s)—would have provided a model for what David might have wanted to see in his own capital city of Jerusalem. Geshur's capital city was the place where David would have married Maachah, and it was also the place that David's son Absalom would have escaped to when he left Jerusalem after killing his half-brother Amnon. After this event Absalom stayed in the capital of Geshur for three years and may even have married there as well. The book of 2 Samuel chapter 14 reminds us that even after Absalom returned to Jerusalem from his northern exile, he did not see his father David for four years. The words in the

Bible show us the poignancy of what truly sounds like a real historical character expressing his dilemma to Joab, a military leader in Jerusalem. Absalom complains in 2 Samuel 14: "Why did I come from Geshur? It was better for me to be there still."

Bethsaida was probably more pleasant to live in than Jerusalem during this time period. Bethsaida sat in the fresh water micro-climate Sea of Galilee, surrounded by pasture and agricultural fields and blessed with abundant drinking water from the Jordan River. The below-sea-level elevation meant it did not have the extremes of temperature like Jerusalem, which sat on a mountain bordering the Judean desert. Jerusalem had none of these advantages. The hills surrounding Jerusalem made it a difficult journey to most everywhere from north to south and east to west, while Bethsaida sat on the famous Via Maris, the main highway of east to west and on a spur of the north-south highway along the Jordan River. Bethsaida was actually larger than Jerusalem in total area, and our research has shown that in the tenth century, the defensive walls of Bethsaida were thicker than Jerusalem's. While size does not always matter in archaeology, it does give us an indication about what comparisons can be made. Absalom is said to have died while attempting to seize the power that he thought he should have been granted as crown prince. He would have gotten a taste for that power not only in Jerusalem, but also in Bethsaida where he resided with his grandfather, the king of Geshur, and saw what real royal power was. The time that he spent in self-imposed exile at the royal city of Geshur did not extinguish his passion for the kingship, rather it fueled his desire to take his rightful place in Jerusalem. If he had been staying in a "backwater" of Galilee, he might have just returned to Jerusalem with his tail between his legs and accepted his fate. Instead he returned to Jerusalem and became obsessed with achieving the kingship. His time in Geshur's capital made a lasting impression upon him. Although he did not achieve power, he left a daughter whose name was also Maachah. King Solomon's son, King Rehoboam, married her and "he loved her more than all his (other) wives and concubines" (2 Chronicles 11, verse 21). These are not just idle expressions of appreciation. The entire Davidic line (in all traditions of the Davidic traditions) saw the connection with Maachah and Geshur as very important parts of the Davidic story. While I have found that Jerusalem is a place where the archaeological layers are inherently mixed and difficult to interpret, it has not stopped archaeologists from trying to find King David and King Solomon amidst the chaos of layers. The search for the Jerusalem of David and Solomon is almost as contested as the Exodus from Egypt.

King David's Palace?

In recent years, the search for King David has centered upon the excavations of the City of David just outside the medieval city walls of Jerusalem. The search for King David's Palace in the City of David, at the outskirts of the Old City of modern East Jerusalem caused quite a stir. Not only because the City of David has been the subject of as many as seventeen hundred excavations in the past 150 years, but also because no artifact has ever been discovered that directly links King David to Jerusalem or the City of David, a "suburb" of the Old City of Jerusalem. When Professor Yigal Shiloh was excavating in the 1970s–1980s in the City of David, it was one of the most exciting excavations I have ever seen. At every moment you expected to hear about the discovery of some history-altering artifact. But even during this period, no one artifact confirmed what the archaeologists needed to confirm the connection between King David and Jerusalem. It is clear from the beginning of archaeology that people were looking for King David. One of the first archaeological projects in the 1850s was to find and verify the relic-tomb of King David that was located traditionally on Mount Zion, where tourists are still taken. In addition, in the past decade, a war of words has developed among Israeli archaeologists about the existence of anything like the developments that would have needed to take place for the United Kingdom of David to have been a reality in tenth century BCE Israel. Some archaeologists argue that in the hundreds of excavation sites that date to the Iron Age, little suggests the major developments written about in the books of Samuel and Kings. These archaeologists and some Bible scholars also wonder whether the lack of major building developments around the country coupled with the dearth of any extra biblical information on David and Solomon indicates that David and Solomon are just literary creations. One side of this debate advocates the rise of Israelite/Judean religion long after the time of King David whereas the other side holds that indeed there are sites with a significant tenth century stratum that would suggest a major building development, such as the one suggested by the books of Samuel and Kings and that the identity of David and Solomon is secure. Wrapped up in this debate, of late, is also another issue: the political meaning of the idea of Jerusalem as the eternal capital of the Jewish people from the time of King David onward. This chapter explores the questions of who were King David and King Solomon? Did they ever really exist, and what do we know about the Jerusalem(s) in the most ancient through the modern period?

The Iron Age

King David was king of what is called by Bible scholars as "the United Kingdom of David" that began at the end of the eleventh century BCE, and his forty-year reign extended into the tenth century BCE. According to 2 Samuel 5:4, he was king starting out in the city of Hebron for seven years and six months, followed by thirty-three years in Jerusalem. He became "king" during what archaeologists call the classical Iron Age (1000–586 BCE). The early Iron Age (1200–1000 BCE) directly preceding the reign of King David is different from the period of David's reign. Though there is a major dispute about whether King David ever existed the way the Bible describes him among archaeologists and Bible scholars, the past century of excavations show a resurgence of building at a number of sites around the historical Land of Israel that come from the tenth century BCE, supporting, in part, the existence of some new initiative at precisely the time when David is supposed to be building his United Kingdom.

Who Was King David?

King David is the standard for all kings of Israel and Judea, and he became a messianic symbol among the Jews and early Christians. He built an empire that stretched from Syria to Egypt and became the symbol of musician, poet, warrior, and politician in world civilization. According to the Bible, David was the youngest child of Jesse, from the city of Bethlehem, and (according to the New Testament) ancestor to Jesus, the famed Rabbi Judah the Prince (according to early Rabbinic literature), and the ancestor of much of the Rabbinic leadership of the early Middle Ages from Babylonia and Egypt (according to later Rabbinic literature). The name David, or a variant of it, is found in the writings of Mari, Old Babylonian, and possibly attested in Moabite writings from the ninth century BCE. It is an unusual name in the history of Israelite and Judean names but not unprecedented. It occurs in the Hebrew Bible over a thousand times and in the New Testament fifty-nine times. David's name is found in a three-letter and four-letter variant. Early texts generally use the three-letter version (in the book of Samuel, for example), and the later texts (such as Chronicles) use the four-letter variant perhaps indicating that the standardized use of vowels was not enough to tell people how to pronounce the name. This also is dependent on manuscript readings of extant texts, but in general, it is clear that the scribes wanted to insure that people knew how to pronounce the name of this important leader. One of the earliest depictions of David found in the sixth-century synagogue mosaic at Gaza, spells his name with the four-letter variant and shows David in all his imagined splendor, very similar to the renderings of Orpheus dressed in Byzantine royal garments and playing a lyre. The Septuagint and Josephus have variants of David in the three-letter version and attempts to render the four-letter version of the name as *Daueid, Daueed,* in Greek lettering.

Who Was King Solomon?

Solomon was the tenth of David's seventeen (or nineteen according to Chronicles) sons and was either born of Bathsheba, daughter of Eliam, as a second son (in 2 Samuel) or Bathshua, daughter of Ammiel, as a fourth son (in 1 Chronicles). David named him Solomon, although according to an early Jewish source, Bathsheba named him. Like David, King Solomon ruled for forty years in the tenth century BCE, and he is reported to have had seven hundred wives and three hundred concubines, although no names of these women are given except Naamah the Ammonitess, mother of Rehoboam, his successor. Solomon's name is *Shelomoh* in Hebrew and is found in other Phoenician variants as *Shelamin* and *Baal Shalem.* These non-Israelite and non-"Judean" contexts suggest that he may have had a "Judean" name as well. The Prophet Nathan calls him *"Yedidiah"* in 2 Samuel 12:25, meaning that he may have had a "throne" or official Judean and a non-Judean name that was used in different contexts. Although the Chronicles traditions give a popular etymology of the name Solomon to mean "he who brings peace," it is also thought to have the original meaning of "replacement" or "compensation" for the loss of Bathsheba's first-born son.

Solomon's name, like that of David is not found in any extra biblical, contemporary literature. Solomon became a symbol of wisdom, justice, and the quintessential ruler in Judaism and Islam. He, like David, is depicted in medieval art for Jews and Christians in illuminated texts. Solomon's name and a "Solomon's Portico" at the Temple complex of Herod is mentioned in the New Testament. According to the Hebrew Bible, in the fourth year of his reign he began the building of the Temple in Jerusalem, and seven years were devoted to its construction. His building projects stretched over twenty years of his reign, and scholars place his reign from 970–960 BCE until 930–920 BCE. These dates are part of a comprehensive history of the period that is aided, in part, by the Egyptian records of Shishak's campaign in Israel and the beginning of the divided Kingdom of Israel and Judea under Rehoboam and Jereboam.

The Critical Study of the Bible and the Search for David and Solomon

As we have already discussed, finding a person who appears in the Bible in the material culture of the period in which he or she lived is also complicated by the differing literary traditions about that person in the Bible. In the case of David and Solomon, the Bible is divided on how to present them. One Solomon tradition holds him to be a wise and benevolent ruler; another tradition holds him to be a ruthless and insensitive leader. While I am not going to psychologically analyze David and Solomon in this book, I will look at how stories about the same person can be so completely different in different collections. The Bible is full of doublets and triplets of accounts that give a totally different perspective on what is seemingly the same event. These differences of opinion result from people's perceptions of an event or are reflections of different oral traditions that were recorded as they were received. In the book of Numbers, chapter 13, for example, Moses sends twelve spies to do reconnaissance in the Land of Israel for the tribes in the desert. The twelve spies come back with two different reports about the same visit to Israel. One group says that the desert tribes cannot overcome the indigenous populations. The other group says they can. In the end, the minority opinion wins the day, but the Bible does not hide the dissent; instead it is incorporated into the story line. People are people, and sometimes one person's perception is different from another's.

Modern literary criticism is another way to view the different perspectives found in the Bible. In general, literary critics think that the existence of varied opinions about David and Solomon are the result of different authors with different information and different writing agendas. Some writers may have had access to them or the official court history, but others may not have had the same access. Who were these authors and why would they hold such different traditions about the same person? Scholars suspect that there were at least two traditions from different ideological camps that wrote about David and Solomon. There are strong differences of opinion among modern Bible scholars over why and where these two traditions originated: Northern Kingdom vs. Southern Kingdom, Pre-Exilic vs. Post-Exilic, Pro-Prophetic vs. Pro-Priestly to name a few. One tradition was in favor of a strong kingship and civil leadership of a non-prophetic, non-tribal and a non-Priestly leader; another tradition would only accept leadership that was tribal, prophetic, and/or Priestly in nature. These two views developed in ancient Israel and are present throughout the entire Hebrew Bible. In the case of David and Solomon, in the biblical books of Kings, Bible scholars have identified what they call an "Early" Source and a "Late" Source, reflecting two totally different views about the whole idea of monarchy of Israel and especially the leadership of Saul, David, and Solomon, the first three kings of Israel. Saul, David, and Solomon emerged as "kings" during the same period of tribal leaders, judges, priests and prophets. Why couldn't the prophets, priests, tribal leaders, and judges continue to rule the people? This changed probably as the people of Israel moved from a group of disconnected "tribes" into a more unified nation with similar goals. They saw that their "nationhood" was emerging to be like the other nations in the ancient Near East and, according to the Bible, they longed for the type of leadership that other nations in the region had. It is not an accident that the Book of Deuteronomy has the only reference to this longing. You can hear the ambivalence. God tells Moses: "I will set a king over me, like all of the nations that are round about me . . . " (Deuteronomy 17:14).

In an example of the so-called "Late Source" in the book of 1 Samuel, chapter 8:1–18, the idea of the kingship is presented as a concession to the will of the people. In the so-called "Early Source" by contrast, in the same book of 1 Samuel chapter 9:1–24, the king is seen as a virtuous divine invention and that Samuel the prophet is involved in its creation. Samuel, the last of these early prophets, who anoints Saul as king, shows his disdain for the institution of kingship in one source, and in the other source he is totally in favor of it. In each of these three cases, you can see that it depends on what source you read to know what the Bible is actually saying. Some literary sources in the Bible vilify David, and others venerate him. The most famous story of King David's early life is the story of his encounter with Goliath. The Early source, for example, that venerates David and kingship, has a long account in 1 Samuel chapter 17 that meticulously builds up to David's victory over Goliath. Another source on the other hand, in 2 Samuel 21:19, has Goliath being killed by one of David's soldiers' named Elhanan, and scholars suggest that the entire event is attached to David's name to bolster his image. The "positive" David sources, such as 1 Chronicles 20, for example, eliminate David's adultery, the murder of David's mistress's husband, Uriah, the sections about how he was reprimanded by the Prophet Nathan, etc. The "negative" David sections include every major flaw in the character of David and take great pains to diminish him as a leader.

The positive information on David and Solomon in the Early Source is usually attributed to an early seventh-century BCE Jerusalem/Judean court source, and the Late Source is the result of the Josianic reforms made in the late seventh century BCE that had a revisionist view of what had come before. Under Josiah, the *laissez faire* attitude that had made the empire of David and Solomon great was now criticized. It is much the same way that modern historians now look back on World War II and the administrations of Franklin Delano Roosevelt and can see them in totally different ways. Some modern historians demonize all of the changes Roosevelt made in the New Deal and to win the war, while others see only the good that these reforms and efforts did.

In the case of the anti-Solomon lobby, 1 Kings 11:1–13, for example, records all of Solomon's excesses:

> He had seven hundred wives, princesses, and three hundred concubines; and his wives turned away his heart. For when Solomon was old, his wives turned away his heart after other gods; and he was not as wholeheartedly devoted to the Lord his God, as was the heart of David his father. . . . Solomon did what was evil in the sight of the Lord and did not remain loyal to the Lord like his father David . . . and the Lord said to Solomon, because his heart turned away from the Lord, the God of Israel . . . because you are guilty of this . . . I will tear the kingdom away from you and give it to one of your servants. However, I will not tear away the whole kingdom; I will give your son one tribe, for the sake of my servant David . . .

These traditions in the books of Samuel and Kings are further complicated by the books of Chronicles. These sources that parallel the history of Samuel and Kings differ significantly when they get to David and Solomon. In Chronicles there is no mention, for example, of Solomon's pagan ways, no mention of David's affair with Bathsheba, and no mention of the rebellion of David's son, Absalom, against his father. The negative elements of the Books of Samuel and Kings are generally left out, and David and Solomon emerge as near perfect leaders. Even the Temple is seen as the master plan of David in 1 Chronicles 28:11–19 although in the book of Kings David is completely disqualified from building the Temple because of his warlike ways. I find that looking for David and Solomon in the Bible is as difficult as looking for Moses. The historical character is often hidden in the twists and turns of the editing process.

The biggest question for archaeologists in the search to find the historical David and Solomon is the lack of extra biblical and unchallenged inscriptional information. Unlike the former period, the Israelites were writing in their own language in the time of David and Solomon. Archaeologists adamantly refuse to accept the existence of a real "David" and

"Solomon" without specific inscriptional evidence from the period of David and Solomon, either from Israelite or non-Israelite sources. If, for example, David was so prominently involved in the lives of so many different peoples around the region, it stands to reason that he would be mentioned in one of these different non-Israelite literatures. If, for example, Solomon conducted international relations with Egypt, marrying into the royal family and importing horses, why wouldn't there be a record somewhere in Egypt that would corroborate this relationship? If, for example, Solomon built a fleet of ships at Ezion-Geber by the port of the Gulf of Aqaba and was contacted by the Queen of Sheba (a kingdom located nearby the port), why is no record of their contacts mentioned in any surviving correspondence/contact in ancient near eastern literature? But no independent corroboration of these events exists from archaeological evidence or source not influenced by biblical tradition, save perhaps an early medieval collection called the *Kebra Negast*, the national epic of Ethiopia. The *Kebra Negast* not only says that the Queen of Sheba visited Solomon but that they had a child together, Menelik, who visited his father Solomon in Jerusalem and brought the Ark of the Covenant to Ethiopia where it rests to this day! The most extreme groups of archaeologists and Bible scholars have said that this lack of evidence suggests that David and Solomon were not real historical characters but were created by writers, perhaps as late as the Persian period, to bolster the Exiles' claims to the Land of Israel. The most radical of these revisionist scholars hold that not only David and Solomon were created to bolster Jewish Exiles identity but also the Patriarchs, the Matriarchs, and Moses. Some even say that these characters were the products of a vivid Jewish imagination of Hellenistic writers writing as late as the second century BCE. These latter group of scholars contend that the writers needed to bolster the Hasmonean's credentials to rule the chaotic Judea of the second century BCE and created a glorious history of Patriarchs, the Exodus, a Tabernacle in the Sinai desert, the revelation at Mount Sinai, the conquest of the Land, the Davidic and Solomonic developments, and the priests and the Temple as an opportunity to show their Hellenistic overlords how significant the story of the Jews was, especially in comparison with the Greek and Roman national epics. According to the most extreme minimalist view, the major accounts of the Hebrew Bible were created wholly out of the minds of these unnamed Hellenistic authors' imaginations and parallels events and people in their own period.

The discovery of the Tel Dan inscription seemed to dramatically change all but the most extreme minimalists. In 1993, at Tel Dan, an excavation site in northern Galilee, an inscription was discovered that was conclusively dated to the ninth century BCE and confirmed that the House of David did indeed exist just as the Bible records. The inscription relates how Hazael, King of Aram, Damascus, (who is known in the Bible and Assyrian records) claims to have killed the King of Israel, Ahaziah, and the King of the House of David, Jehoram, in what can be dated to approximately 835 BCE. It is the first and only inscription that bears the name of the House of David. Its importance is that it witnesses the existence of a line of kings in the ninth century CE that is linked to the King David. The fact that this is an inscription only a few generations after the death of King David and King Solomon and the fact that it is an independent archaeological artifact shows what one discovery can do for biblical archaeology. Although some extreme Minimalists asked if the "House of David" might refer to another David, or tried to read it as the "House of Dod" (meaning "the House of an Uncle" as there are no vowels in these inscriptions and in Hebrew, Dod can be written the same way as David with the three letter spelling of the name), this one inscription has convinced even the majority of biblical archaeologists that the *House of David* was a historical group by the ninth century BCE and that in order for this inscription to have any meaning at all, King David must have been a real person. Was he like the "good" David that the Chronicler wrote about or the "evil" David like the man that the Late Source of Samuel and Kings created, I do not know. Was he good and wise, just and courageous, or someone who lived life in excesses, taking credit for others' work and regretting all of his iniquities? I do not know from this one inscription, but it certainly does give me hope that many other such inscriptions and archaeological evidence will be found and flesh out the rest of the story. But I am sure that based upon the confluence of evidence, a David and a Solomon, who created the House of David were probably real people who really lived in a period in the tenth century BCE. Although we do not know from archaeology if they existed as the books of Samuel, Kings, and Chronicles indicate we do have physical sites that have been attributed to them in Jerusalem, and so I begin our archaeological search for King David and King Solomon in Jerusalem at the place that is venerated as their burial sites.

The Material Culture: The Relic Tombs of King David and King Solomon

The Hebrew Bible has plenty of information in the books of Samuel, Kings, and Chronicles on David and his family but has little information on the place of burial of these important kings, David and Solomon. In

SEARCHING FOR KING DAVID AND KING SOLOMON 119

the book of 2 Chronicles, chapter 32, verse 33, we are told after King Hezekiah finished all of his good works during his reign that he ". . . slept with his fathers, and they buried him in the ascent of the tombs of sons of David." The biblical book of Nehemiah, chapter 3, verse 16, tells us that in the time of Nehemiah, the location of the tombs at some distance from the Temple Mount and was "...down the stairs from the City of David" (putting it in the valley below the Temple Mount in the Persian period or somewhere in the fifth century BCE). "Nehemiah, the son of Azbuk, ruler of half the district of Beth Zur, went to a spot opposite the tombs of David, to the artificial pool, and to the house of the mighty men." (The citation suggests that the tombs of David and Solomon were together.)

Certainly traditions abound, even ancient literary traditions outside of the Bible concerning King David, not only because of the importance of the lineage of David being associated with Jesus' lineage but also because the line of David was seen as the "true" line for Jewish leadership even in the period of the Rabbis. Josephus, writing in the first century CE, has a tradition about the burials of David and Solomon that is particularly interesting:

> He was buried by his son Solomon, in Jerusalem, with great magnificence, and with all the other funeral pomp which kings used to be buried with; moreover, he had great and immense wealth buried with him, the vastness of which may be easily conjectured at by what I shall now say; for a thousand and three hundred years afterward Hyrcanus the high priest, when he was besieged by Antiochus, that was called the Pious, the son of Demetrius, and was desirous of giving him money to get him to raise the siege and draw off his army, and having no other method of compassing the money, opened one room of David's tomb, and took out three thousand talents, and gave part of that sum to Antiochus; and by this means caused the siege to be raised, as we have informed the reader elsewhere. Nay, after him, and that many years, Herod the king opened another room, and took away a great deal of money, and yet neither of them came at the coffins of the kings themselves, for their bodies were buried under the earth so artfully, that they did not appear to even those that entered into their monuments. But so much shall suffice us to have said concerning these matters" (*Antiquities* 7:15.3).

We are not sure where this place of burial is, but it is presumably not the place that has been identified as "David's Tomb" just outside the present Zion Gate in the Old City of Jerusalem. Many religions have relic sites that are established in later periods but are hallowed by the faithful as the site of an event or a person's life or burial. When a monument is established at a holy place, it is nearly impossible to scientifically excavate the site. Whatever we wish to say about these sites, they are venerated by the tradition and they need not be discounted as preserving an ancient tradition. Christianity is filled with relic sites. The site of the Mount of the Beatitudes in Galilee is established by the Church as the site where Jesus spoke his famous pronouncement, the Sermon on the Mount. Notwithstanding the problem that the Gospel, according to Luke, has the Sermon on a plain and Matthew has it on a mount, there is a church established on a mount near a natural amphitheater in Galilee that overlooks the Sea of Galilee that is the established place of this event. Did it really happen there? I do not know. But a long-held tradition that goes back about fifteen hundred years establishes it at that location. There is no archaeological excavation that proves it one way or another. No inscriptions from the first century or first-century evidence point to the spot, but still it is the traditional site. It is a relic for this reason.

Buddhists (and tourists) are taken to a *Bo tree* in southern India and told that a specific tree there is the place under which the Buddha had his revelation some twenty-five hundred years ago. People collect the leaves, and it is seen as a shrine for people to experience the revelation of the Buddha by sitting and meditating there as they felt the Buddha did some twenty-five hundred years ago. The tree was analyzed using carbon 14 techniques to see how old it was. It was seen to be "only" a thousand years old. Did it change the people's view of it? No. I have heard every different type of explanation from the faithful (including that it is a reincarnation of the original tree), but it is still seen as the "real" place that the Buddha experienced his revelation and that is enough for the tourists and many Buddhists.

Relic sites, especially burial relic sites, are very common in Israel, especially for Jews. For example, in Tiberias, the Tomb of Rabbi Meir is a good example of how a tradition can develop from many different sources into one. Today, visitors/pilgrims go to the Tomb of Rabbi Meir (he is called "the miracle maker") and are told that this is the second century CE sage, Rabbi Meir married to the famous woman sage, Beruriah, and one of the great sources for the editing of the Mishnah. Two early medieval travelers, Benjamin of Tudela and Petahiah, both hold that Rabbi Meir was buried in Babylonia and write about his tomb there. By the end of the Middle Ages, the tomb had become associated with a Rabbi Meir. Some traditions associated the burial on the side of the road to Tiberias as the grave of Rabbi Meir Katzin, a public figure in Tiberias from the end of the Middle Ages who saved the community from destruction. Other traditions hold that this is the grave of a famous Rabbi from Paris who came at the end of the Crusader era. Sephardic Jews who came from Spain and from Arabic-speaking countries and Ashkenazic Jews (European) both have a variety of other "Meirs" they associate with the tomb. It seems that they collapsed all of the Rabbi Meir traditions into one, the most ancient, and venerate the spot every year. Perhaps this is the reason that the tomb of King David is both venerated and scoffed at. Although a relic site may be associated with a single religion, some relic sites have become associated with various religions. The Tomb of King David in Jerusalem is one of those.

There are competing traditions for the relic burial sites of David. One group places his burial in his birthplace the town of Bethlehem, but in general, most pilgrims associate the burial place of King David at a site located on Mount Zion in Jerusalem. The Jerusalem site that tourists are shown is a late Byzantine or early Islamic period site. An Arab geographer in 985 CE states that the burial place is on Mount Zion. The medieval traveler, Benjamin of Tudela places it on Mount Zion, but according to his account it was only "rediscovered" in the twelfth century after a Church on Mount Zion collapsed and in the rebuilding efforts, a burial cave was found that contained the legendary treasures associated with his burial. These reports, probably based upon the Josephus passages below, were multiplied in Tudela's account of the "rediscovery" of the tomb in his own time. By the fifteenth century, the established site was the source of debate from local Jews and Christians that resulted in the Mamluke leader taking the site from them and building a mosque over the site. King David was an important figure for Muslims as well. Jewish and Christian pilgrimage to the Mount Zion site of David's burial was restricted from this time through the early modern period. The pilgrimage was made during the year, whenever a pilgrim visited Jerusalem but especially on the holiday of Shavuot, associated with the anniversary of King David's death.

It is perhaps not a coincidence that this David's Tomb is associated with the Last Supper of the Apostles with Jesus immortalized by Leonardo Da Vinci. It would be a little irregular, even in the first century, to hold a Passover Seder at the location of a grave, but eating "memorial" meals at a grave site is known in this period. It is unusual, though, that the Gospels did not explicitly mention eating in the tomb of King David, became this grave is also associated in Christian traditions with the construction of a first century "synagogue." The building of a synagogue in the first century no less around a gravesite would be highly unusual by Jewish practice (according to the Bible—and later Rabbinic interpretation—a Kohen, a member of the ancient Aaronid family, is not permitted in an enclosed location with a gravesite, eliminating a large group of Jews from the site) but not so for the developing Christian traditions. Although David's Tomb is clearly immortalized as a Christian pilgrimage site from the Byzantine period onward, one wonders if it was for its association with the Last Supper of Jesus, a descendant of David, or for its actual association with King David's burial. The Muslims have embraced the location where David's Tomb is located because King David appears in the Koran and other Islamic traditions. This site like the site of the Machpelah, the tomb of Abraham, and some of the Patriarchs and Matriarchs, was a traditional pilgrimage site for Muslims for the past thousand years as well.

But it is only Josephus who really preserved an ancient literary source for a tomb of David and Solomon. He remarks that the tomb, wherever it was, was robbed many times in the past. In the time of King Herod (the first century BCE), for example, the taking of the "treasure in the tomb," was also interrupted by a miraculous intervention:

> As for Herod, he had spent vast sums about the cities, both without and within his own kingdom; and as he had before heard that Hyrcanus, who had been king before him, had opened David's tomb, and taken out of it three thousand talents of silver, and that there was a much greater number left behind, and indeed enough to suffice all his wants, he had a great while an intention to make the attempt; and at this time he opened that tomb by night, and went into it, and endeavored that it should not be at all known in the city, but took only his most faithful friends with him. As for any money, he found none, as Hyrcanus had done, but that furniture of gold, and those precious goods that were laid up there; all which he took away. However, he had a great desire to make a more diligent search, and to go farther in, even as far as the very bodies of David and Solomon; where two of his guards were slain, by a flame that burst out upon those that went in, as the report was. So he was terribly affrighted, and went out, and built a propitiatory monument of that fright he had been in; and this of white stone, at the mouth of the tomb, and that at great expense also. (*Antiquities* 16:7.1)

Josephus' two extensive traditions about the tombs of David and Solomon show his intense interest. In the second century CE, in the time of the "Second" Revolt of the Jews against the Romans, (the Bar Kokhba Revolt), the tomb of Solomon is specifically mentioned, but not the Tomb of David by the Roman historian, Dio Cassius. He writes:

> "Thus nearly the whole of Judea was made desolate, a result of which the people had had forewarning before the war. For the tomb of Solomon, which the Jews regard as an object of veneration, fell to pieces of itself and

Figure 2.2.   The Western Wall with the Gold Dome of the Rock Mosque in the Old City of Jerusalem.

collapsed, and many wolves and hyenas rushed howling into their cities," (*Annals*, Book 5, 69.14).

Even in the second century the tombs were in disarray. The scientific digging in Jerusalem in the past 150 years by thousands of excavations in and around the area have not produced one historical reference to King David or King Solomon from the Iron Age when they would have lived. Many structures and discoveries have been made, but it is still a mystery why one piece of written material has not been discovered confirming King David in the City of David or Jerusalem. Is it just a matter of time, or is it that we cannot find him because he did not exist? Perhaps it is just a part of the mystery of the building projects of Jerusalem over the past three thousand years, so we begin with a study of Jerusalem to understand the problems of the city.

Jerusalem: A Short History

Jerusalem is one of the most controversial and emotionally charged cities on earth for more than two billion Jews, Christians, and Muslims. The city was "officially" destroyed at least twice, besieged to near destruction at least twenty-three times, and attacked more than fifty-two times by outside forces. The city is prayed for by Jews three times a day in the major, statutory prayer services. After eating, Jews pray a concluding prayer that contains the words "*U'Venei Yerushalayim, Ir HaQodesh Bimheira Beyameinu* . . . And build Jerusalem, the Holy City, quickly and in our days," a prayer that is paralleled in every place that a Passover Seder is performed with the final words of the seder being "Next Year in Jerusalem" and on the modern Israeli and Jewish calendars there is even a Jerusalem Day holiday. One of Christianity's first liturgical compilations was from Jerusalem, and Christian liturgy even today inevitably contains references to Jerusalem through its use of the book of Psalms and the New Testament. Islam's direction of prayer (Qiblah), in its initial stages, was toward Jerusalem (as Jews even today direct their prayers toward Jerusalem), and Muslim calendars also include a "Jerusalem Day" as well.

The history of Jerusalem is not simple. The history is a multireligious and multiethnic history going back more than three thousand years and includes Jebusites, Jews, Christians, Muslims, and assorted groups of Persians, Greeks, and Romans. Jerusalem's history begins before there was an Israelite kingdom and King David. The Temple of Jerusalem was the pilgrimage site for Jews and Israelites for nearly five hundred years (tenth to the sixth century BCE) when suddenly the Temple was destroyed. Fifty years later, in the last third of the sixth century BCE, a small band of Jews returned from the Exile of Babylonia to a Jerusalem that had been destroyed and was bereft of Jewish life. After the destruction of the Temple in Jerusalem and the expulsion of the northern (722 BCE) and southern tribes (586 BCE) from the Land of Israel to Assyria and Babylonia, the Jewish history of Jerusalem begins again with the Persian conquest of Babylon and Cyrus the Great's decree that the Jews could return to Judea and Jerusalem and reestablish the "Second Temple" in the end of the sixth century BCE. Two hundred years after this, Alexander the Great's conquest of the region in the fourth century BCE and his introduction of Greek culture changed the face of Jerusalem and Judaism. Although the Jews' appreciation of their Temple in Jerusalem was interrupted by the famous Seleucid Greek Syrian leader, Antiochus Epiphanes in the second century BCE, the Maccabean revolt and success assured that Jerusalem and Judea would be Jewish. The thoroughly Hellenized Herod the Great is given credit for restoring the glory of Jerusalem. His building projects in Jerusalem in the first century BCE finally insured that the Temple in Jerusalem would be one of the greatest religious institutions ever built in antiquity. In this context, the first groups of the followers of Jesus and John the Baptist arrived to see and experience this "Jewish" Temple in the midst of Roman culture and life. After the death of Jesus, Jerusalem, the site of his burial, became a place of pilgrimage for all of the followers of Paul and the Apostles. The destruction of the Temple of Jerusalem created a vacuum in Jewish life that allowed Jews and a new group, the Christians, to seek out new expressions of religious life outside of Jerusalem.

One generation later, in the second half of the first century CE and into the second century CE, the followers gathered in Galilee and in the Diaspora, in house churches in and around the places where Jesus had lived and worked. Jerusalem continued to be a religious center for the Romans even in its destroyed state. Hadrian, in 132 CE, changed the name of Jerusalem to *Aelia Capitolina* (and he changed the name of Judea to Palestine) and transformed the Temple into a site of the worship of Jupiter. The tomb of Jesus' burial in Jerusalem, The Church of the Holy Sepulchre, was turned into a Temple for Aphrodite under Hadrian, and most Jews and Christians were exiled from the city. During the fourth century CE, the Roman Emperor Constantine became a Christian, and his mother, Queen Helena, began establishing churches and Christian pilgrimage sites all around the country and especially in Jerusalem. This means that Jerusalem became a pilgrimage site for Jews and Christians. The major change for Jerusalem occurred in the seventh century CE when Islam conquered not only Jerusalem but also most of the Middle East. The Muslims turned Jerusalem into one of the pilgrimage sites for Muslims. The establishment of the Mosque of Omar (The Dome of the Rock) and the *Al Aqsa Mosque* both on the site of the ancient Temple of Jerusalem clearly established Jerusalem as the third most holy site for pilgrimage after Mecca and Medina. Except for a one-hundred-year period in the twelfth century, when Crusaders retook Jerusalem and reestablished the supremacy of Christianity in the city, Jerusalem remained a site for pilgrimage for Jews, Christians, and Muslims. From essentially 1187–1917, Jerusalem was a Muslim city that carefully balanced the pilgrimage of Jews, Christians, and Muslims to their respective holy sites.

With the rise of modern political Zionism in the nineteenth century, Jews returned to Jerusalem, immigrating both into the Old City and outside the ancient city walls. Before and after World War I, more than half of the population of Jerusalem was then Jewish in the British Mandate Protectorate of Palestine and in Jerusalem. This was basically the state of affairs through World War II. In November, 1947, when the United Nations met to decide on the fate of Jerusalem, the partition of Palestine into a Jewish and Arab state called for the internationalization of Jerusalem as a "corpus separatum." The Jewish authorities accepted this "divided Jerusalem," but the Arabs rejected the UN declaration. At midnight on May 14/15, 1948, the Jews took control of the buildings in the center of the town but were cut off from Jewish enclaves in areas such as the campus of Mount Scopus and east Jerusalem. On June 11, 1948, a cease-fire was proclaimed, leaving east Jerusalem and the Old City in Jordanian hands. Between 1948–1967 the city was divided with a gate used as the border crossing. The border at the so-called "Mandelbaum Gate" near the Old City was used until Monday, June 5, 1967. The so-called Six Day War resulted in Israeli forces taking the entire city (including the Old City). In 1967, the new "united" Jerusalem had a population of 265,000 people: 199,000 Jews and 66,000 Arabs. This population has grown over twofold in the past forty years as have the suburbs now included in the definition of greater Jerusalem. Today, Jerusalem is the largest city of the modern state of Israel as well as its capital. Its population base is nearing three quarters of a million people when you count all of the different suburbs. It is nearly the same size as a large U.S. metropolitan area like Las Vegas. The city limits have grown from 25 acres in its earliest period to 125 acres in the time of Hezekiah to its current size of tens of miles, extending from the outskirts of Bethlehem to the city of Ramallah. It rises 800 meters above sea level and is 33 miles from the Mediterranean Sea and 16 miles from the Dead Sea.

Pilgrims, Preachers, and Travelers: The History of Archaeology and the Ancient History of Jerusalem

In the nineteenth century as the development of new technologies and sciences were underway, the new science of archaeology began in the Middle East and especially in Jerusalem. Many of the earliest contributors to our understanding of the Middle East and Jerusalem were explorers and travelers, and not really scientists. It is a well-documented time with photography beginning precisely in the midst of the period when people could actually more easily travel from Europe throughout the Middle East because of technological advances on the High Seas. Military men from Europe and the United States struck out into the wilds of the Middle East as early as the 1840s.

Recently, when we did an exhibition in our George J. Sherman and Lottie K. Sherman Museum of Jewish Civilization at the University of

Hartford on Jerusalem in the nineteenth century from the collection of a local collector, Hazza Abu Rabi, people were surprised at how much European and American interest there was in the Middle East in the nineteenth century. It was almost as if they all rediscovered the Holy Land and hoped that it would be possible to understand their own religious faiths that during the nineteenth century was being challenged by emerging sciences and university disciplines. Military men helped to further the geographical studies of Palestine and the first scientific mapping of Jerusalem. In 1841, Lieutenant J. F. A. Symonds, a leading member of the team from the British Royal Engineers began the work. He carried out surveys between Jaffa and Jerusalem. A Royal Navy Lieutenant, Thomas Molyneux's campaign was followed by the United States Navy's Lt. William F. Lynch in 1847. Their itineraries included voyages along the coasts starting on the western shore and the surveying of the Dead Sea. Although they often did not say it directly, one gets the impression that many of these nineteenth-century sailors were following in the footsteps of the ancient fishermen and sailors, the disciples of Jesus and John the Baptist. Lynch was the first to make an accurate and detailed map of the Jordan and the Dead Sea. These maps became neopilgrim-like documents that were enshrined in libraries all over the world.

The most colorful character whom we have to thank for much of the earliest documentation of the Temple Mount from the nineteenth century is Count Charles Jean Melchior de Vogue. In effect, because it was done with the full consent of the *Waqf* (Muslim Council) in the 1860s, de Vogue's work included the most complete and detailed monographs on how the mosques looked and their relationship to the more ancient Temple of Jerusalem. Count Melchior de Vogue was one of the first Western researchers who was granted almost free access to examine the interior of the Dome of the Rock where he proceeded to make plans and sketches. He included in his musings many of the known stories surrounding the "Rock" in the Dome of the Rock mosque from Jewish, Christian, Muslim, and Roman sources. He was also known for his architectural studies of Jerusalem and its surroundings. De Vogue was helped by the epigrapher Waddington, who devoted himself to studying the Temple Mount. The results of his research appeared in two illustrated books in the 1870s.

Another key work that gave us information on the Old City of Jerusalem was the work of Charles Wilson (1864–1866) and Charles Warren. Wilson conducted the first detailed survey of the Old City and published the first scientific map of the area. Charles Warren was the first to attempt to follow the ancient contours of the Temple Mount (1867–1870).

Warren, who is best known today for the shafts he dug to burrow below the religiously sensitive areas at the Western Wall, laid the groundwork for scientific work that would follow. After the Crimean War and the ensuing 1856 Peace Treaty, known by some as the Peace Treaty of Jerusalem, the number of Jews inside and outside of the walled cities of Palestine increased. In this early period these Jews were largely supported by charitable donations from pious Jews abroad. New suburbs rose outside the walls of Old Jerusalem. Jewish suburbs with small industries outside of the walled Old City of Jerusalem flourished in the period of 1860–1899 thanks to Jewish entrepreneurs from the United States and Europe. The efforts of Moses Montefiore, Baron de Rothschild, and Baron de Hirsch are legendary, but it was the movement from the Old City of Jerusalem to the new suburbs of Jerusalem that created new interest in Jerusalem among Jews of varying backgrounds in the period 1860–1900. These suburbs often were made up of different immigration groups from Europe to Asia that developed distinctive industries in settlements that now bore a variety of Hebrew names, such as Mishkenot Shaananim, Mahane Yehuda, Meah Shearim, Nahalat Shiva, Mishkenot Israel, Even Israel, Ir Shalom, Sukkat Shalom, Mazkeret Moshe, Yemin Moshe, Beit Yaakov, Beit Yosef, Shevet Tzedek, Shaarei Tzedek, Nahalat Shimon, Shimon HaTzadik, Bet Israel, and the Rehovot HaBukharim. The influence of the Jewish community increased as immigration from different areas of the Diaspora came to Palestine as economic and social conditions worsened in their home countries. Of the eighteen thousand residents in Jerusalem in the 1860s, half were Jews and most still lived in the walled Old City. By 1890 there were forty-three thousand residents of Jerusalem, including twenty-eight thousand Jews, seven thousand Muslims, and eight thousand Christians of various denominations, but by this time almost half of the new residents of Jerusalem lived outside of the Old City.

In 1864, the Palestine Exploration Fund (P.E.F.) was formed in London. Its stated goals were to investigate the archaeology, geography, geology, and natural history of Palestine. Because of the efforts of the early travelers, explorers, writers, and artists, the P.E.F. enjoyed considerable public interest and support. The most well-known results of the P.E.F.'s work were the archaeological expedition reports. The scientific and administrative reports provided new information about Jerusalem that was immediately made available to the emerging scientists throughout the world. Excavations were planned for Jerusalem to uncover its history. Surveying and mapping Western Palestine was a major goal of the P.E.F., and it laid the groundwork for many excavations in the twentieth century.

The research and mapping of Transjordan was the first project of the American Palestine Exploration Society. Two preliminary expeditions were sent out, one under Lieutenant Steever (1873) and the other under J. C. Lane (1875). The Lane expedition included an archaeologist and head of research. The American Palestine Exploration Society failed to complete its mission, therefore the P.E.F. decided to complete the mapping of the Holy Land east of Jordan. Whatever was not carried out by the British and American societies was completed by Gottlieb Schumacher, a German engineer who resided in Haifa. He was engaged in the mapping of Transjordan, on behalf of the German Society for the Exploration of Palestine. Schumacher had been interested in the Holy Land and its historic past. He drew his maps to the scale and format of those of the P.E.F. Many of his writings appeared in the journals of the British and German societies. Schumacher's importance and this work cannot be minimized. Without the groundbreaking and meticulous maps and surveys that were completed by Schumacher, many twentieth-century archaeologists would have been lost when they began their work. At our excavations at Bethsaida, we began by looking through the maps and visits of Schumacher to the area to see what he had found during his work there. We are indebted to this early generation of pre-archaeology for their meticulous and painstaking drawings of people and places.

One traveler who contributed his time to gain the knowledge of the country and especially Jerusalem was the Frenchman, Charles Clermont-Ganneau (d. 1923). He was the secretary at the French consulate in Jerusalem and served as vice-consul in Jaffa until 1882. He carried out his researches in conjunction with the P.E.F. and was employed by the British to perform the most extensive archaeological surveys of Jerusalem. He discovered in 1868, the Moabite (or Mesha) Stele dated to about 850 BCE, which for most of the twentieth century remained one of the key pieces for the Maximalists in their search for biblical veracity. The inscription features the earliest written appearance of the name of the nation of "Israel" and constitutes the most detailed documentary source of information about the kingdom of Moab and its rivalry with the kingdom of Israel in this period. Through his efforts the Stele, which was broken into several pieces, was restored and is found today in the Louvre. His main achievements in the 1870s were his excavations of tombs around Jerusalem. He explored the ridge that begins with Mount Scopus in the north, and the road from Jerusalem to Bethany to the south and the Mount of Olives in between. Charles discovered and published information about numerous first century Jewish ossuaries and ossuary inscriptions in his *Archaeological Researches in Palestine, 1873–1874.*

Among these travelers were illustrators and later photographers too. They gave the world lasting images of the Holy Land and Jerusalem, in particular, that captured the imagination of the West. Even though photography had begun to be used to document the locations, illustrators brought aspects of life and bright and dramatic "color" to the places. One Scottish landscape artist, David Roberts, interested people when he published his drawings of places in the Near East and of the Holy Land. In 1838, realizing his boyhood dream, he embarked on his visit to the Holy Land. His lithographs and journals were published in two, three-set volumes: *The Holy Land,* which appeared between 1842–1845, and *Egypt,* which appeared between 1846–1849. He drew some of the most comprehensive pictorial records of buildings and scenery of the region. At first he worked with travelers' descriptions, but later he toured the areas and created his own drawings of ancient cities. His views of Jerusalem became so iconic that many books on Jerusalem feature his illustration rather than the photograph of the locations they are reviewing. In the 1990s the Bethsaida Excavations Project commissioned a landscape artist, John Lokke, from Nebraska to return with me to many of the places where David Roberts had been in the 1830s. His work, which we displayed in a number of exhibitions, gave people insights into the Holy Sites in a way that photography just could not do. John and I would spend hours in front of the Church of the Holy Sepulchre in Jerusalem where at first he just sketched, and then later he came back to fill in colors and understand the lighting. The most favorite landscapes in our exhibitions were always those from Jerusalem in the 1830s and John Lokke's landscape of the same location in the 1990s. Most people noticed that the artists, Lokke and Roberts, put themselves into the drawings. At one point I remember asking John where he felt closest to his Christian faith in Jerusalem. He inevitably pointed out that drawing of the Church of the Holy Sepulchre in Jerusalem.

One photographer who visited Palestine early in the 1860s was Francis Frith (d. 1898). He made three trips to the Holy Land between 1856–1860, and his photographs of the daily life in Israel and especially Jerusalem were used to assess how far European development of the land had gone by the end of the century. He set out in 1858 with three huge collodion cameras from England. He published a *Holy Bible* (1862) with photos in a limited edition, and his *Photo-Pictures from the Lands of the Bible. Illustrated by Scripture Words* in 1866 was a huge success. It was one of the first collections of landscape photographs of Palestine with the actual photographs pasted into the book. While working in the field, he created his own darkroom in a tent for developing his photographs with temperatures reaching 120 degrees. Upon return to England, he formed his own photography company to produce his work. He argued for the importance of using photographs to give Europeans an accurate view of the country. By the end of the century, images became the standard way for most of the world to assess the nature of the religious sites that they were reading about in their synagogues and churches. I included an early twentieth century photograph of the Western (Wailing) as the opening photograph of this chapter because I have seen it reproduced in countless books and hung in many homes. This photograph captures a moment in history—a time in the Holy Land that has since dramatically changed. If you look carefully, the men and the women are praying together at the Western Wall. This was the status quo of the period, and today when you see the photography of the Western Wall men and women are strictly separated. Without these types of photographs, we would not be able to reconstruct the early or medieval history of Jerusalem.

The growth of European influence created new interest in organized, mass pilgrimages to Palestine by Christians and Jews who lived in the region. After the Crimean War, even Russia exhibited a greater interest in the religious affairs of Palestine. In the following decades, Christian denominations built churches not only to serve the needs of the priests but also to accommodate pilgrims and other travelers. During the same time, foreign institutions opened many schools where thousands of children from different native communities gained the cultural values of Europe. Even though these changes took place elsewhere in the Ottoman Empire, it was only in Palestine that large numbers of travelers and pilgrims gained their knowledge of the Middle East. By the time the Zionist movement began concentrating its efforts on a modern nation in Palestine in the twentieth century, a worldwide Jewish and Christian recognition of the ancient history of Jerusalem began. This would make Jerusalem, a neglected part of the Ottoman Empire in the beginning of the nineteenth century, a place of singular importance in the plans of Jews, Christians, and Muslims in the twentieth century. The division of Jerusalem into two Jerusalems happened as a result of the battles for Jerusalem following the 1948 Israeli War of Independence. The city was divided by a "new" Mandelbaum Gate (similar to Berlin in the post World War II era) leading to two Jerusalems, a Jordanian Jerusalem primarily centered on the Old City and to the east and an Israeli Jerusalem with new symbols of the modern state that included most of the suburbs that were created in the nineteenth century. The political, cultural, and educational centers of the new State of Israel were firmly established in western Jerusalem with the campus of the

Hebrew University of Jerusalem, the Knesset (parliament), and the Israeli Museum anchoring the divided capital city.

After the 1967 war and the reunification of the two sides of the city, Israel began to find opportunities to celebrate with official events the ancient history of a united Jerusalem. Such seems to be the origin of the three thousandth anniversary of Jerusalem. Based on all of the accumulated studies and research on Jerusalem from the nineteenth and twentieth century, the year 1996 was chosen to commemorate David's founding of his United Kingdom in Jerusalem.

I remember how Jerusalem celebrated its "three thousandth" anniversary in a series of events. Even though they may have miscalculated the date of Jerusalem's founding, they were close. Teddy Kollek, the former Mayor of Jerusalem, chose 1996 during 1992–1993 to commemorate the three thousandth anniversary of the founding of Jerusalem as the capital of King David's empire and the center of the cult of the Israelite deity. At the time, there was intense fervor to celebrate Jerusalem (especially in light of peace talks that seemed to be favoring an independent Palestinian state with a capital in Jerusalem) in anticipation of the upcoming millennium celebrations in the year 2000. Most scholars agree that the date (1996) is actually off by a few years (even if we could so precisely pinpoint the date). But the three thousandth anniversary was the culmination of over 150 years of research by Bible scholars, travelers, pilgrims, and now politicians and archaeologists.

Whether the date for the Davidic refounding of the city as a capital of the United Kingdom was right or not, Jerusalem is clearly much older than three thousand years. Archaeology has shown that the city of Jerusalem was mentioned for the first time in Egyptian texts from the nineteenth and eighteenth century BCE as *Rusalimum*, so the city is at almost four thousand years old. But even according to the Bible, Jerusalem was not originally an Israelite site, but rather a well-known Jebusite village encountered by Joshua in his conquest of the land. Joshua 10:1 mentions that a certain "King Adoni-Tzedek of Jerusalem heard how Joshua had taken Ai, and had utterly destroyed it, doing to Ai and its king as he had done to Jericho and its king." King Adoni-Tzedek decided to band together with other area kings and fight Joshua. Joshua 15:63 recounts: "But the people of Judah could not drive out the Jebusites, the inhabitants of Jerusalem; so the Jebusites live with the people of Judah in Jerusalem to this day." It is unclear what "day" is meant, but the Book of Judges 1:8 says: "Then the people of Judah fought against Jerusalem and took it. They put it to the sword and set the city on fire." Although they may have torched the city, the Israelites apparently did not take it because Judges 1:21 states: "But the Benjaminites did not drive out the Jebusites who lived in Jerusalem; so the Jebusites have lived in Jerusalem among the Benjaminites to this day." It is interesting to note this biblical precedent for the current situation of Jews and non-Jews sharing the city.

There are three very important rules in real estate: location, location, location. But this does not seem to apply to the choice of Jerusalem as the national center of the United Kingdom of David. The city is not on any of the major, ancient trade routes. In fact, its inaccessibility seems to be one of the reasons why David selected the site. It was a long climb from the 1200 meters below sea level of the main King's Road along the Dead Sea to Eilat and far from the Via Maris Trunk road along the coast. It was located outside any of the twelve major tribe's section and far from most of the Ten Northern Tribes (near only to the major tribe/state of Judah). By the middle of his life, David had conquered an area extending from Mesopotamia to Sinai, which was the largest extent of any Israelite empire at any time. The surrounding nations desired their lands returned, which David and Biblical authors see as the fulfillment of the Divine will. David's choice of Jerusalem far to the south was out of the way for most Israelites and created special problems for the Ten Northern Tribes when it came to mandatory tithes and visiting for the holidays. Partly because of Jerusalem's distance from the northern tribes, King Jereboam split from the south and formed his own Kingdom of Northern Israel in 922 BCE after the death of King Solomon. For the convenience of his people, King Jereboam ended up establishing two capital sites for his version of Israelite religion—one to the north in Dan in northern Galilee and one just north of Jerusalem in Beth El.

The Jewish Names for Jerusalem: From Shalem to the Place that the Lord will Choose

The name Jerusalem appears to come from two separate words: *Yeru* ("to establish") and *Shalem* (the name of a well-known god of the region; Melchizedek, King of *Shalem,* is mentioned in Genesis 14:18). The name Jerusalem never appears in the Torah (the first five books of the Bible). The Torah does use a "code" word for Jerusalem, but only in the book of Deuteronomy. The rest of the Torah does not seem to have known that the Jews were going to have *only* one place to do their sacrificing and a single capital. This is where an understanding of the Documentary Hypothesis is critical. The book of Deuteronomy always uses the same/similar references. Instead of the name Jerusalem, a "code word" is used in the book of Deuteronomy. Jerusalem is "the place that the Lord your God will choose as a dwelling for His name." These names or something similar are used twenty times in the book of Deuteronomy—six times in chapter 12 and then again in chapter 16 in Deuteronomy the phrases appear. It is clear that they are writing about Jerusalem, but the writer is forced to use a circumlocution "the place that God will choose" because he knows that it will simply be a blatant anachronism. In the time of Moses, there simply was no Jerusalem. It was to be built a few hundred years in the future. But the Deuteronomist is writing about Jerusalem in a time when Jerusalem had been the only capital of the Judean state for nearly four hundred years. In the time of Josiah, the Judean state is not only the only remaining part of the biblical tradition, Jerusalem is the sole place left in the entire country for any type of Priestly sacrifice. The language is remarkable when you see it two or three times: So in Deuteronomy 12:5, we read: "But you shall seek the place that the LORD your God will choose out of all your tribes as his habitation to put his name there. In Deuteronomy 16:2: "You shall offer the passover sacrifice for the LORD your God, from the flock and the herd, at the place that the LORD will choose as a dwelling for his name." In Deuteronomy 16;16: "Three times a year all your males shall appear before the LORD your God at the place that he will choose: at the festival of unleavened bread, at the festival of weeks, and at the festival of booths."

Odd, isn't it, that the Torah authors chose not to introduce the name of Jerusalem here? Even though the name of Jerusalem and its function were well known when the writers of the Torah were transcribing the Torah's text, they may not have wanted to introduce the city before its time, or perhaps it is also an attempt to present the broadest possible selection process for the future. It is possible that these passages allow for the different places that God chose to place God's Name. The 150 years of archaeology in the Land of Israel shows that the most ancient Israelites actually did have many different places of sacrificing throughout the country. Perhaps it is just a slight meaning change; that in the ancient period, before the Deuteronomistic change, the individual was truly able to offer the sacrifices to God—"in [any] place that the Lord your God will choose as a dwelling for his name." Wherever they were; they offered sacrifices. In later Judaism, however, this interpretation changed to mean one holy place and one holy place only—Jerusalem.

The traditional interpretation of these verses is the exact opposite of this view of Jerusalem as the only holy site for God. Judging from the archaeology, these verses might suggest the earlier interpretation to be true—that every place that God chose is a holy place. This has led me to read the Bible in a totally new way. The famous verse of the book of Exodus, chapter 25, verse 2 literally states: "Let them make for me a holy place (*mikdash*) and I shall dwell in them (plural: holy sites)." It seems to imply that there are multiple holy places or altars that would be acceptable. If we take our understanding from archaeology, it is clear that this text in Exodus, written by a Priestly author in the period after the centralization of the Temple in Jerusalem, may be recognizing that there are other holy places where the name of the God of ancient Israel was called upon in that location, outside of Jerusalem. It is such an unusual verse that hundreds of biblical commentaries have interpreted it to mean exactly the opposite. They interpreted it to mean that although the people of Israel will create a single holy place, God shall dwell not in it, but *in them* (in the people of Israel): that the God of ancient Israel was not in need of an edifice to dwell in but dwelt in the spirits of the people. While this is a beautiful understanding, it does not help us understand the archaeological reality.

The name *Jerusalem* appears almost eight hundred times in the rest of the Hebrew Bible but in two very odd spellings. The name is written in Hebrew as *Jerushalayim* in the minority of cases and as *Jerusalem* 622 times; both spellings are pronounced the same way even though the latter spelling is missing the second Hebrew letter "*yud*." Rabbinic interpreters see this as a sign that when the Jews were exiled, God was also exiled. The Hebrew letter "*yud*" forms a major part of the name of God, so the elimination of the "*yud*" follows the exile of the Jews. Grammarians of the Hebrew language relate the missing "*yud*" to the Aramaic form of the word *Jerushalem*, but the original form of the word may hint back to the geological and geographic past of the city. *Yerushalayim* is a dual form in Hebrew. The dual form is found in all words that come in twos, such as hands, (in Hebrew: *yadayim), legs (raglayim), eyes, (einayim)* and so forth. In fact, the name *Mitzrayim* (Egypt) reveals that the Bible understood that there were two parts to Egypt, an upper and lower Egypt, just as it was known in Egypt in antiquity. The modern word *Egypt*, from Greek, has lost this ancient understanding. The reason for the dual form of *Jerusalem* may be because it had an upper and a lower city—the upper city was the location of the Temple/Shrine of the Tabernacle and the lower city was where David ruled, the people lived and the palace was located. Excavations in Jerusalem in the past thirty years show that the upper city is indeed at a higher elevation than the attributed City of David located in a nearby valley. The Midrash and the Kabbalah in the twelfth century explained the dual form in another way. These Rabbis say that there were two Jerusalems, one heavenly and one physical. To this day *LeShanah Habaah BeYerushalayim HaBenuyah (Next Year in the Rebuilt Jerusalem)* is sung on Passover, even in Jerusalem. Why would anyone living in Jerusalem today (after so much building since 1967) sing to "be in Jerusalem in the coming year?" The answer is simple. They are singing not about the political state of affairs in Jerusalem, but rather a metaphysical construct, a future *Jerusalem Shel Maalah-the heavenly Jerusalem* that will descend and bring the heavenly Temple with it. This condition cannot be met in a physical state of Israel.

Another name for the city of Jerusalem is Zion. The word *Zion* appears some 154 times in the Hebrew Bible/Tanach. Curiously, Zion does not appear in the vocabulary of any early biblical writers of the Pentateuch, but figures prominently in the exilic and post-exilic writings. "Zion" originally was the hill next to the Temple Mount as in 1 Kings 8:1: "Then Solomon assembled the elders of Israel and all the heads of the tribes, the leaders of the ancestral houses of the Israelites, before King Solomon in Jerusalem, to bring up the ark of the covenant of the LORD out of the city of David, which is Zion."

Later, however, the word *Zion* became the symbol/code for Jerusalem especially in Psalms and the later prophets. Its use in Psalms is clearly as a poetic parallelism for Jerusalem as well as because it is an easier meter word for poetry writing (Jerusalem has too many syllables while *Zion* only has two syllables, and the last syllable rhymes easier with other words). The book of Psalms is filled with the two parallel statements, Zion and Jerusalem. Psalms 2:6, 9:11, 9:14, 14:7, and 102:21 includes ". . . so that the name of the LORD may be declared in *Zion*, and his praise in *Jerusalem*." In Psalms 110:2 and 125:1, we learn that "Those who trust in the LORD are like Mount Zion, which cannot be moved, but abides forever." Zion and the rock solid faith of the Bible are frequently compared. Psalms 126:1, 128:5, 129:5, 132:13, 133:3, 134:3, and 135:21 show just how important the comparison can be even in liturgical settings: "Blessed be the LORD from *Zion*, he who resides in *Jerusalem*. Praise the LORD!" Many of these psalms are found in Jewish and Christian worship.

Why Zion became a preferred nomenclature for Jerusalem may have much more to do with politics than it does with poetry and meter. After the destruction of Jerusalem in 586 BCE, this indistinct word "Zion" (rather than Jerusalem) may have allowed the Jewish Exiles in Babylonia to write about a more symbolic mountain (*Zion* just indicates a distinctive mountain top) construct rather than the exacting nature of the geographic location of Jerusalem or Judah. The name Zion is used as a symbolic code word for Jerusalem as well as for all of Israel in general.

Jerusalem's geography is important. Jerusalem, similar to Rome, was originally a series of small hill and valley settlements. These hills all had different names. One name, *Ophel*, means a "bulge" or "projection" and appears in Isaiah 32:14. Another hill was *Zion* or Mount Zion, meaning a "distinguished" or "look-out" point. This hill may have been a high point of the city near where the Temple Mount eventually was placed. Another hill located near or at Mount Zion may have been Mount Moriah. Mount Moriah is sometimes connected with the sacrifice of Isaac in Genesis 22, which took place on a mountain in the land of Moriah. As stated in 2 Chronicles 3:1, "Solomon began to build the house of the LORD in Jerusalem on Mount Moriah, where the LORD had appeared to his father David, at the place that David had designated, on the threshing floor of Ornan the Jebusite."

David finally captured the Fortress of Zion (*Metzudat Zion*) in 2 Samuel 5:6–9:

"The king and his men marched to Jerusalem against the Jebusites, the inhabitants of the land, who said to David, "You will not come in here, even the blind and the lame will turn you back"—thinking, "David cannot come in here." Nevertheless David took the stronghold of Zion, which is now the city of David . . . David occupied the stronghold, and named it the city of David. David built the city all around from the Millo inward. And David became greater and greater, for the LORD, the God of hosts, was with him."

Jerusalem's "Chutes and Ladders": Jacob's *Ladder* and *Pillow* in Archaeology

In what appears to be a Jerusalem tradition in the Book of Genesis chapter 28, verse 10, the Bible points out that Jacob departed from Beer Sheva and proceeded toward Haran. Haran, located far to the north of Canaan and one of the main stopping points for the Patriarchs and Matriarchs on their way to Canaan, marks two very distinctive and well-known points in the early Genesis account. Jacob proceeded in a northern direction from Beer Sheva and we have to assume he made his way to the ancient international route to the west of Beer Sheva, along the Jordan rift valley. Genesis 28:11 is very unclear about his journey saying only "he came upon a certain (unnamed) place as the sun was setting and he stopped there for the night." Although we do not know how long his journey took, the Bible assumes that this was an important place and has him perform a ritual of sanctification for the place. That evening he experiences one of the most foundational experiences of all biblical literature. It is connected in direct and indirect ways to many other revelations that are mentioned by commentators in Judaism, Christianity, and Islam as not just any place, but the place where God's name will indeed be called: that is, *Jerusalem.* According to many of these commentators, Jacob's dream took place not just at any place in Jerusalem, but in the place where revelation and religion would continue for the next several thousand years: the Temple Mount. The text of Genesis 28:11–20 continues:

"Taking one of the stones at the place, he put it under his head and lay down to sleep at that spot. Then he had a dream: with a ladder that rested on the ground, with its top reaching to the heavens; and God's messengers were going up and down on it. And there was the Lord standing beside him and saying: "I, the Lord, am the God of your forefather Abraham and the God of Isaac; the land on which you are lying I will give to you and your descendants. These (people) shall be as plentiful as the dust of the earth, and through them you shall spread out east and west, north and south. In you and your descendants all the nations of the earth shall find blessing. Know that I am with you; I will protect you wherever you go, and bring you back to this land. I will never leave you until I have done what I promised you." When Jacob awoke from his sleep, he exclaimed, "Truly, the Lord is in this spot, although I did not know it!" In solemn wonder he cried out: "How awesome is this shrine! This is nothing else but an abode of God, and that is the gateway to heaven!" Early the next morning Jacob took the stone that he had used as a pillow under his head, set it up as a memorial stone, and poured oil on top of it. He called that site Bethel . . ."

This "heavenly ladder," translated from the Hebrew word *sullam,* has (perhaps inaccurately) been translated as "ladder." The corresponding verb, *salal,* means "to heap up" is something like steps or a ramp. The imagery in Jacob's dream probably has its origins in the Babylonian stepped ziggurat or temple tower, which was well known to Babylonian Jewish biblical writers for a thousand years. In Genesis 11:4, for example, the ancient tower "with its top in the sky" was another symbolic rendering of the stepped ziggurat of Babylon. In the Jacob account in Genesis, the stone Jacob used as a "pillow" for his head in Genesis 28:22 is something more than just a headrest. He states that the place where he lay was a heavenly stairway, and in the morning when he awoke he took the stone and created a sacred pillar (*matsevah*-stele) out of the stone to memorialize his experience. According to

Genesis 28:17, this stone and this place became the true and first location of "God's House" or Bethel. This tradition did not disappear, and in fact, it appears to be the basis for an ongoing tradition in Judaism, Christianity, and Islam that associated the later "House of God," that is, the Temple of Jerusalem, with this particular location. This stone and the story of it being located at the stairway to heaven continued into the Islamic period.

Since even before the beginning of the (first) *Intifada* back in 1988, a problem has been brewing in Jerusalem associated with the political implications of Jerusalem archaeology. First, since 1967, the *Waqf* or religious council of Islam, has been in charge of the Temple Mount as it was in the pre-1967 period. Jerusalem is holy to the Christians since the fourth century CE, but Christianity chose, for theological reasons, not to build anything on the Temple Mount and instead chose the Church of the Holy Sepulchre. In the fourth century CE Christians pilgrims began to visit a site called "the footprints of Jesus," a column nearby where pilgrims were shown the place that Jesus grasped a column as he was whipped. The Church had transferred many of the legends of the Temple to the area around the Church of the Holy Sepulchre and held that this was the place where David the King had prayed. Most of these stories were found in the writings of Sophronius, the Patriarch at the Church of the Holy Sepulchre in the seventh century. By the seventh century, the Church of the Holy Sepulchre had become the new center of the world, the place where Adam's creation had occurred and where the tomb and skull of Adam were identified. These legends suggested that the altar that Abraham had set up to sacrifice Isaac (Genesis 22) was there and also Jacob's ladder. So when the Muslims arrived in Jerusalem in 638 CE, two locations were competing for most of the foundational stories that were central to Islam. Sophronius took the Muslim conquerors to Mount Zion, and he showed them the place that the Jews believed to be the Temple. He showed them a dump site at the edge of the Kedron Valley, and from there they extracted a rock, a portable rock which they said was connected with Jacob's dream in Genesis 28. This stone is perhaps the famous *even shetiyah* (Foundation Stone) of the Holy of Holies. Only a few feet square and probably weighing a ton, it may have been used to build the *Qiblah* (the area towards which prayer is directed) of what would become the Al Aqsa Mosque on the Temple Mount. It does not appear to be the famous outcropping of rock that is found inside the Dome of the Rock Mosque nearby. But by the end of the Crusades, the Christians had accepted the idea of the Dome of the Rock as Solomon's Temple area, and many of their biblical traditions were directed there as well.

When Omar Ibn al-Khattab, the second Calif (leader of Islam), entered Jerusalem in 638 CE, he was convinced that the Temple Mount was where Islam should locate the miracles of Abraham, Isaac, Jacob, David, and Muhammad. Omar built something on that Temple Mount, perhaps using stone that Sophronius had identified for him. He also apparently built a small mosque nearby where the Al Aqsa Mosque is today located. The lower slope of the Al Aqsa had great reverence for Islam because according to Muslim traditions, Jesus (who is in the Koran) was born near the Temple in Jerusalem, not in Bethlehem. The place is called the *Cradle of Jesus* and could have been a flat rock area. Why did these Muslim leaders of the seventh century build the Al Aqsa Mosque in Jerusalem and not make it as great as their capital city of Damascus? Scholars think that the the early Umayyad Calif, Abd Al Malik, moved the capital city of the caliphate from Mecca to Damascus and built the Dome of the Rock Mosque in 692–697 CE apparently to make Mecca a secondary site and allow Muslims to see that there were holy sites outside of Saudi Arabia, including Damascus and Jerusalem. The caliph of the later rival Abbasid dynasty in 830 CE, Abu Jafar Al-Mamum ibn Harun, envied his predecessor's achievements at the Jerusalem mosque so much that he erased Al Malik's name from the mosque and put in his own. But Al-Mamun did not change the date on the building, so we know that Al Malik actually built it. It is possible that Al Malik really wanted to create a new pilgrimage site closer to Damascus than Mecca, but it is clear that some of the foundational accounts of Islam are connected to this location as well.

Some Islamic traditions, often not fully documented ones, like a prophet's tale of Abu Hurayra relate that Muhammad said: "No one shall saddle up for pilgrimage except for the three mosques: the Medina Mosque, the Mecca Mosque and Jerusalem." The Jerusalem Mosque is called therefore *Thalith Al Masajid*, the third of the important mosques, and the pilgrimage there involves similar rituals to those associated with the first two mosques; for example, a ritual of circling the rock in the Dome of the Rock, just like Muslims do at the rock in the Kaaba in Mecca.

The Muslim Names of Jerusalem: Aelia, Bayt Al-Maqdis, Al Quds, Sahyun

Jerusalem has had many names according to ancient Canaanites, Israelites, Judeans, Babylonians, Greeks, Romans, and then Christians. By the time of the Byzantine Christians, Jerusalem was known as *Aelius Hadrianus*, the second century CE Roman emperor who destroyed the city after the Bar Kokhba Revolt and then apparently restored the Temple mount to dedicate it to *Zeus Aelia Capitolina*. It is probably for this reason that although the name of Jerusalem does not appear in the Koran, it does appear in Muslim sources as *Aelia*. Paralleling this process of renaming Jerusalem as *Aelius Hadrianus*, the name of the entire area of Judea (and Israel) was also changed. Because Judea had become synonymous in the second century CE with insurrection (after two rebellions against the Romans), the name of the province was officially changed to *Palestina*. The use of this name "Palestine" seems to be a Greek form of the more ancient name known to the Romans: *P(h)ilistina*. From this period onward, the province became known as Palestine and the name continued into the twentieth century. Today, the designations of "Palestine" and "Israel" are politically charged issues that have more to do with modern debates than historical designations. The most indicative change in the past sixty years has been the changing of the name of the main English language newspaper of Israel from the *Palestine Post* to the *Jerusalem Post*. But for almost eighteen hundred years, Jews, Christians, and Muslims alike used the Hadrianic euphemism, Palestine, and it too was indicative of an ancient political debate.

By 750 CE, the Abassid dynasty had taken hold of the Islamic empire from the Umayyads, and they established themselves in *Aelia*. In the ninth century CE, Jerusalem became known in Muslim sources as *Bayt Al-Maqdis*, the Holy House. From the eleventh century CE onward, this became shortened to "Al Quds," the Holy (city). This played on the fact that Islam recognized the existence of the earlier biblical holy places as a part of their ongoing tradition and the existence of the mosques on the Temple Mount. It was also called *Sahyun*, the other biblical name for Jerusalem, Zion. The Kaaba in Mecca was also called by Muhammad, *Sahyun*, or the new "Zion." The Dome of the Rock, *Kubbat asSakra,* is the place of *Al Miraj,* the Ascension of Muhammad to heaven and is connected in Islamic tradition to this rock. The nocturnal journey of Muhammad from Mecca to the farthest point, Al Aqsa, called in Arabic, *Isra,* and his ascent to heaven, called by Muslims *al Miraj* (the ascent), are connected this way: One night the angel Gabriel appeared in the house of Muhammad's wife in Mecca and awakened the Prophet. He ordered Muhammad to dress and to ride with him on a miraculous animal named *Al Buraq* (possibly derived from the three letter Semitic root: *brq*—also associated with the word "lightning"). This miraculous animal *Al Buraq* was, according to Islamic tradition, more than a donkey and less than a mule. Its head is that of a human being, its body that of a horse, its eyes were like blinking stars. After a short and miraculous ride, Muhammad and Gabriel arrived in Jerusalem. According to Muslim sources, Muhammad hitched his horse to what we call today the Western Wall of the Temple Mount. For this reason Muslims call the Western Wall *Al Buraq*. At the rock, Muhammad found a "ladder," a *Miraj* (in Arabic) made of gold silver, and he ascended the "ladder" and guided by Gabriel, he was brought into the upper skies. He met John the Baptist, Jesus, Abraham, David, Solomon, Joseph, and others. He came before the Divine throne. The thousand fiery veils were removed, and he had a near face-to-face encounter with Allah (God). Allah showed him what paradise was like. And according to Muslim sources, he negotiated with Allah over the number of prayer services that were to be done by Muslims to serve Him. God wanted them to pray fifty times a day, and Muhammad was able to negotiate God down to only five times daily. And it is in these sources that we learn that Abu Bakr would be the rightful messenger of the ongoing message of Islam and the first caliph, leader of Islam. The twenty-seventh day of the month of *Radjab*, the seventh in the Islamic calendar, is Islam's *Jerusalem Day*, although other traditions suggest different dates. Later Muhammad's footprints came to be shown to pilgrims when they visited the rock as well as the imprint of the saddle and even the place where Gabriel flattened the rock for his ascent. Some Islamic traditions establish a host of other pilgrimage sites in the area, and many of the Meccan traditions were performed on the Temple Mount in the two mosques.

Jacob's "ladder" had been there, according to Jews and now the Muslim tradition's "ladder" as well; the sacrifice of Abraham's son and his footprints had been there according to the Jews and the Muslims. Noah's ark had come to rest there after the flood in Islamic and Jewish tradition. Resurrection of the dead was to begin nearby the Temple Mount and this tradition was accepted by Jews and then later by Muslims. Some traditions had Muhammad asking to be buried in Jerusalem as well. The souls gather below the rock, navel of the world. One of the early caliphs changed the direction of Muslim prayer from Jerusalem to Mecca, but the importance of Jerusalem was not to be denied. The name for the place, *Al Haram esSharif,* the holy, the revered place, *Al qudsi al Sharif,* is seen as a place of great veneration; not just because of the time that Muhammad spent there but because other prophets of Islam (and Judaism and Christianity) had been there too. The later Muslims, however, the Abbasids, built up Baghdad, but not Jerusalem. These new Muslim movements transferred the holiness from Jerusalem to Baghdad, and they created new interpretations of the Koran that removed the holy places to new locations. It is in this period that Muslim tradition begins to associate the tradition of Al Aqsa not as an earthly domain but in heaven. Following this interpretation, the Shiite Imam Jafar el Saddeq, the sixth Imam of Iraq, held in 765 CE, that only the mosques of Mecca and Medina were holy mosques. By this period, for political and religious reasons, Jerusalem was no longer as important to Islam as it had been in the early generations of Muhammad and the first generations of Islam. "The Al Aqsa [Mosque] is in Heaven," (not in Jerusalem, a physical location) goes the Iraqi tradition of this period. In addition, one finds that the Iraqi traditions go even further in this regard stating that "The Kufa Mosque in Iraq is better than the one in Jerusalem." The Al Aqsa Mosque was finished in 705 CE, but by that time, Islam began to establish holy sites in other places in the Islamic world. Similarly, the later Mamluke Muslims (from North Africa) developed the mosques of Cairo as more important than Jerusalem's mosques in much the same way that the Iraqis had done in the earlier generations.

From Ancient Jerusalem Politics to Modern Jerusalem Politics

Today the politics are more difficult because many Muslims and Palestinians say that nothing on the Temple Mount is intrinsically "Jewish." Since the 1990s, work inside the Al Aqsa Mosque has caused problems. New work inside of the Al Aqsa Mosque has destabilized some of the ancient and medieval walls that surround it. The walls took on a noticeable bulge, and finally it was decided that unless the walls were shored up they might collapse. Unfortunately, the levels of political problems between Israelis and Palestinians have also destabilized the ability of the Islamic authority that administrates the Temple Mount to easily allow Israeli contractors to do the work. Ultimately, the Jordanians were brought in to do the work despite their absence from the area since 1967. Scaffolding was put up, a repair was made, but the problem will only increase as the debris in the mosque is removed to make way for more prayer participants in the mosque, and the wall continues to deteriorate.

Presently no Israeli archaeology is being done on the Temple Mount but Muslims are digging. Unfortunately, clearing for new space in the Al Aqsa Mosque has been going on much to the consternation of Israeli archaeologists. Debris is dumped in assigned sites, and archaeologists do monitor the debris there. It has led to even more tension because some finds have been made in the debris, and unfortunately it is impossible to pinpoint the location of finds on the Mount since the site is not being systematically excavated. The changing of any of the status quo in and around the area immediately causes tension and sometimes violence.

Systematic archaeology of any kind in the area has become problematic, but some work continues. In the past few years Eilat Mazar's excavations in the City of David have yielded finds from the Iron Age through the Persian period. The discoveries, that in earlier periods would have been accepted as part of the long legacy of archaeological data on the city are immediately questioned by an assortment of officials.

In the Friday, August 5, 2005, edition of the *New York Times*, a story appeared noting that Eilat Mazar had discovered what she called: "David's Palace," a large building dating to the Iron Age. Immediately, Hani Nur el-Din, a professor of archaeology at Al Quds University, responded that Palestinian archaeologists consider biblical archaeology as an effort by Israeli archaeologists "to fit historical evidence into a biblical context," he said. "The link between the historical evidence and the biblical narration, written much later, is largely missing," he said. "There's a kind of fiction about the 10th century. They try to link whatever they find to the biblical narration. They have a button and they want to make a suit out of it." (August 5: NYT reported by Steven Erlanger) Unlike other finds, the palace is in its original context. Also, this public building can be comparatively dated to the tenth century by its foundations, which are constructed in the Phoenician style that correspond to other tenth to ninth century buildings in nearby locations. This is significant because the tenth century is the time period of David and Solomon.

The debate over Jerusalem and the existence in the ancient period of David and Solomon is very clear, even among Israeli archaeologists, and has been played out more often in the same *New York Times* article rather than in academic conferences and journals. I was very impressed by the candor of Professor Amihai Mazar, a second cousin of Eilat's and a noted archaeologist of the Iron Age who was quoted in the same *New York Times* article as saying that ". . . there is a debate among archaeologists to what extent Jerusalem was an important city or even a city in the time of David and Solomon. Many think that it was a city but it was small and unimportant in the time of David and Solomon. While others still hold that it was the developing royal city of the greatest of all Israelite kings. Whether archaeology is able to prove one or the other hypothesis is the question. Whether it was or not the city of David and Solomon it is clear that Jerusalem remains a study in archaeological patience and diligence and at the heart of the Jewish, Christian, and Muslim claims and counter-claims to a share in its holiness."

I close with our own observations on the possibilities of discovering something new in places around Jerusalem that have been excavated now thousands of times in the past two hundred years. In 2005 our geophysical team members, Harry Jol and Paul Bauman, accompanied the former chief district archaeologist for Jerusalem, Dan Bahat, on an after-midnight survey of one of the most sensitive areas of Jerusalem, near the Western Wall. In the late 1980s and early 1990s, tunnels were discovered and dug near the Western Wall that have revealed new unexpected secrets of the underground Jerusalem. The discovery of these tunnels and their subsequent excavation was closely guarded information. When they opened the tunnels to the public, near riots broke out and claims and counterclaims of deception and the undermining of the Temple Mount were fired back and forth between Arabs and Jews. The tunnels are still open to the public, but little or no work has been done to see if there are indeed other tunnels and secrets beneath and around the Western Wall. In 2005 our geophysical team revealed that there was probably much to be discovered behind these excavated walls. So one of the most important lessons we have learned about Jerusalem is that it has not given up the last of its secrets, and there is still much to be revealed below the surface of the Jerusalem we see today.

Figure 2.3.   Collecting GPR data in the Western Wall tunnels.

Courtesy Harry Jol, University of Wisconsin Eau-Claire.

3

Searching for Jesus in Galilee and Babylonia

Figure 3.1.   Is this the Key of Peter?

Courtesy Bethsaida Excavations Project

The Key of Peter at Bethsaida?

I have been involved in a number of television documentaries on or about Jesus, the Apostles, the early Christians, the Rabbis, and Jews and Christians in the first and second century CE. During the making of a television documentary, *The Fifth Gospel*, Father Bargil Pixner, a Roman Catholic monk and brilliant archaeologist of Galilee, asked me whether I, as a Rabbi and historian of the period, thought that Jesus and the Apostles really existed. I answered Father Pixner as honestly as I could. My answer was and is that it is just as reasonable that these people existed, just as the Gospels record as not. My answer is based upon the same types of evidence that I collected in the chapter on the Exodus and Mount Sinai. There are so many historical, artifactual, archaeological, geographical, and literary lines of evidence that point to the authenticity of these accounts that it is difficult to interpret otherwise. Father Pixner spent most of his adult life researching the historical Jesus in Galilee, and he took me all over Galilee showing places that have enlightened my own research. In his book, *The Fifth Gospel,* Father Pixner argued that understanding the reality of the land, Galilee and Jerusalem especially, reveals as much as the other four Gospels.

Father Pixner was a person of deep faith and well respected in the Roman Catholic Church. During Pope John Paul II's historic visit to Israel in 2000, Father Pixner arranged for us to present an artifact found at Bethsaida to the Pope. This artifact was an iron door key found near a large fisherman's house in the center of the excavations. A first-century iron door key from Bethsaida had enormous symbolic importance for the Pope. It is clear from the Gospels that Peter, the "ancestor" of the Popes, was from Bethsaida. The key is a very significant symbol for the Vatican and the history of the papacy. The Vatican City flag prominently features keys that are associated with Peter. The keys are linked to Jesus' pronouncement to Peter in the Gospel according to Matthew 16:19: "I will give you the keys of the kingdom of heaven." The key is seen, therefore, not only as a device for opening the door of a house, but rather as a symbol of salvation in the Kingdom of Heaven. I knew, therefore, that the iron door key that we had discovered near the large, first-century CE fisherman's house at Bethsaida was not seen by the Vatican as just any door key. I knew that the Bethsaida door key was viewed by the Vatican as an artifact that was emblematic of what Peter, the papacy, and Christianity stood for.

The key was a unique artifact. The survival of this iron door key in the environment of the northern Galilee was a minor miracle itself. Galilee is rainy and cold in the winters and hot and humid in the summers. These are not exactly the best conditions for the survival of metal. Yet, the key survived and was found with some ancient nails that we think were from the original wooden door for which the key would have been used. The long key doubled as a door handle. Although this design does not match the one on the flags, it is very similar to other ancient keys of the period. The problem was that the key did not belong to us, so we could not just give the Pope the key. Archaeological discoveries in Israel belong to the State of Israel, so we commissioned two well-made replicas. Many museums commonly make copies of artifacts to use in place of a fragile original, and they are usually marked, as our key was, with a single letter "R" for replica. Father Pixner stood with me, my colleague, Rami Arav, and the officers of some of the universities associated with the Bethsaida Consortium as I presented the key to the Pope. I tried to be as scientific and detailed as possible, but recognizing that the entire meaning of the artifact could not easily be broken down to simple data about its discovery and a history lesson about Bethsaida. I remember speaking about the provenance of the discovery, its proximity to the large fisherman's courtyard house, the dimensions of the door, and how Bethsaida was the home of the Apostle Peter. After hearing many versions of what I knew about the key, the Pope simply said four words of recognition to me: "the Key of Peter." He repeated these words to me several times and looked at me for acknowledgement. Finally, I simply looked at him and acknowledged his words and repeated them back to him: "the Key of Peter, the Key of Peter."

This encounter took only a few minutes and when the Pope blessed the copies of the key, I realized how unique the experience had been for him and us. We were the Pope's last interview on that Friday afternoon, March 24, 2000, and by the time the Pope could meet with us at the Tabgha monastery, the Sabbath was beginning. It was for me, as a Jew and a Rabbi, a very spiritual experience. I remember walking back from Tabgha to nearby Kibbutz Ginosar in a light spring rain along the shore of the Sea of Galilee. I debated with myself all of the way back whether I had done the right thing by agreeing with the words of the Pope, "the Key of Peter." On my way back to the kibbutz, I realized something crucial for biblical archaeology and how it affects people. I intellectually knew that what we had presented the Pope was a replica of the key, not even the original key, yet it symbolized something that was far more important and powerful that only archaeology can do. It can create a tangible connection between a literary text and an entire historical tradition. It would take twenty years of excavations, tens of thousands of artifacts, and scores of publications and research to demonstrate what can be expressed in one single, symbolic replica of a key. For the Pope, this was indeed a symbolic "Key of Peter." Even when biblical archaeology cannot prove a direct connection between an artifact and a literary text, it can provide the next best thing—an illustration of what is mentioned in the text. It provides a level of tangible history for both the faithful and the scientist who are in a conversation about the significance of their joint enterprise. The thousands of volunteers who have excavated Bethsaida over the past two decades probably would never have chosen Bethsaida to excavate there if it had been just another Roman city in the small eastern provinces of the Roman Empire. They choose to come to Bethsaida because there is a religious literary history and significance to the site, and many hope that they will find that direct connection. The artifacts we find at Bethsaida provide the public with information that is relevant and available to both the faithful and skeptics. At the moment that I met the Pope, I felt that it was as reasonable as not that this artifact could have been a key of the Apostle Peter of the village of Bethsaida (at least the original could). Science could not easily disprove the pronouncement of the Holy Father, and therefore I felt that we had fulfilled our mission to science and faith.

Father Pixner was the one who convinced the Vatican that Bethsaida was indeed the place where the Apostles and Jesus met, and he even established two holy sites at Bethsaida that are still on the Church's Pilgrim maps of Galilee. But the search for Jesus is also complicated by traditions in Judaism that have tended to create a totally different picture of Jesus in Rabbinic literature. During the making of the CNN television documentary *After Jesus*, I was asked by Jews who knew me, whether I thought that Jesus ever existed. Again, as a Jew, I answered that it is just as likely that a man named Jesus from Galilee existed in history and for whom evidence of his life existed in the same way that events of the Roman period existed for most of the other major people, places, and events of the New Testament.

The Importance of Galilee

Galilee served as an important center of Rabbinic life and culture during a crucial period of rebuilding after the destruction of the Temple and the expulsions of the Jews from the areas around Judea and Jerusalem in the wake of the first and the second Revolts against the Romans. Rabbinic and Jewish life flourished in Galilee and around the shores of the Sea of Galilee between the first and fifth centuries CE. The area went into decline in the fifth century CE after Byzantine and Sassanian conflicts made life in the region a crossroads for the conflicts between these superpowers.

Under the Muslims, the area again became a center of Rabbinic life, and it was in Tiberias that the Masoretes, the grammarians of the text of the Hebrew Bible, established academies that created a uniform transmission and pronunciation for the text of the Bible. It was here, too, that the Rabbis lived among the warring Muslim and Crusader armies in the eleventh to thirteenth centuries. The greatest sage of the Middle Ages, Moses ben Maimon (Maimonides), ultimately found his resting place in Tiberias. Maimonides was born in Spain, worked in Morocco and Egypt, but was buried in Tiberias. Under the Mamelukes and Ottomans, the Rabbis founded in Galilee the greatest academies of Jewish learning of the period. When Jews were expelled from Spain in 1492, many of the greatest sages came to Galilee to continue their work. Two texts provided a new impetus for Jewish religious life in this period: Rabbi Joseph Karo's work, the *Shulhan Aruch* (in Hebrew, literally "the prepared table"), which was composed in the sixteenth century community of Safed (Galilee) that became the basis for all Jewish law, and the Jewish mystical works of Rabbi Isaac Luria, also of Safed. The Jewish mystics continued to flow to Galilee, and Rabbinic life continued on the shores of the Sea despite the earthquakes that periodically destroyed the buildings and walled communities. But the sources of what we know of Jewish communities on or near the Sea of Galilee and in Galilee (and even in what is called today the Lower Golan) in general are preserved in later Rabbinic literature that has been finally redacted in far away Babylonia and is often written centuries after the traditions they are preserving. Often, this would not make a significant difference in our understanding, but when we are trying to understand the historical aspects of Jewish life, especially of specific individuals, cities, groups, etc. from Galilee, it does make a difference.

Jewish archaeology, sometimes called "Rabbinic" or "Talmudic archaeology," is primarily concerned with towns and cities, individuals, and events mentioned in classical Greco-Roman/Byzantine period archaeology which coincide with Rabbinic literature redacted between the first through the tenth centuries CE. This combination of literature of the time and material culture of the period is considered Jewish archaeology. The earliest traditions of Rabbinic literature were centered primarily in Galilee and at the Sea of Galilee. The Rabbis living in the Second Temple Period provided Jewish leadership in Jerusalem, the entire Land of Israel, and perhaps even the far-flung areas of the Diaspora from Italy to Babylonia. The Rabbis began to congregate in Galilee after the disastrous events of the Bar Kokhba Revolt in 135 CE, but Jewish life had begun in Galilee much earlier.

During the Iron Age, the Israelites mixed freely with non-Israelites, and the Ten Northern Tribes of Israel founded an independent nation-state that existed until the Israelites were exiled in the Assyrian conquest of the eighth century BCE. In the sixth century BCE, the Persian influence was felt when the Israelites returned from exile and the Jews established their large Diaspora community in Babylonia with a link directly to the Land of Israel through Galilee. Alexander the Great and his successors left their indelible mark upon Jewish culture in the Galilee. During the early Hellenistic period, Galilee became a battleground as the Jews split their loyalties to the Ptolemian families in the south and Seleucid families to the north. The Maccabean families captured and protected Galilee, and the Romans ultimately saw the area as a strategic link in their road system that connected the eastern and western as well as the northern and southern parts of the expanding empire. The Sea of Galilee sat at the center of this peripheral area of the province, yet it became a crucial lifeline of the empire and prospered in the Roman period. The Herodian families established themselves in the area, and the shores of the Sea of Galilee in the first century CE developed into one of the most creative and prolific areas in Jewish life. It is perhaps because of this fact that Christianity developed in the midst of Galilee and not in Jerusalem, and the whole area served as a refuge for most of the next two centuries for both Jews and Christians.

The Seventh Order of the Mishnah

As Rabbinic culture became the norm in the first and second centuries, and especially after the destruction of the Temple and Jerusalem in 70 CE, Galilee became the new "Jerusalem" of Judaism. The so-called founder of the "new" Rabbinic Judaism movement after the destruction of the Temple in 70 CE was Rabbi Yohanan ben Zakkai. He taught at Yavne in the south of the country but was buried in Tiberias on the Sea of Galilee. The greatest rabbis of the first and second century—Hillel, Shammai, Rabbi Akiva, Rabbi Meir, Rabbi Shimon ben Gamliel, and Rabbi Shimon BarYohai—all worked, and most are buried in Galilee. In addition to the material culture, an enormous amount of literature and information is available about the Rabbinic culture and life in Galilee. Rabbinic literature was assembled early in different collections:

- The Midrash is a series of homilies on specific biblical verses that speak to contemporary traditions among the Jews.
- "The Mishnah" (a Hebrew word referring to study that can also mean "Second" (to the Torah) codifies the traditions developed

throughout the generations among the Jews and were an "oral" literature of traditions that were passed from generation to generation. These traditions, though not directly tied to the Bible, reflect the life and times of the Jewish people. The final edited edition of the Mishnah was collected in this very creative area of Galilee, but its traditions are as old as the Jewish people.

• The Jews of Galilee and the Diaspora immediately began a process of interpreting and developing these traditions that became the literature that we refer to as the Gemara, or more commonly the Talmud.

The Mishnah, formulated by Rabbi Judah the Prince in the third century CE in Galilee, is the basis of Rabbinic literature. Rabbi Judah the Prince used six categories to impose order upon the vast number of oral traditions that were available to him, which in turn imposed a way for others to view the material. Each of the six "orders" or divisions of the Mishnah contains approximately ten to twelve books, for a total of sixty-three different books. Sometimes all of Rabbinic literature is referred to as Sh"as, an acronym for "the Six Orders" of the Mishnah. My work in archaeology has convinced me that in order to understand the Six Orders of the Mishnah, one needs to consider a seventh order of Rabbinic literature, the material culture and context of its origin. The "Seventh Order" is the material culture context itself—the archaeology, the geography, and the geology of the land where it was written. In the case of understanding the Rabbinic understanding of Jesus, the place where it was composed and written down is crucial to understanding what it says. I think the "seventh order" helps impose some order or organization upon an unruly literature. In a parallel example involving the New Testament, Father Bargil Pixner's book and movie, *The Fifth Gospel,* attempts to weave the material culture and geography of first-century Galilee into his understanding of what the first four canonical Gospel accounts meant.

The modern study of Rabbinics began at the same time as modern biblical studies and archaeology and the *Wissenschaft des Judentums* literature of the nineteenth century. Eighteenth-and-nineteenth-century travelers and explorers in Palestine, the Levant and Egypt, such as Edward Robinson, Ernest Renan, and Charles Warren, attempted to link texts from the New Testament and Rabbinic tradition with exact locations in Galilee and Judea. Their reports sparked hopes in nineteenth-century scholarship on Rabbinics that these early site locations would provide direct links with Rabbinic narratives. Works from this period attempt to directly link *exact* Talmudic stories and locations mentioned in Rabbinic literature with places identified by nineteenth century soldiers, explorers, and travelers in the Middle East. This type of identification system proved to be inadequate or theologically weighted in the case of the Hebrew Bible, (called the Masoretic Text or MT), the "approved" Hebrew version of the Hebrew Bible and is even more problematic in the case of the relationship between the Masoretic Text and the Rabbinic figures that approved it.

Another problem associated with nineteenth and even twentieth century biblical archaeology also makes Talmudic archaeology problematic. In the Hebrew Bible and New Testament biblical archaeology search parameters are determined by these two fixed biblical works. Although these works can be and are compared with ancient Near Eastern and Greco-Roman literatures and critical text work is taken into consideration, the parameters of biblical archaeology often begins with the biblical version of an event, site, or life fixed in the canon set of these two works. In essence, an MT archaeological work was "directed" by the thirty-nine books of the canonized Hebrew Bible, and likewise a New Testament archaeological search is "directed" by the canonized twenty-seven books.

Rabbinic archaeology was originally thought to be set by the canon of the books found in the Babylonian Talmud and the Palestinian Talmud. The Babylonian Talmud (BT) was completed in Babylonia in the sixth and seventh centuries CE, whereas the Palestinian Talmud (PT), sometimes called the Jerusalem Talmud, was actually completed in Tiberias in the fifth century CE. In the past fifty years, however, this concept has been challenged by different writers. The determination of Rabbinic archaeology of Israel based upon references found only in the Babylonian Talmud, for example, is suspect, especially when it relates to specific information about the Land of Israel, cities, customs, and so forth in a particular period. Although the Babylonian Talmud has ample information on the life and times of Israel during the Tannaitic and Amoraic periods (first century BCE through sixth century CE, Roman and early Byzantine periods), this information is plagued by textual and factual problems that may be the result of oral and/or written stages of the text's development. In addition, several other issues make a unified "single work" archaeology difficult. First, is the overwhelming size of the Babylonian Talmud and the unwieldy nature of the Talmudic language; the text contains thousands of pages with different Jewish Aramaic dialects from Babylon and Palestine as well as Hebrew. Second, is argumentation in both Talmudim. The third issue is the problematic state of the preservation of Rabbinic manuscripts, primarily because of havoc wreaked upon these manuscripts by Crusades, exiles, systematic burnings, and destruction. In short, there are a number of problems associated with the use of Rabbinic materials to determine reliable information about fixed historical personalities and cities/towns in the Israel of late antiquity. Rabbinic information on Israel, especially information about the earliest period of Galilee and more specifically on the Sea of Galilee, can be used only after it is subjected to serious critical analysis.

The Critical Study of Rabbinic Literature

Can Rabbinic texts provide any substantive and reliable information on historical personalities and cities/towns in Israel in late antiquity? One line of thinking in modern Rabbinic scholarship assumes that Rabbinic literature provides reliable information for modern scholarly analysis. Since the beginnings of modern Rabbinic studies, many scholars have analyzed Rabbinic texts with a critical eye, but most of these scholars accepted information from both attributed and unattributed Rabbinic sources as authentic expressions of historical circumstances. The other line of thinking is that Rabbinic scholarship is not a very reliable source of information, especially historical information. I was taught by scholars in Israel who basically used Rabbinic literature as if it were truly historical information. They analyzed texts in a critical fashion but accepted that Rabbinic literature preserved authentic historical information (not all Rabbinic literature but some). I remember my surprise the first time that I learned that a piece of Rabbinic literature contained a historically inaccurate piece of information. The famous Rabbinic prayer for Hanukkah that is in the official prayer book for the past one thousand years states: "And for the miracles, and for the salvation, and for the mighty deeds, and for the victories, and for the battles which You [God] performed for our forefathers in those days at this time. [It came to pass] in the days of Mattityahu, the son of Yochanan, the High Priest, the Hasmonean and his sons when the wicked Greek kingdom rose up against Your statutes of Your will. . . . "

Unfortunately, we know from the writings of Josephus and the books of Maccabees, that the son of Mattityahu who was the High Priest was *Yonatan,* not Yochanan. Yet it is enshrined in the prayer book because the Rabbis had their own traditions that they trusted more than the writings of Josephus Flavius and the books of the Maccabees. They relied upon their own oral traditions, and thus the texts are not "historical" in the same sense of history that modern historians use. Rabbinic texts do not attempt to be historical in the modern sense.

Over the past forty years, the idea that Rabbinic texts can be relied on for any "historical" information has been challenged by Professor Jacob Neusner and a host of other scholars in a variety of works. Three works from different periods of the vast library of Neusner's writings on this subject will suffice: *A Life of Yohanan ben Zakkai, Development of a Legend: Studies on the Traditions Concerning Yohanan ben Zakkai,* and *In Search of Talmudic Biography.* Professor Neusner's books present a similar thesis about understanding Rabbinic narrative. First, that it is very difficult to understand Rabbinic texts if you do not understand the inner workings of the literature. Second, that this literature is not a good witness of actual events. In *Understanding Seeking Faith,* Volume Two (1987, 143-144), Professor Neusner writes:

> The sources of Judaism of the dual Torah, oral and written, accurately and factually testify to particular moments in time. But how shall we identify the right time, the particular context to which the documents and their contents attest—and those to which they do not provide reliable testimony? Using the canonical sources of Judaism for historical purposes requires, first of all, a clear statement of why, in my view, these sources tell us about one period, rather than some other. The problem, specifically, is that the documents preserved by Judaism refer to authorities who, we generally suppose, flourished in the early centuries of the Common Era. But at the same time, we also know, these documents were brought to closure in the later centuries of late antiquity . . . At the same time, we cannot show, and therefore do not know, that these sayings really were said by the sages to whom they are assigned, and we frequently can demonstrate that the sayings are attributed by diverse documents of the same canon to two or more figures. Along these same lines, stories that purport to tell us what really happened exhibit marks of stylization that show reworkings, and, more important, we rarely find independent evidence, e.g., corroboration by outside observers, of other views of what happened. Not only so, but where sages' stories about events can be compared to stories told by outside observers, we rarely can find any correlation at all, either as to causes, or as to circumstances, let alone as to actual events.

The critical study of Rabbinic literature is important as we compare what Rabbinic literature tells us about Jesus of Nazareth, the Apostles and Galilee with the New Testament, and the archaeology of the period. As we have seen, finding one person in biblical or Jewish history, even a person who became very important, is nearly impossible using archaeology. Before you can actually look for a figure using history and archaeology, you must establish what is known in all contemporary literature about that figure and see why this literature is saying what it does. The Jesus known in Rabbinic literature is different from the New Testament Jesus. So different that you might think that they are talking about completely different people. In fact, they may be dealing with a totally different person.

Why Archaeology Cannot Easily Find Jesus of Nazareth

I am asked by my students why we haven't found any artifacts from the first century that bear Jesus of Nazareth's name. Every summer people come to excavate at Bethsaida hoping that they will find one small inscription with Jesus of Nazareth's name on it. I am not surprised that we haven't found one, and we haven't found an inscription from Jesus of Nazareth in Nazareth either. While people are unlikely to find an inscription, it does not stop them from dreaming about finding one, and it motivates them to sit out in the hot sun for hours sifting through small potsherds at Bethsaida.

I have several reasons why I think that it will be very difficult to find such an inscription. Even if we find the inscription, in a provenanced context, it still might not be accepted by everyone. First, I tell people in our orientation sessions that Jesus may not have been as important in the first century as he became in later centuries. We find that this happens to many famous artists. Artists are so much more important after their deaths that often they despair during their lifetimes about the impact of their lives. Van Gogh is an example of this. When I see what his paintings cost today and remember how he lived in squalor and despair at the end of his life, it demonstrates the problems that archaeologists face in trying to find a single person in antiquity, even someone who was or became important to his followers. Students often do not have the scope of history in mind when they consider the use of archaeology. The names that were used in this period are well known from a host of ancient sources and from archaeology. Yet, because we do not have a last (family) name or specific qualifier, the very common names of the period make it more difficult to know who we have found. The name "Jesus" (assumed to be a transliteration of the Hebrew name, Joshua) may or may not have been the Hebrew name of Jesus of Nazareth. He may have had a Hebrew name that was similar to but not exactly the same as the Greek name, Jesus. Paul, for example, from the same period as Jesus has a Hebrew name, Saul and a Greek name, Paul. Peter, has a Greek name, Peter and also has a Hebrew name, Simon. This was a common practice of the period. The Greek names are not always transliterations of the Hebrew name. Sometimes they are translations of a Hebrew name, and sometimes they are just completely different names that were common in antiquity and were used in different social, religious, and public settings. So the name "Jesus" alone is so common in the ancient world that even if we found an artifact in Jerusalem, Nazareth, or Bethsaida, for example, dated to the first century CE, some would find this enough of a coincidence to relate the artifact directly to the famous Jesus of Nazareth, while others would say that we know this is not necessarily "the" Jesus of Nazareth" but it could be "a" Jesus of Nazareth.

This may seem like a theoretical debate, but it is not. The most recent example occurred over the past few years. There was a discovery in 1980 in Jerusalem of one family cave tomb of ten bone boxes or ossuaries in Talpiot, a suburb of Jerusalem, that listed the names of the family members on six or perhaps seven boxes. The names on the first six boxes included Jesus the son of Joseph, Joseph, Judah, Matthew, Mary, and Mariamene. The producers of a *Discovery Channel* television documentary and a book recently concluded that the bone boxes were all from the family of Jesus of Nazareth. The names on the bone boxes (ossuaries) are all common names of the period. They were written in an unusual way, but they still correspond in many ways to the English equivalents above. The original names on the ossuaries were: *Yeshua bar Yehosef* (Hebrew/Aramaic for Jesus, son of Joseph), *Maria* (Greek form written in Aramaic script for Mary), *Yose* (Hebrew in a shortened fashion of Joseph), *Matia* (Hebrew shortened version of Matthew), *Mariamene e Mara* (written in Greek) and *Yehuda bar Yeshua* (Aramaic for Judah son of Jesus). I will not dwell on all of the details, but suffice it to say that the documentary and book associated with it maintain that "*Mariamene e Mara*" is Mary Magdalene and the producers conclude that *Yehuda bar Yeshua* may be her son by Jesus (the one called *Mariamne* in the tomb). Now there are good academic reasons why the producers and the book associated Mariamene with Mary Magdalene. They are using manuscript readings of New Testament aprocryphal works (works that did not get into the canon but still survived in manuscript form), *Acts of Peter* and the *Gospel of Philip*, some with readings from over a thousand years after the events of the first century CE, but for scholars even these late readings can help unlock an original reading. The other connections include the idea that Jesus had brothers and sisters according to the text of the New Testament so this tomb includes them as well. In short, many of the ideas that are used to connect the names to specific New Testament figures are scholarly arguments that demonstrate the critical study of texts and the value of archaeology in this search.

The name that sparked much of the excitement is "Jesus," the son of Joseph. To understand the excitement and the controversies surrounding the "discovery," one has to first accept the academic study of the historical Jesus and some of its conclusions. Without this basic assumption, the meaning of the discovery is almost unintelligible. Some immediately questioned why it says *Jesus son of Joseph* when Christianity holds that he was not the biological son of Joseph, but rather the son of Mary and God. The modern study of the historical Jesus has concluded that the virgin birth account may not have been an integral part of the earliest versions of Jesus' life. They point to the genealogies of the Gospels of Matthew and Luke and conclude that there were traditions that Jesus was indeed seen as the son of Joseph. But the idea that this was the ossuary of Jesus of Nazareth created a stir because Christianity holds that he was crucified and that on the third day he rose from the dead and so would not have needed a bone box for his bones. The bone box tradition of burial is a two-step burial concept that was used for about a hundred years in the Jerusalem area. First, the dead were buried for about a year in the earth, and only after that the bones were collected from the burial and placed in a limestone box and the box was then put into a family tomb. Sometimes, the bones of a few people would be collected together, and thus, the biblical idea of "being gathered unto their ancestors" was fulfilled. Jerusalemites had become by the first century BCE very careful with those elements that caused a form of ritual impurity (and invalidated Priestly and Temple prescriptions about ritual purity), including the bones of a person, and so they authorized this "solution" of making stone bone boxes that did not allow for ritual impurity to be spread.

However, the faithful argued that if Jesus rose from the dead on the third day, why would his bones need a bone box a year after his death? The modern study of the historical Jesus scholars argued that there were concepts of resurrection in the first century that would have allowed a spiritual resurrection without his physical body, but other also question the entire account of the death and resurrection of Jesus as later Christianity has it. Without the critical study of the New Testament and this modern scholarly questioning of the historical Jesus, the "discovery" of the *Jesus son of Joseph* inscription cannot even be properly understood. But even with this critical methodology, the idea that Jesus was buried in a family tomb in Talpiot did not square with the history of Christianity and the fact that Jesus was from Nazareth, not from Jerusalem, so his family tomb should have been in Nazareth, not Jerusalem. Again, Christianity assigns to Jesus a burial cave where his body was laid out on the fateful day of the crucifixion at the Church of the Holy Sepulchre in the Old City of Jerusalem. It may or may not have been a loaned cave (for the Sabbath) of Joseph of Arimathea, a person who apparently did have a family burial cave in Jerusalem to offer as a place of refuge for the body of Jesus. Jesus would have been taken down off of the cross on the eve of the Sabbath and then on the Sunday following the crucifixion, women visited the burial cave, only to find that the body was missing. The burial cave in the Church of the Holy Sepulchre has archaeological evidence in it to suggest that by the second century CE, this was the known place of the final resting place for Jesus on the day of the crucifixion, and certainly by the Byzantine period the empty cave was certified as the burial place. To overturn an eighteen-hundred-year-old tradition of the Church makes the issue even more problematic.

But the main criticism for the family tomb of Jesus theory, even from the modern scholars of the historical Jesus, seems to be how common these names were in the first century. It is a statistical argument. One must bear in mind not only other ossuaries and what they have inscribed on them, but also the data set of names from the entire first century in documents, monuments, and inscriptions of the period. *Yeshua bar Yehosef* is very common, especially when one considers that the Greek name, Jesus, is not listed alongside the Yehoshua reference. We cannot be certain that Jesus' Hebrew name was indeed Yehoshua because we have nothing else to compare it to. The other inscriptions also beome more and more problematic as you examine each reference. The reference to a *Yeshua bar Yehosef* is important, but there is no connection at all between any literary connections and a family member of this name, and the academic conjecture that Jesus had a son, named Judah, is a form of hypothesis that is not easily explained without an enormous background of study. The Discovery Channel producers concluded that this *Yehuda bar Yeshua* is the son of the same *Yeshua bar Yehosef* and the woman *Miriamne e Mara* in the tomb. Beyond the questions of paleo-DNA and its reliability, the only thing that can be learned from their study is that *Yeshua bar Yehosef* and *Miriamne* are not family. This does not prove that they were married and since there is no DNA comparison to Judah, the hypothesis not only does not satisfy scholars, it is totally unintelligible to the general public. The names on the other ossuaries show us that the people in the tomb are not related to one another, since the inscriptions lacked connections like "daughter of . . . " and "son of . . . " This is one example of how archaeology can be used to create arguments that do not fully contribute to the study of biblical archaeology but do allow Minimalists and Maximalists to be totally confused about what constitutes evidence.

A seventh ossuary, from another private collector, also created its own problem related to the family of Jesus since it lists *James, the son of Joseph, the brother of Jesus* on the side, and the meticulous study of this inscription has revealed parts of it to be unreliable. The fact that the seventh ossuary was in the hands of a private collector, rather than in the original site with the others, immediately created problems for the scientific acceptance of its authenticity, but again, without the modern study of the historical Jesus, the artifact is almost unintelligible as evidence for understanding Jesus of Nazareth. The so-called "James" ossuary led to a public controversy because when it was revealed a few years ago, it was the first such piece of archaeological evidence of the existence of Jesus that had ever been presented. Now, in light of the other six ossuaries from the Talpiot site, the whole question of how valuable these pieces are for the study of Jesus of Nazareth has become an issue. Some asked, is this "the" Jesus of Nazareth, and how is it that he had a brother James?

One part of the controversy revolves around whether or not the inscription is 100 percent the product of one hand in the first century CE or not. Since I had been working on my own study of Jesus in Rabbinic texts, I thought that it was important to compare what can be known from this inscription as well. It appears that the Aramaic inscription of *James son of Joseph* is original, even though it is possible that "brother of Jesus" was an ancient formula that could be validated by other inscriptions. Some people ask how can we know which James and Joseph are meant? James and Joseph are common names in antiquity. If this James is the same James that continued in the Church and died, according to Christian tradition, a martyr's death in Jerusalem in 62 CE, additional information in the inscription, such as "... brother of Jesus," might be important to identify him with the Jesus movement he was a part of. James was particularly venerated by the Church that became the Greek Orthodox Church, so it is possible that the original ossuary of this *James son of Joseph* may have been recognized for special designation as the ossuary of "the" James, who was the brother of Jesus, and the inscription was added to by Church officials in antiquity to distinguish it from any other ossuary with a similar distinction.

Interestingly enough, later fourth century traditions were divided on whether Jesus had any brothers or not. In a number of ancient Church traditions, James was in fact a full brother of Jesus; therefore, the words, "brother of Jesus" may have been added in an attempt to establish without question, a few centuries after the original burial, that this was indeed, the famed James of the Jerusalem Church. Another possibility is that this is an ancient "relic," and the inscription is an ancient addition for establishing the relic's importance. The discovery of these ossuaries immediately started a firestorm on issues relating to the varying traditions about Jesus and the Holy Family, but in order to understand these issues one has to first accept the modern study of historical Jesus information and its methodologies. Alternative Gospels, the so-called Gnostic Gospels, for example, include a panoply of traditions that did not make it into the canonical Gospels and include additional information about his family. In the second century CE, Irenaeus (*Against the*

Heresies) tells us that the Ebionites, a group of Jewish-Christians, denied the virgin birth and believed Mary was the mother of other children, including what would have been biological brothers and sisters to Jesus. Jerome, the fourth-century Church father who worked in Israel on the translation of the Hebrew Bible and New Testament into Latin, in his work, *Against Helvidius*, expressed the view that although Jesus is said to have "brothers" and "sisters" in Mark 6:3 (also Matthew 13:55–56), and James is called Jesus' brother (along with four other men; at least two unnamed sisters), the term used in the Greek New Testament really means the equivalent of "cousins." Eusebius, a fourth-century bishop of Caesarea, had the tradition that James was the son of Joseph's brother and therefore a cousin to Jesus. On the other side of the question is the view held by Epiphanius (*Panarion*) that Mary was Jesus' mother but not James' because Joseph had a wife prior to his marriage to Mary. This view is bolstered by a belief that Joseph was much older than Mary and explains Joseph's early departure from any listing in the Gospel accounts. All of this shows us just how complex it is to contextualize one artifact with the varying textual traditions of antiquity even with a famous person such as Jesus of Nazareth.

Although I differentiate between the early movement that surrounded Jesus and the Jesus of Christianity, it is a difficult task to connect any single artifact with this early movement. Our own experience at Bethsaida has showed us just how problematic it can be. Over a decade ago, we discov-

Figure 3.2.   The Cross of Bethsaida.

Courtesy Bethsaida Excavations Project

ered what appeared to be a "cross" on a piece of pottery at Bethsaida, in figure 3.2, creating enough controversy that this single piece of pottery from Bethsaida appeared on every major television news station for two or three days. CNN, NBC Nightly News, and CBS Evening News all had two- to-three-minute segments on it. We featured it on the first volume of our book, *Bethsaida: A City by the North Shore of the Sea of Galilee,* and many people have asked about the significance of the piece. The shard was not intact as it was missing either the bottom or top of the long cross bar, but it was indeed a very prominent cross from the side of a large jar. The cross (or the crucifix) is probably the most well-known Christian symbol of all time, but it was not used in the first century CE. The fish or symbols associated with fishing were the symbols of the early followers of Jesus of Nazareth, and it was found in many settings in Galilee. But a cross on a single piece of pottery at Bethsaida, home of the Apostles and the place where Jesus first met with them, was unusual because the cross only became the symbol of Christianity in the fourth century CE, some four centuries later than the piece of pottery at Bethsaida. No name appeared on the pottery, but it was found near the fisherman's house where the famous "Key of Peter" had been found. Was it a coincidence, or did the disciples at Bethsaida really use the cross as a symbol of their work in first-century Bethsaida?

The cross was famous for perhaps a thousand years before it was a symbol for Christianity as the symbol of the sun, and the rays emanating out from a center look very similar to the cross as it developed in the West and the East. But the cross on the Bethsaida pottery was not easily resolved. We have found scores of crosses on other pieces of pottery, first-century pottery at Bethsaida, and although it may have become the symbol of the crucifixion in later Christianity, I suspected that it meant something very different in first-century Bethsaida. I think the cross at Bethsaida was, like all other symbols of the early disciples of Jesus, a symbol of the major profession of the Apostles as fishermen. The cross, you see, is not just a cross, it is usually together with an anchor at the bottom as pictured in figure 3.3. I think that the famous cross of Bethsaida was missing the anchor at the bottom, but it still tells us much about how the Jesus movement may have developed into Christianity, taking the symbols of its past with it. Throughout the Coptic Church in Egypt, for example, the anchor cross continued to be used as the symbol of Christianity. I think the anchor, the symbol of the profession of the Apostles, changed into a symbol of the crucifixion of Jesus, as the ancient traditions of Jewish Galilee became the early Church with a new and distinctive identity. At the same time, the ancient Jewish traditions of Jesus of Nazareth faded from memory, and they were replaced in Jewish life

Figure 3.3.   An anchor cross on a pottery handle from Bethsaida.

Courtesy Bethsaida Excavations Project.

with Rabbinic traditions of a totally different Jesus of Nazareth.

Although it's possible that we'll find an artifact to add to our body of knowledge, we are really at the mercy of literary studies in order to understand the historical Jesus. Each of the literary traditions from apocryphal, Church traditions and even Rabbinic texts carry a part of the "truth" of Jesus' life. As the Jewish Jesus movement developed into Christianity, the traditions about Jesus that had been preserved within Judaism seem to have diminished. Church traditions, while distinctive, rarely preserved information that challenged the Church's developing views of Jesus. The Jesus of Rabbinic literature, however, shows an entirely different literary tradition than the Gospels and Church traditions. It may not be informed by the written Gospels or the Church traditions, but as an ancient view, it is worth studying.

The Jesus of Rabbinic literature was in fact known to the Church and regularly challenged in the first three centuries of Christianity. These Rabbinic traditions of Jesus are those produced in Babylonia (and not Israel), and so I call him "Jesus of the Babylonian Jews" rather than Jesus of Nazareth. More important, Christianity never made inroads in Babylonia, and when these traditions were written down, the Jews of Babylonia had scant information on the historical Jesus of Nazareth. Simply put, Babylonian society, in general, and Babylonian Jewry, in particular, knew far less about Jesus of Nazareth than any other Jewish Diaspora community, and yet they produced the only traditions about Jesus that were preserved in Rabbinic literature. Yet, because of the influence of the Babylonian academies and the overarching importance of the Babylonian Talmud, their view of Jesus became the most important source of information for all Jews worldwide. This Jesus is very different than Jesus in Christian sources and Jesus in the Muslim's Koran and the Hadith. Islam has a heterodox view of Jesus. In Islam, Jesus was not crucified and the virgin birth never could occur. He was a prophet, like the other thousands of prophets that had appeared in history to speak in the name of Allah, the universal God. It is perhaps unfair to judge the Rabbinic understanding of Jesus from these late Babylonian sources, but to the Rabbis in the Middle Ages living under Islam and Christianity, these sources relate how Jews in another area of the world received information about a Jew from Galilee. The Rabbis are not the only Jewish source of information on Jesus.

Josephus, the Jewish historian of the first century CE, may have been alive when Jesus was walking through Galilee and the Golan and does preserve a tradition or two about Jesus. By the time Josephus wrote his *Jewish Antiquities*, these traditions were at least a generation after Jesus was no longer living but many of the Apostles were still alive when Josephus was writing. His observations are different from the Jesus of Nazareth found in the New Testament and Christianity but very different from what became the Babylonian Jesus of Nazareth. Many scholars think that Josephus' testimony about Jesus sounds very contrived and formulaic and is missing the pieces of information that only a Galilean like Josephus would have had. Some suspect that the references to Jesus in Josephus were emendations made by well-meaning Church scribes who could not understand why Jesus was not mentioned by Josephus.

In the nineteenth century, as *Wissenschaft* scholars of Rabbinics began to reassess the narratives of Rabbinic literature to reconstruct a critical view of Jewish history, the status of Christians, Jesus, and the entire Greco-Roman period began to be reinvestigated. Before the modern period, many late Rabbinic texts from the Talmudim (and post-Talmudic works such as *Masechet Sopherim*) to the *Zohar*, used, reused, and recombined earlier Rabbinic texts relating to Jesus. In the late eighteenth and early nineteenth centuries, Jews attempted to understand their own history by reinvestigating the historical texts of Judaism. In the early period of *Wissenschaft* scholarship, many of the texts relating to Christianity and Jesus were only partially reinvestigated. Often these texts were reinvestigated with only a minimal commitment to the critical examination of the texts themselves in a rush to determine an overall view of the period. Scholars such as Abraham Geiger, Heinrich Graetz, David Hoffmann, and Joseph Derenbourg, also contributed to some of the modern misunderstandings about the Rabbinic Jesus, precisely because they were perceived to be writing in a time of critical historical research that was totally objective. However, some of this perceived objectivity allowed a newer, more sophisticated misunderstanding of Jesus in Rabbinic literature to occur.

Later Jewish and Christian writers such as Emil Scheuer, Hermann Strack, Louis Finkelstein, George Foot Moore, Gustaf Dalman, Adolf von Harnak, and others began to move toward a "dialogue of sorts" in researching Rabbinic texts in light of New Testament and early Christian literature (and vice versa). The goal of this early twentieth-century work was to determine parallels for the sake of comparison. Unfortunately, this work was often done with a "higher criticism" or overall ideological model in mind, and limited attention was given to the fundamental questions of "lower criticism" or the status of the manuscript readings of the texts themselves.

In the twentieth century, new understandings of Jewish history forced pre- and post-WWII scholars such as Samuel Sandmel, David Flusser, James Parkes, Solomon Zeitlin, W. D. Davies, Ellis Rivkin, David Daube, and many others to reassess the work of the nineteenth- and early twentieth-century scholars. Some Christian scholars were more interested in the "historical Jesus" than earlier generations, and the discovery in the 1945 Nag Hammadi and 1947 Dead Sea Scrolls made the comparison of the varying versions of Jesus' life and history more compelling. Unfortunately, the Jewish and Christian reassessments of the historical Jesus in the post-WWII era were often colored by the Holocaust and its implications. Thus, the post-WWII search for the historical Jesus became a vehicle for the search for reconciliation and dialogue between Jews and Christians. Often, this search was conducted at the expense of the demands of problematics of critical New Testament and Rabbinic textual studies and did not advance our understanding of the Jesus of Rabbinic literature.

Deep-seated passions lurked behind this question of the Jesus of Rabbinic literature in the minds of the general Jewish and Christian population. The Christian view, derived from an interpretation of the Gospels, was that the Jews in general and the Rabbis in particular, were somehow complicit in the conviction and execution of Jesus. Conventional Protestant nineteenth- and early twentieth-century wisdom held that Jesus was a revolutionary against Rabbinic Judaism of his period and therefore that it was fruitless to investigate the Jesus of Rabbinic literature. The use of Rabbinic texts by some nineteenth- and early twentieth-century Christian scholars often tended to reinforce stereotypes known to Christians from Gospel interpretations or to gloss over them completely in order to not worsen developing Jewish-Christian relations in the modern period.

On the Jewish side, the new era of Jewish research in the nineteenth and twentieth century yielded an opportunity to dispel old stereotypes and reresearch ancient topics. After a nearly fifteen-hundred-year history of disputation, ghettoization, and persecution of Jews in Christian Europe and elsewhere *seemingly* in the name of Jesus, the research topic of "Jesus in Rabbinic Literature" was a difficult topic even for dispassionate European Jewish scholars. In the twentieth century, one need only mention the controversies created in the Jewish communities of Palestine and later Israel upon the publication of the scholar (Modern Hebrew) Joseph Klauzner's tomes, *Yeshu HaNotzri* (Jesus of Nazareth), and *MiYeshu ad Paulus* (From Jesus to Paul) and in the United States and Israel over the Yiddish writings of Scholom Asch's *The Nazarene, The Apostle* and *Mary,* just before, during, and directly after the Holocaust in order to understand how deep the question goes in the Jewish consciousness. Most recently, the rise of groups such as "Jews for Jesus" and other so-called Hebrew-Christian groups in the United States and Europe who use such materials to demonstrate one element or another in their group's ideology has complicated the serious research into the topic. In short, it is difficult to write critically about the Jesus of Rabbinic literature without recognizing the history of the issue even in the modern period.

Lower and Higher Criticisms of the Textual Information

One problem of researching Jesus in Rabbinic literature is that modern scholars did not or could not research how these Rabbinic sources originated and were transmitted to determine whether they were reliable sources. "Lower and higher criticisms" are the two names given to the studies of the text that can be done by modern scholars who examine the ancient and medieval textual traditions of a text. The "lower" criticism is comparing the text internally and how the text was passed on from generation to generation. It establishes the problems of the text that can only be resolved by meticulous studies of the manuscripts and to correct errors that may have gotten into the text as it was transmitted by imperfect scribes. There is a singular problem with the Jesus and Christian references in Rabbinic (and other Jewish) texts that will be addressed later in this chapter, but it is the cause of many questions about the reliability of any of the manuscript readings which we use today for research about Jesus. Rabbinic texts were systematically destroyed in the Middle Ages from the period of the Crusades through the Renaissance by overbearing Church officials throughout Europe. Because of this, few complete manuscripts of the Talmud survived into the modern period, and those that did needed to be carefully checked for accuracy. More important, medieval Church officials took to systematically censoring those manuscripts that did exist by changing or exorcising references to Jesus and Christians from Rabbinic texts. As we shall see, even when they were restored by *Wissenschaft* scholars in the modern period, they are not fully reliable. The tension that had developed between Church officials and the Jewish communities of Europe created a situation where texts became a tool for disputes and conversion. Thus, as we speak of lower criticism of Jesus texts in Rabbinic literature, this is a crucial issue. Only after we have done the lower criticism can "higher" criticism be done. Higher criticism involves the comparison of a text with other texts written from around the same time period but which preserve totally different traditions. I have been doing both lower and higher criticism in this book.

It is important to recognize just how difficult it is to compare traditions about Jesus. The New Testament preserves different versions of Jesus' life, and we have to compare and contrast manuscript readings to know exactly what the New Testament says Jesus did and did not say and do. We know that the New Testament writers had different traditions when they wrote their Gospels down in the end of the first century CE, but the manuscripts changed with the development of Christianity. While the physical resurrection of Jesus was known to some writers, others did not have this tradition. When Christianity developed, the resurrection was too important to not be a part of all of the Gospels, so the Gospel according to Mark (Mark 16 just seems to end in verse 8), for example, which does not have a resurrection scene like Matthew and Luke, has a later manuscript tradition which added an appropriate resurrection scene in Mark 16:9–20, which became the norm. Lower criticism allows us to compare and contrast the manuscripts and internal evidence to see what the text really said in its original form. Higher criticism asks questions about what a text means when it is compared to other texts from the period.

Higher and lower criticisms are very difficult in Rabbinic texts because of the problems that Jews faced in maintaining their traditions among Christians and Muslims in the lands of their dispersions. Many studies of Jesus and early Christianity in Rabbinic literature bunch together sources from different periods, assuming that Rabbinic literature was one continuous work. Robert Travers Herford made a first attempt to investigate the different historical layers of Rabbinic texts in his now classic *Christianity in Talmud and Midrash*. In this book, Herford collected possible references to Jesus and Christianity from the Talmud and Midrash. His work, when it appeared in 1903, was a landmark achievement and established the existence of an extensive literature contemporaneous with the New Testament and apostolic teachings and became a source of information on Jesus and the origins of early Christianity. This book demonstrated in stark and compelling ways the complexity of Rabbinic literature and understanding of the development of Jesus in Rabbinic literature.

Ancient Sources for the Jesus of Rabbinic Literature

So how long does the memory of an individual who lived in history survive in popular consciousness? Investigating ancient literature for references of a person helps address this question. Five contemporaneous sources of potential information of the Jewish view of Jesus survived into the modern period. They are the New Testament, Josephus, Philo, Jewish papyri (other writings), and the Tannaitic levels of Rabbinic literature. If

we do "higher" criticism, we can compare and contrast what these contemporaneous sources tell us about Jesus. Do they include information
that is similar to or different from the text of the New Testament? These
last four sources (Philo, Josephus, Jewish papyri/inscriptions, Tannaitic
Rabbinic texts) do not specifically mention Jesus as related in the Gospels
at all. The Tannaitic literature was probably written down for the first
time in approximately the mid-third century CE, and if any Rabbinic
writing is going to reflect a "real" Jesus, it should be in these texts, but it
is not. Josephus recorded in great detail the events and figures of Judaism,
especially Galilean Judaism, which he knew intimately in the first century
CE. But the early Church used and recopied Josephus' writings, which
most scholars think the Church may have emended to feature Jesus. The
Church emended many parts of the New Testament that did not meet
the changing and developing traditions of the Church. Just like the New
Testament manuscripts were changed to reflect Christian traditions such
as the resurrection, we might assume that the same thing happened to the
text of Josephus because it too became a part of Church tradition. I do
not think the Jesus sections of Josephus were originally written by Josephus Flavius, but it is important because whoever inserted it in Josephus'
writings knew that these books were seen as an important Jewish source
of the period for Christian history. Josephus' multi-volume *Antiquities*
starts with the creation of the universe and continues through nearly the
end of the first century CE when Josephus died. His writings are the only
full history of the Jews, from the Hebrew Bible to the New Testament
period and since early Christians saw themselves as the true continuation
of the biblical story, Josephus could not be overlooked. The Jesus section
in Josephus' *Antiquities* 18:63–64 describes Jesus in the following way:

> About this time there lived Jesus, a wise man, if indeed one ought to call
> him a man. For he was one who wrought surprising feats and was a teacher
> of such people as accept the truth gladly. He won over many Jews and
> many of the Greeks. He was the Messiah. When Pilate, upon hearing him
> accused by men of the highest standing among us, had condemned him
> to be crucified, those who had in their first place come to love him did
> not give up their affection for him. On the third day he appeared to them
> restored to life, for the prophets of God had prophesied these and countless
> other marvelous things about him. And the tribe of the Christians, so called
> after him, has still to this day not disappeared.

The context of the Jesus passage in Josephus is odd. The terminology
and extremely formulistic language—"He was the Messiah" and "On the

third day he appeared to them restored to life, for the prophets of God had prophesied these and countless other marvelous things about him"—is very close to formulas of the early Church that refer to Jesus. I have checked numerous writings by Church Fathers from the time of the Byzantine Church, and it is the way that many of them refer to the life of Jesus of Nazareth. Also, in the preceding and subsequent sections in the *Antiquities* (18:62 and 18:65), Josephus writes about a sedition plot against Pilate by a group in Jerusalem and then another group which is planning sedition in Rome. To me, it looks like it was just inserted here because of the Pilate reference, but it is generally the right time period for it to appear (if it was going to appear in Josephus' writings). It is also possible that we are looking at a text that preserves parts of the original Josephus language but were altered to make them fit later Church doctrines. The second Jesus reference in Josephus in *Antiquities* 20:9 appears to have some original Josephus language and some formulaic pieces that were inserted in the midst of it.

> And so he convened the judges of the Sanhedrin
> and brought before them a man James, the
> brother of Jesus, who was called the Christ (Messiah),
> and certain others . . .

I have always been intrigued by the Josephus formulation here: "James, the brother of Jesus." The text became very important when the James ossuary was revealed to the public. The inscription on the ossuary "James, brother of Jesus" is very similar to the way James is described by Josephus. By the end of the first century and into the second century CE, this was one of the ways that James was being referred to. It is possible that this may have indirectly influenced whoever added the words, "James, brother of Jesus" to the ossuary in antiquity. I realized that the same hand of the early Church that may have provided the text in Josephus may have been responsible for the ossuary's rather extensive inscription. These two references are the only evidence in Josephus of his knowledge of a "Jesus" since Josephus' other works, *Wars* and the *Life* lack any references to this "Messiah/Christ." This is extremely questionable, because if Josephus did hold Jesus to be the Messiah, he probably would have written more about Jesus' influence (as he did about the Essenes, for example), but he didn't. Also, Josephus lived almost to the end of the first century in Rome where the influence of the followers of Jesus would have been known. These issues raise serious questions about whether this first-century writer had any substantive information about Jesus.

I think that Josephus, the Galilean expert, seems to have had little or no knowledge of the New Testament's Jesus of Nazareth and his works. Only a vague, wise, and great teacher who is a Messiah, like many others that he mentions in his work. I will point out one other strange fact. Josephus does not even mention Nazareth in his writings, leading many to suspect that Nazareth may not even have been considered a Jewish village in his time period. Apparently, he was so focused on the larger Jewish communities of Galilee that he does not know about these itinerant teachers, such as Jesus, who roamed the smaller villages of Galilee. Many scholars have argued either against or for the authenticity of these "Jesus" sections in Josephus. Some scholars ask: why wouldn't Josephus know of Jesus? Others ask: why would he know of a single individual that was important to a small group in Galilee? This Jesus citation appears in almost all extant manuscripts of Josephus in one form or another, so it is hard to argue that it was emended in the manuscripts. The language and placement of the Jesus passages are a little odd (they interrupt the middle of a totally different discussion), but then Josephus wrote on a variety of issues and people in his writings, and they appear to be placed when he felt it was purposeful. Josephus' knowledge of Jesus of Nazareth, while not perfect, is important.

Josephus often recorded narratives that are reminiscent of, if not word-for-word examples of, traditions found in Rabbinic literature. This is to be expected since even though Josephus was not a Rabbi, he lived in the same time that Rabbinic literature was circulating in its oral phase of transmission. One example of these "parallel" traditions will suffice. Josephus (*Antiquities* 11:8) relates an account of Alexander the Great's meeting with the Samaritans during a visit to Israel, which parallels the narrative in the BT Yoma 69a, telling us something about the common roots of Alexander's information among the Jews. This famous meeting of Alexander and the local sages appears in almost every ancient literature. Alexander's meeting with the Jews is important for us because it is recorded in Josephus and in Rabbinic literature. The Rabbis and Josephus were both using ancient oral sources that they held to be true. Josephus' account contains much greater detail than the Rabbinic text, but the general outline of the story line is the same. A dispute arises between the Samaritans and Jews, Alexander goes to Jerusalem, meets the high priest, prostrates himself before him, sacrifices in the Jewish Temple are guaranteed, and the Samaritans are treated badly by Alexander. Josephus' Jewish Greek account is therefore linked with the Rabbinic tradition, which indicates some link between Rabbinic redaction of legendary materials and circulating Greco-Roman writings. Josephus and the Rabbis maintain parts of legendary materials that were circulating in their world. They chose to include in both of their very different literatures these legendary materials that were meaningful to them both. It is important to note that this Alexander the Great narrative occurs in the Babylonian Talmud without a direct indication of a Tannaitic source. This means that even the Babylonian Jews received some accurate oral traditions about events that occurred in ancient Israel in the Greco-Roman period. One might expect to find something about Jesus. Would it be as accurate as the Alexander the Great narratives is another question. Alexander the Great was seen by the Babylonian Jews as an unusual Gentile who affected Jewish history positively in many ways. Jesus was not seen in the same way by the Babylonian Jews. By the time the stories of Jesus were being written down by the Babylonian Jews, Constantine the Great had created a Christian Roman empire, and the Christians were now persecuting the Jews and ex-pagans in places such as Israel.

But other Jewish communities did have very close contact with Israel, Jerusalem, and the history of the Jewish community there. One very famous source of information on the early first century is Philo Judeaeus of Alexandria. He was born around 20 BCE, so he would have been an adult during the main period of Jesus' life. Yet in all of his voluminous writings, nothing is mentioned about Jesus, John the Baptist, Paul, or any of the other figures of the New Testament. He lived so close to the time of Jesus, was in direct contact with the Jews in Judea and Galilee, and yet seems to know none of this history.

Before I get to the Rabbinic writings, I want to say a word about other Jewish writings that were from this same period and from the same general region and which also do not mention Jesus. I have grouped them under the heading of Jewish papyri or inscriptions, but they are much more than this. Jews wrote letters, documents of all kinds, snippets of history and popular information, and not one of these writings has definitive information on Jesus, the Apostles, or Christians in general. The only references that have come to light recently are the burial ossuaries that we have discussed. I think the only other text that is even remotely in this category is a letter that Bar Kokhba writes condemning the "Galileans," which we think is his way of designating Christians, because they will not join his rebellion.

The Lower Criticism of the Babylonian Talmud: A Sad Tale

Although internal evidence shows that the Babylonian Talmudic text was completed in the sixth century CE, the earliest complete copy of the Babylonian Talmud extant today is only from a fourteenth-century manuscript (Munich, Codex 95). We do have some manuscript fragments of the Babylonian Talmud from the eighth to ninth century CE, but they are just fragments. Textual critics of the Talmud question: how can we be sure what is the correct reading some eight hundred years after its redaction? Unfortunately, it is because the Talmud was burned, and some of its pages were reused for other more valuable Church documents. It is, therefore, hard to say what the Babylonian Talmud originally said about Jesus. We just do not have a good textual witness that is really old. Also, in the Middle Ages there were censors of the Babylonian Talmud (some were converted ex-Jews) who were hired to censor out any negative comments about Jesus and Christianity.

The first printed complete edition of the Talmud was done by a Christian, Daniel Bomberg, in Venice between 1520–1523. Erratic censorship of manuscripts of the Talmud and other Rabbinic literature had been exercised during the Middle Ages, but the printings of the sixteenth and seventeenth centuries systematically and often replaced certain words of the Talmud that Christian (European) censors deemed offensive. Many of these censored texts involved sections concerning Jesus, (Jewish-Christian) sectarians, and various words for "non-Jew," so it is especially difficult to know what the original Talmudic texts did say about Jesus and Christianity. Word replacement was one way of compensating for the deletion, but often, blanks or new cognates were produced to replace the censored words or materials. Jewish printers in the eighteenth and nineteenth century continued this censorship, and although some small and often anonymous works that include the changes made by the censors were produced in the eighteenth and nineteenth century, they are far from complete and often restore the sixteenth- and seventeenth-century wordings that themselves had been censored. Even Sephardic Jews, living outside of Christian Europe, were susceptible to this censorship because manuscripts from European scribes often circulated among Sephardic Jews. In short, trying to reconstruct Jesus in Rabbinic literature is very difficult. One must begin with Tannaitic literature, look at the development of a story in early Amoraic literature, and then see how these Amoraic sources from the fourth to sixth century CE understood the earlier first- to third-century CE traditions.

Jesus in Rabbinic Literature: Tannaitic, Palestinian Talmudic Literature, and the Search for the Lost Stories of Jesus

The recent controversy over the *Judas Gospel* shows us how much we think we know and don't know about stories related to Jesus. The Judas Gospel was originally a part of the 1945 discovery of Christian texts at Nag Hammadi, Egypt. After being separated from the rest of the texts, it has only recently been represented to the public. In the canonical Gospels, Judas is a despicable character. One that became the very essence of what was wrong with the world. Judas betrays his teacher and friend, Jesus. He also is haunted by the memory of his betrayal and given a horrible death that formed the basis for much anti-Jud(aic) sentiment. But the *Judas Gospel* describes a totally different Judas and Jesus. Instead of Jesus being turned over to the Romans by Judas, Jesus instead turns himself in to the Romans. The idea of God's plan for the world, the mission of Jesus, and the role of Judas is all almost reversed from the canonical Gospels. This is not in and of itself remarkable. In addition to the four canonical Gospels of Jesus' life, we have four ancient complete noncanonical versions, seven fragmentary versions of Gospels, four versions known only from ancient quotations in ancient writers, and other sources that would give us a total of over twenty Gospels that were known in the first two centuries of the common era.

Totally unrelated to this are the traditions of the Rabbis that were related in Rabbinic literature. The development of a totally different tradition of the life and times of Jesus in Rabbinic literature begins with the references to Jesus in the earliest layer of Rabbinic literature, namely the Tannaitic level, which contains traditions and is dateable from approximately the first century BCE until the final editing of Tannaitic materials in the mid-third century CE. There is no mention of Jesus of Nazareth (by name) in any Tannaitic literature. In addition, the Palestinian Talmud edited by the fifth century CE (or the so-called Talmud of the Land of Israel) never mentions Jesus of Nazareth by name as well. This enormous corpus of work encompasses hundreds of pages, and the absence of any mention of Jesus of Nazareth in this Jewish "contemporary" literature of the Rabbis is thought-provoking. The Halakhic Midrashim (Sifra, Sifrei, Mekhilta), thousands of pages of narratives that continue to interpret the traditions and times of the Jews in Israel, do not contain any information on Jesus as well, despite the fact that they include long and sustained narratives on many different sages of the early centuries CE. I developed three different hypotheses for the absence of Jesus traditions in Tannaitic (early Rabbinic) literature:

1. These traditions were censored either early on (first to third century) or later (medieval) by Jews or non-Jews because of ideological reasons (the traditions were inflammatory, would lead Jews astray, were against Jewish law or concepts, etc.).
2. No traditions concerning Jesus of Nazareth were known to the Tannaitic Rabbis, those known were not deemed worthy of

preservation in these collections, or the type of literature was not appropriate for their preservation.

3. Jesus of Nazareth, as he was known by the Gospels, was not a significant individual for Rabbinic Jews.

But remarkably, traditions about a Jesus of Nazareth appear in the later Babylonian Talmud (completed in the fifth and sixth century CE), and they seem to have a view of a man who was privy to teachings about magic and healing from or in Egypt, taught these things and other elements to others in public, was not accepted by the Rabbis, apparently was put to death for a variety of different charges, and was seen as connected somehow with the Roman Government! A totally different Jesus. What is unusual here is that if these traditions are talking about a man from Galilee, why didn't the earlier Tannaitic and Palestinian Talmudic traditions preserve these traditions? Why were they suddenly appearing in a Babylonian context? There are named traditions that use code names like *Ben Stada* (Aramaic, literally "Son of the Cross") and *Ben Pantira* (Aramaic, literally "Son of the Virgin"), which can be associated with some known Jesus traditions, and they do add something about his uncertain birth, his powers of healing, his casting out of demons, and his trial in front of either Rabbinic and/or Roman courts, but they never call him Jesus. The *Ben Pantira* quote, found in many Rabbinic versions from Palestine and Babylonia but derived from a statement in the Tosefta Yevamot, established itself firmly in Babylonia. *Pantira* was thought to be a poor Aramiac transliteration of a Greek title (the Greek word *Parthenos,* Virgin and alluding to a Virgin birth) rather than a real name. *Pantera* is explained by the Babylonian Amora, Rav Hisda in the following way: "The husband [of the woman who bore Jesus] was *Ben Stada,* and the [biological] father is called: *Ben Pantira.*" In the BT Sanhedrin 67a, the questioning continues and other Rabbis suggest that the name of the woman who bore the illegitimate child was actually Mary, but she was nicknamed *Stada,* (and so the boy was called *Ben Stada*) because (they made the name into an Aramaic pun) *s'tat da* ("she was a woman who had been turned away") by her husband."

Much of what we hear about Jesus from Babylonian and later Rabbinic texts are confirmed by early Church literature. Justin Martyr (second century CE), Tertullian (third century CE), and Origen (third century CE) have pieces of the same traditions that make up the Jesus in Rabbinic literature. One of the more outstanding traditions is about Jesus being the son of a Roman soldier named *Pantera,* who impregnated a young woman, wife of a carpenter. Wandering about in Galilee, the boy, Jesus, eventually went down to Egypt, learned "magical arts" and then ended up returning and gathering a group of followers. The archaeological discovery of a real person named *Pantera* (Tiberius Julius Abdes Pantera, a Sidonian archer on an early first-century CE tombstone in Roman Germany), who might have been stationed in Israel in the late first century BCE/early first century CE, made the early Christian and Rabbinic texts even more feasible. When the *Pantera* inscription was published in the nineteenth century, scholars thought that evidence of the alternative tale of Jesus' birth had finally been found. Here was the *Pantera*, the father of the illegitimate son, Jesus, as mentioned in these texts. Unfortunately, like the ossuaries mentioned above, we cannot easily relate one single inscription in Germany to texts that were redacted sometime in the third- to fourth-century CE Babylonian texts. This *Pantera* tombstone may just be a Sidonian man named *Pantera* and have no connection at all to the Rabbinic tradition of *Ben Pantira*.

The Gnostic Gospels, the Babylonian and Palestinian Rabbis, and Jesus

So what were the sources of the Rabbinic information in the Babylonian Talmud? Knowing as we do how the oral traditions filtered to Babylonia, we can simply say they were oral traditions that were specific to the Babylonian Rabbis. Some of the information could have come from the canonized Gospels, but the lack of any of the major Gospels themes, such as the imminent *eschaton* (end) and messianship of Jesus, are troubling. Another source of early Christian information provides additional source material. Until 1945, it was possible to assume that the Rabbis possessed oral accounts that were passed piecemeal to Babylonia on trade routes. The discovery of the Nag Hammadi materials in 1945, however, demonstrated that other noncanonized Christian works may have circulated in non-Christian lands, such as Babylonia. A number of elements in the Rabbinic accounts lend themselves to this view:

1. The *Gospel According to Nicodemus*, a rather important Christian work that may have been written in the fourth century CE, contains the BT charge of the illegitimate birth of Jesus and the tradition of Jesus in Egypt where he learned magic just like Moses. Nicodemus was well known in the Christian tradition as being one of the Apostles of Jesus. In addition, it has the stoning and then crucifixion of Jesus by Pilate, apparently with the agreement of the Jews.

2. The Babylonian Talmud lists the five disciples in BT Sanhedrin 43a as *Matthai, Neqai, Netzer, Buni,* and *Todah. Neqai* could be an Aramaic clipped version of the Greek name, *Nico*(demus). The

Rabbis have a tradition in the BT Taanit 19b-20a of a man named *Naqdimon* ben Gurion, a rich individual of Jerusalem, whose nickname was Buni. Todah (Hebrew) is an interesting name since it is also found in the Gnostic Gospel of the *Second Apocalypse of James* and may be the Theudas (Greek transliteration of Hebrew) mentioned in a Josephus *Antiquities* 20:5 reference. In *Antiquities*, Theudas, who rose under Fadus, the procurator in Judea in 45 CE, is said to have: "... persuaded a great part of the people to take their effects with them, and follow him to the river Jordan, for he told them he was a prophet, and that he would, by his own command, divide the river and afford them an easy passage over it; and many were deluded by his words." So, in general, there are some known "Apostles" to Jesus but the names do not correspond to the New Testament Apostles. Matthai is an interesting clipped version of Matthew but in general, it is difficult to find a correspondence between the names of the Apostles in the New Testament and the disciples in the Babylonian texts. The famous Tomb of Jesus ossuary had a Matia (another clipped form) as well.

3. In the Gnostic Gospels, (*The Second Apocalypse of James*, for example), the father of James is referred to as *Thuda* similar to the Babylonian Talmud text name, *Todah.*

4. The BT Gittin 57a account about Jesus in Hell is an odd parallel to the Gospel of Nicodemus' account of Christ's descent into Hell.

5. Some of the Gnostic Gospel traditions were, for example, preserved in the ancient Syriac Church. The tradition about Didymos Judas Thomas, for example, the twin brother and Apostle of Jesus is echoed in the Syriac Church. The *Gospel of Thomas* and the *Book of Thomas the Contender* set out traditions about the two different careers of Jesus and Judah Thomas. The Tosephta Sanhedrin 9.7 has a possible parallel with this. Rabbi Meir states:

"What is the meaning of (Deut. 21:23); 'For a curse of God is he that is hung'? [It is the case of] of two brothers, twins, who resembled one another. One ruled over the whole world, the other took to robbery. After a time the one who took to robbery was caught, and they crucified him on a cross. And every one who passed back and forth said: 'It seems that the king has been crucified.' Therefore it is said; 'For a curse of God is he that is hung.'"

Does this Tosephta preserve an ancient Jewish story about Jesus? The Rabbis, even the Rabbis of Palestine, seem to have some heterodox traditions of the life and the death of Jesus in general. These traditions may be Gnostic traditions that circulated through Syrian and Alexandrian Christianity into the rest of the Middle East, or they just appear to be similar versions of stories that were circulating about Jesus in antiquity. The importance of a physical resurrection of Jesus to some Synoptic writers in the canonized New Testament or normative Christianity is apparent. This is clear in Matthew and Luke, although they do not agree about the number or place of these resurrections. Matthew, for example, has physical resurrections of Jesus in Jerusalem and Galilee, while Luke has only an appearance of Jesus in Jerusalem. The original Mark manuscripts did not contain a resurrection scene at all, although it was added in later medieval manuscripts. In Gnostic Christianity, this main tenet of the Church, the physical resurrection of Jesus, does not appear to be central. In fact in the *Treatise on Resurrection*, the *Exegesis on the Soul* and the *Gospel of Philip*, demonstrate that for these Gnostic Christians resurrection was a spiritual idea and not a physical reality. Instead of the New Testament's *eschaton*, these Gnostic texts offer an "end of history" scenario and the return of the "human sparks" to the Kingdom of Light. The exclusive messianship of Jesus is part of a Gnostic larger scheme in which the different counterparts of the unknown God are manifested in a number of forms. An ancient Christian teacher, Basilides, taught, for example, the existence of six spiritual powers of which the Christ was only one.

These issues may explain, in part, why the Rabbis in Babylonia commenting on the myth of Jesus have no references to the central issues of the NT; that is, the messiahship of Jesus and the Eschaton. Their sources may have been heterodox Christians and Christianity and the details of the Gospel of Nicodemus provide enough context for many of the events mentioned by the Rabbis.

Conclusions

First, let me conclude with a note about how difficult any of this work on Jesus in Rabbinic literature is in light of the treatment of Jewish texts in the Middle Ages and even into the Modern period. Starting in the Middle Ages, learned Christians decided to undertake a systematic censorship of all of the materials that seemed to mention Jesus, Christians, and anything disparaging about "sectarians (*minim*)" or even some references to non-Jews. This systematic censorship continued for another five hundred years. In the seventeenth century, Jewish publishers of the printed Talmud even encouraged their own censorship in versions of the Babylonian Talmud to insure that it would not cause problems for the Jewish communities in Poland. I often feel when I look at the different versions of the traditions about Jesus that the traditions themselves are suspect not only because of this censorship but also because the traditions were often reinserted with emendations that made the Jesus tradition more difficult to follow. They took an already poor oral tradition and made it worse. Trying to reconstruct the "original" Rabbinic tradition is extremely complicated. Second, Jesus in Rabbinic tradition seems to have been accepted in different ways by differing Jewish groups in the Roman period in the region of the Mediterranean. The further removed these traditions are in time and place from Israel in the first century, the more estranged they became from the historical Jesus. Asia Minor and parts of Roman and Palestinian Jewish literature bear witness to this tendency. The relative silence of traditions about the Jesus story in the earliest strata of Rabbinic literature leads me to believe that perhaps nothing was really preserved by Rabbinic Jews in the period of Jesus' life.

Third, Rabbinic traditions seem to not be aware of Josephus' traditions nor does Josephus seem to know of the Rabbinic materials relating to the life of Jesus. This is not unusual since apparently Josephus was written in Greek and not circulated outside of the Roman (and later Christian) world. The Babylonian Talmud and many of the Midrashim were the product of Babylonian (non-Roman) society. The lack of early Rabbinic materials preserved in the Roman period (and influence) gives these Babylonian sources less credibility as representing anything like a historical Jesus.

1. The clear references to Jesus of Nazareth in Rabbinic texts are not necessarily from canonized Gospel information but may capture pieces of oral traditions that were circulating in noncanonized and Gnostic materials.
2. The unclear (but possible) references to Jesus in Rabbinic texts appear to be a mix of uncanonized and canonized traditions of different people that have been "collapsed" together.
3. The possible references to Jesus in classical Rabbinic texts do not present a positive, Rabbinic, heroic image of Jesus. They represent the types of stories that were circulating in the anti-Roman, Babylonian atmosphere where the majority of Jews lived in this period. It is possible that the Jews of Babylonia were not even aware of what Christianity was let alone who Jesus was.

There are a few reasons why I suspect the Jesus traditions did not make it into the earliest layers of Rabbinic literature that were written in the Land of Israel. It is possible that the Palestinian Talmud (PT) in particular did not present these traditions because of the fear of offending the Church, which by the time the PT was redacted had already become anti-Rabbinic in Israel. The absence of any fully developed Jesus of Nazareth story in Tannaitic Rabbinic writings, on the other hand, may be due to the challenge posed by the Jewish leadership model proposed by Jesus' ministry. The absence of Jesus in the Mishnah and Tosefta is similar to the absence of the entire story of the Maccabees from the Mishnah and Tosefta as well. You might assume that Hanukkah, the story of how a ragtag group of Maccabean fighters who took on the Syrian Greeks and won, would clearly be an important part of Rabbinic literature. The entire story does not even appear in the Mishnah and Tosefta, and it is only in the Babylonian Talmud that it appears; it is clear that the Babylonian Rabbis have no idea what the historical events of the story really were. There the Babylonian Rabbis start their discussion of the holiday by asking: "What is Hanukkah?" indicating just how little known it was in Babylonia. Some scholars assume that the redactor of the Mishnah, Rabbi Judah the Prince, left the story of the Maccabees out of Tannaitic Rabbinic literature because they wanted to leave out any mention of another war against Greco-Roman forces. By the time Rabbi Judah finished redacting the Mishnah, it was after two horrific revolts against Rome in 70 CE and 132 CE that resulted in the devastation of the Land of Israel, and it perhaps seemed to him to be prudent to avoid any reference to another historical war in Rabbinic texts. Other scholars suspect that Rabbi Judah left out the Maccabees story from the Mishnah because the Maccabees were not non-Davidic leaders of the Jewish people in the period in which they governed. Rabbi Judah, a descendent of King David, was extremely sensitive to this issue, and the Hasmoneans were not of Davidic stock. Although some of the canonical Gospels tied Jesus to the Davidic tradition (through his father, Joseph), this was not the way Jesus was understood by the second and third centuries. The exclusion of Jesus traditions from the Tannaitic and Palestinian materials, therefore, may point to Judean Jewry's sensitivity to messianic leadership issues rather than complete ignorance of these traditions. By the time the Rabbinic texts were canonized, the Jesus movement was no longer a sect of Judaism but was already a separate Christian movement where Jesus represented a different messianic tradition. Therefore, the original versions of the Rabbinic Jesus, whatever they might be have been, were no longer a part of relevant Jewish religious literature.

The inclusion of a Jesus story in the writings of Josephus has been one of the great controversies in the study of Josephus in the modern period. It is true that the Church maintained, quoted, recopied, and used the Josephus writings throughout the Middle Ages as a major historical source. Therefore, the "formula-like" presentation of "Jesus, the wise man" and its inclusion in the writings of Josephus remains suspect. The obvious absence of a Jesus story in Philo's writings is particularly problematic, although the timing of the transmission of the story and the writings of Philo (first half of the first century CE) and his location in Alexandria may be the question. While clearly there were "Jesus followers" in Alexandria by the second half of the century, the timing of Philo's writing may be crucial. Perhaps information about Jesus did not reach Alexandria until after Philo was no longer on the scene. Josephus, on the other hand, wrote in the second half of the first century when the Jesus account was being circulated to a much larger audience than in the first half of the century. If a story about Jesus developed among the Jews (especially those outside of Israel), its importance must be relegated to the second half of the first century, coinciding with the missions of Paul and the establishment of the Church network that allowed Christianity to develop.

The absence of the named Jesus stories in parallel readings from the Palestinian Talmud is also perplexing. The Palestinian or Jerusalem Talmud is a product of fifth-century Galilee (close to the centers of Christianity in Jerusalem, Caesarea, and Antioch until the academy was closed in the fifth century CE), and one might expect some type of information on Christianity and Jesus. The absence of a named and clear Jesus figure in the Palestinian Talmud may indicate that a variety of different types of Roman period (and post-Roman period) messianic, heretical, and aberrant figures are being alluded to and collapsed into one more comprehensive literary figure in the Babylonian Rabbinic tradition. These traditions are not of the Jesus of Nazareth of the New Testament and of first century Palestine, but rather a composite literary figure who may not have lived at all.

Finally, the Rabbis of Babylonia, writing as they were in the fifth and sixth centuries in a land that was only indirectly informed about the Jesus and Christianity, are particularly unreliable sources of "real" information on Jesus either because the texts were not properly maintained (and therefore cannot be evaluated) or because their information is so faulty as to be unusable as a comparison text. To be sure, the BT narratives may tell us more about the different figures and controversies faced by Babylonian Jews in the fourth and fifth centuries CE than they do about an authentic or historically accurate Jesus the Jew of the first century.

4

Searching Her Stories:
Women in Ancient Israel

0   1   2cm

Courtesy Bethsaida Excavations Project

Figure 4.1.   Livia Julia statuette from Bethsaida.

The study of archaeology can be deeply intertwined with the study of social history, though archaeologists rarely recognize this connection. In particular, archaeology can reveal new and intimate details about the lives of women in the ancient period—details unmatched by other historical records. The study of women in antiquity can be particularly frustrating because of how few written records document their lives, but archaeology has lifted the veil on key details regarding several ancient women.

I have learned about women in ancient Israel at three excavation sites. Bethsaida, Tiberias, and the Cave of Letters have revealed how archaeology can unravel the complex social history of women in antiquity. In the year 2000, when we were excavating at the Cave of Letters, I invited one of the most famous female classics scholars, Professor Hannah Cotton of the Hebrew University, to tell me what she had learned about one of the most intriguing women of antiquity, Babatha. We brought Dr. Cotton to the place where the archives of Babatha were discovered in the Cave of Letters, and she described to us the life of this remarkable woman as understood in her archives. The documents were found in the Cave of Letters during Yigael Yadin's excavations, and at the time it was not known how important the documents of Babatha really were. Dr. Cotton had spent a long part of her career researching these documents, and the moment that she stepped into the area where the archives were found she was nearly overcome by emotion. She said: "I feel like I know this woman." As I sat there listening to her hour-long interview as we excavated (only a few minutes of the interview appeared in the television documentary on NOVA, "Ancient Refuge in the Holy Land") I felt as if she was "channeling" the spirit of Babatha. I think that archaeology has that kind of power when it is in the hands of a scholar who can interpret the social implications of discoveries. Good scholars can reveal elements about ancient people that are not otherwise accessible through documents and artifacts. For this reason, I include research I have done on women in antiquity who may not be well known, but who actually were catalysts in their own periods for an enormous amount of change. Much of this research is a combination of data from literary texts and archaeology.

Women and the Bible

In any book about archaeology and the Bible it is reasonable to look for information on both men and women in antiquity. If the demographics of ancient people were similar to our own, one would expect to find similar

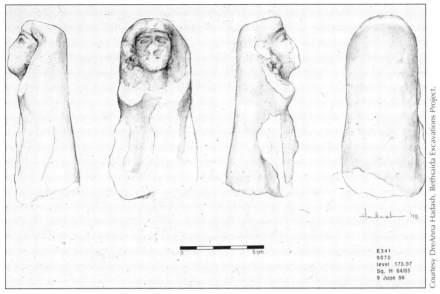

Figure 4.2.   Statuette of a woman from the Iron Age.

kinds of evidence about both men and women. Unfortunately, most archaeology texts rarely deal with the differences in archaeological finds between men and women, even though women are connected to a substantial amount of artifacts and remains on any archaeological site. Although most people don't realize it, the lives of men and women were quite separate in antiquity. The household and its sundry artifacts from flints, cooking pots, storage jars, and spinning whorls were not the exclusive domain of women, but they were used by far more women than men in antiquity. Since these artifacts are the most ubiquitous finds at an excavation, one might think that we know a lot about women in antiquity from archaeology. In fact, we know very little about the lives of women because so little of the textual information that survived is devoted to the lives of women. All of these items would have been a part of any woman's typical day at an ancient site. The feeding and hydrating of the family, the preparation of food for family and livestock, jewelry, cosmetics, and various personal items, all are routine finds at an archaeological site. Women's religion is far less known than daily life. Based on textual information and archaeology, it seems that the religions of men and women in antiquity were probably quite different from each other. The ever-present goddess statuettes at most Israelite sites would have been used by women for protection of the entire family's welfare but were especially a part of women's religion.

One statuette that we found at Bethsaida reminded me of this role. The clay-standing female figurine is holding what we assume to be a tambourine in her hand (figure 4.2). Similar figures are often found around Israel from the Iron Age, representing parts of religious life that we know little about. More complete clay figurines like this one have been located all over the ancient Near East. Her earring and Egyptian Hathor hairstyle demonstrate the type of goddess figurine that would have been common among women of the Iron Age. She was a symbol of hope, enjoyment, and the role of music in her devotion. These finds tell us not only about tambourines, hairstyles, and earrings, but also establish connections with textual references that are often obscured without these discoveries.

In one of the earliest accounts featuring women in the book of Exodus, this tambourine woman has new meaning. Following the crossing of the (Red) Reed Sea, the Israelites join in singing a "Song of the Sea" and Miriam, the sister of Moses, picks up a tambourine and sings and dances to the *Song of the Sea*. Is she fulfilling a common part of women's religion in antiquity? If not for the discovery of small figurines at sites like Bethsaida, we would never be able to fully understand the meaning of the biblical episode at the Reed Sea. This small figurine at Bethsaida connects the people there to a goddess performing a similar task in antiquity. To judge from ancient texts and our archaeological finds of the ancient Near East, many ancient rituals were allocated to women and others to men. In fact, at any archaeological site, it would be very difficult to identify artifacts that were exclusively used by men in antiquity. Yet, studies about ancient women that utilize archaeology are few and far between.

The role of women in antiquity is immense and beyond the scope of this book, but since I have learned about women at three separate excavations, I felt that it was incumbent upon me to share the results of this work, first, to demonstrate how difficult it is to recover information about women in antiquity, and also because the study of women in antiquity through evidence proves the rule about the role of archaeology in illuminating the Bible—it is only as good as the interpreters of the data. Women were mothers, daughters, sisters, wives, and just women in antiquity. We know that women were matriarchs of tribes, judges, prophets, and queens in ancient Israel, and even, according to some modern writers, scribes of some note. *The Book of J* by Harold Bloom and David Rosenberg (1990) suggested that women may have been involved with writing down some of the most important and oldest traditions of the Hebrew Bible. All of these traditions point to a parallel understanding of women's role in society that allowed them a similar status to men in society. However, little of what they did was recorded in the "official" version of the religion of ancient Israel that is communicated to the public.

New studies about the role of the goddess in ancient Israel suggest that the goddess was a very prominent part of Israelite religion until the rise of a more absolute (male God-dominated) monotheism, which occurred perhaps as late as the post-Exile return of the Judeans from Babylonia. The returnees may have done away with the separate roles of the divinities and collapsed them into a single, male God. In *Did God Have A Wife?* (2005), famed archaeologist William Dever concludes that women in antiquity functioned in a parallel "folk religion" that was different from the men's official religion. This folk religion presumably is preserved only in archaeology and material culture and by reading between the lines of the Bible. Archaeology may preserve information on women that would not otherwise be preserved in literary traditions.

Archaeologists have found very few artifacts from specific women in the Bible, although many items used by women in antiquity have been found. Textual information is important to understand these finds, but material findings must be connected with specific women to comprehend how these women really lived. We know much about women in Egypt. For example, women served as pharaoh. Unfortunately, because it was so unusual, little about women's lives was written in Egypt. Our traditions about women from antiquity generally appear to show us how women interacted with men in society. It is rare to find archaeological information that would enlighten us about a stand-alone woman in history, such as Miriam.

Some women of antiquity invite interest in the Bible because they were evil. The Jezreel excavations in Galilee, for example, provided some archaeological background for the life of one of the Bible's most notorious women, Jezebel. Jezebel, wife of King Ahab of northern Israel, of the biblical book of 1 Kings fame is probably the most well known and atypical women of the Bible. In one of the sequences in the documentary by the Biblical Archaeology Society, *From the Ground Down*, Professor David Ussishkin, the archaeologist who excavated ancient Jezreel, was asked if he could relate the story that occurred at "the ruins of a stone tower at Jezreel, from which Queen Jezebel was thrown down, murdered and eaten by dogs." Archaeology had identified Jezreel, the excavations had revealed a large tower, the road going by it was clear, it was from the right historical period. What more do we know about this woman from these excavations? Very little. Who was she? How had she achieved such an elevated position in the northern Israelite kingdom of Ahab? Why was she so despised by the writers of the Bible? All of this cannot be understood from the archaeology, but it helps to see that elements from the story are accurate.

At Mount Tabor, a Galilee site nearby the Jezreel Valley, we have a site associated with the ancient Israelite judge, Deborah, yet no archaeology from the site matches the Iron Age when Deborah would have been judging. She was one of the most famous and successful Israelite judges (eleventh century BCE), yet little or nothing is understood about her life from the archaeology. We would like to know more about why Deborah was able to be a "judge" in a period in which most judges were male. What qualities of leadership did she possess? Did she have a family? Was she different from other women of the period? None of this can be discerned from the archaeology, and the text is basically silent on these issues.

Several infamous relic tombs of women are venerated by Jews, Christians, and Muslims alike. The most famous are the tomb of Rachel, the wife of Jacob, outside of Bethlehem; the tombs of the Matriarchs Sarah, wife of Abraham, Rebecca, wife of Isaac, Leah, another wife of Jacob, who are all buried in the Machpelah Cave in Hebron. One of the most overlooked relic burial sites, the tomb of the Matriarchs in Tiberias includes many of the overlooked women from the biblical period, such as Bilhah and Zilpah, the other "wives" of Jacob; Yocheved, the mother of Moses, Aaron, and Miriam, Tzippora, the wife of Moses, Elisheva, the wife of Aaron, and Avigail, a wife of David. Every time I show these tombs to students they are surprised to learn that all of these women were brought together on this hilltop in Tiberias to be buried together, despite having lived and died in vastly different locations throughout Israel. Little or nothing about these women is found in the texts of the Bible so it is even more curious why their burial sites became important. Some of these relic sites have more reliable and more ancient traditions than others. This latter set of women have few citations in the literary traditions of the Bible, but they were enlivened in Rabbinic and Christian medieval lore. The tombs are considered relics because many believe they date from the ancient Israelite period—yet no scientific information corroborates this identification. How did these sites originate? Some oral tradition of women, often revelations, bring people to this spot. Tiberias, a city on the shore of the Sea of Galilee that was built up in the first century CE, is an unusual setting because so many of the burials of ancient holy figures are found in one location. From Rabbi Akiva's burial spot on top of the hill overlooking the city to Rabban Yohanan ben Zakkai's burial below it, scores of holy Jewish and biblical figures are found in close proximity to one another. These burials were and continue to be pilgrimage sites, usually established in the Middle Ages based upon oral traditions that were transferred into literary traditions by travelers and pilgrims who visited the site.

Although we have a view as to what women looked like in this period, how they dressed, and perhaps even what they did with their lives in general, it is never specific to a single individual. Many anonymous women in the literary traditions of the Bible were given names in later religious literature to personalize them. Some of these women are linked with archaeology, others not. The next sections explore many women that are named and unnamed in the texts of the Hebrew Bible, the New Testament, and in other ancient texts. Four of these women have been brought alive by archaeology and some of the archaeologists that I have known. Livia Julia became a real person through the work of my colleagues on the Bethsaida Excavations Project, especially Dr. Fred Strickert and Dr. Elizabeth McNamer, who spent years researching aspects of Livia's life and death as reflected on coins and texts. Berenice I came to understand through the work of Dr. Yizhar Hirschfeld at Berenice, an archaeological site that is named for her just above the city of Tiberias in northern Israel. Babatha was brought to life by the work of Dr. Hannah Cotton of the Hebrew University who has been writing about Babatha's life for the past two decades. The final woman I review in this chapter is Beruriah, the wife of Rabbi Meir, a Rabbinic sage of singular importance in the second century CE. Beruriah became a real person to me after I visited the graves of the Rabbinic sages and their spouses that are found in the hills around Tiberias and noticed that she was missing. Her absence is as important as her story. I have come to understand from these women much about how textual information informs archaeology and archaeology informs textual information. These four women, Livia Julia, Berenice, Babatha, and Beruriah, who all lived within a century of one another, may or may not known about each other, but their stories do inform us about the period.

Finding One Woman in Antiquity

If finding one man in antiquity is difficult, it is even more difficult to find one woman, even a very important woman, in antiquity. I came to understand how important archaeology and material culture can be in reconstructing the history of women in antiquity when I read about famous women in classical Greece and Rome. Thirty years ago, most of the evidence used to research women in antiquity was primarily from literary accounts. Today it is from both literary sources and material culture/archaeology, but the careful use of the two is rare even today. I first read about the attempts to combine archaeology and ancient texts from Professor Sarah Pomeroy's book, *Goddesses, Whores, Wives and Slaves: Women in Classical Antiquity* (1976). In the book, Professor Pomeroy was able to weave the archaeology of antiquity with all of the classical textual information on a subject like women and arrive at new conclusions about women in antiquity. She recognized the pitfalls that exist on writing about real, historical people in antiquity. Some writing exists on some famous women in antiquity, but most of the literature (often written and copied by male scribes) did not always accurately reflect the true lives of women and their status in antiquity. Instead, the literature reflected men's view of the women through the lens of their own social contexts. The literature's reliability can be judged only by a comparison piece that confirms or denies the literature's assumptions, biases, or portraits. Pomeroy wrote:

> Evidence from the fine arts, including sculpture, vase painting, frescoes, mosaics, and depictions of women on tombstones and coins, as well as objects used by women—e.g., ornaments, kitchen utensils, looms, and furniture—are useful in reconstructing the private life of women. Written evidence that would not be classified as formal literature can be found in the graffiti on ancient buildings as well as in the inscriptions on ancient monuments. (p. xi)

Only by comparing the archaeology and the material culture can one really come to know a single personality in history. This can occur only when archeologists get extremely lucky to discover pieces that really point to a single individual. Looking in antiquity for one individual, even an individual who is very prominent in the later tradition, is like looking for a needle in a haystack. Looking for information about one particular woman in antiquity is even more difficult because unless she was educated and had a relatively important status amongst her peers, her name might not even be preserved.

Women in the Hebrew Bible

If it is difficult to corroborate the existence of a particular named individual in antiquity, even a well-known person, imagine how hard it is to find an unnamed or partially named individual in antiquity. If it is hard to find substantive information on women in antiquity, think about how difficult it is to substantiate information on a woman who is only partially named in the biblical text. In many sections of the first five books of the Bible that scholars assigned to the mysterious writer known as "J," a number of "nameless" women traditions appear. In "J," long narrative sections in Genesis 19:8, 15, 30–38, Lot first offers his nameless two daughters to save his male guest from being molested. Later the text says that Lot had sexual relations with these nameless daughters as part of J's history of the Moabites and Ammonites. In Genesis 19:26, it is Lot's nameless wife who suffers the fate of becoming a "pillar of salt." It is possible that the technique of using anonymous characters in ancient or mythic materials may be the key to J's use of anonymous men and women, or it may be indicative of the actual state of extant oral traditions of ancient materials. So one finds that the wives of Genesis 4:19–24 are listed in detail; yet the wife of Cain is left anonymous in the preceding verses of Genesis 4:17–18. In another J narrative, Genesis 38:2 the text gives unusual information about his family: ". . . Judah saw the daughter of a Canaanite man whose name was Shua."

This anonymous daughter of an anonymous Canaanite—*Batshua* (literally: the daughter of Shua) is transformed into a biblical name and a named individual in later biblical tradition. She, like Bathsheba in the King David story, is called simply Bathshua (literally: 'daughter of Shua') in 1 Chronicles 3:5 as if this is her real name. In 1 Chronicles 2:3, the tradition reflects a change: "The sons of Judah were Er, Onan, and Shelah, the three being born to him by Bathshua the Cannanite." In another J narrative concerning Joseph in Genesis 39:7–9 and again in 39:12 and 39:19, for example, Potiphar's nameless wife is prominently mentioned. If she was so well known and such a critical part of the story, why could no one remember her name? It is important to note that in the famous *Yusuf Sura* in the Koran, the narrative about Joseph is much longer than it is in the Hebrew Bible and oddly enough Potiphar's nameless wife has a name: *Zulaikha*. In this Koranic section, the entire sordid affair is elaborated to the point where we understand Zulaikha's motivation and character, a unique and very worthwhile piece of ancient information about one woman. Is this a piece of the original Bible that has been preserved in the Koran? Much of this is also preserved in Rabbinic Midrash as well. It is hard to say whether these texts really do preserve relevant ancient traditions, but I think they must be considered when trying to understand the status and lives of women in antiquity. The reason why the woman is nameless in the Hebrew Bible may have more to do with the editing process of the Hebrew Bible than it does with our understanding of ancient women.

Chapter 2 of Exodus preserves significant information on the life of Moses and his family. A "J" narrative states: "Now a man from the house of Levi went and took to wife . . . (2.1)." This J narrative includes a nameless sister, a nameless daughter of Pharoh, and others. Some modern scholars assert that the unknown J writer may have been a woman, but for several reasons this seems highly unlikely. I think that J may just not have had more traditions about women than other ancient writers. Other writers apparently did have names for some of these nameless women, and we are lucky that they are sometimes included alongside the J narratives to fill in these details. In the case of the story of Joseph and Potiphar's wife, none of the writers seem to have known her name. Traditions of unnamed men and women may just be a literary technique or may signal that such details were just not transmitted over the generations. A nameless Egyptian beats a nameless Hebrew (Exodus 2:11) when Moses suddenly intervenes, and while this tradition does not have transcendental importance for the story line, in the next sentence, two nameless Hebrews accuse Moses of murder (Exodus 2:13). This is very significant since it initiates the entire cycle of Moses adventure in the desert and his meeting with God at the Burning Bush. The story line continues using the same device as Moses meets a nameless Priest of Midiam and seven nameless daughters (Exodus 2:16, 20) in the continuation of the narrative. This use of an "anonymous woman" device is found again in the P narrative concerning the infamous Moabite woman of Numbers 25, but this may be to heighten the drama of the story. In this narrative, P begins with the nameless "daughters of Moab" and an anonymous "man of Israel" and then proceeds to name names at the end of the narrative. In Numbers 25.14: "The name of the slain man of Israel, who was slain with the Midianite woman was Zimri, the son of Salu, head of a fathers' house belonging to the Simeonites (15). And the name of the Midianite woman who was slain was Cozbi, the daughter of Zur, who was the head of the people of a fathers' house of Midian."

Many books of the Bible demonstrate the importance of certain women such as Miriam, Esther, Ruth, Huldah the prophetess, and especially Deborah who is unique among women leaders of the period. In Judges 4:4–5, we read: "Deborah, a prophet, the wife of Lapidot, judged Israel at that time ... and the Children of Israel came up to her for judgement." While these women were known and held an important status in Israelite society, later Rabbinic commentators could not always successfully integrate them into the system of Rabbinic narrative and life that was developing in Babylonia a thousand years after these women existed. When later Rabbinic commentaries encountered this reference to a woman being a judge in the Bible, they were astounded. Because one of the qualifications for being a Rabbi was the ability to be a judge, this verse implied that women could be Rabbis, something that was not acceptable during the most ancient periods of Rabbinic history. Rabbinic literature totally reinterpreted this text in Judges and concluded, contrary to the literal implications of the text, Deborah was not the judge; she only appeared to be judging as the true judge was Deborah's military commander, Barak. This exercise reminds us that even when we have traditions about women from antiquity, this does not insure that her legacy will be maintained in the ongoing tradition of interpretation.

Unnamed Women Who are Named: Jephthah's Daughter Siela?

The book of Judges if full of unusual traditions about women. In Judges 11:34, the anonymous daughter of Jephthah appears and quickly disappears in an apparent child sacrifice. Jephthah vows to sacrifice 'that which comes forth from the door' if he achieves victory. It appears from the Hebrew Bible that this unknown vow to God is made and is foreshadowing the sacrifice of his unnamed daughter. The text states:

> Then Jephthah came to his home at Mizpah, and behold, his daughter came out to meet him with timbrels and with dances; she was his only child; beside her he had neither son nor daughter. And when he saw her he rent his clothes and said, "alas, my daughter! You have brought me very low, and you have become the cause of great trouble to me; for I have opened my mouth to the Lord, and I cannot take back my vow."

Despite the fact that this story is included in the Hebrew Bible, we know little about this woman and in Rabbinic tradition she became known as *Bat Jephtah*, (literally: Daughter of Jephtah). In Pseudo-Philo's *Liber Antiquitatum Biblicarum*, a first century CE work only extant in Latin, a longer, more developed tradition is presented about this woman. In this work, the daughter of Jephthah is named *Seila*, and her name is interpreted: "that you might be offered in sacrifice." The apparent reference seems to be to the Hebrew word "*Tzeila*"—"her shadow." Jephthah's daughter was given a name at birth that seems to foreshadow her unfortunate demise, much the same way that many other biblical figures have names that foreshadow their future. Although it is pretty clear that name is not in the original Hebrew text of the Bible, it is an attempt by a later writer to give meaning to the life of an otherwise unnamed woman in the Bible. What is important about the Pseudo-Philo reference is that when the woman is given a name, I think we (the reader) have a different attitude toward what happens to her. It lessens the victimization and objectification of Jephthah's daughter. She is a real person suffering a real fate.

But there are also other, unnamed literary women of the Bible who are good and evil characters: an anonymous woman patriot of Thebez in Judges 9; a wise woman of Abel in 2 Samuel 20, and the wise woman of Tekoah in 2 Samuel 14, and the witch of Endor in 1 Samuel 28:7–25. We wish we knew more about them, and in Rabbinic literature we do learn more about them. The books of Song of Songs, Proverbs, Ruth, and Esther do have something to say about women, but usually little is known about women from the same period from contemporary literature much less from archaeology. So it is important when we can actually take ancient traditions about women and compare them with archaeology and understand something about women who are named and achieved a level of fame in their own periods. That is why I chose the four women that I feature in this chapter.

Livia Julia: One Woman Solves Many Mysteries of New Testament Archaeology

When we began to work at Bethsaida over twenty years ago, someone asked me if I was working at Bethsaida or Bethsaida-Julias. I thought they were joking, but it turned out that they were expressing what had become a way of distinguishing the city of Bethsaida in the New Testament from the city of Philip Herod, son of Herod the Great. One Bethsaida was a fisherman's village, the other Bethsaida Julia an imperial city. Even though the first-century historian Flavius Josephus said that they were one in the same, the two names confused people. I became intensely interested in this one woman, Livia Julia, for whom the city of Bethsaida was renamed in the first century CE. I knew that Bethsaida had a long history of important women associated with it. In the Hebrew Bible the stories of Maachah, the wife of King David, and the daughter of the King of Geshur, was associated with traditions in the books of Chronicles, Samuel, and Kings. I had been working on medieval maps of Israel trying to discover how pilgrims imagined Bethsaida and found that many medieval maps named two cities, on two sides of the Sea of Galilee, one was Bethsaida and another Julia. According to Josephus, Philip Herod, the son of Herod the Great, rebuilt and then renamed the village of Bethsaida as the new, larger city of Julia to honor the importance and life of the Caesar Augustus' family. This was quite common in the ancient Near East. The power to rename a city was the prerogative of the ruling family of the region. Philip Herod had inherited the region from his father, and although his inheritance territory was not as well endowed as his other brothers' inheritances in Galilee and Judea, he made the best of it by establishing two different renamed towns to the Imperial Cult of Rome. One city he renamed Caesarea to the north of Bethsaida and the other site, Bethsaida Julia in the south of his realm. Questions persisted about which member of the royal family Bethsaida Julia was named for since Josephus seems to indicate that the city was renamed for the daughter of the Caesar Augustus and not the wife. Augustus' daughter Livia Julia was banished from Rome, while his wife Livia Julia was deified after her death. Which Livia Julia was it, daughter or wife? I knew one thing about traditions regarding women in ancient manuscripts, great care was not always taken in preserving the readings. The question ultimately brought me to understand an enormous amount about the Livia Julia for whom Bethsaida was renamed in the first century CE. Josephus Flavius, who lived in Galilee in the the first century CE, writes that the city's namesake is Caesar's daughter. He states in *Antiquities*, 18:2:

> He [Philip Herod] also advanced the village Bethsaida, located in front of the lake of Gennesaret, unto the dignity of a city, both by the number of inhabitants it contained and its other grandeur, and called it Julias, the same name with Caesar's daughter . . .

In a parallel passage, Josephus in his *Antiquities* 18:28 gives much more detail:

> Philip for his part made improvements at Paneas, which is situated at the headwaters of the Jordan, and called it Caesarea; he further granted to the village Bethsaida on the Sea of Galilee both by means of a large number of settlers, and through expansion of strength, the rank of a city and named it after Julia, the daughter of Caesar.

It does not seem possible that Josephus is really referring to Julia, the daughter of Caesar, because she was banished from Rome in 2 BCE and the city was only awarded to Philip Herod after the death of his father, Herod the Great, in 4 BCE. I did not think that Philip Herod would be so foolhardy to name a city after a disgraced daughter of Caesar. It made more sense that this Julia was the wife of the Augustus Caesar, the mother of the sitting Caesar and who not only was a respected member of the family, but also deified after her death by the Senate of Rome.

So how did Josephus, who knew all these people well (he lived this history) get it wrong? This is where understanding how ancient writers and copyists preserved traditions about women is very important. I think that Josephus did not get it wrong. I think copyists, who recopied the original manuscripts of Josephus, did not pay attention and by the time they were recopying the manuscripts, they did not know the difference between these two women.

It is possible that Josephus himself had flawed information about the Julian family. Much of the information that he had available to him in Rome when he finished his writing is confusing because many women had the same names in the same families. Josephus was writing about this area, Galilee, which he knew a lot about, but the period of the renaming occurred about thirty years before he was living there. But Josephus knew Bethsaida well since he had been injured there in one of the crucial battles at the beginning of the Revolt against Rome in 67 CE.

I think it was a scribal error that may have started in the Middle Ages and was enshrined in the text by copyists who just did not know who Livia Julia the mother and Julia the daughter were. Something like this happens many times in ancient manuscripts. A scribe (usually these are scribes whose native language is not the language of the manuscript they are copying) looks away from his work for a moment and then picks it up again and forgets exactly where he has left off and leaves out the clause (or word). Additional information about the daughter of Augustus, Julia, might somehow have been removed in the process. So it would have read in the original Josephus section: "Philip Herod [re]named it Julia, *the wife of the Augustus Caesar,* which is the same name as the daughter of Caesar." So either it was a dittography, a mistake made when a scribe drops similar words or clauses out during a lapse in concentration, or a creative scribe thought he knew better than the original wording. In any case, it makes more sense that this is Livia Julia, the wife of Augustus Caesar and archaeology helped us correct a thousand-year-old error.

I believe that the Julia mentioned in connection with the renamed city of Bethrampta in Trans-Jordan and this Bethsaida Julias reference are both the same Livia Julia. Livia, wife of Augustus, had been an extremely popular figure in the entire Near East, who was honored with her husband Augustus in the Imperial Cult of Rome on coins and other artifacts. People would have brought tribute (money or goods) to a center of the Imperial Cult, (even to the very humble fisherman's village) especially those sites where a temple or sacrificial center was established. We discovered a small temple and sacrificial areas around the temple at Bethsaida that we have dated to the first century. In the excavations we found some tiny shards of pottery that we have associated with the Imperial Cult, a few bronze incense shovels that would have been used in the incense service and even a small statuette that looks like all of the other known statues of Livia Julia that were preserved around the Empire. Some other centers of the Imperial Cult were probably developed in Israel throughout the period. Upon Augustus's death in 14 CE, Livia was adopted into the Julian family according to the directive of the will of Augustus (she was adopted as a "daughter" of the Julian family so it is not so far-fetched to read that she was the daughter of Augustus in Josephus). The Julian family would give her a distinction that would instantly make her a "royal." She received the title Augustus/Sebaste and the name Julia, which, while guaranteeing succession to her son Tiberius, also raised her status to a level equal with the next emperor. As a close friend of the Herod family, it is no accident that her honors extended to the children of Herod and all of their different territories. Antipas had already rebuilt the town Betharamatha in Perea and named it Livia, later to be changed to Julia. Herod the Great left cities in the south, including Yavne, to his daughter Salome. When Salome died in 12 CE, she in turn, left the cities in her will to Livia Julia, and ultimately they became part of the Emperor Tiberius's holdings in Israel. On the topic of famous names, Salome, is another name that continually causes problems for historians. There are actually four famous first-century Salomes. Salome of the New Testament, who is the daughter of Herodias; Salome the daughter of Herod the Great (and Herod's sister's name as well); and finally Salome the disciple of Jesus.

Livia Julia was very beloved in the eastern provinces of the Roman Empire, and she was honored with different coins minted between the year 15 and 24 CE. It was only fitting for Philip Herod to honor Livia Julia as well. He renamed the city, which by the way, was also very shrewd. The territories of Philip Herod were not the most fruitful areas of the realm of his father Herod the Great. By establishing an Imperial Cult center at Bethsaida, he insured that every traveler from the north, east, south, and west that passed by the city by the north east shore of the Sea of Galilee would have felt a measure of obligation to stop and give tribute. He also apparently issued a coin of his own to honor her and his rebuilding effort and as a method for publicizing his efforts. The issuing of a coin to coincide with the renaming ceremony of the new Livia city of Philip Herod was nothing new in the Roman world. Petty rulers like Pontius Pilate in Jerusalem and others throughout the empire would issue coins after the death of a leader, especially if it was the mother of the new Caesar. The case of Philip Herod and the renaming of Bethsaida-Julia is different because the renaming and the coin that was issued helps us understand much about the entire chronology of the life of Jesus.

The Timing of Jesus' Ministry and the Renaming Ceremony of Bethsaida

The timing of most of the events of Jesus' life, as presented in the different Gospels, is not easily discerned even by the scholarship on the historical Jesus in the past century. Because there are no firm dates for any of the major events of the New Testament, scholars are hard pressed to compare and contrast Roman historical events with the events of the New Testament. Although a general framework for the events of the New Testament is known, there is very little to suggest exact dates. Usually you will see the dates of Jesus' life as 4 BCE–30/33 CE in most historical texts. Those last three years of Jesus' life and even the year of Jesus' birth are questions that have been worked on by scholars of the New Testament. We know from the New Testament Gospels (Matthew and Luke) that Jesus was born in the time of King Herod the Great. Our best information is that Herod the Great died in 4 BCE, so we know that Jesus would have been born before or around 4 BCE (yes, the year 0 is a problem!). The earliest birth year is 8 BCE and the latest is obviously 4 BCE. Since we know that there was a Roman census of the region in 6 BCE, many scholars think that this is the best birth year. On the other side, 26 CE is the earliest year assigned for his death, while 36/37 CE is the latest. Since we know from Roman records that Pontius Pilate was removed in 36/37 CE, the events surrounding the death of Jesus must have occurred before then.

If we take the New Testament chronologies seriously, we find that John the Baptist appeared in the fifteenth year of the reign of Tiberius Caesar which would put John's work in the area north of the Dead Sea in the year 27 CE or the latest, 29 CE. Jesus' ministry is set by the Gospel of John as three years and Jesus' ministry starts with the arrest of John. So we know that all of the major events can be put into these few years. Very little else is known. But one of our colleagues in the Bethsaida Excavations Project, Dr. Fred Strickert had a new theory about the timing of Jesus' ministry from the coins related to Livia Julia's death and the renaming ceremony at Bethsaida.

According to Professor Strickert, the timing of this renaming ceremony for the new city of Philip at Bethsaida and the issuing of a coin may have been done on a very significant date to bring it more attention and give us a clue about why archaeological information on this one woman reveals much about biblical archaeology. Strickert's analysis includes coins issued during the crucial period of 29 CE–30 CE. If Strickert could narrow down the date of the coin issued for the renaming ceremony of the city, it would show that Bethsaida was no longer a "village" but was truly a Roman city. More important, Strickert narrowed down the date to a specific day and month, allowing many of the events of Jesus' ministry to be tracked.

One might expect renaming the town of Bethsaida as Livia Julia to have occurred in 29 CE, the actual year of Livia Julia's death. But according to the coin record, it was probably issued in the year 30 CE. Why did it take place a year later? We know that the death of Livia was surrounded by controversy in Rome. The controversy involved many in Rome who did not want to deify Livia versus those that did. Although Livia personally sought deification during her lifetime, as had her husband, Augustus, this was not granted by her son Tiberius. In fact, because Tiberius was away from Rome at the time of her death, only a simple funeral was carried out for her without him being present. It is unusual. Tiberius was not there for the funeral, and then he ordered the people to mourn her. If he had ordered the people not to mourn, it would have meant that he recognized her claim to deification. By ordering people to mourn her, Tiberius was suggesting that she was merely human. The coin with her name on it issued by Pilate in 29 CE shows that Livia was taken seriously throughout the entire empire, but it is also a coin of mourning. Instead of the grain being straight, the ears of grain on this coin are drooping. Pilate was responding favorably to his patron, Tiberius, by honoring Tiberius' mother but by showing symbols of mourning he was suggesting that he agreed with Tiberius that Livia was not a god.

Philip's actions went beyond just acknowledging the death of the mother of Caesar. Like many others in the empire, Philip wanted to deify Livia. Deification can be a drawn-out process, and eventually she was deified during the rule of Claudius in 41 CE but in 29 CE, it was choosing sides. Thus, the absence of a Julia coin issued by Philip in 29 CE is not surprising. Philip was not going to produce a coin that focused on the themes of mourning, yet by doing nothing he was not insulting the opinion of the present Caesar Tiberius.

A year after the death, such honors for Livia could be considered appropriate. The coin of Julia not only honors her following her death, but also emphasizes her place in the divine pantheon. She has her hands holding ears of grain, a symbol of the goddess, *Abundantia*. A second coin puts Livia and Augustus together, and the inscription on the coin indicates that they both share a part of the divine royalty. Philip knew that by doing this he was honoring the entire royal family and was simultaneously acknowledging that his right to rule came from Augustus, not Tiberius. The ultimate honor Philip bestowed on Livia was not the issuing of coins, but rather the founding of a city in her honor in the middle of his assigned inheritance at Bethsaida.

Most of the people who I have worked with on the Bethsaida Excavations Project have written on some aspect of Livia Julia and her life. Dr. Elizabeth McNamer, for example, has compared her to other women in Rome at the same time as Livia and has created a raison d'etre for why she was a good choice for a city that would become crucial to the entire New Testament. But Fred Strickert's tireless work on the coins of Philip Herod actually resulted in a specific date for the refounding. Dr. Strickert assumes that this celebration took place, as during her lifetime, not on the anniversary of Livia's birth, but on September 21, Augustus' birthday, which honored her together with Augustus. He also developed a unique theory about the why the combined birthdays of Augustus and Livia would make sense. His theory, based upon one single coin type from our excavations can now be used to date the events of Jesus' and the Apostles' ministries in Galilee and Jerusalem. If Dr. Strickert is right and the most likely time for the refounding of Bethsaida Julia was on September 21, 30 CE, he may have unraveled one of the secrets of the entire New Testament dating of the life and times of Jesus. This dating of the refounding of Julia would explain the absence of the name "Julia" in the Gospels. The Gospels have traditionally been known to have recorded events ending with the crucifixion of Jesus on April 7, 30 CE. Even though we now assume that the Gospels were written down only a generation later, if the name Julia had appeared with the name Bethsaida in the Gospels, readers familiar with the Galilee would have known that Bethsaida had not yet been refounded as Bethsaida Julia during Jesus' lifetime and would have seen this anachronism as a sign of an inauthentic tradition. The issue concerning the terminology and the timing of the refounding of the city has additional implications. Although Mark, the first Gospel to be written down, correctly refers to Bethsaida as a *village* (reflecting its pre-30 CE status) at that time, Luke and John use the later designation of a "city." The Gospels of Luke and John were written down after Mark and may reflect what they knew in their own time about the city. This dating of the founding of the city of Bethsaida-Julia to September 21, 30 CE is important for those who have tried, usually in vain, to date specifically the life and career of Jesus in the New Testament. The story in Mark 8 of the healing of the blind man is thought to be one of the examples of a historical Jesus. This story, clearly begins with Jesus showing up at the "village" of Bethsaida and bringing the man outside of the "village" to try to perform the miracle. It is a very unsuccessful "healing" that contains all of the elements of a more "human" Jesus. He must perform the healing multiple times, using unusual methods, and then is finally successful as the blind man (probably the well-known cataracts that afflicted many people in the ancient world) is warned: ". . . do not attempt to [re]enter the *village*." The events of the Gospel of Mark tell us that Jesus went to heal this man at Bethsaida before September 21, 30 CE, when Bethsaida was still a village. If Dr. Strickert is correct, the story of Jesus' healing of the blind man at Bethsaida can help us date the early journeys of Jesus on the northeast shore of the Sea of Galilee that clearly must have taken place at a time before the rebuilding efforts that would have begun in early 30 CE. This event also appears to be early on in the career of Jesus since he is still unfamiliar with his own abilities to heal. Other Bethsaida references "to walking on the water" and feeding of the multitudes seem to be after this initial event and suggest a Jesus that is not only familiar with his powers but a Bethsaida that is now a "city."

I have been asked in many different television interviews if I have learned anything new about Jesus, the Apostles, and the early "Jesus group" from our excavations at Bethsaida. This dating project from one coin and the subsequent archaeological discoveries of what we call the Roman Imperial Cult temple dedicated to Livia Julia on the acropolis of the city of Bethsaida have taught me much about what Jesus, the Apostles, and their followers were experiencing in that city of the year 30 and 31 CE. If we are right, during the events leading up to Jesus being seen walking on the water in front of Bethsaida and the feeding of the multitude on the hills surrounding Bethsaida, Jesus and the Apostles would have seen the daily incense cloud emerging from the Temple of Livia on the acropolis of Bethsaida. They would have been very aware of the Roman Imperial Cult and how it permeated every aspect of their lives at Bethsaida even though they lived far from the centers of Roman influences in the main cities of Jerusalem and Caesarea. What Jesus was preaching and what he was complaining about to the Apostles may have had more to do with these foreign influences and the infidelities of this Roman religious life than it did with what appear to be the critiques of Jewish life and infidelity. We have discovered that Bethsaida was not some religious backwater with poor, unworldly people who followed an itinerant and charismatic Jesus. It was a place where all of the people would have daily experienced the excesses of Roman culture and life and enjoyed imported Rhodian wine and fine jewelry like any other major Roman city. Jesus and the Apostles may have begun their march towards Jerusalem from a place like Bethsaida precisely because their complaints were as much against Roman religious excesses as they were about Jewish customs and life.

All of this began from meticulous work on a coin looking to uncover the history of this non-Jewish woman (Livia Julia) whose name is indelibly connected with the history of Judaism and Christianity because of the importance of the site. Professor Strickert has written a number of articles that chronicle how this one Philip Herod coin and one woman have revealed much about the life of the royal family, the life of Jesus, and the life of the empire as well. He thinks that it was probably no accident then that the Julia coin was reissued in 33 CE, the ninetieth anniversary of Livia's birth and the seventieth anniversary of her marriage to Augustus. Livia was just that important.

Berenice: A Jewish Woman who Almost Was the Wife of the Emperor (26/28–85 CE)

Archaeology and textual information combined again in the investigation of a woman that could have changed the history of Judaism and Christianity. The woman was Berenice, the daughter of King Agrippa I and the place was a mountain overlooking the city of Tiberias. Tiberias, judging from the name, was a very Roman city in northern Israel on the southeast shore of the Sea of Galilee when it was established sometime before the year 20 CE. Until quite recently, it was a "sleepy" town that became a major tourist city in Israel in the past forty years. Tiberias was built by Herod Antipas, another son of Herod the Great, who inherited this area of Galilee upon the death of his father. Built somewhere in the years 17–20 CE, it was named for the Roman Caesar Tiberius, Antipas' patron, but the name is the feminine Greek form (Tiberias) of the name. It was not a particularly "Jewish" city, since it apparently had many burials that were associated with it. These traditions about the city are found in later Rabbinic literature but by the second century CE, it is clear that Jews needed to come to Tiberias to escape the disastrous aftermath of the Bar Kokhba Rebellion in Judea. It continued to have an important Rabbinic presence until the first part of the fifth century CE.

In the 20s CE, Tiberias would have been a very pleasant Roman city on the picturesque Sea of Galilee. In the 1990s, excavations were being conducted around the city of Tiberias at the same time we were excavating at Bethsaida on the northeast shore of the Sea of Galilee some twenty miles away. We would visit the excavations of other excavators on a regular basis and learn about the common regional history that we were all excavating from the first century CE. In the late 1990s I had the pleasure of accompanying Professor Yizhar Hirschfeld around his excavations on the Berenice Hill overlooking Tiberias. Dr. Hirschfeld was a well known and very passionate archaeologist who seemed to never be satistifed with the status quo in his excavations. He always introduced new and inspiring insights to places that others had looked at and made pronouncements. Unfortunately he passed away at the young age of fifty-seven in 2006. At the time of his death he was conducting groundbreaking new excavations in another area of Tiberias. He will be missed by the entire field but also by the people of Tiberias. He had reinterpreted Tiberias in the course of twenty years.

Professor Yizhar Hirschfield excavated a site on a hill overlooking the Sea of Galilee known as Mount Berenice and found remains primarily from the late Roman and Byzantine periods, but it did not stop him from telling me about why he thought the mountain was named for Berenice. I went there with him and he explained the site to me, and I felt that he had a special relationship to Berenice, for whom the site was named. It was hoped, I think, when they started to find the remains of a palace on top of this hill that has traditionally been named after Berenice, that it would tell us the story of a Jewish princess/queen, named Berenice. This was a true Jewish princess/queen of the region, who for a brief moment in history, might have been the wife of the Emperor of Rome, one of the most influential females of the first century in a time when the Jewish people were desperately in need of a champion. It was such a moving story that writers even into the modern period have written about the love affair between an emperor and the Jewish princess/Queen Berenice in drama and poetry. Unfortunately, little about the historical Berenice was found on top of the remains excavated by Hirschfeld, but it did not stop the tour guides from connecting the site with this Jewish woman of the early first century CE. Berenice was a real "Jewish princess." Like other Jewish princesses/or regional queens that we know about from the Hellenistic and early Roman period, her power may have been limited to a specific time period and region, but these regional queens did have some power. We do have archaeological information on the existence of these "vassal" queens and their stories from many different sites around the eastern Roman provinces, and they are important for understanding the history of ancient Israel. Very few of their tombs were preserved from the Hellenistic and Roman periods, and by the Byzantine period, many of these women and their titles no longer had any meaning in the Christian Byzantine life of the Holy Land. Unfortunately, the anchor church found on top of the mountain named for Bernice is from the Byzantine period, some three or four centuries after Berenice's death, and the renovations of the church were done in the Islamic period. It is possible that this anchor church was built upon the remains of the Bernice palace (or burial site), which is a common custom in antiquity, but it is hard to know. Often when a massive architectural discovery is made like the anchor church, archaeologists do not want to destroy the church to search beneath it for an allusive earlier period. Again, the name Berenice was well used in the entire Roman and Byzantine periods, and perhaps the name Berenice does preserve the ancient connection with the famous queen of the early first century CE. In a twist on the old story about Sigmund Freud and his psychological evaluation of the symbolic significance of cigars, sometimes a Berenice Church is just a Berenice Church (without any connection to Queen Berenice). But sometimes remains of a significant church, like the anchor church of

Berenice above the city of Tiberias, may really preserve a historical part of the Queen Berenice epic.

The history of Hellenistic Jewish Queens and their role in Jewish society of the period needs to be understood in the general context of Hellenistic Vassal Queens in Macedonia, Syria, and Egypt. A long tradition dating back to the late fourth and early third century BCE created a new role for a woman as a political and religious leader in societies under Greek and then later Roman rule. Names of these women, such as Arsinoe, Cleopatra, and Berenice are used and reused repeatedly for women whose role as Queen (*Basilissa*) was both Queen Mother, Regent, and King. One of the chief values of these women in this period was to create alliances for petty kingdoms through marriage. Among the Ptolemies of Egypt, women reached an unusual status when no male heir was present in a single generation for succession. Among the Syrian Greeks, (Seleucid) Plutarch and Appian remark that Stratonice, wife of Antiochus I, was appointed by Selecus as monarch with her husband when the king sent his son to rule the eastern part of the kingdom. Polybius holds that Laodice, daughter of Mithradates was appointed Queen by Antiochus III and in such cases the queen was "ruler" when her husband was out of the kingdom or if a minor son was in need of a competent regent. Sometimes an excellent woman would rule with a competent brother such as the role of Cleopatra VII and Ptolemy. This is reflected in the joint appearance of queens on coinage and in royal ceremonies. Mark Antony is the first to feature women on Roman coinage. Fulvia, Octavia, and Cleopatra all appear on these coins for the first time. Cleopatra VII apparently issued her own coinage, but in general, appearances on coins during their lives and after death determine their unique status in this period.

It is in this context that the life of Berenice must be understood. No other Herodian queen comes close to the power sharing and importance of Berenice except perhaps Salome, wife of Aristobulus of Chalcis. This Salome attained the Hellenistic title for a vassal queen, *Basilissa*, as well. On the obverse side of one of the coins Aristobulus issued is the portrait of Aristolubus with the inscription, *Basileus Aristobulus* (King Aristobulus), and the reverse includes the portrait of Salome with the inscription, *Basilisseis Salome* (Queen Salome). From this we know that some type of power-sharing was going on. This was Salome's second marriage. She had earlier been married to Philip Herod, son of Herod the Great, who had built Bethsaida and who had died childless. This fact is important to the understanding of the strange state of affairs that occurred among the Jews in relation to women in this period. Philip Herod had been the first Jew to put his image on a Jewish coin in his area of the Golan. Bethsaida, near the city of Tiberias, was a different sort of region than the rest of Galilee. Philip's inheritance of Bethsaida and the region that was Gaulanitis was not as economically successful as the region of Galilee that Antipas, his brother had inherited. Philip built cities dedicated to the royal family in Rome like his brothers. He built up a city in the north and called it Caesarea (of Philip) Philippi and in Bethsaida, he had dedicated the city to Livia, the wife of Augustus, who had died in 29 CE. If I am right, Philip was something of a "feminist" and presents a different view of the status of women in this period by issuing coins with his image, but also in dedicating the city or Bethsaida for a woman, the magna mater of Rome, wife of the Augustus and the mother of the reigning Caesar, Tiberius. When Philip died in 34 CE, apparently his wife Salome married Aristobulus, and she appears on the coins of Aristobulus. The existence of strong women who appear to have continued to exert influence over their husbands in this period is apparent. Salome bore three sons, Herod, Agrippa, and Aristobulus. Although Salome died between 54 CE and 61 CE, her image is last found on a coin from Nicopolis in 54 CE. Since her husband appears alone on his coins from 61 CE onward, we assume that Salome was no longer living. She must have been a powerful role model for the succeeding generations. Berenice, daughter of Agrippa, with her title *Basilissa*, is found in an inscription in Athens dated to 61 CE.

According to Josephus Flavius, one of the most intriguing Jewish women mentioned in the first century CE was Berenice, daughter of Agrippa I and Queen Cypros. Josephus calls her *Basilis*, which is often just a Greek word for *princess*, but may in fact mean (more in light of other inscriptions and sources) that she was a regional ruler or queen. Tacitus uses the word *Regina* about Berenice. Because few other Hellenistic Jewish women bore this title, and because Tacitus, the Roman writer, mentions Berenice with other vassal kings of the period, it assumes some type of unique state as "regional Queen." This Berenice was born around 28 CE, the eldest daughter of King Agrippa I, then a vassal king with authority of an ethnarch or "regional" king in the Roman Empire region of Galilee. Berenice was first married at thirteen years old to the head of the Alexandrian Jewish community, Marcus, who was son of Alexander Lysimachus the Alabarch. Alexander was the brother of Philo Judaeus, the famous Jewish philosopher of the period, so it means that Berenice must have had some status in the Jewish community of the Diaspora as well as Galilee. Berenice's sister, Marianne, was married to another leader of the Alexandrian Jews, Demetrius. Between 37–44 CE, Agrippa I, grandson of King Herod the Great, consolidated his control of Galilee and Judea (at least in name) so this really was a marriage that would have been important to the Jews of the period. After the death of Agrippa, the succession of procurators began in Judea. Agrippa II did not succeed his father with anything like the power that the earlier Herodians had had. Although the Romans allowed Agrippa II to rule in the north and northeast of Judea, he basically was a figurehead with power to appoint the High priests in the Temple with popular support by Jews in Jerusalem. When Marcus died, Berenice was married to her uncle Herod Pollio, King of Chalcis, who died in 48 CE. According to Josephus, Berenice had two sons. It was during this period that she apparently reconnected with her brother Agrippa II in Jerusalem at precisely the time that her relation, Tiberius Alexander, a nephew of the Jewish philosopher, Philo of Alexandria, had been appointed procurator in Jerusalem. There circulated a nasty rumor. Berenice was accused of being her brother's lover. Now although this was a well-known Roman practice, it would have been a highly unusual Jewish custom in this period. The lack of any reference to this relationship by the Roman historians who write extensively about the man who would be Emperor, Titus, raises serious questions as to the accuracy of this claim, which was made by Josephus after her death in a parting shot in the *Antiquities*. It is possible that this was just done to diminish the near mythological status of Berenice that she had attained during the tumultuous times of the First Rebellion of the Jews in 66–70 CE. The aforementioned Tiberius Alexander was something of a legendary character in the writings of Josephus as well. He was known as one of a succession of pseudo-messianic revolutionaries in the first century CE leading up to the destruction of the Temple of Jerusalem in 70 CE. Tiberius Alexander, the procurator, ordered the sons of the pseudo-messianic revolutionary, Judah of Gamala, Jacob, and Simon, to be crucified causing more strife among the Jews of the period. Jerusalem was in turmoil due to this action and combined with an economic downturn and drought of the period, Tiberius Alexander was replaced by the procurator Cumanus in 48 CE.

By this time, Berenice commanded enormous political and economic authority in this period of the first century. With her brother, she shared property they inherited from the Herodian and Hasmonean families a variety of old first-century BCE estates in the western Jezreel Valley, which in the following bounty years after the drought produced large quantities of grain in the Bet Shearim area. While a large part of the land was owned by tenant farmers or lands taken over by Roman authority and thereby products and taxes were part of Roman wealth, Berenice had a unique status in this time period. Unique in that she was still considered somewhat a Jewish princess but connected to the larger Roman world in breeding and name.

Unique to our understanding of a woman of this period, Josephus tells us of the jealousy Berenice felt for her sister Drusilla, because of the latter's beauty. Her younger sister, Drusilla, married the King of Commagene and even later married Azizus, King of Emesa in Syria. In the early 50s CE, Berenice went to live in the home of her younger brother, Agrippa II, who had by now succeeded their father. At about the same time, Drusilla divorced her second husband and then married Felix, the Roman procurator of Judea from 52–60 CE. Felix is the procurator featured in the New Testament's Book of Acts, chapter 24, who laid the groundwork for the situation preceding the First Revolt against the Romans in 66 CE but also the issues relating to the relationship between the Christians and Jews in Judea in this period. Again, Berenice plays a central role in this unfolding drama. Berenice, similar to other royal families of the Roman period, moved back to be with her brother Agrippa II after the death of her husband, Herod Pollio. She served, as far as the source can be understood, as a judge (formally or informally), and both inscriptions and literature point to the use of the title: *Regina* or *Basilea*, Queen, during this period.

In the New Testament's *Acts of the Apostles*, chapters 25–26, Berenice goes to Caesarea to witness the trial of Paul around 60 CE. Paul is given permission to speak in his own defense. According to Acts 26:27–31, Paul asks King Agrippa: "King Agrippa, do you believe the prophets? I know that you believe. And Agrippa said to Paul: Do you think that you can make a Christian of me in so short a time? . . . Then the king rose, and the governor and Berenice and those who were sitting with them. They said to one another, this man is doing nothing that deserves death or imprisonment." Again, Berenice is apparently serving as a judge, although Paul directs his comments only to Agrippa.

Berenice was married again in 65 CE to King Polemos II of Cilicia directly before the beginning of the First Revolt against the Romans in the north of Israel. He apparently converted to Judaism and was circumcised, but in the spring of 66 CE Berenice was back with Agrippa II in Jerusalem when the palace was burnt down by a Jewish mob and she was forced to flee. Among other attributes, we find a woman who is passionate for her Jewish brethren in the period of the revolt and apparently loyal to the cause. She stood before Florus, the Roman procurator, in bare feet, pleading for him to stop the killing in Jerusalem.

Most notably, especially in relation to biblical archaeology, Berenice was the mistress of Vespasian's son, Titus, and she was apparently in the Roman camp at Yavne as the city of Jerusalem was captured and burnt. She would have been there in the camp when Rabbi Yohanan ben Zakkai was pleading for Yavne and its sages to save Judaism. Josephus, Suetonius, Dio Cassius, and Tacitus write of the love of Titus for her and of her beauty and wealth. For no other Jewish woman of the period, perhaps no other queen in the century, do we have such a full picture of her life and works. Berenice was forty-four years of age at the time, and Titus was in his late twenties. Berenice came to Rome with Titus after the war and may have even accompanied the artifacts taken from the Temple on the ship that took them to Rome. Dio Cassius says that Titus and Berenice lived like man and wife in all respects, and her conduct so exasperated the Romans that Titus ultimately was forced to send her back to Judea for a time. In 79 CE, on the death of Vespasian, she went back to Rome, paid her honor to the royal family and hoped to reestablish herself in the royal court of Rome. It was not meant to be. But this is one of those stories that could have been. What if she had finally been accepted as a royal princess or Queen in Rome and able to marry the Emperor? A Jewish woman in Rome after the destruction of the Temple in Jerusalem married to the Emperor. I have often speculated that she may have been one of the reasons why Rabbi Yohanan ben Zakkai was successful when he asked Titus to give him Yavne for the reestablishment of Rabbinic Judaism. It may have been more for the respect and love of Berenice than for any love and respect that he had for the Rabbis. If so, she may have played one of the most important roles in all Jewish history and yet is relatively unknown, while Rabbi Yohanan ben Zakkai is very well known.

Babatha bat Shimon and the Cave of Letters (104–135 CE)

When I wrote about Babatha in my book, *Secrets of the Cave of Letters: A Dead Sea Mystery* (Prometheus, 2004), I realized that she was one of the few women of antiquity that we know an enormous amount about from archaeological evidence alone and that but for these discoveries we really would know very little about Jewish women of this period. When the Babatha scholar, Dr. Hannah Cotton, accompanied us to our excavations in the Cave of Letters, she sat in the place where the Babatha documents were found and she was nearly overwhelmed by the sense that she was somehow communing with this ancient woman who held all of these documents with her during her lifetime. These documents have been part of the life work of Dr. Cotton and others, and they have revealed much about the second-century life of Jews and women of the period. The Babatha documents are found in the book, *The Documents from the Bar Kokhba Period in the Cave of Letters,* ed. by Y. Yadin, J. C. Greenfield, A. Yardeni, Baruch Levine with additional contributions by H. M. Cotton and Joseph Naveh (Jerusalem: Israel Exploration Society, 2002).

Because Babatha is not known in any literature of the period, save in these documents, many scholars of the ancient world have had to create a whole life for Babatha based upon a careful reading of the documents. We know about her because she hid her documents in the Cave of Letters during the Second Jewish Revolt against the Romans in 132–135 CE, and they were found in readable condition. Why Babatha was in the cave remains a mystery because she apparently had much to lose from her association with the rebels. She might have been in the cave because of her family connections because she was in Ein Gedi at an inopportune moment in the history of the rebellion or perhaps because of a personal connection to one of the commanders of the region. Whatever the reason, her presence in that cave at that moment in history and the time capsule of her life has unlocked a history of Jewish women in the middle Roman period that is so different from the picture that emerges from literary texts, such as the New Testament and the Rabbinic literature, that it demonstrates just what archaeology and social history can do when properly engaged together.

In the Cave of Letters, which Professor Yigael Yadin excavated in 1960–1961, were autographed copies of letters from the mythical Shimon Bar Kokhba (the leader of the Second Jewish Revolt Against the Romans 132–135 CE) and the correspondence and documents of Babatha, daughter of Shimon and Miriam, the second wife of one Yehudah who owned real estate in Ein Gedi. Babatha was born at the southern end of the Dead Sea, in Zoar, during the end of Nabatean reign in the area, and whose documents continue up to the fateful year of 132 CE, the start of the Revolt. These letters and documents, papyri, and leather scrolls bring to life one of the most dramatic and critical times in Jewish history. Indications from the Babatha archives seem to point to a September date for the beginning of the Revolt, but it is possible that the ferment began then and only later developed into a full Revolt. If this is the case, it would explain why counting the time of the Revolt is so problematic. The Revolt is dated from between two and a half to three and a half years, and even up to four years. Our understanding of when the refugees came to the cave depends upon when the Revolt broke out and whether it broke out before or after the Jewish New Year in September. The end of the Revolt is understood by most to be the ninth day of the Jewish month of Av (July–August), Tisha BeAv (the ninth of Av), of 135, before the new Jewish year, in late August, 135. An August, 132 date appears in a document in the *Babatha Archives* and shows no sense that the Revolt had already begun; therefore, some push for a start date of the Revolt in September, 132, sometime after the New Year and the date for her trip to the Cave of Letters.

The Life of Babatha Outside of the Cave: 104 CE–132 CE

Babatha bat Shimon, (the daughter of Shimon) was apparently quite educated, judging from the number of documents and the languages they were written in and the legal maneuvering in which she was involved for over a decade. Others disagree with me and simply say: so what? She had her documents with her, but we have no way of knowing if she understood her documents, she just had them with her. She may have been smart enough to carry them with her but not necessarily literate enough to know what they meant. One wonders if these same scholars would make the same arguments about men who carried their documents with them in the same time period. I assume that she had to be acutely aware of the importance of each document that required a measure of literacy, which we did not know about until the Babatha archive was discovered in the Cave of Letters. We know much about her life from her documents.

She was born in Maoza (near Petra in modern day Jordan), a village at the southern end of the Dead Sea in the district of Zoar (well known from the Bible), part of the mysterious Nabatean realm. Her birth fell very close to the year that the Romans finally were able to annex Nabatea into the Roman Empire in 106 CE. I estimate her birth year to be on or around 104 CE, because by 124 CE she was already a widow with a young son. If Babatha became betrothed at age twelve and a half (as we find in the Talmudim), and Babatha had an eight-year-old son in 132 CE, according to the documents found in the cave, then she was at least eighteen by 124 CE. Her father owned a date palm orchard that was deeded to his wife and ultimately to his daughter, Babatha. The name Baba and Babatha were Idumean names not normally used by Jews. One of Babatha's parents may have been Idumean because her name is archaeologically identified with Idumea. Idumeans were an important "bridge" people between the Jews and the other local peoples of Israel in the time after the Jews came back from Babylonia in the fifth century BCE. Babatha's son is expressly designated as a "Jew" by the Roman legal document. Romans may not have been very aware of the differences between Jews and Idumeans, so the designation may be more of a symbolic way of identifying him as a non-Roman. In fact, the Idumeans were not exactly Jews by choice and not always considered Jews by the other non-Idumean Jews. In 129 BCE, the territory of Idumea was conquered by John Hyrcanus I and the entire non-Jewish population was forced to convert and males circumcised. The most famous Idumean was Herod the Great. In the First Revolt, the Idumeans were not full participants in the Revolt but in the end, Idumea, its territory south of the Judean Hill country and the northern part of the Negev was decimated. Babatha's parents might have come to Maoza precisely because of the problems associated with the First Revolt and left to avoid similar problems. She seems to have been an only child or oldest sister, which created the possibility of her inheriting the control of the property after the death of her parents. She apparently could read, and therefore the importance of the neatly arranged documents (writing may have been another skill) indicates that she knew what some of the content was. She married a man named Jesus in Greek and Yehoshua in Hebrew. Their son's name was Jesus as well. After her husband died, the son had guardians appointed by the court to assure his protection in the event that the mother remarried and he held no inheritance.

By 125 CE, Babatha was married to her second husband, Judah, who was originally from Ein Gedi but who had settled in Maoza. Much of the financial issues of their lives revolve around investments in Ein Gedi. Judah has three productive palm date orchards there. Judah was already married to Miriam, and it is not clear whether Babatha lived in Miriam's household or in another household in Ein Gedi or whether Judah traveled between Maoza and Ein Gedi. In 128 CE, based on the marriage contract of Judah's daughter Shelamzion, Babatha apparently is residing in Ein Gedi with her husband. The fact that his daughter's Greek wedding contract is in Babatha's papers indicates she was financially involved in this relationship. In fact in the same year, in February 128 CE, Judah receives from his wife Babatha a loan/deposit of three hundred denarii. It is a very telling document because it shows how Babatha controlled her own money in their marriage and instead of a loan on interest or minimal interest, she allows Judah to receive the money as a deposit, which is repayable on demand. A little over a month later, Judah's daughter is married to a man in Ein Gedi, and the marriage contract contains an impressive dowry of five hundred denarii: two hundred coming from the bride's father (apparently the deposit of Babatha, her stepmother) and three hundred from the groom's family. Judah's debts, even before he marries Babatha, are carried in this archive, so this marriage contract ultimately ended up being Babatha's responsibility. We do not know what the relationship was between the women, but it is clear that the fiscal responsibility for Judah's daughter was carried by Babatha even after his death. Judah died in 130 CE, and Babatha seized his property.

The last of the documents revolve around the summons and depositions by Miriam and Judah's family who want Judah's property returned. Miriam was a relative of a man named Yehonathan, who is thought to be Bar Kokhba's commander at Ein Gedi. Although in the previous documents,

Babatha appears to be protecting her assets, it would be very difficult in the climate of the new political regime to protect them. If this is the case, the very people who were suing her for return of property were now in charge of the political situation in the area after the beginning of the Revolt. Babatha was now subject to their whims. She was in Ein Gedi to resolve some of the legal problems with the date palm groves that Miriam and Judah's family were disputing. There is an interesting reference in the summons. In July of 131, Babatha is summoned by Miriam, "an Ein Gedian woman, daughter of Beianos, to accompany her in person before Haterius Nepos, legatus Augusti pro praetore, wherever his venue may be to answer why you seized everything in the house of Judah, son of Eleazar Khthousion my and your late husband . . . and equally important to attend before the said Nepos until judgement." If this was the case, and she was being summoned on the properties in Ein Gedi by an Ein Gedi woman, she might have have been in Ein Gedi for the proceedings, right before the Bar Kokhba Revolt began. On August 19, 132, Babatha has a receipt for the guardianship of her son in Petra. But a fragmentary summons from late August, early September, 132, apparently was the continuation of the summons from the year before and may have dragged her back to the court case with Miriam and Judah's family in Ein Gedi. It is quite possible that following the summons, she felt compelled to be in Ein Gedi or nearby to attend the proceedings. She may have been caught up in the Bar Kokhba Revolt quite by accident. Not because of political design or sympathy, not necessarily because of being pushed out of Maoza for her political sympathies, but because of the summons and her devotion to the legal system of the Romans.

It is very possible, therefore, that despite Yadin's attempt to make Babatha a political sympathizer and victim of the Bar Kokhba Revolt, she may not necessarily have been involved at all. She may have been swept up by the events of 132 CE and for her "protection" brought to the Cave by Miriam and Yehonathan's family. Yadin even concluded that one of the bodies discovered in the Cave was Babatha's (because her archives were found across from the niche, it seemed reasonable to assume that she was buried there as well). If he was right, the dating of her documents is crucial. She was in Maoza until August, 132 CE, and she must have come to the Ein Gedi area just as the Revolt had broken out. Because the last of her documents is dated in 132 CE, she may have been brought to the Cave directly after the outbreak of the Revolt and never emerged again. She may have been among the first wave of Bar Kokhba cave dwellers.

Babatha's thirty-five documents are precisely dated and range from 94 CE until August/September, 132 CE. It appears that uniform, day-to-day, uninterrupted Jewish life in nearby Petra and Maoza, where she was apparently living until the outbreak of the Revolt, continued until 132 CE. If nothing else, her documents tell us how international many Jews were because they are written in Nabatean, Aramaic, and Greek. The documents tell us how integrated into the Roman legal system Jews were in this period. It also tells us how people all around the Dead Sea were affected by the Revolt to the point that they ended up taking refuge in caves on the western side of the Dead Sea, despite the fact that there were perfectly adequate refuge caves on the other side of the Dead Sea, nearer to their ancestral homes. In addition, it is clear that Babatha was not an isolated case. The understanding of how extensive a woman's holdings in this period might be is raised by other documents found in the Judean Desert. We read about a number of women and their documents that they kept with them in their final days from other caves around the area in the same period. They suggest that women kept a whole treasure trove of personal documents that they needed to regularly access.

The fact that Babatha's documents were found in the Cave of Letters supports Yadin's suspicion that Babatha had been in the cave, even if she is not one of those people buried there. The question is whether we can conclude that she was a political sympathizer of Bar Kokhba from the archaeological information presented by the juxtaposition of the niche and the documents. This is a part of writing a social history of the period based on understanding the texts and then constructing plausible and often very diverse views of the men and women as if they were indeed real "live" characters. The most recent attempt to understand the life and times of Babatha comes from one of my colleagues in Israel, Dr. Hanan Eshel. He suggested that perhaps Babatha had a companion such as Eliezer, son of Shemuel, and they were not necessarily sympathizers with Bar Kokhba's Revolt but rather were both running away from Bar Kokhba and the madness of the Revolt. Dr. Eshel theorized that there might have been a relationship between Babatha and Eliezer, and this is the reason why this divorced, woman of means, went to this cave of refuge, the Cave of Letters. She was following her companion, Eliezer. The entire circle of people that Eliezer was involved with, including Eleazar, the son of Hayyata, who had had his land confiscated by Bar Kokhba, may suggest that they were running from Bar Kokhba as well as the Romans. Knowing now how powerful Babatha was, one must wonder whether it was the men who led her there or whether she knew about this cave herself from her many First Revolt and Ein Gedi connections. It is difficult to know; but we do know she went to the cave and did not leave with her most precious possessions—her documents. As a postscript, I need to acknowledge that some scholars still maintain that despite the fact that Babatha had all of these documents with her in the cave, she may have been unable to read them. She could have been totally illiterate and just carried these documents because she knew they were important. I acknowledge that it is not possible to say whether or not Babatha could read all of her documents but for a woman who knew enough to preserve these documents and apparently use them when it was necessary, it suggests a high level of knowledge. I usually find that this type of argumentation is circular reasoning for those who continue to assert that women in antiquity were uneducated in most periods of Jewish history. The final example I think proves this assumption invalid.

Beruriah bat Rabbi Hananiyah and Rabbinic Texts (110–140 CE)

I end with the most famous woman of all Rabbinic literature even though we have no archaeological information to suggest that she indeed lived. In digging around the Talmud, you would find that Beruriah is the most unique woman in Rabbinic literature because we have so many authentically formulated traditions associated with her name and because she is the only one who has such a high level of rabbinically sanctioned traditions associated with her name. After studying the Babatha archives, one must assume that the Jewish situation, following on the heels of the Bar Kokhba Revolt, may have allowed women to have a greater role in Jewish life than they might have had before the Revolt. If we are to accept the records of the Jews, Christians, and Romans on the subject of the Second Revolt, the male population of Palestine must have been decimated by the war. Beruriah, the daughter of Rabbi Hanina (or probably, Hananiyah—his name is spelled in a number of different ways in different traditions) was born either before or directly after the Bar Kokhba Revolt of 132 CE. Her mother's name is not known, but if we isolate the different traditions, she had a brother and a sister. Hananiyah's unnamed brother is presented in a horrible incident from Midrash Lamentations Rabbah, 3:6 in which he has become involved with a group of bandits who apparently roamed Israel after the Revolt of 70 CE. This is part of a full tragic biography of Beruriah and her family that one can piece together from as many as twenty different Rabbinic traditions spread over half a dozen different Rabbinic collections.

The story of Beruriah and her family is linked with some of the most famous Rabbinic stories in all Rabbinic literature. The unnamed brother, for example, is featured in a famous discussion of an impure/pure oven controversy that began among the Rabbis in the early second century CE. Ritual purity was a near obsession with the Rabbis (judging from the number of texts that deal with it) and seems to have been an ongoing question in the Rabbinic period even as the central reason for ritual purity, the Temple in Jerusalem, no longer existed (after 70 CE). The question of the "pure or impure oven of Achnai" became emblematic of Talmudic reasoning in general and is used by generations of scholars to demonstrate how the Rabbinic mind works. The oven would have been made out of clay and often the outer part of the oven made from removable clay tiles that were separate from the actual oven itself. It is thought that this example of the impure/pure clay oven of Achnai was connected with the regularization of Temple period laws in the Rabbinic period, and opinions seem to vary among the Rabbis about the strictures of purity in their period. Pottery could easily become impure by the introduction or contact with a source of impurity. Even if the layers of pottery tiling on the outside of ovens would tend to protect the inside from the outside contamination, it was still a question to the Rabbis since it is possible to see the entire oven as one entity or to subdivide it into an outer and inner vessel. Because many of the purity laws were based on the existence of the Temple, the need for these laws in a post Temple environment was problematic to some Rabbis, and some Rabbis did liberalize their views about these contaminations in later generations. In Tosefta Kelim-Baba Qamma 4:16, each sage weighs in on the possibilities raised by different types of pottery ovens that have become impure and how and when they became impure. Rabbi Halafta of Kefar Hananyah, a place well known as a center for Rabbinic pottery making and purity management, states: "I asked Shimon ben Hananiyah who asked the son of Rabbi Hananiyah ben Teradion, and he said: it becomes impure when it is moved from its place." Whereupon the Tosefta then states: "[Rabbi Hananiyah's] daughter [Beruriah?] said: "it [an oven] becomes impure when the outer covering is removed from it." And when this was reported to Rabbi Yehudah Ben Baba, he said: "Better did his daughter rule than did his son." This appears to be in an early period of Beruriah's life but still demonstrates that the recognition of her wisdom may have caused some controversy in her family. In any case, the brother later appears to have joined the marauding bandits who plagued the country during the middle of the second century, especially following the Bar Kokhba Revolt. Beruriah's father was the famous Rabbi Hananiyah ben Teradion, who we find in the Mishnah and liturgy of Yom Kippur (in the Martyrology) that is read to this day by Jews all over the world, because he was burned to death by the Romans with the scrolls of the Torah wrapped around him. In this case she is placed in the center of one of the great arguments of Talmudic history. In BT tractate Sanhedrin 32b we have another indication of her status:

> Our Rabbis taught: 'justice, justice shall you follow,' this means, Follow the scholars to their academies. [for example follow] Rabbi Eliezer to [the city of] Lod, Rabban Yohanan ben Zakkai to [the city of] Beror Hayil, Rabbi Joshua to Peqi'in, Rabban Gamaliel [II] to Yavne, R. Akiba to Benei Berak, Rabbi Mathia to Rome, Rabbi Hananiyah ben Teradiyon to Siknin, Rabbi Jose [ben Halafta] to Sepphoris. Rabbi Judah ben Bathyra to Nisibis, Rabbi Joshua to the exile, Rabbi [Judah the Prince] to Beth Shearim, or the Sages to the Chamber of Hewn Stones.

Here we see that her family would have been from a northern city of Sikhnin and was famous for having refounded a Rabbinic academy there. Sikhnin was a Galilean village that was outside of the Judean center of the Bar Kokhba Rebellion but still may have been caught up in the events of 132 CE.

According to other Talmudic traditions, Beruriah's mother was executed the same day as her father, Rabbi Hananiyah, during or following the Bar Kokhba Rebellion. Her brother joined a rebel band and was later executed by the Romans as well. Beruriah married the noted scholar Rabbi Meir, who formulated the first organization of the Rabbinic traditions that became the Mishnah, the most important codified text of Rabbinic wisdom. Similar to Rabbi Akiva, Rabbi Meir, was (in some traditions) descended from a pagan family that had converted to Judaism. Unlike Akiva who is "ben Yosef" the son of an unknown Joseph, Meir's lineage is never mentioned nor is he ever referred to in any terms but "Meir" without the designation "son of." In a time when the Rabbis were meticulous in preserving the entire lineage of a sage together with his wisdom, Rabbi Meir is an anomaly. According to legend, Rabbi Meir's ancestor, a Roman commander from the family of Caesar from around 70 CE, was marching with his legion toward Jerusalem in a period before the destruction of the Temple in 70 CE. He heard the sound of children studying in the Bet Midrash about what was to come in future times and embraced Judaism. For the most part, the legal references to this woman sage, Beruriah, in the Babylonian Talmud constitute a major group of traditions that do not differ in style and argumentation from other legal discussions of the Talmudim. Beruriah appears to be just like other Rabbinic figures of the period even though she does not have the title Rabbi appended to her name. Beruriah's appearance and views were distinctive. In one case, a legal opinion listed as coming from Beruriah in the Tosefta Kelim-Baba Metzia 1:6 is found in the Mishna Kelim 11:4 as the opinion of Rabbi Joshua. It is either they shared the view, or she was only being recognized by some of the Rabbis. Either way, Beruriah's knowledge of Rabbinic sources, either maxims or formal Rabbinic argumentation, does not seem to be a question in the Beruriah texts.

A number of the passages allude to the personal tragedies of Beruriah's life. It is possible judging from one encounter with a Sadducee that she was unable to have her own children. In this example a Sadducee said to Beruriah:

> It is written [Isaiah 54.1], "Sing O barren one, who did not bear." Because she did not bear children [should she] sing?" She said to him, "Fool! Cast your eyes to the end of the verse where it is written, 'For the children of the desolate one will be more than the children of the favored wife,' says the Lord.

If our interpretation is correct, Beruriah may have been the "barren one" mentioned by the Sadducee, and he may have been alluding to a major controversy about adoption among the Jews of the first and second century CE. Beruriah seems to have been raising Rabbi Meir's children from his former marriage. This would explain why Beruriah is able to so dispassionately explain to Rabbi Meir about the death of his children in another section of Talmud. All of these traditions in Rabbinic literature point to Beruriah's ability to deal with personal tragedies in a way that impressed the Rabbis enough to record them. The story also tells us how Beruriah saw herself as a full-fledged representative of a normative Pharisaic tradition of the period. The adoption question is interesting since it seems that the Pharisees may have readily accepted the idea of adopting children while the more priestly Sadducees were less enthusiastic about adopting children into their families since they come from non-priestly backgrounds. The adoption controversy continued into the second century CE (after the disastrous results of the First and Second Revolts against the Romans) when orphaned or displaced children were no longer able to find their parents and were taken into people's houses and "adopted." The Pharasaic Rabbis searched for biblical precedents and finally found some citations in the book of Samuel and the book of Ruth. In BT Sanhedrin 19b we find a colleague of Rabbi Hananiyah ben Teradiyon discussing the question:

> Now as to Rabbi Joshua ben Korha, surely it is written, "And the five sons of Michal, the daughter of Saul, whom she bore to Adriel." Rabbi Joshua [ben Korha] answers thusly: "Was it then Michal who bore them? Surely

it was rather Merab who bore them!" "But [he answered even though] Merab bore them it was Michal who brought them up, therefore they were called by her name." This teaches that whoever brings up an orphan in his home, Scripture ascribes it to him as though he had given birth to him. Rabbi Hanina says: "This is derived from the following [biblical reference]: "And the women, her neighbors, gave him [the son of Ruth, her daughter-in-law] a name, saying, "There is a son born to Naomi." [But the Rabbi asked:] "Was it then Naomi who bore the child [or Ruth]? Surely it was Ruth who bore him! But [it seems that] Ruth bore him and Naomi brought him up thus we learn that he was called after her [Naomi's] name [because even though she did not bear the child, she "adopted" and raised the child, therefore she is indeed like his birth mother].

In the Rabbinic text, Beruriah finishes her analysis of this discussion and adds: "Why [does the text say]: "O barren one, who did not bear?" [Rather should it say] "Rejoice, O community of Israel, which is compared to a barren woman, which has not borne children for people like you!" This pronouncement shows us not only her wisdom but may reflect a piece of her own personal biography confirmed in other Rabbinic texts.

In writing a social history of one woman in antiquity, we are forced to consider if she was in fact unique because so many literary materials survive about her. In one reference in a later Midrashic collection, Beruriah demonstrates unique characteristics of compassion and wisdom. The story holds that two of Rabbi Meir's sons died on the Sabbath, and she did not inform her husband of their deaths in order not to move him to grieve on the Sabbath, which was prohibited in Jewish Law. Only after the termination of the Sabbath did she broach the subject, using a well-known Rabbinic technique of indirect, often midrashic, storytelling: "Some time ago a certain man came and left something in my trust; now he has called for it. Shall I return it to him or not?" When Rabbi Meir replied "yes," Beruriah showed him the dead children. Rabbi Meir began to weep, and she asked him: "Did you not tell me that we must give back what is given to us in trust?—'The Lord gave and the Lord has taken away. Blessed be the name of the Lord'" (Job 1: 21).

It is curious why the Rabbis included this account because it reflects negatively on one of the key framers of all Rabbinic thought, Rabbi Meir. Additionally, Beruriah, who emerges from most of the Rabbinic accounts as a woman who bests a male scholar in a Talmudic discussion with her superior knowledge, does so here in unusually impressive style. According to one tradition in BT Pesahim 62b, she is known to have learned three hundred Rabbinic traditions from three hundred sages in one day! Even more important, in this account, the ethical reasoning is recorded. She withheld the information from her husband during the Sabbath in order not to cause him extreme grief on the Sabbath. She probably was aware that the principle concerning such news does not mandate that one wait until the end of the Sabbath to relate this information. Her ethical motivation was to wait, despite the fact that the scenario suggests great personal and psychological sacrifice on her part. Her unique "ethic of caring" can be found in an earlier Rabbinic reference as well. In BT Berachot 10a, we are told that Rabbi Meir was being harassed by certain robbers in his neighborhood, and he prayed that they would die. Beruriah discussed this prayer with her husband citing scripture (as all Rabbinic texts do), and she concluded: "So [instead of praying for their deaths] pray that they repent and be wicked no more. He (Rabbi Meir) prayed for them and they repented." Instead of advocating a prayer for death, she advocated a prayer for repentance and the obvious efficacy (Divine approval that is apparent in the results) of her opinion is shown in the text itself. Her ethical sensitivity seems to be so widely known that the Rabbis took pains to preserve many of these Beruriah texts despite the fact that they simultaneously diminish the reputation of her husband, the renowned Rabbi Meir.

Of course having information on the family of a woman in this period is what makes the writing about her life possible. Tractate Avodah Zarah of the Babylonian Talmud has information on Beruriah's sister, who appears as a virgin in a brothel in Rome. It is my thought that Rabbi Meir lived in the period directly following the destruction of the Temple in 80–90 CE because he is still collecting the money for the Temple tributes despite its destruction in 70 CE. He would have had to have been born in around 65 CE and when he died in 135 CE, he would have been seventy years old, a contemporary of Rabbi Akiva. BT Avodah Zarah 17b states that following the 135 CE debacle of the Bar Kokhba Revolt, people such as Rabbi Hananiyah were tracked down and seen as a danger:

> They then brought up Rabbi Hanina [Hananiyah] ben Teradion and asked him, "Why have you occupied yourself with the Torah?" He replied, "Thus the Lord my God commanded me." At once they sentenced him to be burnt, his wife to be slain, and his daughter to be consigned to a brothel.

Did Rabbi Hananiyah have another daughter? It is possible Rabbi Hananiyah had another daughter, but it is also possible that the text is speaking of Beruriah herself being sent to a brothel because the link between the stories suggests a close contact between the Torah scholar, Beruriah, and Rabbi Hananiyah's execution and the brothel story. It is not uncommon for a story with a twist such as this to divert direct attention away from the main character to teach a tradition without demeaning a worthy person. This is similar to the story of the famous scholar known by the title: *Aher* (Rabbi Elisha ben Abuya) as well. The *Aher* (which in Hebrew means "The Other One") designation is used in the Talmud as a designation for the great scholar Elisha ben Abuya so that the Talmud does not have to use his name. Elisha ben Abuya gave up his religious Jewish identity after an experience perhaps related to the Bar Kokhba Revolt. In any case, he was a great scholar so when they quote a story about him, instead of using his real name, they just call him "the other." This may be the reason why they do not use Beruriah's name in the above-cited text. They just call her "his daughter" when they refer to this horrible experience in the brothel. Knowing all of these relationships and trying to create a full social history about the life of this celebrated woman scholar, Beruriah, is complicated because some Rabbinic texts use unnamed traditions in a fashion which is very similar to the way they are used in biblical texts.

In the continuation in BT Avodah Zarah 18a we see that one unnamed daughter was present at the actual execution of her father. We may assume that this is Beruriah since she is one of the few people that has seen such disparate suffering and has been able to find in each of these experiences a significant meaning:

> His daughter [Beruriah] exclaimed, "Father, that I should see you in this state!" He replied, "If it were I alone being burnt it would have been a thing hard to bear; but now that I am burning together with the Scroll of the Law, He who will have regard for the plight of the Torah will also have regard for my plight." His disciples called out, "Rabbi, what do you see?" He answered them, "The parchments are being burnt but the letters are soaring on high." "Open then thy mouth" [said they/she] "so that the fire enter into you." He replied, "Let Him who gave me [my soul] take it away, but no one should injure oneself [commit suicide]." The Executioner then said to him, "Rabbi, if I raise the flame and take away the tufts of wool from over thy heart, will you help me to enter into the world to come?" "Yes," he replied. "Then swear unto me" [he urged]. He swore unto him. He thereupon raised the flame and removed the tufts of wool from over his heart, and his soul departed speedily. And a *bath kol (Divine voice)* was heard: "Rabbi Hanina ben Teradion and the Executioner have been assigned to the world to come." When Rabbi heard it he wept and said: One may acquire eternal life in a single hour, another after many years.

But the Talmudic compilation of Beruriah stories continues with a daughter of Rabbi Hananiyah (Hanina) being consigned to a brothel in

Rome. Although the opening suggests that this is a sister of Beruriah, it is
not clear that Rabbi Meir would have risked so much for his sister-in-law
unless it is a concealed attempt to tell the story about Beruriah in the guise
of "her sister." The collapsing of two separate traditions in the BT is common. Often it involves two versions of a story that have been combined
into one. In this case, the ending of the story, which involves the suicide of
Beruriah, is unusual. It was necessary to combine another tradition about
him in order to create it. In any case, the story is an important part of the
Rabbi Meir legend. Because of this story, Rabbi Meir acquires in some
traditions the denomination "The Miracle Worker" because the use of only
his name immediately invoked a miracle. In Tiberias, this tradition became
the basis for the burial of Rabbi Meir Baal HaNes, Rabbi Meir the Master
of the Miracle. Despite competing "Meirs" who are also proposed, this
tradition of the classic, second century CE Rabbi Meir has persisted. The
original tradition in the Babylonian Talmud, tractate Avodah Zarah 18a-b
reads the following:

> Beruriah, the wife of Rabbi Meir, was a daughter of R. Hanina ben Teradi-
> yon. Said she [to her husband], "I am ashamed to have my sister placed in
> a brothel." So he took a *tarkab*-full of *denarii* and set out. If, thought he, she
> has not been subjected to anything wrong, a miracle will be wrought for
> her, but if she has committed anything wrong, no miracle will happen to
> her. Disguised as a Roman soldier he came to her and said, "Prepare your-
> self for me." She replied, "The manner of women [menstrual cycle] is upon
> me." "I am prepared to wait," he said. "But," said she, "there are here many,
> many prettier than I am." He said to himself, that proves that she has not
> committed any wrong; she no doubt says this to every suitor. He then went
> to her guard and said, "Hand her over to me." He replied, "I am afraid of
> the government." "Take the *tarkab* (an ancient measure) of *dinars* (money),"
> said he, "one half distribute [as bribe], the other half shall be for yourself."
> "And what shall I do when these are exhausted?" he asked. "Then," he re-
> plied, "say, 'O God of Meir, answer me!' and you will be saved." "But," said
> he, "who can assure me that that will be the case?" He replied, "You will
> see now." There were there some dogs who bit anyone [who incited them].
> He took a stone and threw it at them, and when they were about to bite
> him he exclaimed, "O God of Meir answer me!" and they let him alone.
> The warden then handed her over to him. At the end the matter became
> known to the government, and [the guard] on being brought [for judge-
> ment] was taken up to the gallows, when he exclaimed, "O God of Meir
> answer me." They took him down and asked him what that meant, and
> he told them the incident that had happened. They then engraved Rabbi
> Meir's likeness on the gates of Rome and proclaimed that anyone seeing a

person resembling it should bring him there. One day [some Romans] saw him and ran after him, so he ran away from them and entered a prostitute's house. Others say he happened just then to see food cooked by heathens and he dipped in one finger and then sucked the other. Others again say that Elijah the Prophet appeared to them as a prostitute who embraced him. God forbid, said they, were this Rabbi Meir, he would not have acted thus! [and they left him]. He then arose and ran away and came to Babylon. Some say it was because of that incident that he ran away to Babylon; others say because of the incident about Beruriah.

Rabbi Meir goes to Rome to bring her out of this situation of degradation, but the elaborate nature of the narrative suggests that the story has a rather important basis. Disguised as a Roman soldier, Rabbi Meir goes to rescue his sister–in–law in Rome and yet the Avodah Zarah reference is left unresolved. The story of Beruriah is itself not unresolved. The eleventh century commentator Rashi adds another level of impropriety to insure that the history of Beruriah is filled out. The incident, as related in Rashi's commentary on this story in Avodah Zarah 18b, occurred when R. Meir's wife taunted him about the unusual Rabbinic adage (BT Kiddushin 80b) "Women are light-minded." While this seems to suggest that all women are capricious, in fact, in the context it seems to suggest something about how women are more easily seduced and may have little to do with their intellectual abilities. According to Rashi's telling of this Beruriah story (which appears nowhere else in Rabbinic sources), Rabbi Meir replied that one day she would herself testify to the truth of this saying. In fact, there is an incident in BT Eruvin 53b involving Rabbi Meir and Rabbi Yosi HaGalili. According to the story in tractate Eruvin, Rabbi Yosi was once on a journey when he met Beruriah and asked her for directions to Lod, a major Rabbinic center of study in the second century. He asks a longer question than is necessary. Instead of just asking "Which way is Lod," he asks: "By which road do we go to Lod." Beruriah makes the point about sages, who the public assumed knew so much, and yet here was a sage who did not even know which way the great academy of Lod was located. She chides him saying that he should have made his question shorter: "Which way is Lod?" so that he did not engage in a long conversation with a woman [who was not his wife]! She then cites an early Rabbinic saying: "Does it not say: "Engage not in much talk with women" (Mishnah Avot, 1:5), which, although a mild put-down of her gender, is intended to demonstrate just how much she understands about Rabbinic life. When, subsequently (again according to medieval commentator Rashi), Beruriah was enticed by one of her husband's disciples, she demonstrates just how problematic these relationships between Rabbinic fellows and women can be. In fact, Rashi may have interpreted the BT Avodah Zarah story as emblematic of this bold woman, Beruriah, and appended his own insights into the psyche of a woman like this. In this story, Beruriah committed suicide (following her adulterous relation) and her husband, Rabbi Meir, ran away to Babylon because of the shame attached to the adultery and suicide. The story ends with Rabbi Meir in flight to Babylonia.

Many possible tragedies in Beruriah's life are linked together in Rabbinic texts. According to some of these texts, Beruriah lost her father in the Revolt. The Jewish people suffer exile and destruction, and she experiences all of it. She personally never had any children and her husband's children die under her guardianship. Her obvious Rabbinic knowledge does not bring her happiness or respect in these texts. And, as we mentioned above, according to some Rabbinic traditions, these tragedies culminate with her suicide in Rome in the midst of the charges of sexual impropriety and far from her husband and homeland. I included Beruriah with Babatha because both seem to prove the rule that there were women of great stature who lived in the second century CE and who were the equal of many men in their life choices, wisdom, character, and courage. Without the archaeological information from Babatha, Beruriah would always seem like a literary anomaly. Without Beruriah, Babatha seems to be so unusual that she can be discounted or minimized. Together they form a view of strong Jewish women who faced tragedies and made choices, often under the watchful eyes of strong men. In the case of Julia Livia and Berenice, we have two ancient women whose legacies are not well known by the general public and can only be reconstructed by careful comparison of archaeology and ancient literary traditions. Together they tell us much about the life and times of men and women in the Roman period.

5

Searching for Synagogues:
A Lost Synagogue Ritual
Recovered by Archaeology

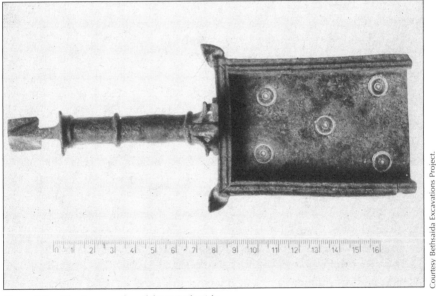

Figure 5.1.   The incense shovel from Bethsaida.

Courtesy Bethsaida Excavations Project.

I became interested in exploring how, when, and where synagogues first originated for two reasons. One reason is that for more than twenty years we have been excavating at a Jewish first-century CE site, Bethsaida, and everyone who visited the site inevitably asked me "where is the synagogue?" They reasoned that if this was a Jewish village/city, it must have had a synagogue. The second reason why I am so curious about where and when synagogues originated, is that there is so little evidence of synagogues in the Land of Israel before the destruction of the Temple in Jerusalem (even up to the Bar Kokhba Revolt). Archaeologists that I asked about where and when synagogues began, just rolled their eyes at the suggestion that there were any Rabbinic synagogue buildings in the Second Temple period in Israel. In 150 years of excavations in the Land of Israel, very few (perhaps four) synagogues were found in the historical borders of Israel during the Second Temple period, and all seem to be connected with the Revolt. But the New Testament, Rabbinic texts, and even the Galilean Josephus suggest that "synagogues" existed. So were there synagogues in the Second Temple period in the Land of Israel or not?

Certainly synagogues are not found in the Hebrew Bible. It is usually reasoned that synagogues were born in the Diaspora, either in Babylonia or from the Mediterranean Diaspora, and were created as a vehicle for Jews to experience a measure of Judaism when they could not make regular pilgrimages to Israel. The "edifice complex" of creating new institutions that paralleled the religious buildings of other peoples in the far-flung Diaspora of the Jews is very well documented in Egypt and the Aegean. In Egypt, the Egyptian Jews in the post-First Temple destruction period of the sixth century BCE, created their own temples for sacrificing. After the return from the Exile, the status of the Second Temple was not completely certain. By the third century BCE, there were synagogues in northern Egypt. Even in the time of the First Temple, other institutions were competing for the hearts and minds of the residents of Israel and Judah. In the Iron Age, there was the Temple in Jerusalem and altars throughout the Land of Israel that are linked with specific sacrificial duties of the Israelites and later the Jews of the Bible. But even this is controversial. The altars or high places of the Hebrew Bible were created in spite of the ancient biblical (Deuteronomy) dictate of a single, centralized shrine at only one city. That city became Jerusalem, but only after King David had established the city and followed other places where the Tabernacle and Ark of the Covenant had rested from the desert of Sinai until it was brought to Jerusalem by David. The fact that at many archaeological sites from the north to the south of Israel we find altars and high places that were built throughout the Iron Age raises the question of whether the Deuteronomistic concept of a single, centralized shrine in one city was a late biblical innovation or whether the altars and high places in these Israelite and Judean cities are all built by and for non-Israelites and Judeans. In many of these cities (that must have included Israelite and Judean homes) there were statuettes and god/goddess figurines. All of this had led archaeologists to conclude that although leading biblical monotheism was a goal of ancient biblical religion, this goal continued to be difficult to achieve in the reality of people's lives and communal settings. The Prophets rail against the inclinations of what we can only assume was the accepted practice of what I call "polytheistic monotheism." It was an Israelite and Judean monotheism that included many different gods and goddesses of lesser orders and powers that the general community could count on for daily needs and questions. The God of ancient Israel was the God who had created the universe, but he was not always available for the daily and rather mundane needs of the people. Although this is not the official line of biblical monotheism, it certainly appears to be the way the people of ancient Israel dealt with their daily religious needs, turning to lesser gods and goddesses to fulfill a whole spectrum of daily needs for food, water, fertility, conflict resolution between neighbors, etc. Throughout the world we find similar arrangements where Christian ministers are forced to accept the popular beliefs of the people and integrate their popular beliefs into the mainstream religion.

So the beginning of the search for synagogues in Bethsaida began with the question: "Where was the synagogue?" No synagogue has been found in twenty years of excavations although a structure that we have been calling a first-century Roman Imperial cult temple was recently hailed in a Polish article as "the synagogue of Bethsaida!" Bethsaida was a first-century city that was inhabited by Jews and that judging by its size might have had a synagogue. I suspect it did not have a synagogue, and if it did, it probably was part of a large house complex and not an independent structure. My own research on synagogues in ancient Israel has shown that synagogues in Israel, in the period while the Temple was still standing in Jerusalem were an extremely rare commodity, if they existed at all. My research led me to question what a synagogue was in the first century as it is mentioned in the Gospels and the writings of Josephus Flavius. I sought to learn not only whether synagogues existed in the first century, but also to unravel one of the most ancient rituals of the Tabernacle and later the Temple that I think persisted into the rituals of the synagogue. This ritual of incense burning has helped me to understand how and why synagogues developed as replacements for and symbolic renderings of rituals from the Tabernacle and the Temple.

A real controversy exists in Israeli archaeology about when synagogues began in Israel and the Diaspora. A modern synagogue is an architecturally unique structure oriented toward the east or Jerusalem that is used for rabbinically-defined regular prayer services and Torah-reading ceremonies. This concept of a synagogue was probably formalized in Israel only after the destruction of the Temple in Jerusalem in 70 CE, perhaps in reaction to other competing definitions of "prayer places" of early Christians and Samaritans. By the Second Temple period, the synagogue was well developed in the Diaspora.

The meaning of the Greek word *synagogue* evolved over time. During the Second Temple period, the Greek word *synagogue* meant either a group of people and community or an institution and building. The word *synagogue* more closely translated to the Hebrew *Bet Knesset* (Congregation House). A Jewish synagogue in Second Temple period was probably also a *Bet Midrash* (House of Study), but not a synagogue the way we think about it today. In the Diaspora, the Greek word *proseuche* (prayer place) was the preferred translation of the Hebrew concept of a *Bet Tefillah* (A Prayer House), but its activity was independent, prayer-oriented, and in the Diaspora apparently located in its own building. The word *synagogue* (a gathering place) was a common word to pagans. Early Christians even used it as a synonym for the Greek institution of the *boule* (meeting place) until the middle of the third century CE. The early Christians also used *synagogue* as an alternate name for an "ekklesia" or church.

The most ancient synagogues (or something like what became "a synagogue") were probably built in Babylonia during the Babylonian Exile after the destruction of the First Temple in 586 BCE, and people often point to the book of Ezekiel for evidence of their existence. The Prophet Ezekiel accompanies the Exiles to Babylonia and helps them keep hope to reestablish the Temple in Jerusalem at the same time that he establishes a place of worship and public gathering for the Exiles. We have never been able to search for and properly excavate at sites that are associated with Jewish (especially Rabbinic) history. The first-century Jewish historian, Josephus, agrees with the statement in the Tosephta Sukkah 4:6 that in Alexandria, Egypt, there was an enormous synagogue so big that the Hazzan would wave flags for the people to answer "Amen!" He is referring to a famous first-century-CE synagogue that he probably knew well. Philo Judaeus, a card-carrying member of the Alexandria synagogue, confirms this assessment in his own writings. Thanks to excavations in the past thirty years we know that the oldest preserved (and documentable) synagogues were probably found in the Greek islands and Egypt. A Greek third century BCE inscription in Egypt that dedicates a synagogue in lower Egypt to the King Ptolemy and his sister Berenice (and entire family) is one of about eight inscriptions that document synagogue activity in Egypt from the third through the first century BCE. The Greek island of Delos (the birthplace of Apollo), Athens, Sardis, and Ostia in the port of Rome also have Second Temple synagogues with distinctive buildings. They all seem to emerge in the third century BCE following the model of Egypt. The Dura-Europos in Syria had a great, decorated synagogue also in the early centuries of the Common Era, but it is hard to know how much earlier it had developed there. What is clear is how much archaeological documentation about synagogues there is outside of Israel but so little in the Land of Israel.

But why? Rabbinic literature uses the term *Beit Kenesset* and speaks about 480 "synagogues" of Jerusalem that were destroyed in the Jewish war against the Romans in the year 70 CE. But, no synagogues have been found there in 150 years of excavations, and only one small inscription with the word *synagogue* has been found there. The inscription, from the time of the Second Temple, is a dedication stone for a synagogue that was used as a place for foreigners to gather. This is very telling. Perhaps the synagogue was a foreign hostel-like place built for the pilgrims so they would feel comfortable. One also wonders whether the Greek word in its local usage in Israel of the Second Temple period indicated a separate and unique building as it did in the Diaspora or a general gathering place perhaps inside of a house or other structure where people came to "think" or meditate. Perhaps synagogues were house synagogues similar to house churches that were the first gathering places for early Christians, and looking for separate edifices is fruitless in the early period. In addition, when the Temple was still standing in Jerusalem, did it make sense to have a competing religious institution like a synagogue? To date, only a few synagogues from the first century CE (or earlier) have been found in Israel. In the first season of the excavation of Masada in 1963–1964, the archaeologist Yigael Yadin suggested that a strange structure adjoining the casement walls around the mountain top fortress was a synagogue. This was the first synagogue ever discovered from the Second Temple period in Israel. His find renewed the issue of Second Temple synagogues in Israel. Yadin wrote in his popular book, *Masada* (1966, 185), ". . . If what we had just unearthed was indeed a synagogue, then this was a discovery of front rank importance in the field of Jewish archaeology and certainly one of the most important finds in Masada. For up to then the very earliest synagogues discovered in Israel belonged to the end of the 2nd or beginning of the 3rd century AD. There were no remains of any synagogue from the period of the Second Temple."

After the discovery at Masada, the sites of Herodium and Gamla each were deemed to possess a synagogue (with a potential fourth of Magdala in Galilee). The fact that only three Second Temple synagogues have emerged raises serious questions about the importance of the institution before the second and third centuries.

The three synagogues at Masada, Herodium, and Gamla became the archetypes for the Second Temple synagogue in Israel. But they are all different from one another, and they are not the Rabbinic style that would be so popular after the Second Revolt. I visited what had been known as the fourth Second Temple synagogue in Israel at Migdal, on the Sea of Galilee, and it is very hard to identify it as anything but a public building. These synagogues at Masada, Herodium, and Gamla do not share many characteristics other than the existence of interior columns, built-in seating, a rectangular shape, as well as an additional storeroom, which was the identifying factor for the synagogue, built into the corner of the room for some unknown reason. The entrances to the Gamla and Herodium synagogues face south to Jerusalem, and the entrance to the Masada synagogue faces east; but the orientation of the seating is all over the place. These three synagogues lack the main literary and later standardized architectural parts of all synagogues. They have no "Seat of Moses" (well known from the Rabbinic literature), no "Bima" or Torah shrine, no standardized setting in the city (the Gamla synagogue was located near the city wall in a large public building, the Masada synagogue was built in the former reception hall of King Herod, and the Herodium synagogue was placed in the dining area of King Herod), and no standardized seating plan (Gamla and Masada had benches on four sides of the hall, whereas Herodium had benches only on three sides).

Despite the lack of standardization, the main problem for making these synagogues the prototype for the Rabbinic synagogue of Israel is that these archaeological sites are associated with the Zealots. These sites are also associated with refugees fleeing the Romans during the First Revolt, and so the existence of a structure for synagogue use in this period might be an "emergency" measure rather than a regular operating institution. It would be difficult to use the Zealots as the "founders or preservers" of the synagogue concept because they were not necessarily followers of the Rabbis. But things changed starting in the second century CE, after the Second Revolt against the Romans (132–35 CE) when almost all the remnants of Judaism in Israel were wiped out. The Second Revolt, known as the "Bar Kokhba Revolt," was the final attempt by the Jews of Israel to reestablish the sovereignty of Israel and the Temple in Jerusalem. After this failed revolt, the Jews apparently decided to take a different direction—establishing synagogues.

Hundreds of synagogues were built in Israel in the third, fourth, and fifth centuries. Many have floors with zodiac and Roman symbols together with Jewish artistic iconography. The synagogue in Israel is, therefore, a product of the Diaspora idea of an independent religious institution and the earlier concept of a native Jewish gathering place and even an ingathering location for Diaspora pilgrims. After 70 CE, the synagogue was meant to replace the now-destroyed Temple in Jerusalem, but it was not intended to be exactly like the Temple and have Temple rituals. In short, the synagogue rituals, familiar in modern religion, are often ancient Temple rituals that have been reformed in some way to fit the demands of the people.

Incense: Israelites, Jews, and the Rest of the Ancient Near East

My own interest in how incense was used in antiquity began with the discovery of an incense shovel (figure 5.1) from the Roman period in 1996 at Bethsaida but has been continually piqued with new discoveries from the Iron Age at Bethsaida. We discovered at Bethsaida, two similar objects that were Iron Age tripodal pottery cups that were in a basin on a stepped altar at the Iron Age city gate. The objects had two columns of holes around the outside of the cup and when we looked into the pottery parallels from other locations throughout Israel, other scholars were calling similar objects incense burners.

Because all work in archaeology requires looking for parallels and then assessing the function of an object under investigation, the incense burner became an important discovery for understanding not only the stepped altar of Bethsaida, but also how incense was used in antiquity. Unfortunately, no burned incense marks appeared in the cups to indicate that it had indeed been an incense burner. My colleagues from the Bethsaida Project have been investigating all of the parallels of the incense burner at other sites in Israel and Jordan, and most of the cups appear without burn marks. All of this has made us reassess the use of the cup. The holes indicate that it may have contained water, milk, or other liquid libation on the stepped altar. The problem is that we tried, using experimental archaeology, to create cups like these out of pottery with the same number of holes and spacing, and we found that the liquids never quite flowed neatly through the holes. Recently, a colleague from Creighton University, Dr. Nicolae Roddy, has raised the issue that the tripodal cup may have been for dry incense shaking (like a salt and pepper dispenser) or for scenting of a sacrifice. This last suggestion would explain why there were no burn marks on the cups, but they could have been used to bring fragrant incense to the stone basin where a fire would be made and the fine grains of incense could be shaken out and burned in the basin on the stepped altar. In many ways this parallels the function of the incense shovel that I write about in this chapter, but it also seems to indicate an object that parallels one of the roles of the Havdalah spice boxes that have been in use by Jews for over a thousand years. In fact, most of our research on these artifacts have raised important questions about how ancient incense ceremonies were conducted.

Incense was a well-known part of rituals in the ancient Near East and the Mediterranean. In the myths of the Greeks, Romans, Egyptian Pyramid texts, Phoenicia, Ugarit, and Assyria, as well as the Hebrew Bible, incense was a part of medicine, religion, politics, economics, and the cultural and social milieu of the ancient world. The aromatic smoke of incense was used to offset the acrid odors that clothes, the body, and even cemeteries had, but it was also used to alleviate some serious diseases. Incense also had the ethereal and symbolic property to conjure up an image of heaven as well as the ghosts and goblins that most people thought inhabited their world. Incense was apparently used in private homes, in burial processions or graveside ceremonies, and in public religious ceremonies. Although its purposes are well described in Ancient Near Eastern literature, the particulars of its private use and its ongoing use in religious ceremonies that originated from the Ancient Near East, such as Rabbinic Judaism, are not well known. An incense service was an integral part of the Temple service in Jerusalem, and a well-formulated series of incense pronouncements appear in rabbinically sanctioned liturgy. It is generally assumed that no incense service continued past the first century CE.

Archaeological excavations starting in the Iron Age in Israel have identified what are thought to be three separate places for incense burning; in pottery incense burners, on stone altars, and in specially created stone bowls. These are only partially confirmed in ancient literature. Apparently, after the incense was burned, the ash and often the coals upon which the incense were burned, were immediately transformed by the ritualistic act of transferring the ash and coals by a ritual object—an incense shovel. In probably the most visible public display of incense, Leviticus 16:12–13, the Day of Atonement ritual indicates that the high priest was to take in one hand a shovel with charcoal and in the other hand incense and then combined the two on an incense altar. Apparently the high priest put the incense on the charcoals in the shovel, and then the incense cloud gave him protection while he proceeded to perform the rest of the rites of the Day of Atonement. The use of incense in the Bible is, therefore, seen as a protective and demonstrative act that would have made an extreme impression upon the general population who did not participate in the rest of the expiation ceremonies of the Day of Atonement, despite the fact that they were impacted by its success or failure.

Jewish and Christian Ritual and the Incense Service

Many "non-Jewish" or Christian rituals or ideas are really an integral part of Jewish rituals in a certain period and then were, for whatever reason, removed from Jewish life. In the nineteenth century, Jews began to modify their lifestyles and religious behavior in light of changing social and political conditions. The "Reform" movement, and especially the historical-positivist school of Jewish research that characterized some of the early reformers, came up with "new-old" results. When Jews in synagogues in Western Europe, for example, began to give topical sermons in the *lingua franca* of the country in which they lived, they were accused of mimicking Protestant Church practice. In fact, research of Rabbinic scholars like Abraham Geiger, Zechariah Frankel, and especially Leopold Zunz revealed in the nineteenth century that many Christian rituals and practices were, in fact, derived from Jewish practices that Jews had abandoned or so dramatically changed that they no longer were similar to the Christian practice. Nineteenth-century scholars demonstrated that far from mimicking Christian practices, many "innovations" of Jewish practice in the nineteenth century were just a restoration of an ancient practice.

Similarly, some modern church rituals evolved from Jewish practices that the Jews later abandoned, such as the use of incense. The Jews abandoned the use of incense just as the Christian Church was making it an integral part of the church service. Today, we associate the ritual burning of incense almost exclusively with Christian services.

The Incense Shovel of Bethsaida and Synagogue Iconography

On May 7, 1996, a bronze, short-handled incense shovel was found in an extremely disturbed Hellenistic-early Roman layer of occupation near a Hellenistic-Roman structure being excavated at Bethsaida. This discovery raised questions about the religious meaning(s) and use(s) of the incense shovel in general and at Bethsaida in particular. Incense shovels of this type are exceedingly rare in Israel, and the discovery and examination of the entire archaeological context of these incense shovels is rarer still. In the Bar

Kokhba "Cave of Letters," Yigael Yadin found three incense shovels together in a basket in one locus and another shovel in a different locus. The incense shovels were found together with other bronze objects, and Yadin assigned the making of the shovels to the first century CE and their production to a non-Palestine locale. According to Yadin, this was "the largest collection of Roman metal vessels found to date in Palestine and the neighboring region." Together, the four incense shovels found in the caves were of four different sizes, which may suggest similar, but distinct, purposes. Little more than 135 shovels have been identified and classified worldwide, and most lack an exacting archaeological context. The documented shovels appear in and around what might be called Hellenistic and Roman ritual sites and in burial caves. Most of the shovels come from the eastern parts of the Roman empire, and the Bethsaida shovel is possibly the only one in Israel that comes from a documented archaeological city context and not from a hoard, a random discovery, or a private collection. The meaning and purpose of these shovels has been debated because the incense shovel is prominently found in synagogue iconography of the third through sixth centuries. Yadin's impression, for example, was that the incense shovels he found in the Cave of Letters were part of the booty taken by Bar Kokhba's troops. In his book, *Bar Kokhba* (1978), Yadin states rather ambiguously: ". . . of the units of the Roman Legions or the Auxilia, which carried them about for ritual purposes." He was not sure what the ritual purposes were, but he, similar to other investigators who had written on these bronze shovels, assigned them to some ambiguous pagan ritual. In addition, although Yadin himself pointed out that the incense shovels figure with a number of other well-known Jewish symbols, such as the lulav (palm-branch), ethrog (citron), and menorah (candelabrum) in synagogue iconography of the third through sixth centuries, he does not address the point of why synagogue iconography would adopt a pagan ritual object for presentation in a Jewish building.

It is, of course, possible that palm branches, citrons, candelabra, and incense shovels, were originally non-Jewish symbols that Jewish artisans adopted for use in synagogues either with full knowledge that they were also pagan symbols or perhaps out of ignorance of pagan practices. There is evidence that all of these symbols, including the shovels, were meaningful in Jewish and non-Jewish circles of the period. Moreover, the quintessential Jewish symbol, the seven-branched menorah, described in the Bible was actually forbidden for use by the Rabbis following the destruction of the Temple in 70 CE, and its appearance in synagogue iconography is itself problematic. In order to accommodate this Rabbinic injunction, small changes were sometimes made to a menorah so that it was slightly different from the Temple menorah. The

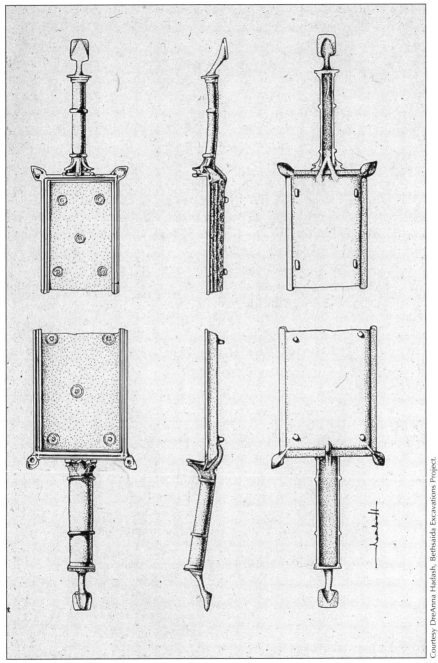

Courtesy DreAnna Hadash, Bethsaida Excavations Project.

Figure 5.2.   The insence shovel of Bethsaida (top) and the Cave of Letters (bottom).

synagogue was not intended to be a replacement for the Temple. The symbols of the synagogue were intended *to remind* the worshippers of the Temple, not be an exact copy of the items in the Temple. This is especially true in regards to the use of the incense shovel in synagogue iconography. More importantly, all of the other symbols continued to not only represent past Temple rituals, but also be active reminders of Rabbinic practices. An oil Menorah was lit on Hanukkah and was used in regular daily service. The Shofar symbolized Rosh Hashanah and the central practice of blowing the Shofar during the services on Rosh Hashanah and Yom Kippur. The Lulav and Etrog symbolized the central practice of the waving of the Lulav and Etrog during the service of the fall pilgrimage holiday, Sukkot. The incense shovel may have symbolized either the daily incense service of the Temple or the Leviticus 16 incense service of the Day of Atonement. In either case, the symmetry of daily High Holiday and Pilgrimage holidays (Sukkot) of the Rabbinic liturgy and practice is suggested by the appearance of the incense shovel on the synagogue mosaics. Incense shovels clearly continued to be a symbol during the Rabbinic period, and the use of incense by the Rabbis continued during most of the Classical Rabbinic period.

Literary Evidence for Jewish Incense Ceremonies and Use

Although the use of incense in the Temple in Jerusalem is well documented, Jewish uses of incense outside of the Temple are not. Scant references to incense burning in one's home could be documented from Tobit 6:17–18 and 8:1–2, although there the incense burning seems to be linked with a marriage ceremony of some kind. One well-known non-Temple Rabbinic use of incense is in the *Havdalah* (literally "Separation" from the Sabbath) service. The use of the candle and wine in the *Havdalah* service appear to be ancient and linked to their respective uses in initiating the Shabbat, but the use of the spices to end the Shabbat was debated until the Middle Ages. The reason given for the use of the spices, "to revive the depressed spirits of the Jew following the end of the Sabbath," seems oddly out of place for the rationalist Maimonides and many other explanations given in the medieval period. The spices, while not burned, have a ritualized purpose and holder ("*Hadas*"), which by the Middle Ages resembled some of the incense burners found in Jewish burials from the Roman period. In addition, Rabbinically ordained blessings were said over a variety of naturally occurring events, including pleasant smells of trees and incense. The special blessing (on spices) '*al hamugmar* is apparently placing incense on top of live coals after dinner or a meal to heighten the senses. This was probably a Hellenis-tic-Roman custom that became ritualized in Rabbinic Judaism. Apparently, it became ritualized into the third (*seudah shelishit*) meal of Shabbat, close to the end of Shabbat, and ultimately passed into a ritual after the end of Shabbat to insure that it would not involve the desecration of the Shabbat. Even into the Middle Ages, a type of ritual holder for this burning incense was called "*mahtah*," or shovel. Despite Rashi's use of the historical word "*mahtah*," it is clear that by the fifth and sixth century the ritualized incense burner was no longer a "shovel." While it is possible that a short-handled bronze shovel may have continued to be used as a ritual transporter of the incense, evidence from both literary and archaeological sources points to the use of a conical incense burner in the medieval synagogue.

It is also difficult to assess the possibility of synagogue incense use because hundreds of Talmudic discussions involving incense usually focus on biblical and Temple practices and do not always state the place of com-monly performed rituals. The reasons for the incense used in the Temple, listed for example, in the thirteenth century *Moreh Nevuchim* (*Guide to the Perplexed)* of Maimonides, gives the impression that his insights are drawn more from contemporary awareness rather than any historical tradition. So, he states: "Since many animals were slaughtered daily in the holy place . . . there is no doubt that the smell of the place would have been like the smell of slaughterhouses, if nothing had been done to counteract it. Therefore, it is commanded to burn incense there twice every day, in the morning and the evening, in order to give a pleasant odor to the place and to the gar-ments of those who officiate there" (part III, chapter 45).

Because nowhere does the Rabbinic literature state that this was the reason for burning incense, Maimonides may be alluding to a contempo-rary practice of burning incense in the synagogue "to give a pleasant odor to a place and to the garments of those who officiate there."

One classical Rabbinic citation, relating to a ruling Rabban Gamliel, (who lived when the Temple of Jerusalem was still standing) suggests that an incense burner was used in an official capacity outside of the Temple for what *halachic* (legal) sources would call *hidur mitzvah*—making aesthetically pleasant an already commanded practice. BT Beitzah 22b relates the three controversial rulings of Rabban Gamliel, one of which concerns the burn-ing of spices on a festival.

> He (Rabban Gamliel) furthermore gave three lenient rulings: One may sweep a dining room and put the spices (on the fire) on a festival, and one may prepare a "helmeted kid" on Passover. But the Sages forbid these.

The Babylonian Gemara relates that this refers to the perfuming of clothes; not a ritual burning of spices. But the actual incense burning in the synagogue on holidays is alluded to in the discussion:

"And one may not put the spices [on the fire] on a Festival, but in the house of Rabban Gamaliel they did put. Said Rabbi Eleazar ben Zadok: Frequently I accompanied my father to the house of Rabban Gamaliel and [observed that] they did not put the spices [on the fire] on a Festival but they used to bring in iron censers and fill them with the perfume of the incense on the eve of the Festival and stop up the vent-holes on the eve of the Festival. On the morrow when guests came they opened the vent-holes with the result that the room was automatically perfumed. They said to him: If so, it is permitted to do the same even on a Sabbath" (BT Beitzah 22b).

This same discussion is found elsewhere in the BT and seems not to have been resolved during this period. Most medieval decisors did not allow "incense burning" at the close of the Sabbath, festivals, although Rabbenu Gershom and Rabbenu Tam are in favor of using incense on these occasions. The large number of conical incense burners found in Syrian locations may have led to the designation of this incense burner as a *Damasca*.

In the Rabbis' narrative insight from daily life, such as in BT Berachot 53a, where the observation is made that Jewish women use incense for witchcraft, it is difficult to determine whether this is a historical insight or a contemporaneous one from the late Roman-early Byzantine period. Midrash Shir HaShirim Rabbah 5:1 states:

> Formerly God used to receive sacrifices from on high, as it is written, "And the Lord smelled the sweet savor" [Gen, chapter 8:21]. Now he receives them below, and so it is written, "I am come into my garden, my sister, my bride. I have gathered myrrh with my spice." This refers to the incense of spices and the handful of frankincense.

The Babylonian and Palestinian Talmudim contain second-century CE narratives about the Abtinas family, who were the incense makers for the Temple, and note that the recipe for the ritual incense was not lost after the destruction of the Temple in 70 CE. The incense that was a part of the synagogue service, however, probably had no direct connection to the incense ritual of the Temple but rather was a way to provide a fragrant environment to the building, link the people indirectly to Temple rituals of old, and provide a defense against lurking demons and evil spirits. Clearly the Rabbis associated the incense symbol with the healing of sins and atonement as well as possessing the power to overcome a variety of other problems. The use of spices for personal hygiene and stimulation were not forbidden; on the contrary, in the context of so-called Oriental or Middle Eastern cultures, incense burning was a recommended and highly meritorious part of daily life.

Given the importance of incense burning, why didn't the Jewish artisans and Rabbis of Israel choose to put conical incense burners in the synagogue iconography? There are a couple of reasons. First, it appears that some did. Professor Edwin R. Goodenough, who surveyed the Dura-Europos synagogue extensively in his *Jewish Symbols* volumes, did not find any incense burners in the synagogue iconography there. Second, they may be there. If upon closer observation there may be several conical incense burners in a number of different contexts of the Dura-Europos synagogue and they could be described as incense shovels. Dura Europos is important. Fort Europos was a Hellenistic and later a Roman-period walled city built on the right bank of the Euphrates River at what must have been seen as the crossroads of Europe and Asia in what is today Syria. It had an impressive synagogue that has some of the most extensive painted walls ever found anywhere. It shows us a picture of how these Jews, who designed these painted walls in the third century CE, thought many of the biblical and post-biblical scenes looked in their own times. Although they are still removed by over a thousand years from the Tabernacle and the Solomonic Temple in Jerusalem, they still attempted to show what they thought the Temple and many of the practices in the Temple looked like. They may have captured some of the grandeur of Herod's Temple in a period only three hundred years removed from the destruction of his Temple in Jerusalem. They are priceless reminders of how little we know about the Temple and the Temple practices.

In four of the panel paintings found on the walls of the synagogue, Professor Carl Kraeling, in his book *The Excavations of Duna Europos: The Synagogue* (New Haven, 1956), located depictions of conical incense burners and an incense shovel. In the panel of the "Ark in the Land of the Philistines" (WB 4, p. 101–2), for example, although the right side of the mural is supposed to represent the ravaged Temple of Dagon, the implements in the right-lower corner of the mural resemble the elements of the Roman Imperial Cult more than Ancient Near Eastern/Philistine wares. A number of elements closely resemble objects found at the Dura-Europos Hellenistic and Roman excavations, including an incense shovel (#17) and four conical shaped incense burners (#11–14). Carl Kraeling noted a number of these different free standing incense burners in the murals. In the "Consecration of the Tabernacle and its Priests" (WB2), on the two sides of the menorah, and the "Wilderness Encampment and the Miraculous Well of Be'er" (WBI), two items to the right and the left of the menorah can be distinguished as freestanding incense burners. The bronze incense burners on the two sides of the menorah in the "Consecration of the Tabernacle and its Priests" show incense smoke coming out of the top of the conical shaped object. In the "Destruction and Restoration of National Life" panel (NC I, p. 119, Kraeling), a freestanding conical incense burner is found as well. The incense shovel was apparently known in the city of Dura-Europos in antiquity. In another part of Dura-Europos excavations from the Roman period, one finds within a niche, a drawing of an eagle mounted on a horned altar with an individual off to the left side of the altar holding a shovel with a square pan that closely resembles the bronze incense shovels that we have been reviewing.

In the same excavations from the Hellenistic and Roman periods, two glazed clay incense burners (one conical) in the temple of Atargatis adorned with the sacred animal, the deer, were discovered as well as a bronze incense shovel from a private building near the temples. Although it might have been possible to preserve a conical incense burner in mosaic form, this was probably seen as a post-Temple innovation and not representative of the Temple ritual. In any case, the conical incense burner was separate from the incense shovel, which may have continued to have the role as a transporter of the incense to the burner. The incense shovel seems to have been depicted as a part in the Temple ritual but not a biblically ordained part of the service. Finally, in the latest periods of synagogue iconography (that is, sixth century), the conical incense burner may have already been proscribed as a symbol because of its use in Church ritual.

Evidence for an Incense Ritual in the Synagogue?

The incense shovel found at Dura Europos in the excavations from the Hellenistic and Roman period, which was similar to the ones found at Bethsaida and the Bar Kokhba Cave of Letters, was also assigned as a pagan incense shovel and assumed to be a "brazier." In the same excavations from the Hellenistic and Roman periods, two glazed clay incense burners (one conical) in the temple of Atargatis adorned with the sacred animal, the deer, were discovered as well as the bronze "brazier." The Dura-Europos incense shovel is freestanding with decorations in an ornate fashion. The presence of the two clay incense burners suggests that the brazier was a shovel for transporting incense and not a receptacle for the burning of incense. Despite Yadin's perception of slight traces of burning on his shovels (which has never been confirmed), incense burning does not appear to be

Figure 5.3.   The mosaics of the synagogues of Israel: Symbols Temple Rituals that persisted in the Synagogue—the Lulav, Etrog, the Menorah, and the Incense Shovel. From the Hammat Tiberias synagogue of the fifth century CE.

the primary purpose of the shovel. It was an incense shovel for handling the fine ground incense that would have been brought to an incense altar or an incense burner.

Archaeological evidence exists for a freestanding bronze incense burner in the early Hellenistic period in the Ancient Near East. These Hellenistic incense burners, or censers, generally are in the form of a cup with one side of the cup elevated and decorated with knobs. The handle is sometimes in the form of an ibex facing outward. Examples of bronze incense burners are also found in synagogue excavations and in iconography in Israel even into the Byzantine period. In the fourth century synagogue of Beth Shean, which features a mosaic of an incense shovel, archaeologist Nehemiah Zori found a two-part conical bronze incense burner that had four feet and could be freestanding, although it had a bronze chain connected to the upper part for hanging. The decorated sides of the "pan" or receptacle were ornate with bronze latticework and resembled the side panels of the Dura-Europos Hellenistic pan. Zori, who excavated the synagogue, says that the side panels of the burner are designed to look like animals. Zori also saw that this incense burner is similar to those some found in Syria and dated the incense burner to the sixth or perhaps seventh century. This is the same synagogue where a mosaic with an incense shovel was found in what is known as Beth Shean A. It is interesting that two incense service-related artifacts were found in this one location. An incense shovel is featured in the synagogue mosaic while an entirely different type of incense burner was found in another part of the excavations. The incense burner and the mosaic are clearly from different periods. The earliest stratum of the Beth Shean mosaic is assigned to the fourth century CE, while the incense burner found in the sixth/early seventh-century CE remains of the Beth Shean synagogue resembles those which were a part of the Byzantine church service. One explanation of the discrepancy is that the two may represent different developments of the same incense ritual. Another explanation is that the two elements were two parts of the ongoing incense ritual in the synagogue. The shovel may have continued to be used only for transporting incense to a conical incense burner.

All of this suggests that incense burning was not in fact a "Christian" practice, but rather a Roman and Jewish practice through the fourth century CE. The Byzantine Church did not at first accept the use of incense in services, apparently because of the Imperial Cult use in the pre-Christian period. Trypho and Irenaeus, in the second century CE, saw incense as a spiritual metaphor. Irenaeus states that "The incense is the prayers of the saints." This trend of valuing the importance of incense continued into the third century, as witnessed in the writings of Tertullian, perhaps because of the attacks of Marcion against the practices of the Hebrew Bible. Marcion attacked the practices associated with the Hebrew Bible, such as the burning of incense in the Tabernacle and Temple, and it is clear from the writings of Tertullian that this was part of his arguments about the inclusion of the Hebrew Bible in the canon of the Bible for the Christians.

In addition, during this period, trade in incense by Christians was forbidden. Arnobius, in his assaults against heathen practices denigrates the use of incense in the late third and early fourth century. Although early Christians did use incense at graves, presumably to cover the odor or against "evil spirits" that would have been thought to hover around the graves, it was not a Church ritual until the fifth and early sixth centuries. As Christian identity became secured in these centuries, many of the rituals that had been part of either the pagan or Jewish past were now seen as less threatening. A Byzantine incense shovel from Sardis, decorated with a large cross and very similar to the ones described above, demonstrates that the shovel was being used as early as the fourth century CE in some Christian contexts. The shovel shows the development of this type of utensil in Christian ritual, since later the incense shovel was replaced by the bronze conical censer in eastern and western churches. The introduction of the incense into services with blessings took place in the late fifth and early sixth centuries, and by the ninth century it became a regular part of eastern and western Church ritual.

But it is the late Roman and Byzantine period synagogue iconography, which features the incense shovel as a major symbol of Rabbinic Judaism, that raises the possibility that it was a synagogue ritual during the fourth and fifth century CE. Because the menorah, Torah shrine, lulav, ethrog, and the shofar did survive as important and active parts of the synagogue ritual (and not just passive symbols as they became the central parts of synagogue rituals for Rosh Hashanah and the holiday of Sukkot), it is possible that such an incense-burning ritual might have survived as well. Whether it was performed with a conical burner or on an incense shovel is not clear, but the iconography suggests that the shovel was a part of an active synagogue ritual. It may even have been a part of the Yom Kippur incense synagogue service that survives in synagogue liturgy to this day or the daily liturgy, which also features readings about the daily incense offering in the Temple.

But even though the material culture suggests that it was an active part of the synagogue ritual, the question remains if there is any literary evidence to bolster this claim. Very little is known about rituals of the synagogue in the Amoraic-Geonic (late Roman and Byzantine) period for a number of reasons. One reason is that the standardization of Rabbinic practice took place at the end of this period (tenth to eleventh century), and any practices discontinued in the medieval synagogue were not written about after this period. Remnants of variant practices can be found in "polemic" responsa literature written by the Geonim to criticize variant practices of certain communities in Palestine and the Diaspora as well as the Karaites. Rabbinic literature is the main source of our information on the synagogue and Babylonian Judaism and its practices became the predominant standard for Rabbinic Judaism. One of the main targets for this polemic responsa literature is directed against the Karaites, who criticized the "Rabbanites" for introducing practices into the synagogues that were not included in the Bible. Some of these practices continued into medieval Rabbinic Judaism, while others did not. For example, the introduction of the practice of the ritual lighting and blessing of Sabbath candles in the period of the Geonim survives; Rabbi Saadiah Gaon took the final action of obligating Jews to kindle the Shabbat light and say a blessing over its light apparently in reaction to the Karaite Sabbath practice of not lighting candles or any other fire even before the Sabbath begins. Even though the earliest Rabbinic collections advocate the lighting of candles before the Sabbath, the establishment of methods for keeping oil lamps burning on Friday evening, the Karaites would not allow any of these Rabbinic innovations.

While the Rabbis and the Karaites were at odds with one another over theological interpretations and religious authority issues, they were most prominently separated by the Rabbinic development of ritual not mentioned specifically in the text of the Bible and Temple rituals directly transferred to the synagogue—clearly enhancing the position of the synagogue and the Rabbis. Both seemed improper to the Karaites. In the Rabbinic prayerbook that began to be developed in the period of the Tannaim and Amoraim (first to fifth centuries CE), the incense service of the Temple figures prominently both in the opening and closing of the morning services. The incense service that was performed in the Temple was a powerful ritual for the senses of those who gathered to see it. The burning incense cloud would have been a palpable and very visible symbol of Divine presence. The fact that it was so prominent in the Temple worship would have been seen by the Karaites as something forbidden for non-Temple worshippers. Thus, when I was looking for a reference to a possible incense service in the Amoraic and Geonic synagogue, I looked for it in the writings of one of the most famous interlocutors of the Karaites, Rabbi Saadiah Gaon.

The ritual of incense is clearly suggested again in a polemic against the Karaite Daniel al-Qumisi in the writings of Rabbi Saadiah Gaon in the tenth century CE. The polemic implies that the Rabbinic Jews were still performing an incense service in their synagogues while the Karaites were not. Al-Qumisi's writings (as many of the controversies and the Rabbinic responses) are preserved only in manuscript form and express some of the major differences between the Rabbis and the Karaites. In the ninth and tenth centuries CE, these differences necessitated Rabbinic responses. The

Gaon Natronai ben Nahshon, for example, composed a treatise refuting the Karaite views on the Jewish calendar (the Rabbis had a different calendar of holidays than the Karaites even though they were both reading basically the same Torah), and this dispute is only preserved in manuscript form. Once the controversy was finished and the Karaites were no longer seen as a threat, the Rabbis apparently felt no need to preserve the original content of the arguments, and so it is amazing that we have any of these works at all. This is the case of the incense ritual that is preserved in a manuscript that was found in a Cairo synagogue Geniza, a burial site for worn texts was established in most synagogues, at the end of the nineteenth century. Scholars, such as Dr. Solomon Shechter, saw in these manuscripts a way of learning about parts of Jewish life that were sublimated to the established rituals of medieval Rabbinic authority. In a manuscript that is now preserved in Cambridge, England (the Geniza from the Egyptian synagogue was brought to England and studied there), the Karaite Al-Qumisi writes about his dispute with the leader of Rabbinic Judaism of the period, Rabbi Saadiah Gaon:

> . . . If they say that we should burn incense and light candles because they (synagogues) are a "Temple in miniature," we will say to them: it is not as you argue, even more so, God forbade that the incense and the lighting of candles in synagogues because there is in this pagan worship, because they are placing the synagogues in the same level as the Temple of God (in Jerusalem) in the holiness and the doing of these things. . . . this is forbidden to put the synagogues in the same level with the Holy Temple in regards to the bringing in of impurities, because synagogues are not holy. And every one who lights candles in them or burns incense in them because they are holy is transgressing the commandments of God and is making holy that which is not holy and is not preparing his heart for the God of his fathers. . . . but those who obligate the lighting of candles and the burning of incense in synagogues are the Rabbis, and they bring evidence (to support this view) of the holiness of the synagogue from the writing that it shall be a "Temple in miniature."
>
> (*Rabbi Saddiah Gaon's Translation of the Torah*, ed. Moshe Zucker [New York: Feldheim, 1959], p. 5)

Al-Qumisi condemns the Rabbis for making their synagogues into a *miniature Temple* that includes rituals from the destroyed Temple of Jerusalem. Goodenough in his assessment of the incense shovel (Vol. IV, 1954, p. 199ff), presents a number of sources that also seem to imply that the burning of incense continued in the period following the destruction of the Temple. Evidence of open-top square box incense burners associated with Jewish burials may reflect refinements of the incense shovel burner.

Goodenough's anthropological approach to the use of the incense burner among Jews found that it continued in the East but not in the West. Evidence for incense burning in synagogues and at home can be found among Ethiopian Jews, Syrian Jews, and especially among Yemenites up until the modern period. They are mostly incense burners similar to the Eastern Orthodox tradition of Christianity. Although the incense burning may have survived in some Eastern Jewish rites of those who mainly lived under the authority of Islam, the Western and Eastern European Jewish rites removed the incense ritual entirely from the synagogue, perhaps because it was too similar to medieval Church ritual. Jewish liturgy continued to have a disproportionately large number of readings on incense in the daily, Sabbath, and holiday services, but no active ceremony is associated with it. But I think that perhaps, even in the Western and Eastern European synagogue, a vestige of the incense service survived in an unlikely but opportune place in the liturgy. The mystical Medieval Jewish tradition also incorporated elements of the incense service, and perhaps even the conical incense burner, into a new/old ritual called *Havdalah* performed with an ornate "spice box" (*Hadas*) at the end of the Sabbath.

Similar to other parts of the synagogue service, the Rabbis in Eastern and Western Europe seemed to move to a new level of symbolic understanding of the mysteries of the Temple—from one physical symbol of the Temple service to another physical symbol of the remembrance of the Temple in liturgy and ritual. In the service, three elements were woven together—the incense holder or spice box, the lighting of the lights, and the wine. The service became an opportunity, not to burn the incense, but to enjoy the smell. What is interesting to me is that this new ritual may preserve one of the most ancient forms of worship. Placed in a container with holes, the fine incense was shaken and the smell of the incense enjoyed by all who were present at the ritual, just as we think the original tripod incense shakers found at Bethsaida were used thousands of years ago.

But it appears that incense burning was going on for almost three thousand years in Jewish life until it was discontinued in the early Middle Ages. In the time of the Hebrew Bible incense was also burned at Bethsaida and at worship sites all over Israel. It was used in the Temple of Jerusalem, the Livia Julia Temple at Bethsaida in the Roman period, and apparently continued in the synagogues of the Golan that have the tiny incense shovels engraved on stones and on mosaics on the floor. Incense has always symbolized the Divine because the incense cloud could be seen from miles away and continually reminded the people at work that God was with them wherever they were.

6

Searching for the Teacher of Righteousness at Qumran and in the Dead Sea Scrolls

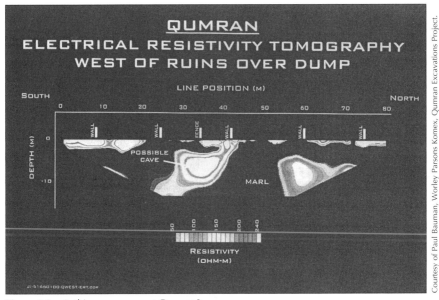

Figure 6.1.　Is this a new cave at Qumran?

Courtesy of Paul Bauman, Worley Parsons Komex, Qumran Excavations Project.

Archaeologists return to a previously excavated site for a variety of reasons. The development of new archaeological techniques can allow them to do research which was not possible in a past excavation. This is what happened with our ground breaking new work in the Cave of Letters using ground penetrating radar, electrical resistivity tomography, and fiber optics to see under the rocks without lifting them up. Archaeologists can also return to a previously excavated site because a new theory about the occupation of the site emerges, which demands a retesting of the old theory. This was also the case in our return to the Cave of Letters site. Many archaeologists return to a site if too much time passes between the original excavations and the publishing of the results, and people question the validity of the research or if many new questions emerge. This is the case of the excavations at Megiddo, Jericho, and Jerusalem, which were done repeatedly as new techniques for excavations were developed. Sometimes political, social, or economic reasons demand that a site be re-excavated. Sometimes major construction of a dam, a building, or roadway threatens the context of the archaeological site so a new excavation will be done of an old site. New literature and especially new social histories that raise new questions that were not asked in previous generations is another reason to reinvestigate a site. Acre (Akko) and Caesarea are two enormous sites that have continually amazed archaeologists even as social historians have changed their understandings of the relationships between Muslims and Crusaders in Medieval Acre and Pagans, Jews, and Christians in a city like Caesarea. In some cases, political fortunes of an area change. A site, which may have been located in the territory of one authority, group, or government, may be ceded to another authority, group, or government, and the new group wishes to assess the status of this "new/old" site or begin an excavation that was never conducted. Although there are numerous reasons to reinvestigate sites, we returned to Qumran primarily to examine it again with new technology and to test out new theories.

Bethsaida, Qumran, and Yavne: 67 CE–1967 CE

I feel a personal and intellectual connection to Qumran and the other excavation sites. Bethsaida was located in an area just over the 1948 cease-fire line between Israel and Syria and only after the Six Day War in 1967 did the area become accessible for all archaeologists. At the modern city of Yavne, in southern Israel, there is an ancient mound that has never been fully excavated, even though Yavne is perhaps the single most important name of a Jewish city around the world. The reasons behind why the ancient mound of Yavne was not excavated are complex, but it would not have been possible before 1948. The new modern city of Yavne grew up around this ancient mound after 1948, and the ancient mound, which had formerly been occupied by a local Muslim community, has only recently become the subject of new interest. Since 2003 our Yavne Excavations Project has been involved in figuring out the most important places to excavate and how to understand where to excavate on the mound using ground penetrating radar and electrical resistivity tomography to direct our work. After the Six Day War, Qumran suddenly became available for new archaeological excavations because of shifting political barriers.

Bethsaida, Qumran, and Yavne were all villages that played key roles in first-century Judaism, and they share unusual connections in the modern period as well. Bethsaida was a part of the beginning of the Revolt against Rome in 67 CE, Qumran was destroyed by the Romans on their way to siege Jerusalem in 68 CE, and Yavne was the place where many of the Rabbinic refugees gathered after the destruction of the Temple in Jerusalem in 70 CE. Just as Bethsaida and Qumran became the proving ground for the early Christians and some of the ideas that became a part of Rabbinic Judaism, so too, Yavne became a proving ground for Rabbinic Judaism after the destruction of the Temple in 70 CE. It was at Yavne that Rabbi Yohanan ben Zakkai pleaded his case to save what was left of Judaism to the new Emperor Titus. There was another reason why Yavne was connected to Bethsaida. From the time of the Roman conquest of Israel by Pompey in 63 BCE, Josephus in *Antiquities* 13:395 makes Yamnia (the Greek name of Yavne) a Roman and not a particularly Jewish city. It was Livia Julia (the same woman for whom Bethsaida-Julia is named), the wife of Caesar Augustus, who received the city in the will of Salome, the sister of Herod the Great, who had earlier received and given the city to his sister in his will. Livia Julia, in turn, gifted the city in her will to Tiberius her son, (*Antiquities* 18:158), and thus it is not a far cry to understand how Titus ends up sitting in the city at the conclusion of the war against the Jews in his siege against Jerusalem. It was the famous Jewish Princess, Berenice, who accompanied Titus to Yavne as well. Rabbi Yohanan ben Zakkai, the Emperor Titus, and Berenice together with Livia Julia form a triangle of connections for me, and working at Yavne has provided me new views about an ancient city.

Yavne, like Bethsaida, is an example of a Jewish mixed population city. Two generations after Rabbis Yohanan ben Zakkai and Rabban Gamliel established themselves at the city, it lost its major Jewish presence. Yavne became the "Second Jerusalem" after 70 CE but by the Bar Kokhba Rebellion, some sixty years later, this was no longer the case. In the period following the Bar Kokhba Revolt, its fortunes declined and the nearby city of Lod became the center of Rabbinic activity. It is even possible that the city's fortunes declined even quicker than we imagined. We created archaeological projects at Qumran, Bethsaida, and Yavne for basically the same reasons— because political and social conditions allowed us to examine the site for the first time in years, and because we had new technologies and theories that would allow us to do work that no one else had done before us.

The Mystery of Qumran

Qumran is perhaps one of the famous and controversial sites in Israel. The five Qumran excavations conducted by Father Roland de Vaux in 1951, 1953, 1954, 1955, and 1956 have never been fully published, and the short digging seasons, of between two to five weeks, did not allow him to fully excavate the site. There have been other expeditions that have excavated at Qumran since the 1950s. Our expedition had new theories and techniques that we were going to test at Qumran—a primary reason to return to this site. Despite or perhaps because Roland de Vaux was the first to conduct scientific excavations there, his theories about Qumran have become deeply entrenched among some scholars and caused great skepticism among others. The theories about the relationship between Qumran, the caves, and the cemetery have raged for more than sixty years with no resolution. Many new social histories have been written about Qumran. If the *"scandal"* of the Dead Sea Scrolls was that for more than fifty years they were not published (and this has been remedied by the final publication of the Scrolls by the new committee by 2002), it is an even greater scandal that the original results of the five excavation seasons have never fully seen the light of day. Many assumptions were predicated upon preliminary information that was circulated and then canonized within popular and professional writings, but the original research was never fully published. More important, to publish the research of archaeology some fifty years after the excavations took place is a difficult enterprise. Unlike the Scrolls, whose translations and investigations were aided by the upgrading of technologies over the past fifty years, the original archaeology is diminished by the recent technology boom. Because none of the newest techniques and technologies were used in the original collection, we are captives to assumptions that were tested and put forth in the 1950s and not in the twenty-first century. No systematic and comprehensive use of modern technologies was ever seriously used at this important site in the past fifty years. The site was in Jordanian hands until 1967. Since the 1993 Oslo Accords the entire area just south of Jericho has been moving toward Palestinian control, raising major questions for future research. In 1992–1993, as a possible peace treaty with the Palestinians loomed and the Israel Antiquities Authority launched "Project Scroll," the largest single archaeological project ever undertaken by the then recently re-organized Antiquities Authority of Israel to look for more scrolls in the caves along the Dead Sea. It was launched specifically to see if any caves were left to excavate. The Authority used conventional search techniques, generally without the benefit of new technology. Archaeologists fanned out throughout the region and investigated as many sites as possible in a relatively short period. In the end, this massive operation of Project Scroll received mixed reviews among some scholars and disappointment from others. Small finds were made, without the benefit of any modern techniques. Our proposal at Qumran for 2001 and 2002 was much bolder. It included a ground penetrating radar scan of the entire site and the marl (a coarse mixture of clay and limestone that is as hard in some places as concrete) close by and an electrical resistivity tomography scan of the edges of the settlement to see if any undiscovered caves and buildings were left to be excavated. The investigation of the enigmatic cemetery was one of the main objectives.

Our journey to study Qumran began in the summer of 2000 with a short visit to Qumran in July, 2000, as we prepared to do our excavation of the nearby Cave of Letters. Paul Bauman, our geophysicist, Harry Jol, our ground penetrating radar geologist, famed Dead Sea Scrolls scholars, Lawrence Schiffman, Steven Pfann, who had also worked on the Scrolls, and I visited the Qumran cemetery to see if any work could be done in the cemetery in future years. We had brought sophisticated equipment to Israel for the John and Carol Merrill Cave of Letters Project in 2000, and I was wondering whether we could contribute to other important sites on the Dead Sea near the Cave of Letters, especially if we brought our scientific team and equipment to Israel again. We had no license to conduct tests, and we did not want to run afoul of the Antiquities Authority of Israel, the agency that licenses all official excavations in Israel. Paul Bauman and Harry Jol, our lead geoscientists for the project, were simply afraid that their equipment would not function well given the extreme heat and salinity of the soil at Qumran. Just as we had not known if their equipment would function well in the Cave of Letters (it did), they needed to see for themselves where they might be able to work and make a contribution to the scholarship on Qumran. Before we even built a plan for doing anything, we needed to have them assess the situation. This look-see at Qumran was intended to determine if it would be worthwhile to even start applying for a license and where their equipment might really provide new results.

The idea of working in the cemetery of Qumran made the most sense. Today, in many parts of the world, cemeteries cannot be excavated as they were in the excavations until the end of the first half of the twentieth century. Today, religious sensibilities regarding graves and the fact that Qumran has become a very public tourist spot would not allow any serious excavation in the cemetery to take place. This despite the fact that it is the single largest and most important mystery of Qumran. Most scholars up until we began our work did not even know how many graves there were in the cemetery! Estimates widely differed from seven hundred (low) to fourteen hundred. Plus, the gradual undermining of the entire area (because it is tectonically active) and because of the diminishing aquifer and water table, graves were being lost yearly from the elevated position of the cemetery. Who were these people that were buried there has always been one of the mysteries of Qumran. So many theories abound precisely because no one knew how to do serious work on the cemetery without excavating it. As we went around the cemetery in the summer of 2000 Paul walked over a number of graves with a totally noninvasive method that did not require a permit to see if the graves would be good candidates for a full electrical resistivity tomography and magnetometry scan (not a metal detector). In one grave Paul immediately detected a very strong signal of metal. He asked me if they buried people in metal coffins in antiquity, and I naively answered that although lead coffins had been found in Jerusalem and elsewhere, they should not be expected in an "Essene" cemetery like this. The grave had been severely eroded on top but not excavated, and some of the stones had been removed for use in other nearby graves, but the visual observation yielded the clear contour of a grave. The signal indicated there was a very large metal object in the grave. The signal continued over the contour of the entire grave indicating the metal object was approximately six feet long (the length of the grave) and three feet wide. It was clear that it was just below the surface.

Our minds raced as we stood there in the middle of the cemetery of Qumran as to the possibilities. We were people who dreamed of the secrets of the Dead Sea Scrolls, and we stood in the middle of the most important possible discovery in the cemetery with no license to excavate. Was it premodern or modern debris buried for safekeeping in this cemetery? Was it the lead coffin of a later second-to-third century rich pilgrim or traveler from Syria or Mesopotamia, who did not make it to a Jerusalem cemetery and ended up buried in this cemetery? Was it a scroll like the Copper Scroll hidden in the grave for safekeeping? Lead coffins were known in Jerusalem in the second and third century CE and were the approximate size and shape of the signal, but the site was apparently destroyed by the time this lead coffin style had come into vogue. Was it part of the famed but allusive treasure of the Copper Scroll, the scroll found in nearby Cave 3, which listed the metal treasures of the Temple in Jerusalem? We were so surprised that we did not know what to do.

Because we did not have a license to excavate and the cemetery is so large and confusing, we feared we might not be able to pinpoint the exact grave among the many graves. We had GPS coordinates, but the cemetery had so many graves, side by side, that when we left the grave to examine the rest of the cemetery we left one student, Chris Morton, to guard and photograph it. We were lucky that we documented the entire event. Years later some would claim that we had planted the metal in the ground. Chris Morton stood in this grave in the hot sun and meticulously documented everything around the site. When we came back two hours later, we recorded the location in GPS coordinates (now together with the photographs) and rated the state of the grave, then returned to our excavation base camp at *Metzokei Deragot,* a youth hostel located in the upper hills beyond Ein Gedi.

We resolved to contact the Antiquities Authority immediately and to give a full report. This was not just a mystery, it was a significant find and it was in need of immediate attention to insure that no one would "raid" the grave or pilfer what was in it before we got there with permission to do a salvage operation. The possibility of a metal coffin got us all thinking that this was an important location to return to and that there might be other strange anomalies in the cemetery. Of course, we had to start with a license, and we would need the full array of technical equipment, as well as raising money for the excavation. We would do scans of graves and get a full view of what was inside the graves without excavating them. We were afraid to leave this mysterious grave for another year, but had no choice.

We went to work on the Cave of Letters in the summer of 2000, and we vowed to get back as soon as was feasible with a license and the funding to properly do the project. To their credit, John and Carol Merrill came to the rescue again to help fund the Qumran Excavations Project. Just as they had been interested in the Cave of Letters, so too John and Carol Merrill were interested in Qumran. John Merrill in particular was very interested in the story of Qumran and the Dead Sea Scrolls. His book, *Sons of Light* (Harrow Press, 2004) that he was working on all during our work at the Cave of Letters is a historical fiction book on the people who lived and died in this area. It remains one of the best books I have ever read on the daily life of the people who were involved with the Scrolls. I am proud to say that John and Carol continued to follow our work as we went back to see if we could get a license to work at Qumran.

When we arrived back in January 2001 for a visit with other archaeologists to plan out our work for the coming summer, we found that the grave with the metal in it had been totally excavated! I remembered how despondent we all felt, and how genuinely motivated I was to make sure that this did not happen to another grave at the cemetery. How many more of these graves contained mysteries that had never been explored? We did not know. The story was featured in *Biblical Archaeology Review* in March/April, 2001, and it was on the basis of this and the other aspects of our petition that a license to re-examine the cemetery and Qumran was granted with our lead archaeologists, Hanan Eshel and Magen Broshi.

When we returned in July 2001, with license in hand, we discovered, to our amazement, that the coffin had *not* totally been excavated! The bottom was still sitting beneath some of the dirt at the bottom of the grave allowing us to remove it and have it tested. Whoever had tried to remove the metal coffin had left the bottom sheet of metal still at the bottom of the now six foot deep grave. We also remembered the small fragment that the student had taken in the summer of 2001 and armed with our license, we began to officially analyze the metal type. Preliminary analysis revealed something so out of the ordinary that it shocked even the metallurgy researchers. It was not lead, it was zinc! A lead coffin this size would have weighed several hundred pounds and would have been difficult to carry for great distances. But a *zinc* coffin was much lighter and had the same advantages of a lead coffin. A sealed zinc coffin would have allowed a corpse to be shipped from far away and to travel well for ultimate burial in this far-flung cemetery. Whoever was entombed in this zinc coffin had gone to great expense to be buried in this area of the world. The discovery of the coffin's remains proved that the coffin had not been a mirage. Some small nails and small fragments of bone were found in the grave, along with the bottom section of the zinc coffin. The shape of the metal indicates zinc sheeting was hammered onto a wood frame.

Had someone seen us poking around the cemetery in July 2000, and gone back to see what had caught our interest? Had they used a metal detector in the cemetery and discovered the now revealed top of the metal coffin? Who were these unknown grave robbers? Remember, Qumran is a public and a privately developed tourist site. It is close to the road but a difficult climb up to the cemetery. After hours on the Dead Sea, the roads are empty enough for people to arrive, complete their business, and leave nearly undetected. Although protected, it is a large area. A team of people like us, walking around in the cemetery in broad daylight with specialized equipment, could have caught the attention of a tourist, a worker, a bus driver, a driver, etc. After our visit, it would have been possible to locate the metal coffin using standard metal detectors. Experienced grave robbers could have dug the grave quickly in the middle of the night, and the metal coffin would have been spirited out of the cemetery without anyone seeing them. It's the coffin's disappearance and our frustration with what we perceived to have been the loss of what might have been a great discovery that pushed us on in our efforts to fully explore the mysteries of the subsurface of Qumran.

The Rest of Qumran

Qumran is not like other archaeological sites in Israel and perhaps unlike anything else in the entire world. It is an archaeological site in direct proximity to the place where the Dead Sea Scrolls were found. It holds great significance because of the discovery of so many scrolls in one location and because the of the scrolls' connection to the study of early Christianity and Rabbinic Judaism. In the short period of fifty years, millions of words, and tens of thousands of articles and books in many languages have been written about the Dead Sea Scrolls. Never has so much been written on so little. But so much hinges upon an interpretation of the archaeological site associated with the Scrolls (that is, Qumran) that I was surprised to find out how little is really known about the people who lived and died at the site. If Bethsaida on the Sea of Galilee was the first place where the Apostles and Jesus gathered to discuss their apocalyptic ideas, many speculated that Qumran on the Dead Sea was the place where many new ideas were carried out in daily life. People sat in the Judean desert site and speculated on when and how the physical existence of the universe would be changed over to a more spiritual and Divine existence. The two sites could not have been more different from one another. The lush valleys of Galilee was where Bethsaida was located. Bethsaida had large courtyard houses and smaller fishermen's houses on a fresh water Sea of Galilee. Qumran, on the other hand, was in the forbidding Judean desert on the undrinkable Dead Sea, with heat that reached over 120 degrees in the summer and did not seem to have a residential section with houses. Could Qumran be the Jewish village from which the nascent Christian movement drew some of the incredible eschatological visions? The "eschaton" (Greek word which deals with the "End of Days" or messianic era) is one of the most important themes in the New Testament and although Second Temple Judaism has some eschatological visions in it, the Dead Sea

Scrolls are permeated with End of Days speculation. Bethsaida seemed to be the Garden of Eden in comparison with Qumran that could easily pass for a reminder of the judgment of Hell.

The buildings of Qumran, the nearby caves, the now empty cisterns and pools, and the cemetery stand as silent witnesses to the original purposes and people associated with the Qumran site. Perhaps more than anything else at Qumran, the cemetery actually contains the remains of the people of Qumran and although we cannot excavate it today, we could find out if the graves contained significant artifacts without excavating the graves. I knew that grave artifacts had been found in the excavations of the graves in the 1950s and 1960s; the question was what we could find in the graves. That is what makes it so archaeologically significant. Over a thousand graves could easily be counted, containing the most significant pieces of information on the site, and we had a way of gaining some of that information without excavating. There has been speculation almost from the beginning of the excavations in the 1950s that some of the founding fathers of early Christianity must have lived and died there. As a result, work in the cemetery has been both important and fraught with problems. Who were these people in the graves around Qumran? Were they all members of the Essene sect or was this a premier place of burial that had been used and reused during many different periods as people moved from north to south and east to west. We hoped that we could figure out who used the cemetery, when, and why.

Working in a cemetery, especially such an important cemetery, is a very complicated proposition in Israel in the present period. For those who have seen the problems faced by anthropologists, universities, museums, and many indigenous peoples over burials that have been disturbed and bones that have been displayed, stored in warehouses, and often disposed of in extremely insensitive ways, it is a familiar and tragic tale. Anthropologists, archaeologists, and researchers have often revealed how little they really cared for and understood the subjects they studied. Native Americans have become more and more militant about rigorous standards of reverence and conduct with regards to their burial sites. The 1990 Native American Graves Protection and Repatriation Act in the United States requires all federally funded institutions to inventory their Indian skeletal remains, notify the descendants, and return the remains if the descendants so desire. In Israel, in this same period, a variety of forces have created a new limitation, which makes any systematic excavation of cemeteries nearly impossible. Even though the law is basically justified by Jewish law, it is nearly impossible to excavate grave sites even from the Stone Age. Non-Jewish cemeteries and burial sites are treated the same as Jewish sites. In short, the groups are polarized, pitting "science" and "faith" against each other. Because there is so much mistrust (by the religious of the motives of the scientist) the possibility of conducting even a respectful excavation of cemeteries and burial sites has become extremely limited. The message that has begun to be heard is simple: bones, even ancient bones, may not routinely be used as subjects for research even when the research may yield significant results such as the tracking of genetic and ancient diseases from bones through the study of DNA. We live in a time when it is both possible and efficient to do this, and the need to do this has become an important research goal for science. Past problems, however, and the sense that the research community does not honor the religious traditions of the people whose bones are used, have led to these severe restrictions. Perhaps a rapprochement of sorts can happen when science restricts its research to specific issues and is able to see the value of returning the bones to the graves from which they were taken when research is complete.

This is part of the problem as we approached our work at Qumran. Since the 1960s, when Salomon Steckoll finished his excavations at the Qumran cemetery, no other sanctioned excavations have taken place at the cemetery. Despite this, even a cursory study of the present state of the cemetery reveals that graves have been robbed, raided, and illegally excavated, but no systematic excavation using modern scientific techniques and methodologies (that have emerged only in the last thirty years) has been done. What we proposed to do was to provide a new way to excavate a cemetery—to provide information in a *noninvasive* way about the graves without having to excavate them. If a grave had been excavated, robbed, or raided, we were permitted to collect information from inside the grave but not excavate an untouched grave. This was a solemn and extremely important study that had no precedent in Israel. It was also risky because we did not know how much information we might be able to collect in the highly salinated soils of the Qumran cemetery.

Secrets of the Cemetery of Qumran

The cemetery of Qumran has been noted by many since the mid-1850s. F. DeSaulcy and the Rev. H. B. Tristram came in the mid-1850s as well. Tristam wrote: "We found at intervals many indistinct rows of unhewn stones, which, if at all the remains of human constructions, carry us back to a ruder period than the flints of our gravel beds . . . " Three reports from 1874 seem directly connected to the first understanding of the significance of the cemetery of Qumran. The first expedition there in October 1873 was conducted by Clermont-Ganneau, who saw the ruins of Khirbet Qumran as insignificant but viewed the cemetery as extremely important. He apparently excavated two graves at the place he called "Khirbet Gomran." They did not really know what to make of this site along the Dead Sea. The name of the site, *Gomran*, (the way they heard it and transcribed it from the local Bedouins) is thought by some to preserve an ancient or premodern association with *Gomorrah*, of Sodom and Gomorrah fame. Clermont-Ganneau's results are the first pieces of information about those buried there. Lieutenant C. R. Conder's December 1874 survey at Qumran does not add any information to the site. It is clear that at least fifty-five graves have been excavated since 1873. Forty-three graves were excavated by Father Roland de Vaux. As many as twelve graves were excavated by Solomon Steckoll between 1965–1967. A variety of "other" graves are empty (at our counting in 2002 there were more than ten others that were excavated and left open) for a total of sixty-five. Many of these have been clandestinely robbed/raided or excavated in the years between 1967 and the present. During the summer of 2001, we were permitted to survey the cemetery using noninvasive technology and to systematically investigate the already excavated tombs. We had a broad mandate for mapping and surveying the area, but we also knew that the cemetery was one of the most important and untouched sources of information for the understanding of Second Temple Judaism and the Dead Sea Scrolls.

The Latrines of the Essenes

In 2002, we extended our work and had a variety of different research projects that we simultaneously carried out throughout the entire site. Professor Philip Reeder of the University of South Florida, chief cartographer for most of our archaeological projects for the past decade, mapped the entire water system from the caves to the site and any other "map-able" work we did from the caves to the cemetery. One of the most interesting and unheralded work we did involved what we called "the latrines of the Essenes." One of the problems that most excavators associated with Qumran (because of the site's association with the Dead Sea Scrolls) was where they established their toilets. While toilets are usually not one of the primary areas of research for archaeological excavations, it is an interesting question at Qumran because of the hygiene and purity rituals found in the Dead Sea Scrolls that are associated with the people who lived at the site. In the Roman period, public latrines were established in many major cities, but little or nothing is known from smaller villages. We know that whoever occupied Qumran was interested in hygiene and purity rituals and since the Dead Sea Scrolls makes a point about establishing toilets outside of the village, we thought it was a worthy archaeological project. Toilets are very important in every village. Latrines were mentioned in the Hebrew Bible and were a part of the daily rituals of the life of the Israelites and the Jews. Most ancient peoples recognized that sickness and disease were parts of life that needed to be controlled and that raw sewage in the middle of a village was neither healthy nor dignified. For a variety of reasons, the Dead Sea Scrolls set out very extreme rules for personal hygiene that necessitated the siting of the bathroom in a dignified but close location. I remember the first time I read about the issue was in the book, *The Dead Sea Scrolls: Fifty Years After Their Discovery,* edited by Lawrence Schiffman, Emanuel Tov, and James VanderKam. In the book, archaeologist Jodie Magness' chapter "A Reassessment of the Excavations at Qumran" (2000, 708–719) speculated on where the toilets of the Essenes might be located. She thought that she had identified a latrine inside one of the buildings of Qumran. I could not imagine that if these Qumranites were so meticulous in their bathing and purity rituals, they would allow a latrine inside of the village. If these Qumranites were the people who wrote the regulations found in the Dead Sea Scrolls, they certainly would not have established a toilet inside of the village. It is true that it is possible that there were later uses for the build-ings at Qumran, but if we were going to be looking for the latrines of the first-century Essenes and especially those people associated with the Scrolls, we had to be looking at a site removed from the village of Qumran. They must, I reasoned, have positioned it outside of the village and in a place that would fulfill their biblical and sectarian guidelines. We followed up on this lead after receiving information from fellow archaeologists and knew that we had the type of equipment that could easily detect groupings of rocks that would have formed the bowl-shape seats that people used even in an-tiquity. Our work included meticulous mapping and even GPS coordinates of the places that we worked so we could create scientific maps for future excavators. It really did not fit the scope of the work we were doing, but it was one of those issues that tells us something about some of the basic customs of biblical life.

Toilets are not the most interesting archaeological topic for the public, but they tell us something about the way that the groups of Qumran may have mirrored a custom that was written about for the first time in the Bible. Private and public toilets are known in antiquity in formal and less formal settings. Even with the advent of indoor plumbing (which was found in homes in ancient India in the Bronze Age!), toilets remained, perhaps for obvious reasons, in a place that was set aside from the village or city. When we began our work at Qumran, I was reminded of the quotation from the Book of Deuteronomy 23:12–13: "You shall have a place outside the camp and you shall go out to it; and you shall have a stick with your weapons; and when you sit down outside [of the camp], you shall dig a hole with [the stick] it, and turn back and cover up your excrement. Because the Lord your God walks in the midst of your camp . . . therefore your camp must be holy, that he may not see anything indecent among you and turn away from you." The idea that hygiene was connected to holiness and that there was also a question of modesty involved seems to permeate this text. In the time of the Deuteronomist, the people of Israel and Judah lived in settled cities and not in the desert in camps. The fact that this citation is found in the Book of Deuteronomy tells us that this may have been an admonition to the Jews of the seventh century CE cities as well as the villages. But where were you supposed to put latrines when Jews moved from the desert camps to cities? How far outside of the walled cities of antiquity did one need to go?

As we have mentioned before in this volume, Jews in the Hellenistic and early Roman period were very concerned with not only physical purity and washing (they developed many ritualized ways of dealing with almost every form of bodily fluid) but also a form of ritual purity that is very different from the physical purity. Ritual purity was a spiritual state of being as much as it was a physical state of being. The Rabbis would later establish that based on their reading of the Bible, there were at least seven or eight categories of ritual purity. Ritual purity issues were so important that they fill nearly *one-quarter* of all early Rabbinic discussion. There is no doubt that starting in the Second Temple period the idea of physical and ritual purity occupied the Jews. One could say that at the time (Second Temple period) the Jews could not control their own political destiny in the face of Hellenism, they used ritual laws to create a spiritual and private way for controlling their own identity and destiny. While Romans were bathing in their bathhouses as a part of Roman culture, Jews were bathing as a part of Jewish culture. The Rabbinic rules are manifold, complex, and varied among different Jewish groups. It is clear that the Qumranites were as obsessed with this issue as any other group in this time period. Perhaps they too could not control their political destiny, so they began to more tightly control their spiritual destiny, especially with regards to purities. Thus the search for the latrines, using ground penetrating radar and electrical resistivity tomography provided another opportunity to understand how the site was conceived. But once we had all of this information, we needed to carefully map the different pieces of the research. Dr. Philip Reeder created what is really a simple snapshot of the daily life of the Qumranites through his mapping of the site. The mapping of Qumran, the caves, the latrines, the water system, and the graves tells us what the daily life of the people of Qumran was like from sunup to sundown. No one has ever done a complete map of all these things, and it is this map that is one of the major achievements of the work that we did over the two years we worked there. For the first time some one could see distances and spatial relationships that must have been very important to the people of Qumran.

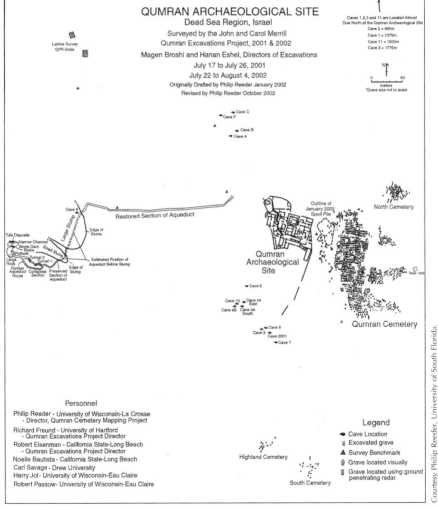

Figure 6.2.   The mapping of the latrines, the aqueduct, the caves around Qumran, and their relationship to the cemetery.

The latrines were important because they could connect the village with the Scrolls. The purities issue is only one of the complications with regard to the latrines. Another complication for the "outhouse" system was the added prohibition of extended travel outside the camp/village/city on the Sabbath day. The Sabbath, that begins for Jews on Friday afternoon at sundown and ends on Saturday night when the stars emerge in the heavens, is nearly twenty-five hours. If one were forced to stay within the boundaries of the village during the Sabbath and were unable to relieve oneself outside of the village until after the Sabbath, the situation would be untenable. The Sabbath boundaries (of a village or city) were a subject of great concern for later Rabbinic authorities as well since during this time a person was not supposed to leave their village or city. The Jews relied upon an interpretation of a passage in the Book of Exodus. The Book of Exodus, chapter 16, just says that one should not leave "your place" on the Sabbath day. While the Book of Numbers, chapter 35 speaks of a buffer zone of 1000 cubits (a cubit is 18 inches, or 1500 feet) as a distance outside of the Israelite camp which was used for grazing of flocks, it is not clear that this is a permitted buffer zone for travel outside of the camp on the Sabbath. The distance from the Israelite camp to the Holy Tabernacle/Tent that included the Ark of the Covenant (which in some traditions is pitched outside the Israelite camp) in the Book of Joshua, chapter 3, is 2000 cubits. If the Holy Tabernacle/Tent was the central shrine of the Israelites for daily and Sabbath worship and was located 2000 cubits (3000 feet) outside of the Israelite camp, then the Israelites would be permitted to go 2000 cubits outside of their living space. All of this does not clarify how far outside of the city/camp one was permitted to go on the Sabbath in biblical times for the purpose of relieving oneself, but it did give the Rabbinic interpreters some parameters for discussion.

Unfortunately, all of these arguments changed in the Roman period when plumbing and sewage systems were built in major cities, and public and private bathrooms could be built in the city. But little changed in the small villages. For the most part, in villages like Qumran, the latrines would probably have been placed outside of the village. The Rabbis, on the basis of the biblical precedents, established clear standards that prohibited travel beyond 2000 cubits outside of a city on the Sabbath day, including for the purposes of latrines. While other Sabbath regulations prohibited commerce, it was possible to travel 2000 cubits on the Sabbath, including presumably for daily needs. This Rabbinic interpretation must have been somewhat of an innovation since the Karaite Jews some eight hundred years after the Rabbinic innovation still would not leave their own ("place"—their

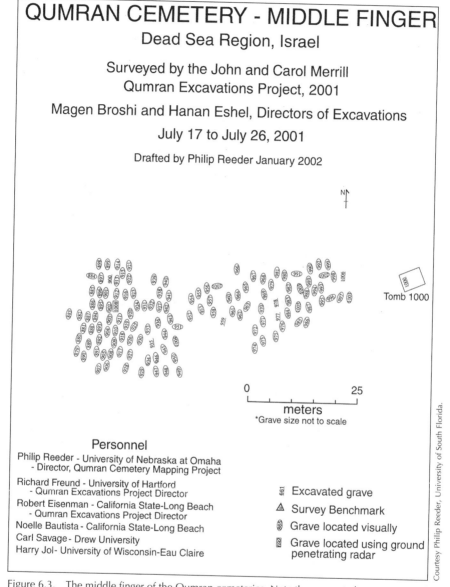

QUMRAN CEMETERY - MIDDLE FINGER

Dead Sea Region, Israel

Surveyed by the John and Carol Merrill
Qumran Excavations Project, 2001

Magen Broshi and Hanan Eshel, Directors of Excavations

July 17 to July 26, 2001

Drafted by Philip Reeder January 2002

Tomb 1000

0   25

meters
*Grave size not to scale

Personnel

Philip Reeder - University of Nebraska at Omaha
  - Director, Qumran Cemetery Mapping Project
Richard Freund - University of Hartford
  - Qumran Excavations Project Director
Robert Eisenman - California State-Long Beach
  - Qumran Excavations Project Director
Noelle Bautista - California State-Long Beach
Carl Savage - Drew University
Harry Jol - University of Wisconsin-Eau Claire

Excavated grave
Survey Benchmark
Grave located visually
Grave located using ground
penetrating radar

Courtesy Philip Reeder, University of South Florida.

Figure 6.3. The middle finger of the Qumran cemeteries. Note the excavated graves 977 and 978 and tomb 1000.

homes) on the Sabbath day! One wonders if they had indoor plumbing, or if they are a reflection of the Qumranite reality in a later period. The Dead Sea Scrolls tell us that some members of the sect were prohibited from leaving the village on the Sabbath. Nearly twenty-five hours without relief.

Since Qumran was not inhabited by Rabbinic Jews, and it had its own peculiarities. The latrines would still have to be located within a short walk of the village for daily and Sabbath use. Two noted Dead Sea Scrolls and Qumran scholars, Joe Zias and James Tabor, had been looking at sites for the Qumran latrines around the village of Qumran in the late 1990s, and in 2001–2002 we used our license for a full physical geological and geophysical survey of the area surrounding the village of Qumran and for its mapping to help look for areas where the daily latrines might have been located. The Dead Sea sects were adamant about ritual purity and hygiene, but they also needed to seek a place of refuge, near to the village that was not easily seen by the villagers and protected also from the sun, which they held in particular regard. It seemed to us to be an interesting subproject of the Qumran work we were already doing, so we added it to the list of scientific goals that we established for our work. But where to start? Although Qumran is small by archaeological standards, the overall site from the caves to the aqueduct system (which we were mapping) to the cemeteries is many square miles. While we thought that our search would be limited to 3000 feet outside the village, there were only a few accessible sites that would fit with the strictures of the Scrolls. So we looked for geological features that might direct us to "discreet" areas that might fit all of the ancient literary information.

The most discreet area within the arc of 2000 cubits was behind a large rock outcropping that blocked off an area about 20 feet long. It is a rock outcropping that has probably been there for millions of years and provides not only some protection from the sun, but also blocks the view of the village. That is where we began. But distance was still a question. While there is some discrepancy among the Dead Sea Scrolls as to how far away the toilets needed to be established away from the site, there are some pieces of information that are important in the Scrolls. The *Temple Scroll* mandates 1000 cubits or 1500 feet. The *War Scroll* mandates that the placement of latrines should be at a distance of some 2000 cubits, or 3000 feet. The *Temple* and *War Scrolls* seem to indicate a permanent installation of some kind. Josephus Flavius, who seems to know the Essenes quite well, gives one more piece of information.

[On the Sabbath] they do not even go to the toilet. On other days they dig a trench a foot deep with a pick—such is the nature of the hatchet which they present to initiants—and wrapping their mantle about them, *that they may not offend the rays of the deity, sit above it.* They then replace the excavated soil in the trench. For this purpose they select the more retired spots. And though this discharge of the excrements is a natural function, they make it a rule to wash themselves after it, as if defiled.

Josephus' point is that the site needed to be in a place that would not offend the "rays" of the deity, so we assumed that it was a place that was blocked off from the sun's rays and not in the village itself because the Scrolls clearly make defecation a ritually polluting activity. With three geoscience faculty in the field, we looked for the place where the site would be located and a natural blocking of the sun was present. The cliffs of where the first major scrolls and the aqueduct system were found to be too far away. The latrines were found through ground-penetrating radar and electrical resistivity tomography to be some 2500 feet from the farthest edge of the village. The rounded shapes of rocks below the surface were regular, and they were located behind the massive rock outcropping. We felt it was important, but since it was not part of our immediate work at the cemetery or the geophysical examination of Qumran, it was left for a future excavation. We were not surprised to read in a 2007 *USA Today* article that the latrines were now being clearly identified in the spot that Paul and Harry had located in 2002. It was only one of the unheralded subprojects we undertook during those two summers of work at Qumran.

New Parts of the Aqueduct, the Cemetery, and Caves

We investigated and found evidence for other caves that may have ringed the site in antiquity. Using the electrical resistivity tomography equipment, we followed a hunch that we had about where possible buried caves at the site of Qumran might be located. We knew that caves #7, #8, and #9 were located directly at the southern edge of the village of Qumran so we checked these areas and found that indeed there were other smaller caves that hugged the edge of the village. We even found that there was evidence for these caves having been used for living purposes since a mat for sleeping and various pits and seeds were found there. The big question for us was whether there were caves located directly adjacent to the main buildings of the village. We knew that de Vaux had begun his excavations of the main buildings in November, 1951. The conventional wisdom in 1951 was that all of the caves filled with scrolls were located far from the site. That is where caves #1 and #2 had been discovered. This turned out to be incorrect. Some caves were located at Qumran.

One of the main things that an excavation director must decide in the beginning of an excavation is where to establish a place for the "dump pile" for the dirt that comes out of the excavations. This is a crucial decision that has significance for the entire life of the excavation. At Bethsaida we had found that inevitably, wherever we placed our dump pile was the place that we needed to dig next! It was just the sad reality of not knowing where the major finds could be located. Often the placement of the dump pile is key to the entire excavation's success, since you do not want to be dumping in an area where you might need to excavate in the future. At a place like Qumran it seemed to me a fateful decision. De Vaux placed his dump pile on the west side of the site just beyond the buildings facing the wadi below. He dumped thousands of pounds of dirt over the side of the site that he thought was not a part of the Qumran story. In 1952 de Vaux realized that the local Bedouins had been excavating a cave just across the wadi from the site of Qumran. It was cave #4, where approximately 20,000 fragments from over 580 manuscripts were housed. If de Vaux had known that caves #4, #5, and #6 were located so close to the main buildings of Qumran, he never would have established his dump pile where he did.

In 2002, I went to Paul Bauman, our geophysicist, and said that we needed to see if there was anything in the dump pile from the excavations of 1951. Paul's work, which is figure 6.1 at the beginning of this chapter, tells the story. Some 15 feet below the present surface of Qumran, directly adjacent to the main buildings, Paul discovered what looked like a cave. It still remains to be excavated. This was only one of the many different sub-projects we worked on and were unable to complete because of the time and resources we had available.

We came to some remarkable conclusions as we did our work. We mapped and carefully assessed the original aqueduct system that brought water to the site in antiquity. Since little detailed information was known about the cemetery, we took little for granted. We did not assume that there were 1400 or 700 graves, for example, because no one had ever exactly counted them in a scientific study. We did not assume that the graves were of the Essenes or Qumranites or even Bedouins. We did not even assume that it was clear what the parameters of the cemetery were today or in antiquity. Geophysicists, geologists, and geographers are used to starting from scratch and producing a totally new understanding. No systematic map existed of the entire cemetery. Steckoll's well-known plan of the cemetery had serious disabilities. It did not conform to the reality of the cemetery plan or the geographic and cartographic standards of the 1960s when it was produced. The de Vaux plan, which was produced and reproduced in a number of forms, does not conform to the reality of the cemetery as we found it. We did not start from the premise that there was only one cemetery. De Vaux and others speak of "cemeteries," mostly because of natural and artificial "borders/separations" between them. The fact that other cemeteries to the far north of the Khirbet Qumran settlement and to the far south across the Wadi Qumran are sometimes mentioned in the same breath as the main cemetery, which contains itself four distinguishable parts within a few hundred meters of the Khirbet, also complicates the matter. We limited our focus to what we call the "extended" main cemetery within a few hundred meters of the Qumran site, while recognizing the existence of other cemeteries in the area.

Surprises

The first surprise was presented by Dr. John F. Shroder, Jr., our chief geologist for the Bethsaida and Cave of Letters projects and now the Qumran excavations. He concluded by a site survey that the northern prong of the main cemetery, which is today separated from the rest of the site by a modern road built in the first half of the twentieth century, was originally connected to the main cemetery. The modern asphalt road probably was built upon a part of the ancient cemetery. The natural erosion, which has also split the four "fingers" of the cemetery, has taken graves into the wadis below. In addition, while the famous earthquakes in the area did have some effect upon the cemetery and the site of Qumran, the infamous Jordan Valley (Syrian-African Rift) rift and fault line, which had been identified so prominently in most of the studies as the culprit for most of the damage in the cisterns, Shroder concluded that the earthquakes may not be the main culprit at all. According to Shroder, the subsidence and erosion have caused the most damage. The earthquakes have not helped the site, but the continuous subsidence and erosion have caused significant damage to both the cemetery, the village and caves.

This new information about the earthquake damage impacts many of the theories about the two periods of occupation of Qumran. Many thought that the earthquake of 31 BCE was the dividing line of choice between different levels of occupation. I have been at the site listening to guides telling people that a certain crack in one of the cisterns can be precisely dated to 31 BCE following the earthquake. What if what had been once thought to be the evidence of an earthquake is really just evidence of regular natural subsidence and erosion, combined with some indirect effects of earthquake damage in the area? Would this change our theories of the occupation periods of Qumran? I think so.

The second biggest surprise was the distance between the settlement and the cemetery. Today a sign marked "Cemetery" appears over 75 feet back from the large settlement wall that separates the cemetery from the

Qumran site. The sign is there to inform Jews and non-Jews that they were entering a cemetery. This signage is actually an important issue for modern-day Jews as Kohanim-Aaronids who are prohibited from entering a cemetery (for reasons of ritual purity, Jews from the line of Aaron the priest are not supposed to enter cemeteries except in limited circumstances) even in this period after the destruction of the Temple.

When I have heard guides speak about the cemetery, they often refer to the distance between the settlement and the cemetery as an indicator of the "Jewishness" of the settlement. They are generally referring to the Rabbinic norm cited from Mishnah Baba Batra 2:9, which states that the cemetery should be 50 cubits (75 feet) away from the settlement. This Rabbinic tradition has been "over-interpreted" to fit the existence of the cemetery as it appeared to many visitors (and may perhaps have been part of the creation of the reality of the settlement's touristic presentation). The tradition is really much more complicated than many are led to understand in the Mishnah of Baba Batra: "Carrion, graves, and tanneries must be kept 50 cubits from a town. A tannery must only be placed on the east side of the town. Rabbi Akiva, however, says that it may be placed on any side except the west, providing it is kept 50 cubits away."

The term here is graves and not cemeteries. Although they are often used interchangeably, in this case it apparently refers to a large number of graves, which is the problem. In the related Mishnah and Tosefta Baba Batra traditions, "dove cotes" are mentioned as well. It appears that the text is addressing the problem of regular placement of graves and other extremely "pungent" (smelling) enterprises and not addressing the issue of "ritual" purity of cemeteries per se. In addition, this is in connection to the place where living quarters were found directly adjacent, which is not the case at Qumran. No living quarters are adjacent to the cemetery, so what might the purpose of the wall be? In fact, the traditions concerning formal cemeteries in open-air locations as we know them today are quite unusual. Mishnah tractate Sanhedrin 6:5 places *batei qevarot* or *batei almin*, two different terms for "cemeteries," at the disposal of the court for the burial of people or commoners who did not otherwise have a family cave or other cave to be buried, or who were executed by the court. The idea of a cemetery of the size and scope of Qumran is really unlike the rest of burials in any other part of the country. Only Jerusalem's Mount of Olives cemetery rivals it in antiquity, size, and scope. In general, the Jewish custom of burying in the ground may have been the preferred form of burial among the Babylonian Jews while the Bible seems to indicate that burial in a family cave was the preferred custom in the Land of Israel. Around the world this same debate seems to have played itself out. In areas where caves were prominent, it seems logical to prefer family caves, but in areas where caves are not easy to find, it seems logical to assume that inground, cyst burial would be preferred. But Qumran seems to defy the norms of the Land of Israel because the area around Qumran is filled with many caves and during this time period the Qumranites seem to have preferred the inground burial to cave burial.

This is significant if one assumes that the Qumranites may have either originated in or come from or gone to Damascus in some incarnation of the *Yachad* (the name that is used for those in the religious group of the Dead Sea Scrolls) community. So it is possible that the Qumranites buried in graves because they were influenced by a Diaspora custom. Cemeteries like the one at Qumran may have served other purposes as well. A Diaspora Jew who died on his or her way to Jerusalem for pilgrimage would have needed a communal cemetery of this type and would have expected inground burial. Cemeteries in the biblical period were provided for mass burials, for multiple burials, for commoner burials, and for criminal burials. In short, either Qumran is an emulation of a distinctive Babylonian-Jewish burial practice, or it may just be a totally different burial practice of an isolated sect and visitors were buried there, according to their burial practices. Even in those cases where Jewish burials are grouped together in the scope of the numbers at the Qumran cemetery, the placement of the stones and the orientation of the graves (north-south and east-west) and other issues begin to make the cemetery unique. The orientation of the graves seems to suggest that different groups were burying in the cemetery with differing burial customs. One of the arguments for the "Jewishness" of the burials has been the distance of the cemetery from the settlement. But even this is problematic after our investigations. Some of the burials seem to be very close (30–45 feet) to the walls of the city, suggesting that they may not have shared the Rabbinic strictures about purity.

Documentation of the cemetery varies. If one looks at photographs of the cemetery from the 1980s, it seems that the "Cemetery" sign was actually closer to the settlement than it was in the 1990s. We used the sign as a benchmark for mapping. As we used our ground-penetrating radar in the area west of where the "Cemetery" sign was positioned in 2002, we began to see graves below the surface that were much closer to the settlement than the "Cemetery" sign would indicate. In fact, using ground penetrating radar, we identified twenty graves closer to the settlement than the present "Cemetery" sign would accomodate. Many of these burials were oriented north to south along the walls of the settlement, and the graves all appeared to have been dug at a depth of two meters (six feet) or more. These were both indicators of the ancient Jewish cemetery and not later non-Jewish burials. Some graves were as close as 30–45 feet away from the settlement. So it would appear that in antiquity, the settlement was much closer to the cemetery than Rabbinic standards would allow. This does not surprise me because the Qumranites do not profess to be "Rabbis" nor should they be expected to keep Rabbinic standards (so they did not have to put their cemetery 50 cubits [75 feet] away from the settlement). But I have noticed that many good researchers feel it is necessary to compare Rabbinic standards and customs to assess archaeological sites associated with Jews in the Second Temple period. In general, it is hard to use Rabbinic injunctions to establish the "Jewishness" of Qumran or many other sites that date to the late Second Temple period precisely because the Rabbinic standards reflect the reality of the later Rabbi Judah the Prince, as much as they may represent ancient Second Temple traditions. While many people like to use Rabbinic injunctions to evaluate "Jewishness," Rabbinic texts were only organized quite late (third century CE) and demonstrate much variation within the diverse collections of Rabbinic literature. In fact, the arguments that most people make about "purity laws" at Qumran and the Dead Sea Scrolls should be only vaguely compared with Rabbinic purity standards because Rabbinic purity laws are for people who lived and interacted with a vastly different population than the Yachad group.

But Rabbinic injunctions do provide us with ancient Jewish information that can help us interpret what would otherwise just be stone walls. Our excavations at Qumran came upon a building in the midst of the cemetery, and we asked ourselves what this building could be? In Rabbinic tradition it was common to have a dwelling place, a building in the midst of a cemetery for a variety of reasons (for security, mourning, caretaker, etc.). One reference in the Babylonian Talmud in particular caught my eye with regard to whether the building in a cemetery might be included within the boundaries of the village. In BT Eruvin 55b it states: "What is meant by "Ruins"?—Rav Judah replied: Three walls without a roof on them. The question was raised: What is the ruling in the case of two walls upon which there was a roof? Come and hear: The following are included in the Sabbath boundary of a town. A sepulchral monument of the size of four cubits by four, a bridge or a cemetery that contains a dwelling chamber . . . " For the Rabbis, the existence of a building/monument in the middle of the cemetery (that may not have a roof but has walls) was a part of the Sabbath boundary of a village, much the same as the building that we suddenly found in the middle of the Qumran cemetery was a place that was directly connected to the site of Qumran.

Tomb 1000 (The Mausoleum)

When you are trying to number every single grave in the vast cemetery of Qumran, you have to assign numbers to every single tomb. Tomb #1000 or the location of the mausoleum/mourning enclosure we found is located on an impressive hill overlooking the entire cemetery and the village of Qumran. Because Tomb #1000 is located on such a prominent hill above the settlement, it would make an appropriate place to bury the most important member of the Qumran/Dead Sea Scroll community: that is, the mysterious *Teacher of Righteousness*, mentioned many times in the Scrolls as the leader of the community. It is equally possible that this was an even more ancient location for a dwelling of a cemetery caretaker (Qumran's history does include an Iron Age) and that it became a mourning enclosure or mausoleum only later. What we first found in 2001 in Tomb #1000 were parts of two bodies arranged in a haphazard fashion and clearly in secondary burial. The bones were from a younger woman and an older woman as determined by our Israeli physical anthropologist, C14 tests were performed (first century CE), and the bones were reburied at the site. That summer an article appeared in *Time* magazine titled: "Bones of Contention" because the Essenes were known to have been celibate so it is difficult to understand how women would be buried at the Qumran cemetery. Some joked that we had found the mysterious leader of the Qumran sect, the *Teacher of Righteousness*, and that the leader was a woman! The incomplete skeletons of the women and their haphazard burial inside of the Tomb #1000 building convinced us that those women were not the end of the story, but the beginning of the story. Tomb #1000's secrets were left for the summer of 2002.

Tomb #1000 was different. The zinc coffin had been discovered in tomb #978, and tomb #977 adjacent to it had been excavated as well. Tombs #977 and #978 are actually in exact alignment with one another. Whoever robbed #978 must have thought that #977 might contain a similar treasure and opened it as well. Tombs #977 and #978, both in perfect north-south alignment, are at the bottom of the hill in front of Tomb #1000. Many other graves are located nearby in a haphazard arrangement that suggest different attempts to fit in a variety of different burials. While some seem to be oriented east-west, this too is a misnomer. Very few graves are perfectly oriented north–south and perfectly east–west. Most are nearly north–south, and a few seem to totter on the brink of going one way or another. But the east–west orientation also betrays part of the problem. These east–west graves (of which some we already noted were shallow graves and had another, deeper grave below them) also had odd gaps associated with them. These spaces indicated to us that the rocks had been borrowed from a north–south grave and reoriented to east–west. It is difficult to know if everyone of these east–west graves was created in this fashion, but it is clearly a pattern. The cemetery of small stone heaps do not leave sufficient space to indicate a systematic burial pattern from one single period.

The area where the mausoleum is located is about 12 feet up from the last graves below and is today and probably was in antiquity the highest point in the entire Qumran area. It overlooks the Dead Sea and is a spectacular view at dawn and sunset from the site of Qumran. Right beyond it sits a modern Israeli army watch post and bunker. They were apparently created before the 1973 war in anticipation of a Jordanian attack. It is a great location. It looks out upon the wadis below and the road north and south. It's high enough above the settlement to scan the hills above and the east–west road from Jerusalem. The students from California State University, Long Beach (CSULB) who worked he site—Dennis Walker, Hanan Eisenman, Sarah Eisenman, and Ron Dubay—were sent for this summer project by Dr. Robert Eisenman, their teacher and mentor, to provide some of the workforce in our efforts in July, 2001. After we finished excavating possible caves identified by Dr. Eisenman back in the early 1990s, his students agreed to work on our cemetery study. Working in a cemetery is not as interesting or exciting as exploring a new cave, but it was for us, just as important. When we started making discoveries at the mausoleum, almost everyone went to work there. Small finds had been made in the interim days including pottery, more sections of walls, and a door space. At first it appeared that the site might prove to be a destroyed watchtower. It is the most prominent location at Qumran for a variety of reasons. Our interest in the hill was piqued by the presence of the zinc coffin and its proximity to the elevated point and the fact that it is the only "structure" in the cemetery. Raised mausoleums are not unusual in antiquity, but a watchtower was more what we thought about. There was already one large watchtower at the northwest of the Qumran settlement, perhaps this was another. With the idea of the Essenes as simple people, the possibility of a mausoleum and a zinc coffin were already testing this hypothesis to the maximum. We had come to Qumran to resurvey and excavate the two caves of Professor Eisenman's earlier expedition and to check the entire cemetery for signs of other "special" burials. We looked especially in the area around the zinc coffin and discovered that the area where the mausoleum was eventually defined contained a burial and other buried objects. The remarkable thing about the mausoleum was the rather defined walls. So the goal was to see if this was a watchtower with a floor on such an elevated hill. We did find Roman period pottery in the burial area of the mausoleum. Because we did not find much pottery anywhere else in the cemetery, it reinforced the possibility of it being a settlement watchtower, although the vessels appeared to be of a different quality from the simple jugs, plates, and dishes found at the Qumran site. This is highly unusual because the many theories of who was buried in the cemetery hinged upon all of the burials being similar. The mausoleum is not like anything else in the cemetery. We were not the first people to discover this wall on top of the hill overlooking the settlement, although we are perhaps the first to see it for what it was—not just one wall but four "walls" of a structure. The wall was mentioned by de Vaux in his original report but for him it was just a series of arranged rocks. He calls it simply "carré"—"squared." The wall was really a series of four walls with a door/opening to the north in the center of a structure, creating a room similar to the size of most of the small rooms in dwellings in this time period, 5 feet by 5 feet, except in this case with a burial in the center of the room. In front of the burial, in shallow secondary placement, were the bones that we found in 2001. Preliminary anthropological evaluation of the bones found in 2001 revealed that they were buried at a depth of perhaps a foot to a foot and a half and comprised more than one body (too much cranial material for one person) in this shallow secondary placement. The bones appear to be of two women (by the pelvic remains of the body), and the shallow placement in front of the main burial may indicate that they were not buried but put in the structure. I have worked with bones in this region before, and often they are well preserved by the salt, sand, and low humidity. The bones presented the physical anthropologist with a picture of two women from the first century (dated by carbon 14 from the teeth). First, a larger woman in her thirties and another smaller woman or child who may have died after rocks fell on them in the room or who had their bones removed to that location after death. But the finding of first-century women buried in a building in the cemetery of Qumran raised questions about whether the whole cemetery contained men and women and whether the ascetic (and celibate) Essenes were the only ones buried in the cemetery. In *Time* magazine the article on our excavations in the summer of 2001 was entitled: "Bones of Contention" but the main contention was not over the women inside the building but what still lay buried in the middle of the building.

The Earlier Bones of Contention

The state of the bones found at Qumran is an interesting and a newly reinvestigated question. The bones recovered from the north-south burials by de Vaux's excavations in the 1950s were sent to be analyzed in Germany, and they disappeared. In 1998, Joe Zias, former paleopathologist for the Antiquities Authority of Israel and several others found out what happened to the missing bones. The Qumran bones from Roland de Vaux's excavations were originally sent to Germany for study by Gottfried Kurth (died 1990) who visited Qumran on February 24, 1956. The bones were studied by anthropologists in Germany until the lab closed in the 1970s. The anthropologists brought the boxes of bones to their homes in Germany and placed them in storage. They admit now that they did not know what to do with the materials when the lab closed. Zias restudied the bones with simple but remarkable results. He demonstrated that the east–west burials where the women and children were found were clearly late burials because of the wear patterns of bones and especially teeth which had been buried for two thousand years versus only a few hundred years. The life patterns of the people buried in a later period, especially Bedouin bones and teeth, also expresses itself in terms of the numbers and pitting of teeth and the poor diet is reflected in the breaks present in the bones. In short, the state of the bones tells much about the people even when it is not possible to do carbon 14 dating of the bones.

Although the carbon 14 testing of some of the bones from the de Vaux excavations proved them to be recent, this research was fraught with problems not the least of which were the mishandling of the bones for nearly fifty years. The state of the bones did not allow full tests to be performed in well-controlled conditions. Zias concluded that some of the bones, possibly those of the women and children, found at Qumran were late, probably premodern Bedouin bones. He hypothesized that the Bedouin were probably using the ancient Qumran burials for their own burials, but instead of burying at a depth of 6 feet (as the ancient Qumranites were doing), the Bedouin buried at a shallower depth. They used rocks from the ancient Qumran burials to hold down the dirt and prevent wild animals from entering these shallow graves. Usually, and this is key, they buried on top of an already existing Qumran grave. Because the dirt and rocks were there, this was not an unusual Bedouin practice.

The study of the east-west orientation of the graves was an important part of our study in July 2001 and again in 2002. In the cases that we checked, we concluded, using the ground penetrating radar, that the east-west graves that de Vaux had excavated and which are found in the middle of the cemetery were 1 to 1½ feet in depth. These are the burials identified by Zias as Bedouin burials. In the case of the mausoleum, this is even more important. The women's bones found in the mausoleum were only buried at 1½ feet in depth. Below them, were the bones of the original occupant of the mausoleum. We do not know for sure who was the original occupant of tomb #1000, but we have good reason to speculate on his identity. He was probably the most prominent figure in the writings of the Qumranites, the *Teacher of Righteousness*, and it is not an accident that buried near the mausoleum was the zinc coffin of perhaps a prominent disciple, perhaps brought from a great distance to be near the most prominent burial place for the most important person at Qumran. There is much speculation about who the mausoleum belonged to, and most speculation by researchers of the Dead Sea Scrolls hinges upon the identification of the mysterious *Teacher of Righteousness* in the Scrolls. It is all based upon understandings of the Qumran site and the Dead Sea Scrolls, which only recently have been finally published. What follows is a summary of the recently published results.

The Developing Theory of Qumran and The Scrolls

Since the 1950s, the reigning theory has been that Qumran was a monastery-like place where the Essenes lived and died. John the Baptist may have been a member of this community, and possibly even Jesus for a time. It is there that a majority of scholars feel the asceticism of both John and Jesus was born as well as their eschatological view of the world created. A proto-Christianity if you will. Professor Lawrence Schiffman of New York University has countered the proto-Christianity view with the view that the group represents a form of proto-Rabbinic Judaism. These are only some of the innovations and controversies that have come up over the past sixty years since the Scrolls were discovered. All of these views affected the way people thought about the cemetery. Despite the possibility that non-Qumranites coming to visit Qumran and had died and were buried in the cemetery or the possibility that there were some married Essenes, no one challenged the "celibate" monastery theory until the 1990s. This has changed and affects our understanding of who is buried in the cemetery and who lived at Qumran. No standard work in the field presented all of the views of the "new" school of archaeologists who challenged the monastery theory until recently. In addition, since the new editor in chief of the Dead Sea Scrolls publication team, Dr. Emanuel Tov, and his team of scholars had completed their work, a statement about the final stage is important as a summation to put an end to incorrect assumptions.

Many other caves still exist in the region. Research, even our own research into unexplored caves at the Qumran site, may yield yet more scrolls. The major archaeological finds from Qumran are from the Hellenistic to early Roman periods (there was an Iron Age settlement as well) and stretched over approximately three centuries from 250 BCE–68 CE. The interpretation of the finds tries to establish a relationship between this village, the caves, and the scrolls, although this is part of the problem. Usually we work on an archaeological site and stay focused only upon the archaeological site as our central research goal. From the beginning, there were many combined issues in this site—the caves, the scrolls, and the site of Qumran.

Some archaeologists will place an archaeological site into the larger regional survey and compare it to other sites in the area. In this case, the relationship between the Qumran village, the caves, and the scrolls became much more complicated because of the importance of the scrolls. Nothing had ever been found like these scrolls in the area. It forced archaeologists and most researchers to develop a hypothesis as they worked on the scrolls and the archaeological site of Qumran. Six hypotheses are presently held by most researchers on Qumran. These hypotheses differ greatly from one another, but everyone accounts for the caves, village of Qumran, the scrolls, and even the cemetery in their formulation:

> Theory 1. Qumran was a religious community of Essenes, a well-
> known sect of ascetic Jews, who wrote the Scrolls and lived in
> caves or tents near the public buildings. The Essenes developed a
> religious purity ethic that required regular ritual purification in the
> many ritual baths and pools. The nearby cemetery includes many
> people who lived there and their extended families who wanted to
> be buried there.
> Theory 2. Qumran was a fort and/or trade/customs checkpoint on
> the road to Jerusalem. The contents of the nearby caves were put
> there to be safeguarded in anticipation of the impending war
> against the Romans in the first century CE unbeknownst to the
> soldiers. They used these caves near the fort because it was a well
> known location for easy future retrieval of the scrolls. The many

pools provided a useful bathing spot, and very few soldiers lived there, so no large living quarters were necessary. The cemetery is the result of fighting in the area associated with the revolt against the Romans in 68 CE.

Theory 3. Qumran was a first century BCE–CE Roman villa rustica/ manor with swimming pools. The contents of the caves have nothing to do with this settlement except that it was used as a clear point of demarcation for people wishing to deposit their texts there and perhaps retrieve them later. The cemetery also has nothing to do with the main life of the villa but may have provided a useful place for burial of the dead from the region over a long period of time.

Theory 4. Qumran was a ritual purification center used by pilgrims coming to Jerusalem in the late Second Temple period. Those who came there often brought their texts to study and live for short purification periods in the caves, like a retreat center. The caves were known to many people who had used them over the years, and so they began to store their books there. The cemetery is filled with people who died on their way back and forth to Jerusalem or from the semipermanent residents, and so the place became known as a place of burial for pilgrims from many places.

Theory 5. Qumran was the "New Jerusalem" of a group of dissident Jews opposed to a variety of the policies of the Jerusalem priesthood. This group may have lived in caves or tents nearby Qumran. This group wrote some of the scrolls and recopied many of the Dead Sea Scrolls. Those who resided there were opposed to the teachings of the *Wicked Priest* of Jerusalem and provide the basis for proto-Christianity of Jesus and John the Baptist. Their daily purifications and rigorous religious life was an attempt to fulfill the eschatological promises of its founders. The cemetery of Qumran was for the community's residents and their extended families.

Theory 6. Qumran was used for different purposes over the more than three centuries that it actively existed in antiquity. It was used by Essenes, dissidents, pilgrims, soldiers, and "gentlemen farmers." The caves provided shelter, places of refuge, solitary places for study and introspection, and convenient storage. The different architecture, pools, ritual baths, and buildings are the result of changes and improvements made by the different groups who did not coexist in the location at the same time. The cemetery was used by all these groups and even by later travelers and Bedouin living in the area.

Scholars have chosen one or more of these theories and then move on to interpret the scrolls in light of the theory they have chosen.

The Discovery and Provenance of the Dead Sea Scrolls

Many versions of the original discovery of the scrolls exist. Here is my version of the Qumran story. In either late 1946 or early 1947, two Bedouin shepherds explored a cave near the ruins of (Khirbet) Qumran at the northwest corner of the Dead Sea. They took leather scrolls from the cave and sold them to an antique dealer in Bethlehem. After the initial discovery, many Bedouins and archaeologists searched for more manuscript caves and found another ten caves (caves are numbered: 2–11; caves 3, 5, 7, 8, 9, and 10 were undisturbed). Twenty-seven caves dating to the Bar Kokhba era (Second Jewish Revolt) have also been found. While most people speak of thirty-plus caves that have yielded manuscripts, these are but a small fraction of the caves that exist along the Dead Sea and Judean desert. There are hundreds of caves. Most have not been heavily researched or analyzed. They may yet yield more information about the period. The most famous cave at Qumran, Cave 4, which is located near the Qumran settlement, contained more than twenty thousand fragments of about 580 texts. To date, there are over nine hundred texts among the scrolls. Many fragments are of the same texts. The most common are Genesis, Deuteronomy, Isaiah, and Psalms. This tells us what the people who deposited the texts there were reading. The original excavations at Qumran began a couple of years after the discoveries of the scrolls and always clouded/confused the discussion of the scrolls and the excavations. Father Roland de Vaux of the French school of Archaeology in Jerusalem, the *Ecole Biblique*, excavated the ruins of Khirbet Qumran and discovered three large features of the site: (1) traces of an aqueduct; (2) a community center with a complex consisting of a tower and rooms for various purposes; and (3) a cemetery. The chronology of discoveries of the Scrolls and the excavations of Qumran is important.

1946–1947	Cave 1 with the first Scrolls accidentally found.
1949	Cave 1 identified and excavated.
1951–1956	Five seasons of archaeological work at Qumran.
1952–1956	Ten more manuscript caves discovered.
1967	The Temple Scroll is recovered.

The dating and authenticity of Qumran and the Dead Sea Scrolls is very important. Though one or two scholars questioned their antiquity it is generally understood that these are the oldest Hebrew evidence of the Hebrew Bible. The Scrolls are the oldest evidence that the Hebrew Bible is an ancient document, and these manuscripts predate the next oldest exemplar of the Bible by about one thousand years! Because of the lack of ancient Hebrew manuscripts of the Bible, Bible scholars at the beginning of the twentieth century had begun to construct theories that the Hebrew Bible may not have been as ancient as it was first thought. Some of these theories were constructed as part of larger anti-Semitic ideas that were developing in Central Europe, but the fact that there were no ancient Hebrew manuscripts of the Hebrew Bible did give these "scholars" an opportunity to speculate on a very late date for the Hebrew Bible and bolster Christianity's view as the "True Israel." The discovery of the Dead Sea Scrolls changed all of that. For the first time there were manuscripts of almost every book of the Hebrew Bible in ancient Hebrew and dating back to the Hellenistic-early Roman period, before the advent of Christianity. At the beginning of the 1950s, some suspected that the scrolls were medieval or even worse, modern forgeries. There had been a scandal involving scrolls at the end of the nineteenth century, and it was difficult for people to believe that scrolls dating back two thousand years could have been preserved even in the dry caves by the Dead Sea. This speculation ended early. But the Scrolls turned out to be much more than just manuscripts of the Hebrew Bible. Thirty percent of the Dead Sea Scrolls are copies of books of the Hebrew Bible. Every book except Esther is represented. The book of Nehemiah is also not in the collection of nine hundred manuscripts, but it was probably connected with the book of Ezra that was found. Fifty percent of the collection were quasi-biblical texts that did not make it into the canonized Bible and which we would classify as similar to the Apocrypha and Pseudepigrapha. The most unique discoveries were sectarian texts, compositions representing the specific rules and beliefs of a Dead Sea sect community, which made up 20 percent of the nine hundred different manuscripts found.

Modern science had emerged to allow different types of dating, including carbon 14 tests. The Qumran site is dated through coins, pottery, and organic materials such as produce and linens found in archaeological contexts. The main activity of occupation(s) of Qumran is dated from circa 250 BCE to 68 CE, and it is seen, almost like Pompeii, as a relatively unoccupied and hostile place until the present period. The caves are different. The caves have been in use for tens of thousands of years. They were used for storage, living, and refuge right up to the present period. The scrolls are dated by means of paleography, the radiocarbon method, and internal historical allusions. The scrolls range in date from the third century BCE to the first century CE and are without doubt authentic.

What do we know about the relationship between the scrolls, the caves, and Qumran? That is a big question that is still the basis of controversy. We know that the scrolls are connected with Qumran due to the proximity of the caves to Qumran, as well as the similarity of artifacts and pottery found both at Qumran and in the caves. This does not mean that all of the scrolls and all of the caves are connected to Qumran, but at least some of the caves and their scrolls are connected with Qumran. The connection of the caves, especially some of the jars found in the caves, with the ancient settlement was conclusively proven by a number of scientific methods over the past sixty years. The pottery of Qumran not only has a particular style, it also has a specific chemical makeup that links it to the clay of Qumran and the caves. Some people had speculated that the scrolls, especially those in the jars, had been made in Jerusalem and brought to the caves of Qumran for safekeeping. Although it is possible that the scrolls were written in Jerusalem and brought to Qumran for storage in jars from Qumran, it is clear that there is a connection between Qumran and the caves. Because the pottery in which some of the scrolls were stored was from Qumran, it is assumed that the Qumranites wrote some of the scrolls as well. But who were the Qumranites? The identification of the Qumran community has proven elusive but has been resolved within some parameters. Once we know who the Qumranites were, it is possible to figure out who different scholars speculate might be buried in the cemetery and especially in tombs #1000 and #978.

There are five major theories about the residents of Qumran and people buried in the cemetery. Many books and articles elaborate on these theories in great detail, but I think it is worth knowing the differences between the theories in brief. The five leading theories for the identity of the Qumranites are:

Theory 1. The Qumranites are the Essenes.
Theory 2. The Qumranites are Jerusalemite refugees (of all kinds).
Theory 3. The Qumranites are "disaffected" Sadducees (also from
     Jerusalem but specifically Sadducees).
Theory 4. The Qumranites are a sect of Zealots, followers of James
     the Just or John the Baptist, and can be called a group of proto-
     Christian Essenes.
Theory 5. The Qumranites are "disaffected" Pharisees (also presumably
     from Jerusalem but specifically connected with the Pharisees.

The Pharisees, Sadducees, Essenes, and Zealots are all mentioned by Josephus Flavius in his works from the first century CE when presumably Qumran was still functioning. For the purposes of this book, it is most important to know that a controversy exists and that it has not been resolved by the translations of the Scrolls or by the sixty years of excavations at the site of Qumran.

From Scrolls to the Teacher of Righteousness

From the very beginning of the discovery of the Dead Sea Scrolls, one person stood out. The leader of the sect was known by the mysterious designation, the *Teacher of Righteousness*. At the outset, many thought that the *Teacher of Righteousness* was the author of most or all of the scrolls called "the Rule of the Community," the Thanksgiving Hymns and even the War Scroll. Some even held that he had written the Temple Scroll. Research has proven that these scrolls could not have been written by the same person in the same period. They are the product of different hands in different periods. Most scholars, however, acknowledge that the *Teacher of Righteousness* must have been involved in the writing of at least some of these texts.

The fifteen references to the *Teacher of Righteousness* in the Qumran texts have yielded two basic schools of thought about the role of the Teacher. The majority school of thought holds him to be one individual in one time period, and the minority school of thought holds that like other leadership positions within Judaism in the Hellenistic and Roman periods, the "Teacher" is a leadership position that passed from individual to individual in different time periods. My view is a middle position: the original *Teacher of Righteousness*, probably from the middle of the second century BCE, was a special/specific priest, (perhaps even an officiating high priest in the Temple in Jerusalem or just one of the many qualified priests), who had worked in the Temple and who left and founded the Qumran group. At the site of Qumran they found the ruins of a more ancient settlement from the late Iron Age. The site was on a well-known ancient highway from north to south, so it is not difficult to imagine that people might have established a village there in the Iron Age. But just as the site was refounded in the Hellenistic/Hasmonean period and refounded in a later period of its Roman period existence, I think there were multiple leaders and multiple Teachers of Righteousness in the settlements at Qumran during the Hellenistic and Roman periods. The idea that the community would follow the dictates of a single, dead leader that had led them into the desert may seem to have support from the early Christian movement but would have been a difficult in Jewish idea the first century BCE. It is perhaps an idea that made sense to early Christian scholars who studied the Dead Sea Scrolls, who saw everything discovered at Qumran as precursors to Christianity, including the "dead" *Teacher of Righteousness* as a precedent for the role of Jesus in early Christianity. I see the *Teacher of Righteousness* as other Jewish leadership in the Greco-Roman period. One in which another *Teacher of Righteousness* continued after the death of the original and either followed the dictates of the earlier Teacher or initiated his own views; new leaders for each successive generation of Qumran.

The Literary Evidence for the Origins of the Title: Moreh HaTzedeq

The concept of a "Teacher"/*Moreh* as a leader in Judaism is difficult to trace. The term *Moreh* is not a standard designation in the Hebrew Bible and it appears that it was fashioned during the Hellenistic and Roman periods when a variety of new titles were created to accommodate new leadership roles in Judaism. This word *Moreh* was used in the Rabbinic period in a variety of ways, but it lacks a clear precedent in the Hebrew Bible for the title. In the Hellenistic period, the official Greek title of "Teacher" (*didaskalos*) appears to have been known to the author of II Maccabees. II Maccabees begins with two texts written as "letters" and is only a digest. Most scholars think that it was written by a Hellenistic Jew called Jason of Cyrene, perhaps as a condensed version of a longer five-book account of the court history of the Maccabees, which was finally redacted around 100 BCE by an Alexandrian Jew who was a Pharisee. This would place the terminology of the "Teacher" in the historical context of the first *Teacher of Righteousness* in the second century BCE. It is in II Maccabees that the Jewish usage of the official title of "Teacher" regarding an individual who is also a priest is found in 1:10b:" . . . the people of Jerusalem and in Judea and the Council of Elders and Judas, to Aristobulus, *didaskalos* of King Ptolemy and member of the stock of the anointed priests, and to the Jews in Egypt, greeting and wishes for health."

Aristobulus, was a "Jewish teacher" who received a Ptolemian court title, *didaskalos*, and apparently was the source of information about Judaism for Ptolemy VI Philometor. It is possible to theorize that the title "Teacher" was an imitation of the Ptolemian court title that came into Judaism at this period and was translated into the Hebrew term "Moreh" at this time. The title was so well known in the period of the Septuagint, the Greek translation of the Bible, that it is used unambiguously in the translation of Esther 6:1 in a distinctive usage: "But the Lord removed sleep from the king that night and told his *didaskalos* (teacher) to bring him the books, in which were registered the events of the day and to read it to him." Josephus Flavius uses *didaskalos* in his writings in a number of ways. He uses it for teachers of children, teachers of the Law, and even as teacher of ethical conduct. He uses the term to describe the Sadducees in a very particular way: ". . . for they think it an instance of virtue to dispute with those "teachers of wisdom" (*didaskalous sophias*) whom they frequent."

It is important to remember that Josephus is writing in Greek for a very literate non-Jewish audience. From this we learn that the term may have been Sadducean terminology that was adapted to describe one of their leaders. The Josephan use of "Sophia" is consistent with other Greek writers of the period with regard to "wisdom" and is also a cognate for righteousness in Greek. If so, Josephus is referring to the Sadducean origin of the title: *Teacher of Righteousness.*

The Hebrew concept of *Tzedeq*, righteousness, is rendered by a number of different words in the Hellenistic period. The noun, *Tzedeq*, appears over one hundred times in the Hebrew Bible, although only rarely in the Pentateuch and never in the earliest strata of the Bible. The verb and even the noun *Tzedaqah* appear regularly, but the literary concept of a theoretical concept of *Tzedeq* as righteousness/justice does not. It is, of course, a favorite concept of the later Hebrew literary prophets and is found in the writings of Job, Psalms, and Proverbs. The preferred term/noun or title in the Hebrew Bible is a *Tzadiq*, a righteous individual and *Tzedaqah*, but no *Tzedeq* and certainly no *Moreh HaTzedeq*. This seems to suggest that the concept of a *Moreh HaTzedeq* emerged from outside of the sphere of ancient Israelite terminology in a later period.

The standard concept of Greek justice is a form of wisdom, developed from the time of Plato and Aristotle and was transferred into Judaism through the Septuagint and later in Jewish intertestamental literature and from there into the NT and Christianity. The use of the standard translation of the noun *Tzedeq* in the Septuagint: *Dikaios, Dikaion, Dikaia, Dikaiosune,* and *Diakaioma* in the Hellenistic period is important because it is also the word that translates a variety of different other theoretical concepts of the Hebrew Bible, such as *Tzedaqah, Meisharim, Mishpat, Din, Mitzvah, Yosher, Naqi, Nadiv, Tamim, Shalem, Tahor, Emet,* and *Hesed.* By the time of the writing of the New Testament, the concept and the terminology is established as *dikaios* and *dikaiosune,* words that appear some two hundred times in the New Testament. In the Intertestamental period, Ben Sirah, Wisdom of Solomon, Maccabees, Tobit, Baruch, Susanna, Philo, and Josephus, etc. all gingerly use the terminology although not in the same quantity and quality as the New Testament. All this points to the concept developing greater and greater meaning in the Hellenistic period.

Identifying the *Teacher of Righteousness* in the Hellenistic and Roman Periods at Qumran: The Results of the John and Carol Merrill Excavations at Qumran in 2002

Attempts were made to identify the *Teacher of Righteousness* in different periods because of varying interpretations and inferences in the sectarian Dead Sea Scrolls materials. Some held that the original Teacher of Righteousness was Ezra the Scribe (fifth century BCE), others Onias III (second century BCE), Onias IV (second century BCE), Menahem the Zealot (first century CE), and others saw him as Jesus, John the Baptist, or James the Just (all three are from the first century CE). One of the sources of information about the Teacher is not only the texts but also the archaeology of the site. Because of the different time periods in which people lived at Qumran, ranging from the Iron Age through the Hellenistic-early Roman periods, and even some small settlements through the Byzantine period, it is difficult to know who is buried in the cemetery. It is likely that people from all of these time periods are buried in the cemetery. Even modern and premodern Bedouin may have used the cemetery because it was such a convenient and well-known burial spot on a major, ancient north-south highway. The possibility that a person such as the *Teacher of Righteousness*, who is mentioned in a sectarian text found in the caves of Qumran, is indeed buried at Qumran seems logical.

It is important to know in which time period(s) the Teacher functioned to determine if tomb #1000 is his burial site or the burial site of another important leader in the Qumran community. If the latter is the case, and the person lived and died among his followers, the mausoleum we found in the summer of 2001 and then excavated in 2002, is of great significance, for scholars who research the scrolls.

The Teacher directly and indirectly appears in a variety of Qumran texts: Qumranic manuscripts of a *Commentary on Habbakuk* or *Pesher Habbakuk*, a *Commentary on Psalms* or *Psalms Pesher*, a *Commentary on Micah* or *Pesher Micah*, and other sectarian texts such as the *Community Rule* or *Manual of Discipline*, MMT (*Miktzat Maaseh HaTorah*, a Halakhic letter which was the foundational document of the group), the *War Scroll*, and the *Damascus Document*. These manuscripts are not complete, and it is clear that the

Teacher of Righteousness permeated many of the Qumran texts. A variety of texts from different time periods of the Qumran community were preserved in different locales. The *Damascus Document*, for example, (designated by Qumran researchers as CD or Cairo-Damascus) refers to a copy of the manuscript found in Cairo but which may have originated with a community in Damascus. This Cairo manuscript, discovered in a special area of the Ben Ezra Synagogue known as the *Geniza* or Holy Storage (or holding area for manuscripts that were considered holy because of their contents but for a variety of reasons were no longer usable by the congregation) is an amazing story itself. When repairs were being made to the synagogue, they discovered a long neglected storage area that contained manuscripts dating back over one thousand years! This area yielded thousands of manuscripts of Jewish documents that had been preserved and copied over a long period of time and carried by Jews until they no longer were serviceable. In Jewish law, a holy manuscript needs to be stored or officially buried after it is no longer usable. So the holy storage area in the Ben Ezra Synagogue had a copy of a document that speaks about a holy community of Jews that either went into exile in Damascus, Syria, or into exile to another location from Damascus. Why would a text that mentions the *Teacher of Righteousness* from the obscure Qumran Essene community appear in the Cairo Synagogue Geniza one thousand years after the sect no longer exists? No one knows for sure but we suspect that it may have to do with the Teacher of Righteousness. If the *Teacher of Righteousness* continued to function as a Priestly and an authority figure in the synagogue, it explains why the Cairo Geniza of the Ben Ezra Synagogue had a copy of the Damascus Document. Because the document appears in the Qumran caves and because of its references to Damascus (perhaps a code word for the Diaspora), it appears that a link exists between the exile of these Jews from either Damascus to Qumran or from Qumran to Damascus. There is also a clear indication of the Jewishness of the Qumran settlement and the importance of a messianic figure (Cairo-Damascus Document 20.1) "of Aaron and Israel" but from the line of Tzadoq, a competing family within the Aaronite descendents. So the Teacher may be a link to an ancient Priestly authority figure that survived in the synagogue.

According to the Damascus Document, the Teacher was a prophet who discerned the "truth" for the Qumran community against a "*Wicked Priest,*" a Priestly and political enemy of the *Teacher of Righteousness* who is charged with corrupting the Temple and the Priesthood. He apparently drove the *Teacher of Righteousness* from Jerusalem, conspired against him, and even pursued him to his "House of Exile". The *Man of Lies* is a student of the *Teacher of Righteousness*, who rebelled against the Teacher and formed his own group, the "Seekers of Smooth Things," which separated from the Essene/Qumran community. The Damascus Document makes the *Man of Lies* appear to be both an apostate and a military leader. According to the eschatological plan of the sectarian literature that survived, the vehicle for the punishment of the *"Man of Lies"* group and the corrupted priesthood and Temple of the *"Wicked Priest"* would be a group that is known simply as the "Kittim," a code name for the Romans. While none of the sectarian documents (or "pesher" commentaries) were written directly by the Teacher, scholars assumed they reflect his influence. These commentaries are the "proof-texts" for the coming judgment and seem to coincide with historical events. The longest and best preserved of the "Teacher" texts are *the Habakkuk Pesher* and the *Psalms Pesher* that were found in caves 1 and 4. These documents mention all three key figures, the *Wicked Priest, Man of Lies,* and *Teacher of Righteousness.* The documents are written in a code that would be understood by the followers. Sometimes a second level of code was used, and the word "wicked" stands in for the *Wicked Priest* and the word "righteous" alludes to the *Teacher of Righteousness.* But it appears that the writers know that the readers would understand.

In the 1950s, when many of the scrolls were first made public, speculations about the possible identity of the *Teacher of Righteousness* were presented. Theodor Gaster, for example, writing in his 1956 *The Dead Sea Scriptures*, held on the basis of the Damascus Document that the *Teacher of Righteousness* was raised up "some twenty years after the beginning of a 390 year period of Divine displeasure." Depending on how timing is reckoned, the *Teacher of Righteousness* could be placed at the end of the Persian period, more specifically in the time of Ezra and Nehemiah. More important, the possibility of the *Teacher of Righteousness* being the fourth-century BCE Persian named Ezra the scribe, who was a priest, was raised early on by Gaster. But in the same document it states that "about 40 years will elapse from the death of the *Teacher of Righteousness* until all who have taken up arms and relapsed in the company of the *Man of Lies* are finally destroyed," and this appears to anticipate another future *Teacher of Righteousness* who will appear later. To be fair, Gaster and others recognized the difficulty of taking texts that were purposely ambiguous about the identity of the *Teacher of Righteousness* and attempted to move the debate to the ideas of the scrolls rather than the individuals. Early on in the debate over the identity of the *Teacher of Righteousness*, it became clear that there were those who wanted to historicize him into a single individual while others saw the office of *"Teacher of Righteousness"* as an ongoing and developing role in the Yachad group.

The historicizers came to the conclusion that the *Teacher of Righteousness,* the *Wicked Priest,* and the *Man of Lies* all lived in the period of the Maccabees, or the second century BCE. They saw all manner of historical reflections in the writings that alluded to events that they connected to this period. For the historicizers, the *Teacher of Righteousness* would have been Onias III, the last legitimate Zadoqite high priest, who was assassinated at Antioch in 170 BCE according to II Maccabees 4. The *Wicked Priest* would have been Menelaus, high priest from 172 BCE onward, who embezzled funds from the Temple, instigated the murder of Onias III and the priest who oversaw the accommodationists of Antiochus Epiphanes IV. Jason, the founder of the pro-accommodationist/Hellenization movement in the period of Antiochus IV, according to II Maccabees 4, would have been the most likely candidate for the *Man of Lies.* Professor Lawrence Schiffman, one of the most prominent Jewish commentators on the Scrolls has stated most recently that there was only **one** *Teacher of Righteousness,* but several other officers who served as leaders of the community after his death. On the basis of his analysis of MMT, a document composed in the Hasmonean period (153–63 BCE), Schiffman placed the Teacher's reign as leader of the sect not in the second century BCE, but rather in the first century BCE (Herodian period: 40 BCE–4 BCE). The differences of opinion over the positioning of the *Teacher of Righteousness* leads me to conclude that perhaps all of these researchers are correct. A *Teacher of Righteousness* did lead the group in the second century BCE when it was established. Another *Teacher of Righteousness* led the sect in the first century BCE and finally another Teacher emerged in the first century CE.

The question is whether the Qumran group invented the new term "Teacher" or whether they used a known title of leadership among Jews of the Hellenistic and Roman periods. In much the same way that the title *Rabbi* was just one of many different leaders who had the title in the same period, the *Teacher of Righteousness* was a title accorded to the leader of this sect of people on the Dead Sea. The use of the title of *"a"* *Teacher of Righteousness,* as opposed to *"the"* *Teacher of Righteousness,* fits the model of Jewish leadership titles in general. First, the title "Teacher" is a possible title of leadership in Jewish literature of the Hellenistic and early Roman period. The New Testament uses the technical term "Teacher" in John 1:38–39 and 20:16 to refer to a *Rabbi* and to insure that it is understood. When we survey the Rabbi's history of their development in the beginning of the Mishnah Avot, for example, we find that Hillel and Shammai, who lived in the first quarter of the first century CE do not have the title Rabbi before their name, but the generation after Hillel and Shammai, Rabban Gamliel, and Rabban Shimon ben Gamliel, do have the title appended to their names.

The title was new enough, however, that even in the second century, emended texts of the New Testament had to add explanations of the "Rabbi" title. John 20:16 states: "Jesus spoke to her, Mary and she said to him: Rabboni, *that is to say, Teacher.*" The emendation suggests that the writer needed to interpret the title Rabbi with the more common title, "Teacher." *Didaskalos* seems to be the more well-known and ingrained terminology, and the Rabbi title seems to be less known. Similarly in John 3:10, Jesus answering Nicodemus says: "You are a teacher of Israel and you do not know these things?" John's tradition is quite distinctive. Jesus is a teacher in John 3:2, 3:10, 8:4, 11:28, and 13:13–14. In fact "teacher" is a title of leadership in the New Testament equal to or greater than "rabbi."

In the Synoptic Gospels, "Teacher" is a clear title for Jesus, most often in the vocative, in Matthew 8:19 and Mark 4:38. In Luke 2:46, Jesus is in the Temple amongst the "Teachers" (*didaskaloi*), and most important in Luke 3:12, John the Baptist is seen as a "Teacher." The Teacher in the New Testament is apparently known as being a priest and sage.

The Dead Sea sects seem to have a number of different levels of leadership beyond the Teacher of Righteousness, and most scholars have no trouble assuming that these titles continued from generation to generation among the Essenes. It is difficult to understand why there would be only one Teacher of Righteousness, and yet there were other leaders who appear during the entire history of the sect. I assume that just as there were a *Paqid* and a *Mevaqqer*, an "Overseer" and "Exchequer," who are mentioned in these texts and who continued their positions into later periods, so too there were multiple "Teachers." Even more important, because there is no continuation of the title of *"Paqid"* and *"Mevaqqer"* into the later Rabbinic and Roman Jewish world vocabulary of leadership, I assume that these titles became extinct. The title *Moreh HaTzedeq*, however, continues in Rabbinic literature.

Back to the Sources: The "Teacher" in the Rabbinic Tradition

Regarding the possibility of an ongoing tradition of *"a" Teacher of Righteousness* in the first century CE, the most famous passage of the scrolls involving the Teacher is found in the Damascus Document 1:3–11:

In the era of wrath—three hundred and ninety years from the time He [God] handed them over to the power of Nebuchadnezzar king of Babylon—He took care of them and caused to grow from Israel and from Aaron a root of planting to inherit His land and to grow fat on the good produce of His soil. They considered their iniquity and they knew that they were guilty men, and had been like the blind and like the groping for the way twenty years. But God considered their deeds, that they had sought Him with a whole heart. So He raised up for them *a Teacher of Righteousness* to guide them in the way of His heart.

Although later historians dated Nebuchadnezzar to 587 BCE and calculated the 390 year period to end in 197 BCE before the Hasmoneans, Jewish tradition, (which this Damascus Document may be following) in the Rabbinic medieval *Seder Olam Rabbah*, Nebuchadnezzar is dated to 423 BCE, which would place the first *Teacher of Righteousness* in the last decades of the first century BCE. The leader of "Israel" and a leader of "Aaron" would have had to possess a priestly background and perhaps a Davidic lineage. Early on in the discussions of the scrolls, it was determined that there were three eschatological leaders: a prophet on the level of Moses, a Messiah of Aaron, and a Messiah of Israel. The famous passage (9.11) in 1QS Manual of Discipline reads: "They shall be ruled by the first laws with which the men of the community began to be instructed until the coming of the prophet and the messiahs of Aaron and Israel." 1QS gives numerous pieces of information about the presiding officer, the *Mevaqqer* in charge of the property of incoming recruits to the community (6:20) and another officer, the *Paqid* who is the head of larger groups. The *Mevaqqer* is an overseer of multiple groups (14:9) and who was apparently head of the laity and the *Paqid* was head of the priests. Although it was thought that the two figures were different overseers they may have been fused into one position in later generations of the sect.

This seems to be in accord with the idea of the later Jewish tradition as well. The Midrash on the book of Psalms is a early medieval commentary on one of the most important books of the Bible in Qumran and the Jewish world during the Roman period. More copies of Psalms appear at Qumran than any other book. It was used by Jews and Christians as a prayer book even before their liturgies were canonized. It was a book that was used by many people in the Roman period to help chart the way that Jewish leadership would and should be. The Midrash commentary tries to do the same thing. Psalm 102, verse 16–18 (Revised Standard Version translation) states in the Bible: "When the Lord builds Zion anew, [He] appears to her in his glory, if He regards the prayer of the destitute and does not despise their prayer. Let this be recorded for a future generation, so that a people yet unborn may praise the Lord." The verse seems to say that only God will be able to build Zion anew. The late Midrashic collection on the biblical Book of Psalms 102 cites a tradition in the name of Rabbi Isaac (a third-century source) that adds some significant information about a Jewish leader who was known to the Rabbis and called the *Teacher of Righteousness*: "[King] David had in mind the [future] generations, that will have neither prophet, nor priest, nor *Teacher of Righteousness* (*Moreh Tzedeq*), nor Holy Temple to atone for them."

While the title of "Moreh" is found in Rabbinic literature, it was not known to be a title in the Rabbinic period for a distinguished figure, but this tradition actually tells us that it was known to the Rabbis. This figure is apparently a well-known figure of leadership of the Jews, especially in Israel, into the Tannaitic and Amoraic period. The Midrash Psalms states that there was an ancient figure who held a similar status to a priest and a prophet called the Teacher of Righteousness. The collection, Midrash Psalms, has been thought to be a literary product of the classical Geonic period (eighth to tenth centuries CE) and probably from Palestine. Although the collection was put together in the Geonic period, a very active codification period in Rabbinic literature, it is seen as representing Rabbinic traditions from an earlier period. The appearance of the title *Moreh Tzedek* in a text codified in the Geonic period means that the title may have still been meaningful for the readers and copyists of this text. In what is the last use of the title, *Moreh Tzedek* appears as the name of a polemical text from fourteenth-century Spain. The continued use for nearly 1,500 years in Jewish sources suggests it was indeed a well-known leadership title.

Searching for The *Teacher of Righteousness* in Early Christian Literature

The words *Teacher of Righteousness* do not appear in the New Testament, despite very intense interest in both the title "Teacher" and the concept of "Righteousness." Other words, in addition to *dikaiosune, dikaios,* etc., can be masking the Christian concept or perhaps the combined title does not exist in the Christian community despite the interest in both terms. Another term, *Sophos* and *Sophia,* that is usually a translation of *Hacham/Hochmah, Binah, Musar, Tevunah, Daat,* and *Machshavah,* can also be a cognate for *Tzedeq, Etzah, Lekah,* and a variety of other words in Hebrew. The title of "*Moreh*"/Teacher is not in the Hebrew Bible and appears to be a later distinction that was meaningful for Jews that was different than the designations of prophet, priest, wise man/woman, judge, etc. that will be raised later. The parallelism in the DSS appears as well in 1QH1.34ff, where the words "Sages" and "Righteous" people (*Hachamim* and *Tzadiqim*) are paralleled and the *Nevonim* of Aaron and the *Hachamim* of Israel are paralleled as well. *Sophia/Sophos* is a concept of ethical conduct, academic wisdom, cunning, skill, practical wisdom, but also, piety. The title of "Teacher" is used throughout the NT of Jesus and into the later Church writings in the second and third century. Even Paul is called "*didaskalos* (teacher) of the people" in 1 Timothy 2:7.

Another term, *kalodidaskalos,* is rarely found in Greek literature but again has been created by Pauline writers in order to describe a position in the community. *The Teacher of Goodness-Kalodidaskalos* is found in Titus 2:3. In chapter 3 it continues: "(1)But you speak of things that are sound teachings (2) the aged men ought to be sober, serious, discreet, sound in faith, love and endurance (3) the aged women, in like manner, in deportment as becomes sacred individuals, not slanderers, not given to much wine, and *teachers of goodness*." The use here demonstrates that the title is not a formal title as in the Rabbinic text but still to describe a role, perhaps a new role amongst the women. Titus, who apparently is not circumcised and is a gentile Christian that we know nothing of from Acts. He is first distinguished by Paul in Galatians as one of his companions that represents him in Crete. The term, therefore, seems to be an original creation and not from his knowledge of either the Jewish or gentile communities.

The Evidence of a "Teacher of Righteousness" in the Byzantine Period Synagogue

It is possible that positions or titles were actually circulating in a number of different versions in Jewish communities in Asia Minor. One such combined title seems to recall the *Moreh Tzedeq* of Rabbinic texts and the Qumran texts. It is found in the synagogue inscription from the late Roman period at Sardis as "Teacher of Wisdom [or Righteousness]" in Greek, *sophodidaskalos,* but presumably in other manifestations as well. The ancient synagogue of Sardis has an inscription of a donation by a member of the community who is both a priest and a *sophodidaskalos*. "The inscription suggests that a four pillared structure was the object which the *sophodidaskalos* gave and that from this that place he taught. The fact that the *sophodidaskalos* had a role in the synagogue, was a priest, and continued to have a title that is found in Rabbinic literature of the period seems to indicate for an ongoing Rabbinic leadership role for this figure into the Byzantine period when the inscription was done. In the Roman period a number of these different types of leadership roles were maintained. The "*Archesyna-gogos*" is another term that is only found in the Hellenistic-Roman period and may correspond to a Hebrew term as well. The *sophodidaskalos, the Teacher of Wisdom [or Righteousness]* may have been adapted to distinguish it from the Rabbi, but it apparently still maintained a Priestly position. If it is another version of the "Teacher" of Qumran, it would confirm the ongoing use of the title in the Rabbinic period that indicates that it is right to suspect that:

1. The title of "Teacher" was well known among Hellanistic Jews, and then later the followers of Jesus and Paul and the Rabbis continued the use of this title beyond the first and second century CE. The use of the title *Moreh Tzedeq* in the Psalms Midrash and in the use of *sophodidaskalos* in the Sardis synagogue for a priest and official leader within Rabbinic Judaism is significant. The use of "Teacher" in the Synoptics (Luke) Gospel of John and is a respected role between prophets and miracle workers in Pauline language that combines *vomodidaskalos* and *kalodidaskalos* as a point counterpoint for different types of Rabbinic and Church leadership.
2. It appears that Qumran's use of this title is part of another link with Rabbinic Judaism (and for some period early Christianity) that continued after the destruction of the Temple.

Conclusions: Archaeology and the Scrolls

Now that I know that a "Teacher of Righteousness" was a known term in the Jewish and Christian circles in the first, second, and third centuries CE, it makes more sense to see the discovery of the burial in Tomb #1000 as one of the "Teachers" who led the people of Qumran. More important, the discovery of the single grave inside of a building on top of the most prominent hill overlooking both the cemetery of Qumran and the entire village of Qumran signals to me that this would be the place where they would have buried the most important leader of the community. I remember that as I worked to excavate the building every day at sunrise (we began before sunrise because it was so hot). I noticed how the sun could be seen first from this elevated position. As the sun rose from the east and came over the mountains of Jordan, you could see that this location would have been one that people of the village would have seen from every part of the village. It seemed to most of us that the most reasonable explanation for this location was that it was the site of the burial place of the leader of the village and the mysterious Teacher of Righteousness from the Dead Sea Scrolls.

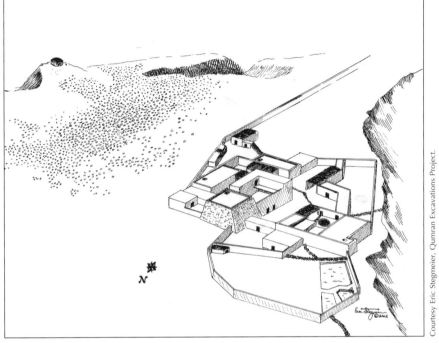

Figure 6.4.   Reconstruction of Qumran, the cemetery, and the mausoleum of the Teacher of Righteousness on top of the hill to the east.

7

Seeking Mary, Mother of Jesus; Miriam, Sister of Moses; and the Well and Bathhouse of Nazareth

Figure 7.1.   Mary's Well, Nazareth.

When I was flying home from Spain from our Burgos excavations in 2005, I had the opportunity to read a small article in the *International Herald Tribune* that caught my eye. It was a story about the so-called "house of Mary," in of all places, Loreto, Italy. It simply stated that a house in Loreto, Italy, has stones that have the same origin as stones found in the Grotto of the Annunciation in Nazareth. I could imagine how such a thing could have occurred. The industriousness of religious people never ceases to amaze me. I could imagine that over a period of centuries, monks and other religious pilgrims could indeed have brought stones from the Holy Land to Loreto, Italy, and created this house. This is the basis of many of the relic sites, perfectly logical in the world of religious pilgrimage.

What this story in the *International Herald Tribune* did not write about was the industriousness of the monks who may have brought the stones from Israel or Nazareth over centuries. Instead it included the legendary account that is told about Mary's House in Loreto by the locals. According to this account, Mary's House from Nazareth was transported, like Dorothy's house in the *Wizard of Oz*, intact from Nazareth. It is akin to the mystical night journey of Muhammad from Mecca to Jerusalem in the Koran or reminiscent of the biblical Elijah the Prophet's visitations to the houses of Jews worldwide on the evening of Passover, and Santa Claus's ability to visit the homes of all Christian children worldwide on Christmas Eve. Mary's House from Nazareth was transported to Italy for pilgrims to enjoy and feel her presence there. This is the essence of relics. They give us a sense of the person, place, or event often in our own locale.

Relics can be found in the most unlikely places, and they are often large structures. There is a site on top of a mountain called Ararat in Turkey that has the outline of a large wooden ship, way above the treeline and it has the dimensions of the Ark mentioned in the Genesis story of Noah's Ark. It is amazing that scientists and Bible scholars alike have seen this ship and have accepted the Genesis account as true based on seeing the contours of this enormous ark on top of this mountain. We have to be sure when looking at something that purports to be a biblical object that it has a scientific context that can be validated. In the case of this ancient Ararat ark, the pieces of the mystery were evaluated, and it is clear that the ark was only twelve hundred years ago, while the ancient story of Noah's Ark purports to be very ancient—at least four thousand years old. So what is this boat on top of this mountain? A relic, built by the very industrious monks of this region to celebrate where they felt the event of Noah's Ark happened. Is it the real place? We cannot really know without further study, but it is clearly where these monks, twelve hundred years ago, felt it happened. They may have had an oral tradition that this was the place and decided it was only right that pilgrims see for themselves the grandeur that they knew had been there. Today it is a tourist site and little will be done to mar the enthusiasm of willing tourists to the area, but the Ark's mysterious history is similar to the history of many other relic sites. They cannot be scientifically validated.

As we began to work in Nazareth, I wondered if I would be engulfed by the relic-seekers and the pilgrims. I really had no idea what I was getting myself into when we accepted the call to excavate a bathhouse found near the famous "Well" of Mary in Nazareth. I was shocked, for example, when a colleague came and told me outright that I was foolish to work in Nazareth, looking for a connection between the ancient Well of Nazareth and the "supposed" Bathhouse of Mary nearby. He stated outright the problem that I had never before heard. "It is ridiculous," he said. "There wasn't even a village of Nazareth in existence in the first century CE. The village developed only later, after the story of Jesus became important in the Byzantine period. Looking for the Well of Mary in Nazareth was like looking for witches and goblins." What started as a straightforward archaeological investigation suddenly took on huge archaeological and religious importance for many people as we delved into what was clearly a sacred cow of archaeology. Was Nazareth a well-known village or city in the time of Jesus? The excavations of the Israel Antiquities Authority (IAA) in and around Nazareth tells us it was. Nurit Feig, who has excavated Iron Age cave burials and Iron Age and Hellenistic fortresses that ring around the city to the north, indicate that there were many different locations that spiral out from the famous Roman city of Sepphoris and which indeed lead down to the modern city of Nazareth. The fact that there were massive Byzantine structures in Nazareth, a Roman road system that went through and by the city, and an ancient well of large proportions all point to the city as being in existence from the Iron Age onward. Our own excavations in the Bathhouse cisterns, which had Middle Bronze Age pottery in it, and the thousands of fragments of Roman pottery in the water channel leading to the mouth of Mary's Well, all point to a settlement in this area in the Roman period. We had come to investigate a part of biblical lore that brought me closer to understanding not only Nazareth, but Mary, mother of Jesus, and the life and times of Jesus.

The call came this way. Maha Darawsha, who was a graduate of Haifa University's archaeology program and a resident archaeologist for the Antiquities Authority of Israel, was a graduate student who began working with the University of Hartford in 2001. She had been recommended to us by Michal Artzy, a rather famous Haifa University professor of archaeology. Maha lived in the Nazareth suburb of Iqsal and had been involved in many of the projects in Galilee leading up to Pope John Paul II's visit to Israel in 2000. In Nazareth and the surrounding Arab villages, many new and ancient sites were excavated and renovated for the visit of the Pope to the area. In the basement of one of the buildings near the ancient Well of Nazareth a bathhouse was discovered. The bathhouse was well known in local lore as having been rebuilt by the mayor of the city of Nazareth in the late nineteenth century. So the archaeologists excavating the nearby Well of Mary did not feel it was necessary to scientifically excavate this bathhouse. The couple who leased the store where the bathhouse was found were Orthodox Christians, and began speaking about the bathhouse not as a nineteenth-century Turkish period bathhouse, but as the bathhouse of Jesus and Mary. It was just this type of mystery that our technology could help us solve. Was it ancient or was it modern? Was it a relic built in the Byzantine period, Crusader period, or was it solely the product of a nineteenth century developer? That mystery was important enough for us to have my colleague, Maha Darawsha, work together with us and the Antiquities Authority of Israel to solve.

Mary's Well

Mary's Well is at the north end of the city of Nazareth in Israel. Uphill on Paul VI Street from the Church of the Annunciation, you come to Mary's Well. The water of the well was well known in legends for centuries. People went on pilgrimages to the well since the water was said to heal all ailments. The main spring of the well, which for twenty centuries has supplied Nazareth, is right under the Crypt of the Greek Orthodox Church of Saint Gabriel. This building, topped by a slim stone bell tower, was restored in the middle of the eighteenth century.

In fact, the location of the Mary's Well site is not as clear as people think. Archaeologists located one site on the basis of its use in the nineteenth century as an active well for the general public. A small portion of this well was excavated in the 1990s down to a Roman layer as they prepared for the millennium celebrations of the year 2000 and the visit of Pope John Paul II to Nazareth. By the 1950s the well had dried up and was no longer being used as a public well as the Israelis began regular sewage and water service in the Nazareth area. This well, at the corner of Mary's Well square, was a public well and a relic site visited by many people up until the present period. The dried up well is now a small dump with little sense of its majesty and importance of antiquity.

The main controversy is not whether there was a well or a bathhouse there—the controversy centers around the age of the well and who may have used it. After five years of work, I can say that the well was in use in the first century, and it is possible that the bathhouse was connected to the well in this ancient period, but until we have an undisturbed area to excavate it is hard to know. "Undisturbed" is the operative word. The entire area around the bathhouse was refurbished in anticipation of the Pope's visit in 2000. The bathhouse was discovered when the coffee shop proprietors decided to excavate the basement themselves. When we began our work, we discovered that the bathhouse was presently located in the basement of a coffee shop directly adjacent to the ancient well of Nazareth. How ancient might this bathhouse have been? We discovered a mystery that we have yet to fully solve. I can say with some confidence that the bathhouse in the coffee shop of Mary's Well is from the Crusader period, but we discovered that it was probably built upon an earlier bathhouse, but that has yet to be resolved. If it was confirmed as a first-century bathhouse next to the ancient well and near St. Gabriel's Church of the Annunciation, we realized that it might potentially contain artifacts related to the New Testament's Holy Family in Nazareth.

Another problem is also whether there was a "Jewish" Nazareth of the first century CE from which Jesus, Mary, and her husband Joseph all came from. We know from many excavations in the area that burial caves were in the area around Nazareth for thousands of years that provided a local population with a place to bury. When I went to see Mary's Well for the first time, I did not realize that a real controversy surrounds the existence of Nazareth in the first century. Because Nazareth is not mentioned in the Hebrew Bible, in Josephus Flavius's many works, nor in the writings of Paul nor in the many volumes of the Talmud, some scholars began to think that a historical first- century village/city of Nazareth never existed and that the New Testament writers created this "mythical" city. Although the city name of Nazareth might not have been known in antiquity, it is also possible that Nazareth is simply not mentioned in these other writings because it was a small, out of the way, village. It happens that a city that is important to one writer is not in the writings of another writer for many different reasons. The appellation "Jesus of Nazareth" may not be referring to a city of Nazareth but perhaps a locale or a geographic element in a setting. But the Gospel writers were writing for an informed ancient public, even if this public was not necessarily living in Israel at the time of their writing. But the absence of the city name does not, necessarily, imply that a settlement was not located in the area where Nazareth is today. Remember: the absence of evidence is not evidence of absence, primarily when settlement information is associated with Mary's Well and other places around the modern city of Nazareth. The well is an ancient water source, as shown through the pottery finds, and this place where the city of Nazareth is located is in fact surrounded by hills (with many burial caves), and this is a part of the Netofah Valley. Although the city of Nazareth is called a "polis" or Greco-Roman "city" in the New Testament, it may have been something less than a village in this period (and the Gospel writers do use the Greek words for "city" and "village" almost interchangeably). But the presence of this major well in the north of the city would have been a place where people would have gathered in antiquity, this is for sure.

Most major wells in antiquity attracted people to the area, and a village or city developed around the water source. The fact that this well was located in this area from time immemorial makes me suspect that despite the lack of a mention of a city "Nazareth" in most of the literature, it is probable that a village would have sprung up in this location. More important is that the renaming of a city, after the fact, is also common in antiquity. The city of Yathrib was home to Muhammad in the first years of the rise of Islam. The city was renamed after this famous resident and called Medina (Medina means "city" in Arabic) because it was the city of the Prophet Muhammad, and today is known only by that name. Because we find groups with the "Nazarene" or "Notzri" designation in Rabbinic writings, we can assume that the designation was a well-known location, associated with characteristics of the location or an actual village name. If these designations are talking about something to do with the Hebrew root of *Nazareth*, which means "bud" in Hebrew, they may just allude to the valley's fruitful nature. The name Nazareth may have been a designation that moved from alluding to the location's fruitful nature to a city. By the third century, Nazareth is a city mentioned by Julius Africanus and then later in the *Onomastikon* of Eusebius. All of these and many counterarguments are well known to me now, but when I first got to Mary's Well, I learned only about the positive, Byzantine records that securely located it in the place where we were brought to in Nazareth.

Mary's Well is mentioned in the very first records of pilgrimage sites in Nazareth by Jerome and Egeria. In 670 CE, after the Arab conquest, the pilgrim Arculf saw two churches in Nazareth. One was built over the house of Jesus under which a crypt with Mary's spring was found, and the other was at the site of the present-day Franciscan Church of the Annunciation. In 2001, while visiting Nazareth, we visited the coffee shop near Mary's Well. Mary's Well itself was carefully excavated by Israeli archaeologists in anticipation of the Pope's visit to Nazareth, and the water system from St. Gabriel's Church was a part of their work. The basement of the nearby coffee shop had been dug by the proprietors, and what they discovered was what appeared to be a bathhouse. Their "excavations" contained artifacts dating back to the Byzantine and perhaps Roman period but unfortunately, they did not undertake their work with archaeologists so it is difficult to assess what they found. They had dug out the basement for storage space for their shop and had found a very large structure with arched/vaulted ceilings, a marble floor, and a fireplace. It was a small bathhouse by Roman standards, but when the Israeli archaeologists looked at it in the year 2000 in the midst of their own excavations at Mary's Well, they designated it to be of Ottoman origin and from the nineteenth century. It was, therefore, not an antiquity (antiquities in Israel date to a period before 1750 CE) and not in need of scientific oversight.

If indeed, it was a Roman bathhouse, it should have been an elaborate structure, with vaulted ceilings, and marble dressed walls, including both the *caldarium* (hot room) and *frigidarium* (cold room). The caldariums were heated rooms, each warmed by one or more furnaces and a sophisticated system of hypocausts (furnaces) for warming the floors. The hypocausts were made of piers of one-meter stacked clay bricks, with mortar. From these furnaces, the hypocausts were sufficiently warmed to heat up the entire room above. The smoke escaped through numerous flues in the wall, providing effective heating for the whole room. Most of these elements are present in the bathhouse at Mary's Well, but they also correspond to similar bathhouses from the Byzantine through the Crusader periods. The Roman bath required fresh water for its use. The only source of water in the vicinity was located a few meters to the southwest, Mary's Well. Since 2001, other scholars have looked at the bathhouse and raised questions. Heavy metals had been found in the dirt sampled, including gold and silver particles mixed in with the calcium carbonate. In our excavations we committed ourselves to dating the entire location and searching to see when and if it was linked up with the Roman water system located only a few feet from the edge of the bathhouse.

We visited other bathhouses in the area of Galilee and Judea from the late Roman-Byzantine period and compared them with the Nazareth bathhouse. The bathhouse at Kursi, on the Sea of Galilee, another site associated with early Christianity, shows why this study of heavy metals is important. A team of archaeologists from the *Jerusalem Center for Biblical Studies* and the Antiquities Authority of Israel uncovered a late Roman-period (third-early fourth century CE) bathhouse complex near a previously excavated Byzantine monastery. Inside the 26-by-36 foot bathhouse were three dozen women's rings and other pieces of jewelry. This jewelry would have been brought into the bathhouse, left there or forgotten in the water, and remained to be found some sixteen hundred years later. Bathhouses are notoriously good places to search for personal items, especially small pieces of jewelry, such as rings, earrings, and necklaces. It is the equivalent of going to the gym or spa today, putting away your personal items in a locker or on a bench, and forgetting about them after you are dressed and on your way. Lighting in these ancient bathhouses would have been minimal. So the possibility of finding personal effects from people from Nazareth in the midst of this bathhouse associated with Jesus, Mary, and Joseph seemed to be of a good possibility. Even one item, like a comb, a piece of jewelry, pottery, glass perfume, or other personal items, engraved with a name from a bathhouse so close to the places associated with Jesus and his family would be of enormous importance. Perhaps Minimalists would say which Jesus, Anna, Mary, or Joseph, but in the end they would be placed in close proximity to a venerable Church (St. Gabriel's) associated from the Byzantine period with the holy family. These types of items in the bathhouse at Nazareth, especially with its location adjacent to the site of Mary's Well, would be significant in the study of Nazareth and early Christianity.

Are There Roman Period Bathhouses in Israel?

In spite of the Antiquities Authority of Israel classifying the coffee house bathhouse as from the Ottoman period (and not in need of any specialized excavation or investigation), we found three items that immediately caught my attention. First, the proprietors claimed to have found Byzantine and perhaps Roman period finds, including pottery, oil lamps, and coins (from the Roman, Byzantine, and Crusader periods) in their nonscientific excavations. Unfortunately anecdotal information is very unreliable and not part of a good archaeological report, but it does raise the question of what could possibly be there. The shopkeepers also claimed to have found Crusader remains that they used in decorating throughout in the coffee shop itself. Since the Crusader remains are indeed in the shop and prominently displayed, one has to take seriously their contention that these items were indeed part of their work. Second, the bathhouse was buried under three layers of street debris at the same level as the Mary's Well excavations that had already been dated to the Roman and Byzantine period. We spent one morning just digging up thousands of early Roman period cooking pots that clogged the Well near the Roman period piping. So there is evidence (nearby) that confirms that the water system was in use in the Roman period. Third, was the structure of the bathhouse itself. We examined the literature on Roman baths in Israel and then visited them and compared how they were constructed to the bathhouse in Nazareth. They were indeed similar.

Emmaus, for example, a site in the Ayalon valley near Latrun on the old Jerusalem-Tel Aviv road that ascends from the Coastal plain to Jerusalem, is a city that like Nazareth had existed for a long period of time but that was a middle-sized city in the time of the Maccabees onward. It was probably a mixed city, of pagans and Jews, by the first century CE. The Roman Fifth Legion was located there during the First Revolt (66–70 CE), but it is still mentioned by Rabbi Akiva and the sages and well known in the Talmud. In BT Shabbat 147b, the Rabbis refer to the public bathhouse there by the Greek-derived name *demosion loutron* public bathhouse. Byzantine Christian writers connected the bathhouse's curative properties with the visit of Jesus to Emmaus, and the present structure that resembles the bathhouse in Nazareth but was not built until the third century CE. The Roman arches that channeled the water below the floor are built using bricks that resemble the arched channels and the brickwork of the Nazareth bathhouse. The mosaic and extensive improvements of Emmaus were made in the Byzantine period.

In the area of Judea, Beth Zur, a city situated on the old Jerusalem-Hebron road, some 30 km. to the south of Jerusalem, has the makings of an early bathhouse structure. This is really a complex of baths in the period of the Hasmoneans (and even earlier in the Hellenistic period), but it would be the equivalent of what we might find at other places below the Byzantine level. The presence of springs in this area made it possible to have had formal baths in the earlier period, but no fuller work below the Byzantine-level impressive bathhouse was done there to test the hypothesis that the baths dated from an earlier period. Perhaps a formal bathhouse was there in the time of the first century, but the standing structures excavated indicate a third-century-CE origin. The vaulted entrances of massive work that took place during the Crusader period are reminiscent of the same vaults that we find preserved in the walls of the Nazareth bathhouse. They are very low on the walls of the Nazareth bathhouse and very high up on the walls of the Emmaus bathhouse. This was my first clue that the Nazareth bathhouse that we were looking at might be only a later incarnation of the original bathhouse level.

This is common. The hot water in a bathhouse destroys the plastering and bath works over a relatively short period of one hundred years. Hammat Gader, east of the Sea of Galilee, and its baths may originally date from the second and third century as well, but today they are clearly from the Byzantine period. According to the Talmud, an entire cadre of second- and third-century-CE Rabbis (Rabbi Meir, Rabbi Yehuda HaNasi, Rabbi Yonatan, Rabbi Hanina ben Hanina) visited the site of the Hammat Gader baths indicating that its use was widespread. Again, as in the Emmaus case, it is possible that an original structure existed and was rebuilt and extended. The Byzantine structures are impressive at Hammat Gader, but clearly new and better structures were put up over the original hot springs. The indicators that link it also with the Nazareth structure are the Roman arches of brick in the channels of water below the floor and the limestone walls built without mortar and floors paved with slabs of clay like limestone that could be polished. Similar to Emmaus and Nazareth, massive Crusader arches are found at the site.

Hammat-Tiberias is another bathhouse and synagogue located in the area around Tiberias but located in the Talmudic period one mile outside of the formal city boundary until it became unified (especially to include the bathhouse and springs). Today, thanks to the new excavations of Yizhar Hirshfeld in Tiberias, we know that the ancient city of Tiberias actually is much closer to the Hammat Tiberias bathhouse than we originally suspected. According to the Talmud, Tiberias was a particularly problematic place for Rabbinic settlement until the second century CE when it was "purified." Its original founding as a Roman city by Herod may have had something to do with it, although the Rabbis attribute burial impurities to their prohibitions. In any case, the Hammat Tiberias site excavations reveal an extensive building layer from the Byzantine period onward long after the Rabbis of the first and second century had been visiting it. But this is generally the rule, once a site was chosen for a bathhouse, it was generally the site for reconstructed bathhouses in other periods. Basic issues for bathhouses such as grading, the water table, access routes, etc. were made in one period and therefore made this place the preferred place generation after generation.

Also on the Sea of Galilee, Bet Yerah (Khirbet El Kerah) has another Roman bathhouse with clay piping that resembles the clay piping bringing the water from Mary's Well to the bathhouse in Nazareth. The clay piping that is found in the walls there also resembles the clay piping at Nazareth. Again, many developments that (like those at Hammat Tiberias) include the development of a Byzantine era synagogue alongside the bathhouse, something that in the Roman period probably would not have been done, but later, as the Jews in this area became more prominent, was added.

Beth Shean or Scythopolis, located at the junction of two important ancient roads from the Jordan and the Jezreel Valleys, has a number of bathhouses. One major bathhouse was started in the Roman period but went through many changes until it was destroyed in the earthquake of 749 CE. Again we have the example of a Roman period bathhouse that was reconstructed in the same place in the Byzantine period. This is the largest bathhouse unearthed to date in Israel. The clay piping and brick arches that held up the floor are extremely prominent and very similar to the Nazareth bathhouse. The site of Scythoplis was important as a city of the Decapolis in the early Roman period. Although the Byzantine bathhouse is seen by the tourists, we suspect an earlier bathhouse was destroyed in the famous earthquake of 361 CE and then updated by residents.

But there are real Roman-period bathhouses in Israel. In the south of the country, the situation for comparisons with the Nazareth bathhouse is actually quite interesting. The most famous bathhouse of Herod the Great at Masada does not have the same Roman brick arches that hold up the floor, but the piping in the walls is similar to that found at Nazareth. It is important to remember that each region had its own materials that were used in the preparations of something such as a bathhouse. It is also important to note that Herod's bathhouse was a private bathhouse of a king, very different than the type of bathhouse that would have been in Galilee for the public. Perhaps it is the unique construction that was done at Masada by Herod's engineers or perhaps it is another design, but the stacks of blocks that make up the pillars that held up a mosaic floor is different than the brick arches found in the above-cited examples and as we will see the ones found in the rest of the Negev. Similarly at Herodion, the floor is held up by similar pillars, again from the period of Herod the Great in the first century BCE. It is distinctive perhaps to Herod's builders, although the styling of the pillars seems to differ even at other sites.

The Negev was geographically Jewish until the middle of the first century BCE when it was conquered by Obodas III, a Nabatean, who was probably a collaborator with Herod the Great in the creation of the Judean kingdom he ruled. In the first century, during the reign of the King of the Nabateans, Rabbel II (70–106 CE), the Nabateans developed eclectic but highly Hellenized structures that were unique to them. Maha and I visited many of the Nabatean Roman period bathhouses to see if they too used local materials to construct unique bathhouses and to compare them to the Nazareth bathhouse. In the midst of the Negev, in places such as Mampsis (*Mamshit* in Hebrew and *Kurnub* in Arabic), a bathhouse exists with the same sort of Roman arched bricks for holding up the floor but this time without the additions of the Byzantine period found in the north. At Avdat, again in the Negev, the bathhouse has the same Roman brick arches for holding up the floor and a limestone floor. Although the original literature on most of these bathhouses suggested that they were originally built in the Roman period, most experts today have declared most of these "Roman" period bathhouses to be from the Byzantine period. Most of these bathhouses were put up in the Roman period and then changed in the Byzantine period either because of the earthquakes that affected the area or because the bathhouses needed to be updated. One might think that a bathhouse would only be put up at a prominent location, but Avdat, Masada, and Mamshit are very far from the major centers of population. A bathhouse and formal bathing was a part of the life of people who lived in Israel from the first century CE onward.

The other more important item in the evaluation of whether a bathhouse in Nazareth even makes sense in the Roman period in an apparently Jewish village, has to do with the entire development of the bathing practices of the Jews in the Hellenistic and Roman periods. The Rabbis debate the importance of the Roman bath but at the same time established their own bathing facilities. Rabbi Elai states (BT Shabbat 33b) regarding the positive contributions of Roman society in the second century CE context writes: "Aren't the accomplishments of this people wonderful, they set up markets, bridges and bathhouses." In the Hellenistic and early Roman period, a parallel Jewish institution to the Roman bathhouse, the ritual bathing facility, the *mikveh*, was established, usually in or close to a bathhouse.

A Mikveh and Bathhouse?

Many times during our work at Nazareth we considered the importance of a bathhouse in the Roman period for the Jews. In reality, bathing was not only important to the Romans, it was important to the Jews and they ritualized their bathing practices. One of the most important innovations in Jewish bathing practices was a specialized pool that would have been a part of any Jewish bathhouse complex: a mikveh. Although bathing for ritual purposes is mentioned in the Hebrew Bible, no specific structure is mentioned in the Hebrew Bible. One has to assume that when the Hebrew Bible speaks about bathing in "running water," a natural water source is probably implied. But somewhere in the Hellenistic and early Roman period, the bathing rituals were performed in a bath that roughly parallels the different baths that the Greeks and Romans must have brought with them in their conquests of the Near East. As I mentioned before, although Rabbinic texts are only codified in the third century CE and are not excellent parallels for all archaeological discoveries before this period, often we have no other way of making sense out of the development of a ritual.

A mikveh is an architecturally unique structure used for Jewish ritual immersion that is approximately 6 feet by 2 feet by 2 feet and, according to Rabbinic standards, contains at least 40 seahs (191 gallons) of collected rainwater. The definitions of its size and exacting standardization are defined by the Rabbis in the earliest collections called the Mishnah, Tosefta, Midrashei-Halachah, and Aggadah. The mikveh was central to the Rabbis and postbiblical Judaism but emerges fully formed in the Rabbinic period without a clear precedent. It was a part of the public needs as a road or other public building. Rav Ashi remarked: "Our Mishnah states: 'And all public needs may be performed' [the language of the Mishnah]. What does [the Mishnah] mean '*all* [public needs]'? .... 'They [the leaders of the community] go forth to clear the roads of thorns [obstacles], to mend the roads and highways and to measure the [ritual] pools[*mikvaot*]; and if any [ritual] pools be found short of forty [cubic] se'ahs of water they train a continuous flow into it [to ensure] forty se'ahs'" (BT Moed Katan 5a).

While the Hebrew Bible does not mention a structure called a "mikveh" (literally Hebrew for "collected [water]") there were examples of baths in early Greek life as early as the fourth century BCE. The move of the Jews from small villages to larger Greek-like cities would have provided guidance about how to immerse in more formal city settings as opposed to rural settings. Only in the period of the Septuagint and Apocrypha do we find even a hint of the need for a special washing place constructed for this purpose. It is also clear that in Jerusalem of the late Second Temple period and in the great building clamor in Palestine in the fourth to sixth centuries CE, mikvehs (of the above definition) can be found throughout Israel, although not in great numbers. Professor Jacob Neusner over some twenty years of research has come to the conclusion that the mikveh was a unique structure of 40 seahs of water and was rabbinically integrated in Jewish law as a post-Yavne, second-century-CE-Ushan (Usha was a center of Rabbinic study in the second century CE) innovation of the Rabbis. Given what excavations in the past thirty years have found, the mikveh, a Jewish ritual stepped bath, probably emerged as a parallel to Roman bathing pools alongside the innovation of Roman bathhouses. They were copying, in the earliest incarnations, the most obvious models of bathing pools like the stepped Greek and Roman baths known later by the names of *impluvium* (piscina), which was rectangular and shallower than the mikveh, a *confluvium* found in an atrium-style home, and a "ritual" dedicated bath referred to as a *nympheum*. They were also expressing a unique Jewish bathing ritual alongside the Roman bathing rituals of the same period. The fact that no origin for the unique structure of a mikveh has ever been posited leads me to believe that this hypothesis needs further investigation. If I am correct that in the first century CE the Roman bathhouse had fully developed alongside a mikveh complex, a place like Nazareth would be a great place for the two to coexist. I have no doubt that standardization, according to perhaps Rabbinic definitions, both of synagogue construction and mikvaot began in the second and third century CE. This would be a natural progression after the destruction of the Temple in Jerusalem in 70 CE. I have to admit, however, that the existence of purity laws associated with Jerusalem may have pushed the development of the mikveh into a much earlier period. By the late Hellenistic-Early Roman (through first century CE) period, the existence of mikveh and bathhouse complex would be a natural combination. I believe that the Greco-Roman origins of the practice may lie in this period. Furthermore, the desire to rabbinically define a likely commonplace practice may lie at the core of its proliferation. It is not just the Essenes at Qumran that saw as essential the bathing process. David Small earlier initiated questions about mikvaot in the early Roman-late Hellenistic period in his article titled: "Late Hellenistic Baths in Palestine" in the *Bulletin of the American Schools of Oriental Research* (1975, 59-74):

> The material is now so abundant that Palestine challenges Italy as the most fruitful area for the study of late Hellenistic baths. Many of these baths resemble their Italian counterparts and current opinion is that they were the result of Rome's early influence in Palestine.

The question of course is whether the Roman influence that resulted in the innovation of the "mikveh" or whether the Roman baths in the eastern provinces tapped into an already existing practice of Judean baths that were formalized into the innovation of the mikveh. The question is relevant because it affects not only the mikveh, but also our perception about the rise of synagogues that also seem to have emerged in the late Hellenistic-early Roman context and resemble quite closely the construction of the Hellenistic *bouleterion*.

The earliest examples of baths that could be mikvaot date from the Maccabean and Hasmonean periods or the Ptolemian/Seleucid Greek periods. In the case of the mikveh discovered at Masada, Yadin had similar thoughts in his book *Masada* (1966, 164–5):

This find immediately suggested to us that what we had discovered was a ritual immersion bath—Mikve in Hebrew—and this we announced at our routine press conference. The news that we had brought to light a mikve from the period of the Second Temple quickly spread throughout the country, arousing particular interest in orthodox religious quarters and Talmudic scholars; for the traditional Jewish laws of the Talmud relating to the ritual bath are quite complex, and no mikve has so far been discovered belonging to this very period, the period when much of the relevant traditional law governing the mikve was written and enacted.

The mikveh was not a subject of archaeological speculation in the nineteenth and twentieth century mainly because most of the archaeologists did not have the background to recognize architectural structures as mikvehs. Unfortunately, beginning with Yadin's recognition of the mikveh at Masada, a long line of reconsiderations of architectural assumptions have begun. Roni Reich, for example, reexamined a stepped cistern excavated at Gezer by Macalister and then William Dever and Joe Seger and declared it to be the earliest mikveh ever identified from the Hasmonean period from the time of Simon Macabee (141 BCE). In part his reinvestigation of the structure was prompted by a rereading of I Maccabees 13:48, ". . . he resettled it with men who observed the Torah . . ." What were they observing? Rituals like mikveh. The literary information is difficult. There is no mention of an architecturally unique structure being created there, yet Reich was able to reinterpret a cistern to a mikveh. It is not clear that all of the reassigned stepped pools are mikvaot, but it is clear that the formal and later ritual bathing practices of the Jews in the late Hellenistic and Roman period made these bathhouses and mikvaot indispensable in Jewish cities in Galilee.

The Return to the Bathhouse

In 2002, we returned to Nazareth with a full geophysical team (ground penetrating radar and electrical resistivity tomography equipment from the University of Wisconsin and Komex International in Canada) to look again and to survey the site for possible excavation. Our work revealed that this bathhouse definitely had another deeper layer to it that probably led to ancient Mary's Well complex of antiquity. It is a self-contained location in Nazareth. The shopkeepers at the coffee shop called *Cactus* were very enthusiastic. Elias and Martina Shama-Sostar were eager for our excavations to confirm the authenticity of the bathhouse in their basement as a first century bathhouse. Most important, they were believing Christians who held from the start, that this was Mary's Bathhouse. I was interested in looking through their collection of photographs from the beginnings of their "excavations" of their basement. The first thing I was shown was a plaster-like bathtub they discovered (and destroyed) as they dug through the rubble below the street level of their shop. The digging out and the reconstruction of the site by the Shama-Sostar's from the start made the possibility of doing a systematic excavation there nearly impossible. So much had been disturbed during their work that a scientific and systematic excavation was very difficult, but it was important to assess the situation as it was in order to move forward. We did preliminary studies in 2002 and in 2003 returned with a full team and equipment with a license to excavate if necessary when we determined where it might be profitable. From the start, many people were interested in our work because of Mary, Jesus of Nazareth, and the whole family of Jesus who would have lived in close proximity to the site of Mary's Well in this period. The collection of carbon datable materials was key to our study. Israel's Weizmann Institute's top professional, Elisabetta Boaretto, measured Accelerator Mass Spectrometry technology at the NSF-AMS radiocarbon laboratory in Tucson, Arizona. The results from the carbon 14 tests revealed that our floor was in use in the twelfth century CE. But that was only the beginning of our work.

The three geophysicists that we worked with all concluded that the floor that we had extracted our samples from was not the original floor of the lowest level of the bathhouse. The GPR confirmed that levels below the present level that Elias and his wife had excavated looked like ancient floors. Our samples indicated that the bathhouse dated from at least the Crusader period and that it had been reconstructed. But the enormous vault in the middle of the coffee shop showed us that the present level of the coffee shop was not the original level of the bathhouse. The large and long vault was just above our heads as we sat and drank our coffee. For this to be the ceiling vault, the ancient floor had to be at least 10 to 15 feet below our feet. We knew that we had to excavate, and we had to excavate in a place that had not been as disturbed as the coffee shop was. After nearly two years of negotiations, the Kawar family who owns the building where the coffee shop and the surrounding stores are located, gave us permission to excavate an untouched area of the original bathhouse if we could find one to excavate. We began our excavations in 2005 and continued in the summer of 2006. We hunted for a place to excavate that did not disturb the floor of a business and yet was scientifically meaningful. We finally ended up digging in the cisterns of the bathhouse, which was a cavernous structure that had been used for trash collection and was very far below the bathhouse at the coffee shop. We excavated for three days in the cisterns, digging through modern concrete that had replaced the ancient plaster that would have lined the bottom of the cisterns. The cisterns for the water system clearly went down to the Middle Bronze Age. Small pieces of pottery from jugs and plates were found, photographed, and catalogued. The existence of small pieces of pottery seems to mean that there was runoff from the well and the ancient sewer system down into these cavernous cisterns three to four thousand years ago. We are still waiting for one of the stores on either side of the coffee shop to become unoccupied so we can excavate another unexcavated part of the bathhouse down to the level of the Roman period. However, the storeowners on both sides of the coffee shop have active businesses and would not relish our digging up their expensive tile floors and excavating some five to six feet down. The history of Judaism and the early history of Jesus and his family in Nazareth in this time period will have to wait until we have a clear place to excavate the rest of the bathhouse.

Mary's Well and Bathhouse of Christian Legend

Mary's Well developed as did other Christian sites because it was at the right place at the right time. It was on the road to the city of Tiberias in Nazareth and in the city of Nazareth that two completely different literary traditions grew about one of the seminal events in the lives of Jesus and Mary: the announcement (*annunciation*) of the birth of Jesus. According to both Christian versions, the "annunciation" took place in Nazareth. According to the Roman Catholic version of this story, it took place when Mary was in her home. According to the Greek Orthodox version of this story, it took place at a well. According to the version preserved by the Greek Orthodox church and to be found in the noncanonical gospels, this "Well" is the true place of the annunciation; the Archangel Gabriel is said to have announced to Mary that she was to become a mother while she was going to the well to fetch water. In fact in the canonical gospels, there is no mention of the well, but it was known in a number of early Christian writings.

> In the *Gospel of Pseudo-Matthew*, chapter 9: "And on the second day, while Mary was at the Well to fill her pitcher, the angel of the Lord appeared to her saying: Blessed are you Mary, for in your womb you have prepared an habitation for the Lord. For, lo, the light from heaven shall come and dwell in thee and by means of thee will shine over the whole world."
> In the *Proevangelium of James*, chapter 11: "She took the pitcher and went out to fill it with water. And behold, a voice saying: Hail, you who has received grace; the Lord is with you. Blessed are you

among women. And she looked around on the right hand and
on the left to see whence this voice came. And she went away,
trembling, to her house, and put down the pitcher and taking
the purple (linen), she sat down on her seat and drew it out. And
behold, an angel of the Lord stood before her saying: Fear not
Mary for you have found grace before the Lord of all and you
shall conceive, according to his word."

In the *Infancy of Thomas*, chapter 11: "When he was six years old,
his mother gave him a water jar and sent him to draw water and
fetch it home. As he jostled through the crowd, the water jar was
broken. Jesus then spread out the cloak he was wearing, filled it
with water and brought it to his mother. When his mother saw the
sign that had occurred, she kissed him and kept within herself the
mysteries she saw him performing."

(*The Other Bible*, edited by Willis Barnstone [San Francisco: Harper
and Row, 1984] pp. 383–405)

The Proevangelium of James contains the information about Mary for the
first time receiving her annunciation of the miraculous events of the birth at
the well, something that is missing in the Gospel of Luke. Even her name
was used to be tied to the well. *Maris stella*, says Jerome, (the fourth century
CE Bible translator) "a drop of water, *maris*" as if *Mary is water*. So the water
of the well becomes more than just a place for water, it is Mary herself. The
well was a metaphor of the "superabundant, eternally clear foundation of
grace that flows from there through all the worlds" (Goethe's *Faust*, 1245–
52). The healing waters, springs, and wells are associated with many of the
apparitions of the Virgin Mary. Miraculous cures are associated with the im-
bibing of these waters, such as places like Lourdes. But the story of the well
is found in the writings of many key Christian writers in the Middle Ages.

Saewulf (1102–3 CE): "The city of Nazareth has been entirely laid
waste and overthrown by the Saracens, but yet the much renowned
monastery points out the place of our Lord's Annunciation. The
fountain near the city bubbled out most clearly, still surrounded as it
used to be with marble columns and slabs. From this fountain it was
that the Child Jesus together with other boys, *often times drew water
for the use of His Mother.*"

Fetellus (circa 1130 CE): "Twelve miles from Tiberias is Nazareth, a city of Galilee in which Jesus was brought up. Nazareth is

interpreted a flower. In the synagogue at Nazareth Jesus opened the Book of Isaiah and expounded out of it to the Jews. On the highest point of Nazareth, towards the east, a remarkable fountain arises, from which in his boyhood, *Jesus used to draw water for His Mother's service and his own.*"

Theoderich (circa 1172 CE): "Four miles from Tabor towards the west, on the road which leads to Acre, stands the most glorious city of Nazareth in which is a venerable church, which enjoys the honor of being the cathedral church of a bishop, and which is dedicated to our blessed lady Mary. . . . A fountain in this city flows forth through a spout fashioned in marble like the mouth of a lion, from which the child Jesus often used to draw water and take it to his mother. This fountain is said to derive its origin from the following event: Once when the boy Jesus came to draw water from the well, his pitcher was broken by his comrades in their play and he drew the water and carried it to his mother in the lap of his tunic. As she refused to drink it, as he did not seem to have brought it in a sufficiently clean manner, he as though in a rage, flung it out of his lap on the ground; and from that place where it fell the fountain, which still flows, is said to have burst forth."

The Travels of Sir John Mandeville (14th century), chapter 13, ("Galilee") includes the additional information that the well had a place to bathe attached to it: "Thence men go through the plain of Galilee to Nazareth, which was once a big city; but now there is only a little unwalled village. In Nazareth was Our Lady born, but she was conceived at Jerusalem. Our Lord took his surname from Nazareth. There Joseph wedded Our Lady, when she was fourteen years old. There the angel Gabriel greeted Our Lady, saying, *Ave, gratia plena! Dominus tecum*, that is, Hail Mary, full of grace! The Lord is with thee. In that same place is a chapel, built beside a pillar of a church that was there in the old days; Christian pilgrims make great offerings there. The Saracens look after this chapel very strictly because of the profitability of the alms-giving. The Saracens there are very evil, much crueler than in other places; for they have destroyed all the churches that used to be there. There is the Well of Gabriel, where Our Lord *used to bathe* when He was young. And from that Well He used to fetch water for His mother, and she used to wash His clothes there."

John Poloner (circa 1421 CE): "South of Acre, yet turned away a little to the east, is Nazareth, the beloved city, where the flower of flowers budded from the root of Jesse. It is seven leagues from Acre. There is the Savior's own city. Jesus was called a Nazarene because he was brought up therein. Here bubbles up a little fountain, from which the boy Jesus was wont to draw and fetch water for His mother."

From these different accounts, we learn that it was a well-known site for Christians starting in the Byzantine period and continuously until the modern period. The Well was known for drinking water and for bathing. If it was known for bathing, it may or may not have been a bathhouse, but it may actually explain the medieval traditions that were circulating about a famous Jewish well with healing powers as well, Miriam's Well.

The Well of Mary, Mother of Jesus and the Well of Miriam, Sister of Moses

Mary's Well may be connected to a very famous legend of the Jews concerning the "Well of Miriam," the sister of Moses. Mary of Nazareth is known in Hebrew and Aramaic sources by her Hebrew name Miriam. Even in the Koran, the name of Mary of Nazareth is confused/conflated with Mary, sister of Moses, because of their obvious significant meanings to the fledgling Christians and Jews. Similar to Mary's Well that became a place for pilgrims to achieve spiritual healing, the Well of Miriam was a famous Well that accompanied the Israelites in the desert finally resting permanently as a located site in Galilee after the entrance of Joshua into the land.

The Well of Mary may not be a strictly Christian or pagan creation or amalgamation of legends. It may also be based upon Jewish legends as well. In the Hebrew Bible, a story emerges from the need for water for the Israelites in the Desert in the Book of Exodus. In Exodus 17:6 a miraculous spring of water gushes forth from a rock. According to Jewish Midrashic (Amoraic) traditions that emerge in the third to fifth century CE, the Well of water is called: "Miriam's Well." It is not mentioned in Tannaitic (first to third centuries CE) sources but is prominent in Amoraic sources in the Babylonian and Palestinian Talmudim, Midrash Aggadah, and Medieval collections (BT Shabbat 35a, Bereshit Rabbah 18:22), meaning that at precisely the same time that Mary's Well may have been functioning in Nazareth, the Miriam's Well accounts were proliferating in Rabbinic sources. It is quite possible that the Miriam's Well tradition, because it does not exist in Tannaitic or early

Rabbinic sources from the first to third centuries CE, may have been created after the existence of Mary's Well in Nazareth had become a well-known Christian site. The Mary's Well site in Nazareth may have sprung from the oral legends of Miriam's Well and became concretized in a very specific way at Nazareth among Jewish followers of Jesus of Nazareth. It is impossible to know which came first: the Jewish legend of a miraculous Well associated with Miriam or a miraculous Well associated with Mary.

Because of the nature of miracles that "break" the order of nature of this sort in Rabbinic Judaism, Rabbinic sources place the creation of Miriam's Well on the second day of creation of the universe. This Well of water accompanied the Israelites through the desert and according to some other versions it disappeared with Miriam's death, while in others it continues to exist. The miracle of the Well of Miriam was created at the beginning of the world and on the second day of Creation according to late *Midrash Pirke D'Rabbi Eliezer* 3. It was the same Well that Abraham demanded back from Abimelech, King of the Philistines in the Book of Genesis. Upon the entrance of the Israelites into the Land of Israel in the time of Joshua, the Well was hidden, according to some sources, at a certain point it was located near the Sea of Galilee. Other sources like the Midrash Tanhuma say that Miriam's Well will be enjoyed in the Messianic era and had the Israelites not sinned in the desert, it would have continued to be used in their conquest of the Land. The famous *Kaftor VaFerach* text, which chronicles the travels of the medieval Jewish traveler, HaParchi, records traditions about the well. Medieval Kabbalists believed that drinking from the Well of Miriam gave them an opportunity to pursue more deeply the secrets of mysticism. As they gathered in the mystical Galilean city of Tzefat (Safed) in the sixteenth century, some thirty miles to the north, they seemed to know that it was in Galilee somewhere. In the Middle Ages Miriam's Well continued to be a Jewish legend of significance with tales of the well moving from river to river, from one location to another on the termination of the Shabbat. Just like Mary's Well, Miriam's Well had healing powers but for the Jews these healing powers were strongest at the end of the Sabbath. One of these late Midrashim relates how a leper once bathed in the waters of the Well of Miriam and he was instantly healed, similar to the tales we told of Mary's Well by Christians in the Middle Ages. Many medieval Rabbinic sources place the Well of Miriam near or in Tiberias or in a secret location by the Sea of Galilee. In a second of the Jerusalem Talmud (PT) and in other medieval Midrashim the undisclosed location near the Sea of Galilee places it somewhere in Galilee. Some traditions place the Well of Miriam closer to the location of Nazareth than others, but most place it in Galilee. One tradition says that standing on Mount Carmel and looking over to the east from the Mediterranean Sea, one can see the Well of Miriam, putting it much further west than the Sea of Galilee.

I do not know who derived the tradition of a miracle well from whom. The Rabbinic idea of Miriam's Well seems to emerge at precisely the same time as Mary's Well in Nazareth. They may have drawn from each other's interests in a miracle well. We have no indication of the Well of Miriam before the second and third centuries CE. Whether it is originated with Christianity and was borrowed by the Jews or whether it originated with the Rabbis and was borrowed by the early Christians is difficult to know. This borrowing of sources in antiquity is well known, especially when a name is similar or the same as another source. Many examples are found of this practice in sites associated with specific names. In Tiberias, for example, the Tomb of Rabbi Meir Baal HaNes is one of the most important sites of pilgrimage in Israel today, after Jerusalem, Rachel's Tomb, on the way to Bethlehem, and the Machpelah (Cave of the Matriarchs and Patriarchs) at Hebron are Jewish relic sites for modern Jewish pilgrimage. In reality, the site of Rabbi Meir's tomb in Tiberias is unusual given the literary accounts of his life and death. Premodern records do indicate the burial of a Rabbi Meir in this tomb, but it is not connected to the second century CE sage of the same name until the eighteenth century. This has become a legendary place for people to come, donate money, light candles, and pray in the hopes of being protected against illness and danger but most prominently for barren women hoping to conceive. The most exciting part of the "Well" legends is that they may be connected to a bathhouse and may explain one of the most vexing stories found in Rabbinic literature. The Rabbinic story involves the impregnation of a virgin through no sexual intercourse in a bathhouse and is one of the few ancient parallels to the Christian version of Mary's virgin impregnation. The story is found only in Jewish sources stemming from the early Byzantine period, but the sources speak of an ancient form of artificial insemination that was known to occur only in the warmed waters of ancient bathhouses.

The Roman Bathhouse and the Virgin Birth

The waters of the Roman bath provided a regular place for people to visit. Roman baths are found throughout Galilee and Israel; the most famous baths are the ones that have been restored in Tiberias, Beth Shean, and Masada, and some are connected to water sources and others rely on seasonal rain or water channels and piping. The bathhouse was a water source par excellence. The "Well" of antiquity was not small as it usually provided an entire village with a source of water for bathing, cisterns, drinking, and cooking. The account in the *Alfa Beta d'Ben Sira*, a Rabbinic text of unknown origin, has the birth of Jesus Ben Sira as the result of a miraculous impregnation that was produced following his mother's visit to a bathhouse. Here is the original text with short summaries of some sections and some of my added comments in parentheses [ ]:

> [God] does great things beyond our understanding, miracles beyond number [Job 9:10]. If it says "great things" why does the verse say "miracles"? It is thus because the sages interpreted each one. Come and see the miracles that are done and the great things that are beyond understanding. It is said that three were created in the world in order to fulfill this biblical saying. Miracles without number: It is said for the three that were born without any physical [sexual] relationship between the parents. They are the mother of Ben Sira, the mother of Rabbi Zera, and the mother of Rav Pappa. All were great scholars in the Torah and in good deeds . . . How is it possible that they gave birth without physical (sexual) relations? Once they went to the bathhouse and entered into the water the seed of an unknown person entered into them and they gave birth from this.

The Ben Sira case connection to Jesus of Nazareth is very compelling because while little is known of Ben Sira except from the biblical book that bears his name, *Jesus ben Sira*, the fact that he used the Greek name Jesus may have connected him to the Jesus of Nazareth traditions in the minds of the Rabbis. The Rabbis of Babylonia, as we have seen, had very little knowledge of the canonical Gospels and so connected issues related to Jesus of Nazareth with traditions that they knew. The book of Ben Sira, which did not get into the canon of the Bible, was known to the Rabbis. *Yeshua ben Elazar ben Sira* was probably a Hebrew-speaking Jew that lived in the early second century BCE, but his book resembled the book of Proverbs that did get into the canon of the Hebrew Bible. The Rabbis knew enough about him to mention the book in the BT Hagigah, Niddah and Berachot, and the Tosefta. According to the book of Ben Sira, the grandson of the original Ben Sira translated the book into Greek in the second century BCE and translated his name as Jesus. This may have caused the beginning of the confusion for the Rabbis. The second confusion is that the Book of Ben Sira contains many pithy wisdom sayings, very similar to the New Testament sayings of Jesus of Nazareth. Because a part of the book of Ben Sira was found at Masada, we know this book still claimed a Jewish audience into the first century CE. The wisdom of the book is cited by the Rabbis some eighty-two times in early and late Midrashic texts and even using the citation form: "as it is written" (which is normally reserved only for accepted biblical passages). All of this suggests that although the book of Ben Sira did not make it into the final codification of the Bible by the Rabbis, not everyone felt that it should be excluded. I think the confusion between Jesus of Nazareth's sayings and Jesus ben Sira's sayings may have doomed the work for the Rabbis. The canon, that was decided by Rabbis in the second century CE, was very affected by the Christians, who by then were discussing what they considered to be appropriate reading. I think this confusion between Jesus of Nazareth and Jesus ben Sira may also have carried over to the Rabbinic work, *Alfa Beta d'ben Sira,* and the Rabbis were giving their own understanding of what was developing in Christianity concerning the virgin birth. Virgins played a role in the Roman period religious mind not only because of the importance of the Vestal Virgins of Rome who were part of crucial rituals to the Roman State but also their virginity was a much prized part of Roman mythology. From time to time, a Vestal Virgin would in fact become pregnant or be accused of having had sexual relations and although a cruel punishment awaited the pregnant virgin in Roman society, some Vestal Virgins were in fact accused and did not suffer the punishment. One wonders if a similar line of thinking to the Rabbinic Ben Sira story was used to vindicate the pregnant vestal virgins that were not punished. Either a bathhouse impregnation or oftentimes sources tell us that a god had impregnated a woman. Because the Vestal Virgins were also priestesses of the gods of Rome and their virginity was a mark of their "reserved" status, a lot was riding on their virginity for the integrity of Rome. A water ritual (albeit not the one we are speaking about) of vindication was known in Rome for an accused virgin. She appealed to the goddess Vesta to vindicate her honor and had the power given to her to carry a sieve full of water from the Tiber to the Vestal temple.

The fact that the story of a *sine concubito* impregnation in a bathhouse is known only from the Jews in antiquity would not be unusual if the Jews were passing on a tradition that had been known in the Roman world. The concept is found in Jewish texts throughout the Middle Ages and into the premodern period. It is related as well in the early Middle Ages (ninth century) by the Rabbi Hai Gaon in *Teshuvot HaGeonim* and was even used by Amatus Lusitanus, a sixteenth-century Marrano physician to clear a nun from suspicion of fornication after an apparent miscarriage. It is strange, but if Mary's Well was not only a well, but also a Roman bath and well complex, it might better explain in antiquity the idea of the virgin birth among Jewish readers in antiquity.

Mary's Well was not a well-known canonical New Testament image. It seems to have been known only by a handful of ancient writers. The common word "Well" appears only once in the canonical New Testament and appears only in the apocryphal New Testament works. The word for well is a well-known classical Greek word that even Rabbinic language copies as a cognate word in Rabbinic texts—*pegei* in Hebrew. This corresponds to the Hebrew word "*ma'ayan*" which is usually referring to a fountain or naturally occurring water source. In Hebrew, the Well of Miriam is referred to in Rabbinic literature as a "Be'er" or "Bor" indicating a cistern-like dug well. It is not clear that a dug "well" was actually meant in the New Testament reference or whether it was referring to a more amplified water source like a fountain and bathhouse complex. In the NT John 4:6, both of the words for a cistern-like well and a fountain-like spring were known. The word *pegei* is used in the New Testament, but this is alluding to the ancient biblical "Jacob's Well." The word corresponds better to a spring or a fountain of a spring but the other word is *phrear*—the dug well is used in the same verses of John 4. They are used interchangeably. Was the original Nazareth story set by a spring, a well, or a bath and ritual purification area with a large water source? That is very hard to know.

The wells are the subject of legends beginning in the first century CE primarily because of the importance of Mary in the developing Church. She is not only the Mother of Jesus. She is the mother of God and so connected with every type of supernatural ability that Jesus and God have associated with them in the Mediterranean world. Mary also had unique abilities and characteristics as a symbol of fertility and the godhead. She is the Mother of God, the Second Eve, the Receptacle of God's Grace and Being, and Possessing the Face of Christ. Although there is little in the Gospels about her, she is the subject of much speculation and insight in the early Church. Some people believe she has made appearances at locations associated with the experiences of her life. Mary's appearances began in 40 AD, probably before she died, to James the Apostle in Saragossa, Spain. She has been appearing to others at irregular intervals throughout the two thousand years since she gave birth to Jesus. In Spain, in particular, the Virgin Mary was extremely important and connected to James, who is buried in the Church of Compostela in Spain. After James returned to Jerusalem, he was executed by Herod Agrippa in about 44 CE, the first apostle to be martyred for his faith. Several of his disciples took his body and returned it for final burial in Spain. The local queen, observing several of the miracles performed by James's disciples, converted to Christianity and permitted his body to be buried in a local field. Eight centuries later, a cathedral in honor of St. James was erected after his gravesite was rediscovered by a local hermit. The hermit found the burial site after noticing an unusual star formation. The site for the cathedral was called Compostella (starry field), and it is a major pilgrimage site to this day. Spain and the Iberian Peninsula was a particularly popular place for the reappearances of Mary. In the 1600s, in Agreda, Spain, similar apparitions are documented as well as in Fatima, Portugal, in 1917; in Tuy, Spain, in 1925; and Garabandol, Spain, in 1961. In Italy, other locations in Europe, Latin America, Asia, and in North America, the sightings of Mary have appeared from the fourth century through the twenty-first century. But the continuing factor of the Well of Mary is found in some of these apparitions. Throughout February to July, 1858, Bernadette Soubirous had sightings of Mary, and she was told to dig in the ground and a new "well" or water source appeared that is very similar to Miriam's Well in the desert. Thousands of healings are associated with the bathing or drinking of this water at the site in Lourdes, France, indicating that the moving Well of Mary/Miriam had taken root in yet another location. One last tie may connect the Well of Miriam and the Well of Mary. In Islamic tradition, Mary, mother of Jesus and Miriam, sister of Moses and Aaron are often transposed. It implies that at least in the popular religious outlook, the two, Mary and Miriam, were interlocked in the minds of the oral traditions that circulated among people in the ancient near east. Miriam is the original Hebrew name for the Greek name Mary, so the exchange was facilitated by the change in languages.

Conclusions

The public well, which was for centuries Mary's Well, was shut down during the modernization of the sewage systems in Nazareth in the 1960s. No water is directed to the monument that stands in the original location where Mary's Well stands and although it resembles the public well that locals knew over the past one hundred years, it is just a building that looks like a well. During the course of our work at Mary's Well, I would notice the occasional tourist who would arrive expecting to find water flowing from the reconstructed Well. Unfortunately, I would tell these tourists that the only water that can be found is the original source of the well that emerged out of a cave in the Church of Saint Gabriel. They would reluctantly go there seeking Mary's healing (there is a running water spring inside the back of the Church) and would sprinkle or drink the water there. The vast majority of people never did quite feel that they experienced Mary there because the Church of Saint Gabriel is an eighteenth-century

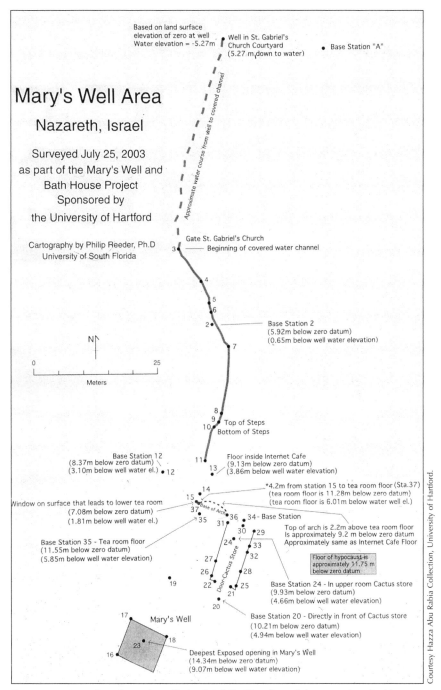

Based on land surface
elevation of zero at well
Water elevation = -5.27m

Well in St. Gabriel's
Church Courtyard
(5.27 m down to water)

Base Station "A"

Mary's Well Area

Nazareth, Israel

Surveyed July 25, 2003
as part of the Mary's Well and
Bath House Project
Sponsored by
the University of Hartford

Cartography by Philip Reeder, Ph.D
University of South Florida

Gate St. Gabriel's Church
Beginning of covered water channel

Approximate water course from well to covered channel

N

0   25
Meters

Base Station 2
(5.92m below zero datum)
(0.65m below well water elevation)

Top of Steps
Bottom of Steps

Base Station 12
(8.37m below zero datum)
(3.10m below well water el.)

Floor inside Internet Cafe
(9.13m below zero datum)
(3.86m below well water elevation)

*4.2m from station 15 to tea room floor (Sta.37)
(tea room floor is 11.28m below zero datum)
(tea room floor is 6.01m below water well el.)

Window on surface that leads to lower tea room
(7.08m below zero datum)
(1.81m below well water el.)

Base of Arch

34- Base Station

Top of arch is 2.2m above tea room floor
Is approximately 9.2 m below zero datum
Approximately same as Internet Cafe Floor

Base Station 35 - Tea room floor
(11.55m below zero datum)
(5.85m below well water elevation)

Door-Cactus Store

Floor of hypocaust is
approximately 11.75 m
below zero datum

Base Station 24 - In upper room Cactus store
(9.93m below zero datum)
(4.66m below well water elevation)

Base Station 20 - Directly in front of Cactus store
(10.21m below zero datum)
(4.94m below well water elevation)

Mary's Well

Deepest Exposed opening in Mary's Well
(14.34m below zero datum)
(9.07m below well water elevation)

Courtesy Hazza Abu Rabia Collection, University of Hartford.

Figure 7.2.   Mapping of Mary's Well, St. Gabriel's Church, and the mysterious bathhouse.

structure that for the most part looks and feels like a modern building. But for many of these tourists who sat in the cool basement of the *Cactus* café, where they were served coffee in the presence of the ancient bathhouse and the Crusader ruins around them, it felt like they were in the presence of a real religious experience and drank their coffee with unusual gusto. As we continue our work there we may never be able to prove that Mary, the mother of Jesus, bathed and had her annunciation there, nor can we prove that this was the water source from which Jesus served his mother Mary, but it is still a very compelling place in an evangelical triangle of sorts between the Well of Mary, St. Gabriel's, and the bathhouse.

8

The Search for Bar Kokhba: One "Biblical" Character Who Was Found

Figure 8.1.   Bar Kokhba Coin-inscription reads right and left of the palm tree trunk "Shimon" [Bar Kokhba/Kosiba] and the reverse side-not seen here-reads: "For the Liberation of Jerusalem" (Courtesy Carolyn LeClair Posey, Bethsaida Excavations Project).

The Debate over the Interpretation of History

T hroughout this book I have dealt with what I perceive to be the biggest controversy that has emerged over the past two decades—the controversy of "revisionism," which dramatically changes our understanding of the past based on new evidence. Recall our discussion of "Minimalists" and "Maximalists" in the introduction. It is important to note that while revisionism goes on constantly in almost every generation of scholars, there is a difference between the recent trends toward revisionism in biblical archaeology in the past two decades and as a necessary corrective among scholars. In every generation new scholars posit new ways of looking at the same materials that their teachers and their teachers' teachers have presented to them. In general, revisionism was reserved for the elite scholars to hash out and did not trickle down to the general public. It was an academic debate, which is a good and healthy part of scholarship. Sometimes small correctives from these scholarly debates would find their way into the public's general perception of history. In the most recent controversies, though, the revised ideas are presented to the public as fact rather than a point of scholarly debate.

Revisionists seek to "turn on their heads" current theories of culture, art, and history. Today the work of many of these revisionists is immediately picked up by news services and printed as if the previous generation's views have suddenly been superseded. This phenomenon works both ways. The immediacy of information available from Internet and mass media can push a minimalist or maximalist theory immediately into public attention as if it were already a proven fact. A recent example was presented by a student in one of my classes. I had just spoken about Herod the Great in class, and she announced to the class that Herod the Great's tomb had been found in Israel. Shocked, I went to the Internet and indeed, Ehud Netzer had presented a sampling of decorated pieces from the archaeological site of Herodium and theorized that this was from the tomb of Herod the Great. In the past, this type of information would have been written up, presented in scholarly conferences, and debated, and eventually it would be presented to the public. Today a theory is presented immediately as fact in the mass media, with a corrosive effect upon many of the traditional understandings of biblical and postbiblical events, people, and places.

Recent articles in the *New York Times* and *Wall Street Journal* have deeply affected the overall understanding of biblical history because the general public reads these articles and just assumes that long-held conclusions have been overturned. The crux of the issue involves how much evidence is enough to confirm or deny long-held conclusions about the Bible. I am surprised to see how quickly newspapers are ready to publish new, revisionist theories about anything in the Bible. The same newspapers that would consult an unnamed background source and two named sources to corroborate a news story about a modern politician (for fear of getting the story wrong) are ready to publish one professor's musings about whether Israeli archaeology is legitimate archaeology or not without any further evidence to support the story. Biblical history, and, most important, the sites and individuals who are defined in the Bible, are not easy to track down and they usually require two or three steps of methodologically sound research to validate. So, while newspapers are not the best place to publish academic research, newspapers often publish stories on the Bible because people are so fascinated by the subject.

Without evidence from any independent sources outside the Bible itself, it is nearly impossible to confirm the historicity of figures such as Abraham, Isaac, Jacob, Moses, Joshua, Elijah, King David, Solomon, Jesus, Mary, and a host of other people in the Bible. Even with an independent and outside source, doubts can arise, as we have seen throughout this book. Which Abraham, which Joshua, which David, which Jesus? The "independent" sources that are usually invoked come from the world of archaeology. Recent discussions have centered upon whether the histories of these ancient figures were all constructed hundreds, or perhaps thousands of years after the fact and that there may never actually have been a real historical figure by the name found in these texts. This is why extreme revisionism can make outlandish claims. Biblical archaeology and its discoveries rarely supply specific information about an individual, place, or event in the Bible. Biblical archaeology supplies general background information about an event that is from the same historical period as a more specific individual or event. The Minimalists say that "background" provided by archaeology demonstrates only that "background" and little or nothing else can be learned from the evidence found from a period including architecture, comparative ancient literature, iconography, coins, pottery, etc. These elements do not demonstrate the historical existence of any of these figures, and they certainly do not validate any specific event. In fact, this general background points to the absence of exact information on these individuals as evidence that these individuals ever existed. In terms of this, the Minimalist (or extreme revisionist) might simply state the axiom: *The Absence of evidence (of specific people, places, and events) is evidence of the absence (of specific people, places, and events)* and get away with it. Conversely, it is clear that the only evidence sufficient to convince a Minimalist of the absolute veracity of a claim would require so much specificity that it would render the scientific method nearly unworkable.

Extrapolation from logical inference is the basis for the Maximalist case. The Maximalist states that the existence of extensive archaeological background points to a convergence between the accuracy of literary accounts and the meaning of the material culture. To the Maximalist, the background of archaeological evidence is evidence of an accurate background in the literary account. According to Maximalist logic, if the Bible is correct in its general outlines of biblical life, it should be accurate in terms of the details of the characters as well. If the Bible has historically validated information about simple questions of daily life, ceremonies, styles, forms of communication, law, etc., this should validate all statements and information in the Bible. Not all Maximalists will accept the accuracy of all statements, but they will argue for more legitimacy to be given to those areas of the Bible that have more validation from outside, independent (albeit general) sources. It is tantamount to how legal proceedings can convict a person of crime on the basis of circumstantial evidence.

Now I can see how extreme Maximalism is untenable in an age of scientific reason. Do we really think it is right to convict someone of murder just on the basis of circumstantial evidence? But Maximalists and Minimalists have polarized our understanding of ancient history. Did Moses really exist? Did Joshua conquer Jericho as described in the Book of Joshua? Did King David really conquer the nations and areas described in the Book of Samuel and Kings? If so, why isn't there exact archaeological evidence to confirm any of these literary accounts? The debate involves the Hebrew Bible in particular, but also New Testament studies as well. One cannot fully confirm the historical existence, let alone meaning of the messages of John the Baptist, Jesus, and Paul without falling back on a scant series of ancient literary references and a scant fewer archaeological artifacts. What biblical archaeology does best is its great deficit. It provides the background of a life, a place, an event—not a life, place, or event in itself (to use a classic Kantian term).

Only in very rare instances does archaeology actually confirm the existence of any individual and tell us something substantive about the person. The case of Bar Kokhba, the famous leader of the Second Revolt against the Romans, is just such a rare instance. The discovery of letters signed by Bar Koz(s)iba (better known as Bar Kokhba) electrified the entire State of Israel in 1961. It was the discovery that gave Jews and biblical scholars new hope to find information from other biblical figures, even more hope than the Dead Sea Scrolls had provided. It is also the discovery that ultimately drew me back to the Cave of Letters in 1999.

I brought our technology and our staff of experts to the cave to see if there were other discoveries that could tell us more about the biblical past that perhaps is not told in literary accounts of the period. I had previously written about the discoveries from the Cave of Letters in 1997, during the fiftieth anniversary celebrations surrounding the Dead Sea Scrolls in Israel. In 1996, we had found the incense shovel described earlier, which was similar to an artifact that had been found by Yigael Yadin in the Cave of Letters. I concluded that the artifact was from the Temple of Jerusalem, and that the Cave of Letters had been in use during the First and the Second Revolt. This simple scientific hypothesis caused enormous controversy that pushed me to develop a full excavations project of the Cave of Letters to search for new evidence. The entire episode was chronicled in my book, *Secrets of the Cave of Letters: A Dead Sea Mystery* (2004), and a NOVA documentary entitled "Ancient Refuge in the Holy Land," so I will not review the conclusions here. I felt that it was important to write about Bar Kokhba in this book because he is one of the few biblical characters whose existence has been proven through archaeological evidence. His story also proves that you should not discount the possibility of discovering a cache of documents, like the Bar Kokhba letters, in some new excavation.

Son of the Star

One of the ways that people in antiquity were determined to be "special" or "designated" by Heaven for a special destiny was for a celestial event to be connected to their life. For example, one reads in the Gospel of Matthew, 2: 1–2 "Now when Jesus was born in Bethlehem of Judea in the days of Herod the King, behold, Wise Men from the East came to Jerusalem, saying, 'Where is He who has been born King of the Jews? For we have long seen His star in the East and have come to worship him.'" Even earlier during the spring of 44 BCE the appearance of a star in the Heavens was seen as prefiguring the death of Julius Caesar. So too, the career of the leader of the Second Revolt against the Romans in 132–135 BCE, Simon Bar Kosiba was linked to the Heavens. His name, according to the rabbis was not *Bar Kosiba* but rather, *Bar Kokhba*, Hebrew/Aramaic for "Son of the Star," and many Rabbis of ancient Judaism believed he was the anointed and awaited messiah of the Jews. It is probably no accident that in 130 CE the appearance of Halley's Comet may have prefigured his rise to fame and the beginning of his revolt which ended with a disastrous defeat and the destruction of the remaining Jews in the south of the country who had survived the First Revolt. Rabbi Akiva himself, announces in PT Taanit 68d that Bar Kosiba is the fulfillment

of the verse in the book of Numbers 24:17: "There shall come a Star out of
Jacob, the ruling sceptre shall rise out of Israel." Rabbi Akiba, the leading
Rabbi of the period was opposed by others who said: "Akiba, Grass will
have grown out of your [dead bones] jaws until the Son of David appears!'

The Cave of Letters documents are different than most archaeological
document discoveries like the Dead Sea Scrolls because they are personal
letters that basically agree in general with the portrait of Bar Kokhba written in the Talmud. Among the two complete letters written by Bar Kokhba
to Yeshua ben Galgoula and found at Wadi Murabba'at (the so-called:
"Chief of the Camp") is one regarding the participation of the Galileans in
the revolt. He writes: "From Shimon ben Kosiba to Yeshua ben Galgoula
and to the men of the fort, peace. I take heaven to witness against me that
unless you mobilize *the Galileans* who are with you every man, I will put
fetters on your feet as I did to ben Aphlul" (Y. Yadin, Barkokhba, p. 137).

"The Galileans" is an unusual term in Bar Kokhba's writing and may be
directly connected to the usage in other first and second century writings.
In my research I have found that there was no standard language for the
"Christians." "Galileans" may simply have been a general term for Christian
followers because the movement that became Christianity originated in
Galilee. More important, the letters connected to the literary texts of the
Rabbis by the tone suggests a person with a demanding, paranoic, courageous, short-tempered commander. In Midrash Lamentations Rabbah, it is
reported at the end of the war that Bar Kosiba became convinced that Rabbi
Eliezer of Modi'in wanted to surrender the city of Beitar, the last stronghold.
Bar Kosiba respectfully waited until Rabbi Eliezer finished praying and then
he had him brought and directly asked him if this was the case. Rabbi Eliezer
gave him a noncommittal answer and then suddenly Bar Kosiba "became
angry, kicked him and killed him." According to the Rabbis, Bar Kokhba was
known for the most ruthless recruiting tactics of any commander in Jewish
history, including amputating a finger of the recruited soldiers to insure that
they indeed were committed to the cause of the Revolt.

These letters were not intended to be historical documents, but because
they are signed by Bar Kokbha, we have the opportunity to compare these
documents with what other texts preserved in Judaism, Christianity, and Roman literature say. These letters from Bar Kokbha give us details of the time
and insights into his personality, but do not give answers to the larger questions of the period. But they do prove that he was a living, breathing human
being and for this, biblical archaeology owes an enormous debt of thanks.
We now know more about Bar Kokhba than any other key Jewish/Israel-
ite/biblical character from all of ancient Jewish history. It does not prove that

all of the other key Jewish/Israelite characters in the Bible are as real as Bar Kokhba, but it suggests that we need to continue to look for the evidence.

The Bar Kokhba Revolt and the Minimalist–Maximalist Controversy

The case of the Bar Kokhba Revolt is an excellent example of how far the Minimalist and Maximalist interpretations of biblical and even ancient history can be verified. The ancient Jewish, Christian, and Roman literary accounts agree that the Bar Kokhba Revolt engulfed the larger Jewish population of Palestine and parts of the Diaspora. In these accounts, nearly six hundred thousand Jews were killed and more than nine hundred villages destroyed. They paint a picture of an extensive Revolt, which either achieved its goal of reaching Jerusalem and then got pushed back or nearly achieved it. The latest revisionist view has been prompted by the archaeological picture that has emerged. Most of the Bar Kokhba finds in caves and tunnels around Judea point to an intensive campaign in this area. Little or no remains outside of this area leave some scholars such as Professor Menahem Mor at Haifa University in Israel thinking that the Bar Kokhba Revolt may not have been as extensive or even as successful as was first thought. Some Minimalists contend that it was a small Revolt that never even achieved its main goal; that is, the recapturing of Jerusalem. The Temple is dramatically portrayed on some of the Bar Kokhba coins. Some Bar Kokhba coins feature the Temple and the Table of Showbread in-between the columns of the Temple. They indicate the year of the "Freedom of Jerusalem." In some instances the coins list the name of the High Priest Eleazar. But ask the Minimalists: "So what? Does this all mean that the Temple or Jerusalem was ever really recaptured or were they just indications of propaganda and aspirations?"

Ancient literary accounts tend to point to the fact that the Temple was retaken by the rebels, but archaeology is very scarce on this point. Nearly ten thousand Bar Kokhba coins (many were being restruck over Roman coins and the locations where the vast majority of these coins were found is in doubt since they were not systematically excavated but rather found and only later identified) have been found in areas around the greater Judean province area but very few in Jerusalem and its closest suburbs. Of the 13,629 coins found in Jerusalem up until 1982, for example, only three are Bar Kokhba coins. A fourth Bar Kokhba coin was from Ramat Rachel near Jerusalem. This coin information has led some historians to argue the Minimalist position more intensely. Some scholars do hold that Jerusalem was retaken and Temple worship reinstituted for a short while. This last point is important because if Jerusalem had been taken and Temple worship reinstituted, it would certainly have been an event that would have commanded the interest of the entire Jewish Diaspora and population of Palestine in this period.

Other evidence with regard to the size of the Revolt is brought from Roman records of another sort. Professor Werner Eck from Koln University, a military historian of the Roman Empire, has categorically proven from Roman legion records that as many as twelve Roman legions from as far away as Britain were sent to put down the Bar Kokhba Revolt. He argues that this corroboration from an outside source may indicate the "real" presence of a large Roman fighting force in second century CE Palestine and may mean the Bar Kokhba Revolt was as brutal and destructive as the literary accounts say. He carefully reviewed the Roman records of this period and came up with remarkable information that gives greater credence to the Maximalists. He found that the 10th Legion was forced to abandon Jerusalem until the reinforcements showed up. The 22nd Legion was brought from Egypt, but was routed and apparently wiped out. Eck found that this 22nd Legion disappears from succeeding lists of Roman legions. The Second Trajana, the Third Cyrenaica, the Sixth Ferrata, the Third Gallica, the Fourth Scytica from Phoenicia and Syria, the Fifth Macedonica, the Tenth Gemina from Mauretania, and the Seventh Claudia are among the legions that were sent. Why were so many legions sent if the Revolt was so small?

What has the Minimalist/Maximalist debate contributed to our understanding of the Cave of Letters? It affects substantially our understanding of how desperate the people in the Cave might have been and our perception of their state of mind going in. Were these people like the Masada residents of 73 CE? Were they being hunted down by the Romans and therefore desperate to hide and survive at all costs? Or were they just hiding from the Romans and intending to return to their homes in Ein Gedi and elsewhere? Were these the last survivors of the Bar Kokhba Revolt or just a group who did not want to be bothered by the Roman presence?

Yadin, a Maximalist, held that the Cave of Letters and the cave across the way, the Cave of Horrors, represented the desperate last effort of the revolt. He assumed that the revolt was a colossal failure and that these people of the caves represented in a sense, the end of Jewish autonomy in Palestine until Yadin's own days. Yadin argues that the skulls found in a burial niche tell us of their inability to bury their own dead in a proper place. And so they end up living with their last precious possessions in the cave of the living "dead." In the post-Holocaust Israel of Yadin, the caves were a stirring symbol of the new Israel's commitment to a continuing struggle. The caves, guarded from above by the Roman camps, provided a place for them to resist and die. Bar Kokhba became the symbol of the Jewish nation even before the 1967 war. The Bar Kokhba Revolt, in a sense, did not end with the people in the cave. Artifacts found in the cave such as the single fragment of the Psalms and the nineteen bronze ritual artifacts in a basket tell us how they hated pagan religion and sought religious and political freedom from Rome. It indicated an ongoing historical war of which this was just the opening battle. Modern Israel represents the culmination of the war. On Lag B'Omer, May 11, 1982, the State of Israel buried in a state funeral the bones found in the burial niche of the Cave of Letters and in the Cave of Horrors.

For the Minimalist, the Cave of Letters is a microcosm of the small revolt of Judeans who foolishly tried to match the might of the Roman emperor. The Judeans were part of a fringe movement that was not well supported by the Jews of Palestine. Their end is another example of how fringe zealots bring destruction upon themselves. Their possessions and letters are indicative of a middle- and upper-class group that was fleeing from the Romans stationed in their own particular village of Ein Gedi. They stole nineteen bronze artifacts from somewhere in Ein Gedi and hid in the cave to escape detection. They also represent a Jewish fringe group because they do not keep the standard Jewish practice of burying and plac-ing the bones together in a burial chamber. Rather they separated the skulls of their dead into baskets and kept them in the burial niche. All in all, a small, lunatic fringe using strange and desperate means to survive, but by no means representing the will of the entire Jewish people.

These debates of the Minimalists and Maximalists in Israel also bear a strange resemblance to the political divisions of the Israelis in the post-Inti-fada, post-Lebanon world of modern Israel. Many Israelis, tired by the fifty years of bloodshed and flag-waving, have begun to reinterpret the mission of the state and their own history. Post-Zionists now readily tell a tale of Israel's need to insure that small groups of overzealous settlers will not bring an-other destruction upon the Jewish people. Minimalism fits the new "vision" of an Israel that need not rest upon the myths of the past or put itself in the position of having to flee into caves to survive. The silent majority of Israel recognizes that the will of the majority is to accommodate the "other."

Evidence from Coins

As I wrote at the beginning of this volume, I call myself a "Maximalist-Minimalist" in most areas of biblical archaeology. Information from coins found in the Jerusalem area is used by both Maximalists and Minimalists to make their points. If the rebels did achieve their goal of retaking Jerusalem and the Temple Mount, they must have done it like the Maccabees with an initial attack on the Temple *before* Hadrian had the chance to call for other legions from around the Empire. The troops would be called up only after Hadrian realized that his own troops could not control the situation. Since Hadrian had been in the area in 130 CE he may have thought that the Temple was the crux of the issue—not the Jewish Temple, but the temple that Hadrian intended to build on the Temple Mount to honor Jupiter. Did Hadrian begin building the Temple of Jupiter in 132? Did the Jews then rebel? Or did the Jews rebel because of the generally oppressive measures of Hadrian? Did Hadrian build the Temple of Jupiter on top of the Temple Mount after the war? It is hard to imagine that Hadrian would begin building a major cult site on top of what he knew to be a sensitive religious site without having a large contingent of troops on hand. Hadrian and his advisors knew the Roman accounts of the First Jewish War. They knew the problems caused by even simple displays of Roman power in the time of Pontius Pilate and the procurators.

The Bar Kokhba coins were generally restrikes of classical Roman bronze and silver coins over the images of Roman emperors and pagan symbols. Coins were excellent sources of propaganda precisely because everyone used them. Hadrian decided to rename the city of Jerusalem *Aelia Capitolina* and rename Judea as Palestine to further detach Jewish aspirations from Jerusalem and Judea. He minted *Aelia Capitolina* coins to commemorate this event. The discovery of two *Aelia Capitolina* coins together with four Bar Kokhba coins from the El Jai Cave in the Nahal Michmash area seems to indicate that the building of the Temple of Jupiter on the Temple Mount by Hadrian began before 135 CE and that the rebels were preparing to restrike the *Aelia Capitolina* coins as Bar Kokhba coins. Although it is possible that the coins were deposited by a casual visitor in the El Jai Cave after 135 CE, Hanan Eshel and Arieh Kindler, one of the world's leading coin specialists on the Bar Kokhba Revolt, concluded that the Hadrian coins prove that the building of the Temple was the main cause of the Revolt. Kindler, in particular, has made a science of understanding what the Bar Kokhba coins tell us about Hadrianic forays into the Middle East in general. Kindler has looked at all the Hadrianic coins and discovered that how Hadrian is depicted in the coins may tell us more about the man than was first suspected. Kindler's "psychology of coins" has important implications since his interpretations tells us that the coins of *Aelia Capitolina* were minted by Hadrian late in the 120s CE (128–129 CE) rather than the earlier "assumption" made by varying historians that the city renaming of

Aelia Capitolina was done after the war. It is possible that *Aelia Capitolina* was the renamed Jerusalem both before and after the war, but certainly Kindler's evidence is insightful. On the early Hadrian coins, Hadrian has a portrait of himself that differs from coins later in his career. The portrait on the coins, therefore, tells us when the coin was minted. The *Aelia Capitolina* coins have a more flat-topped, round-faced Hadrian which is more in line with coins from the 120s CE than it is from the late 130s.

In addition, we know that Hadrian had been adopted into the Emperor Trajan's family. He so valued this privilege that he listed his father's name on coins during his building phase of the 120s CE. After the horrible Roman troop losses of the Bar Kokhba Revolt, however, he did not list his father's name. It is as if he was embarrassed or was taking full responsibility for the results—something which matches his letters to the Senate in this period. On coins from the Revolt, only his name is listed on the coins. During the building process, it appears that he had been trying to demonstrate the continuation of the policies of his "adoptive" father and to show how proud he was to build up the Roman Empire in these areas. The coins were apparently minted after the renaming of the city was accomplished. They are found together with the Bar Kokhba coins because like the other Roman coins found in Bar Kokhba coin hoards, they were going to be restruck by Bar Kokhba to create new coins. Between Hadrian's visit in 129–130 CE and before the end of the Revolt, Hadrian had renamed Jerusalem as *Aelia Capitolina* and was in the process of perhaps making the ancient site of the Temple in Jerusalem into a Temple dedicated to Jupiter. This sparked the Revolt and the rest is history.

The Chronology of the Revolt

It can be helpful to see the chronology of the Second Revolt, which ultimately affects our understanding of the events in the Cave of Letters. Here is what I think happened:

1. 129–131 CE: Hadrian actually made two trips to Palestine. He first visited in 129 CE on his way to Egypt. His presence at Gerasa is evidenced by an inscription. On his first trip Hadrian would have seen the state of the Temple Mount and Jerusalem. He probably decided that he would undertake the restoration of the ancient site, as he did elsewhere in the empire. He would have ordered the beginning of work on the new Temple to Jupiter on the Temple Mount and minted coins in honor of the event. This would have sparked the beginnings of the opposition movement that resulted

in the coalescing of a Revolt. The other cause of the Revolt was apparently a growing anti–circumcision movement. While Dio Cassius says the *Aelia Capitolina* project initiates the Revolt, the *Scriptores Histoiae Augustae* say it is the prohibition against circumcision that does it. The *Aelia Capitolina* coin minted in honor of the initiation of the work shows tethered oxen preparing the ground for the *Aelia Capitolina*. If it was commemoration of the completion of the work, an actual Temple of Jupiter would have been more appropriate. Coins were used as commemoration devices. The iconography suggests an early point in the construction. Hadrian remained in Egypt through 130 CE. In the beginning of 131 CE he returned to Palestine apparently to see the progress of the work.

2. 131 CE: He would have seen the preparations in Jerusalem for the inauguration of his Temple of Jupiter.

3. 132 CE: Bar Kokhba and his rebels seize the construction site. Bar Kokhba coins are minted in celebration of the initial victories. They may portray a hybrid temple that incorporates elements from the Hadrianic Temple and the Herodian and/or imagined Third Temple. With his initial victories, Bar Kokhba has access to coin hoards created around Judea and Samaria that had been gathered for Temple tithes and reconstruction since the destruction in 70 CE.

4. 133 CE: Hadrian sends for major reinforcements. Bar Kokhba rebels begin "guerrilla warfare." They begin living in tunnels around Jerusalem and Judea. Restriking of coins begins as bronze becomes scarce. The caves used to store the coin hoards are the same caves that had been known from the First Revolt that stored the Temple tithes collected from 70 CE onward. Temple Mount has been lost to the rebels. Coins with other symbols of redemption are chosen (grapes, lyres, palm trees, amphorae, freedom of Israel/Jerusalem/Zion, redemption of Israel). In the early coins a Temple priest, Elazar, is named on the coins. His name is/was later removed.

5. 134 CE: Bar Kokhba coin hoards are created around Judea and Samaria in anticipation of victory.

6. 135 CE: All Hadrianic reinforcements arrive in anticipation of major battles.

7. 135 CE (August/September): Beitar and Bar Kokhba rebels are defeated. Some rebel groups escape to caves in the Judean desert in the hopes of escaping destruction. The Roman armies decide to initiate a search and siege policy similar to the one exercised by

Vespasian and Titus during the end of the First Revolt.

8. 136 CE: Eusebius describes the ultimate transformation of Jerusalem into a full Hadrianic *Aelia Capitolina* after the complete destruction of the Bar Kokhba Revolt.

If the coins tell us anything, it is that in this period "dreams/hopes/aspirations" were not normally stamped on coins. One does not usually appoint a High Priest in anticipation of the coming time when his services will be necessary. If the Bar Kokhba rebels were able to take the Temple mount and Jerusalem for even a short time, they might have begun to issue coins only after the fact. If they were driven from Jerusalem by the end of the first year, it would stand to reason that no Bar Kokhba coins would be found in those areas. By the end of the first year of the Revolt, Bar Kokhba coins were probably being issued from rebel headquarters outside of Jerusalem. The rebels were clearly motivated by the real circumstances of reclaiming Jerusalem forever and not simply exercising "wishful thinking."

Conclusions: Why Digging through the Bible Is So Important

I conclude with Bar Kokhba because he is the biblical character I have come to know most personally through my investigations. My attempts to know Abraham and Sarah, Moses and Miriam, King David and Solomon, Jesus and Mary, Rabbi Meir and Beruriah, Livia Julia, and the Teacher of Righteousness have largely been intellectual pursuits illuminated by archaeological discoveries. I have spent great amounts of time in significant places including Mount Sinai, Bethsaida, Qumran, Jerusalem, and Nazareth, but I never felt that I really knew much about the daily life of the individuals that I was tracking until I began studying Bar Kokkba. I have traced most of the places that Bar Kokhba and his army used during the period of 132–135 CE. I have gone through the tunnels of Herodium where they hid and attacked Roman forces on the road nearby, investigated the Bar Kokhba caves in the Judean desert, and spent a month of my life in the Cave of Letters where the rebels were holed up during the end of the Bar Kokhba Revolt. I have found Bar Kokhba coins, his letters, his pottery, his clothes, his firewood, his water sources, his latrines, the burial places of his soldiers and their families, and I can tell you what they ate, what they read, and can even tell you about their typical day in the cave. I slept in the Roman camp above the Cave of Letters and visited the Cave of Horrors across the valley, witnessing what these Bar Kokhba fighters might have seen as they looked out from the cave. I sometimes felt their despair, fear, and exhaustion as we worked in the Cave of Letters with the lack of air cir- culation that surrounded us every day. Perhaps it is because I spent so much time devoted to Bar Kokhba that I really felt that I knew him, but learning about his life so intimately has motivated me to try to gain the same deep understanding of other biblical figures that are equally manifested in the places where they lived, worked, and died.

How can we, living thousands of years after the Bible, really know the biblical figures who appear only in a literature so far removed from our reality? My suggestion in this book is that we carefully analyze the Bible for clues by investing the same type of time and thought as we would for any other modern problem. When we use the scientific method to analyze the Bible, the result is never the same Bible that we knew before, but it re- mains a rich and meaningful text that speaks to a new generation. When we compare this new biblical understanding to the results of archaeology, we confront real men and women who lived and died, real places and events that we can share, even though they happened a world away from us.

Appendix

Exploring an Archaeological Site

Archaeology is the study of antiquities or ancient artifacts. During the last twenty years of our excavations at Bethsaida, much has changed in the way we do archaeology in the field, thanks to technology leaps that brought us from a pencil, drafting board, and protractor to GPS and computer software that can continually update every single find at a site. Some archaeology is done in laboratories, some occurs in libraries, but the cornerstone to all of these studies is field excavations. Until recently, professional archaeologists hired laborers and often just supervised their work in the field. The famous scene from the *Indiana Jones* movie where thousands of local paid laborers digging up massive sites is still employed in some countries, but not in all countries. In most scenarios today, archaeologists take the finds back to a lab, analyze them with the help of experts who had never been in the field, and then write up the results. These results were in turn written about and then used by literary scholars of the Bible and other disciplines for pure research. The results were slowly and often selectively disseminated so that both scholars and the general public heard some of the information about the discoveries but not all of the results. Unfortunately, by the time the final results were published, very few people could remember the earliest assumptions that may have changed dramatically in the interim. The experience of the discovery and the dissemination of the meaning of the Dead Sea Scrolls demonstrates just how frustrating this process can be. It took more than fifty years for the discoveries made in 1947 to be fully understood.

Today, especially with the availability of the Internet, the situation is very different. Many very educated people write books on archaeology for the general public, the bulk of the work is done by educated volunteers, and every day is an opportunity to educate and learn about the particulars of the archaeology and its meaning. Many of the chapters in this book began as lectures for our dynamic and motivated volunteers on site and at our base camp. The entire enterprise of archaeology at a dig lends itself to a fruitful teaching and learning environment, which can motivate students and archeologists on faculty throughout a long academic year.

If you have never been on an excavation, be aware: Excavations are carried out by manual labor. A tractor assists in heavy-duty jobs, but the bulk of the work is done by individuals lifting, sifting, cleaning, and sometimes removing rocks and dirt. Work in the field consists of excavating, recording, photographing, and surveying. The location of the dig is called a *tell* (a mound comprised of the remains of a succession of previous settlements). The tell is divided into a network of squares of 5 by 5 meters. Today, this can be transferred immediately into a map database with GPS coordinates. Finds can be easily transferred into this computer grid. Each square or architectural unit is known by the term *locus*. As soon as architectural units are created, the excavation begins. Walls, floors, etc. are carefully excavated and cleaned for reconstruction. Finds are collected in baskets. Finds and baskets and the development of each locus are recorded in a field diary and on a locus card. All records are computerized, but we also keep a written (hand-copied) record as a backup. "Murphy's Law" that states if anything can go wrong, it will, is very true in archaeology. This has taught us that even with the most sophisticated technology and computer systems, the best way to insure that the daily work is properly recorded is to do it by hand on site. Preliminary analysis of finds is done daily at the site. With proper supervision and training, volunteers work their way through the different tasks so that at the end of a three-week session they have done almost every task from lifting rocks to recording and explaining finds.

At a dig, volunteers can be engaged in all tasks, including excavating, measuring, recording, surveying, drawing, restoring, photographing, and pottery analysis. They do not need previous training in archaeology to participate, and trained students or professionals are welcome as long as they are able to work in the collaborative atmosphere with inexperienced volunteers. All volunteers receive guidance and instruction in every phase of the excavation, including the recording, surveying, and treatment of finds. They also help in the daily cleaning and sorting of pottery and contribute to the weekly surveys of the work on the tell, in which a volunteer representative of individual loci summarizes the current progress in each area. Three to five volunteers are assigned to a locus. Each locus has a locus supervisor. Each area in the tell has an area supervisor. Area supervisors are generally faculty/staff members of different disciplines who are skilled in the techniques of keeping the daily log, supervising the actual digging, and doing on-site evaluations of the thousands of pottery pieces found every day of varying sizes.

Finds are truly made at every moment at an excavation site. Small fragments of pottery are sifted, and decisions about keeping or throwing away in the dump pile very small fragments have to be made at every moment. The area supervisors have to make judgment calls based upon years of experience. Mentoring the area supervisors is the chief archaeologist or director of excavation, who oversees the different loci supervisors and assorted staff on the expedition and is the final arbiter for finds and procedures on site. The expedition staff may also include a photographer, geoscientists of different backgrounds, a surveyor, an architect, a recorder, a pottery and sometimes a metal restorer, and the expedition administrator.

What are we trying to teach with biblical, Jewish, or Christian archaeology? Are we really teaching the Bible, Judaism, or Christianity? No, biblical archaeology is not really teaching the Bible, Judaism, or Christianity. We are teaching about the Bible, Judaism, and Christianity, but it is really not an "official" version of the Bible, Judaism, or Christianity. Archaeology does tell us about how scholars think the Bible, Judaism, and Christianity developed by giving a comparison. I am sometimes asked whether I want to bolster an individual's faith and reconcile the Bible, Jewish, and Christian tradition with modern scientific discoveries. I cannot say that this is my intention. I do want to create an inquiring, creative mind using archaeology. Archaeology lends itself to shaping a creative mind because it utilizes the scientific method. I think that the study of the Bible, Judaism, Christianity, and Islam in the university should meet the same standards that we hold for the teaching of other liberal arts. Archaeology is one of the ways to direct the academic study of religion in the university. I use archaeological information in most of my own Jewish historical studies. I am at my heart a Jewish intellectual and social historian who sees the world through my Jewish spectrum of experience, and I am informed equally by material culture as well as the traditional texts of Judaism, including the Bible, and I try to strike a balance with material culture and traditional textual information. I try not to allow traditional understandings of the text to color my view of new material cultural information, but I do not allow traditional understandings of the text to be forgotten when examining new material cultural information.

As a professor in a nondenominational university, I keep in mind a few caveats: I try not to dampen students' spirits by showing just the ambiguities of archaeology or the scientific method to create total chaos in their modern view of the world. I try not to "diminish" the importance of a student's personal religious convictions with regard to the Bible and its import. I also try not to diminish the texts of the Bible and Rabbinic or Christian interpretations of these texts to emphasize the importance of the archaeological data or interpretations of the data as regard to biblical sites. I always favor the scientific method over no method at all just because it is the scientific method that has gotten us here, but I always encourage students to study the Bible in any context that they can in order to become more familiar with the text.

Archaeology is an exciting way to introduce often extremely sophisticated students (who are also often quite skeptical and jaded) to a moving and "real," "hands-on" study of the Bible and Jewish history. It is impossible to provide the same feeling for the reality of the history through books. Archaeology appeals to students as an objective science. The fact that material culture and writings are ancient (read in their original and pristine state) and can be "discovered" (really rediscovered because most of these things were not lost but rather thrown out or abandoned) is equated in students' minds as being verifiable, quantifiable, and therefore scientific and true. Nothing could be farther from reality. The "rocks do not really speak"; the artifacts and writings have come down to us often by a very subjectively influenced processes of history and are intelligible only through the process of subjective interpretation that is open to speculation and reasonable hypothesizing. But archaeology is more objective than the say thousands of years of interpretation that biblical and Rabbinic texts enjoy. However, artifacts are subject to the same types of intellectual wrangling and hermeneutics as biblical interpretation.

In my course on biblical archaeology at the university, in my first class, I exploit the inherent interest of students for the unknown ("mystery") aspects of archaeology while lowering their expectations of what really can be "known." I discuss how interpretation is a part of the process (but often this process includes their own informed rational interpretation). The other aspect that students recognize is that the main "nuts and bolts" of archaeology are not the big discoveries but the small finds that add up slowly to a larger picture. The cumulative argument of archaeology is often missed by the cinema and popular culture. A picture, which, unlike the interpreted model of the rabbis and later Jewish historians, is always an unknown (at the beginning) to the archaeologist but ultimately becomes clear through hypothesis and evaluation. The scientific method teaches us a simple rule: The better the hypothesis fits all of the evidence available, the better, the "authenticity" of a bibilical text.

Acknowledgments

I am first and foremost indebted to my fellow archaeologists, geoscientists, historians, Bible scholars, Judaic Studies faculty, donors, and volunteers who have worked with me over the past twenty years and contributed to my own knowledge base. I hope that I will acknowledge most of the people who made contributions to the present work but, in the off chance that I miss some of you, many other names and affiliations can be found in the numerous publications, papers, press releases, documentaries, and interviews that led up to the writing of this book over the past decade. In particular, I would like to thank Dr. Rami Arav of the University of Nebraska at Omaha, who has tirelessly worked on the Bethsaida Excavations Project with me and some twenty other directors to unravel the mysteries of Bethsaida, Galilee, and the Sea of Galilee during the past twenty years and was always there to answer my questions. He has been a veritable encyclopedia of information, and he never tired from listening to my archaeological insights. The ideas and many versions of the chapters in this book have been presented at professional conferences of the American Academy or Religion, Association of Jewish Studies, and the Society of Biblical Literature (regional, national, and international conferences), American Schools of Oriental Research, Geological Society of America, and the Association of American Geographers over the past eighteen years, and I am thankful for the feedback I received at these conferences. This book is intended for the nonspecialist in archaeology, religion, history, and biblical studies and is not intended to take the place of the more academic tomes that are also available. Any errors that have occurred in the reporting of the data in this book is my responsibility alone. The results presented here, however, are data that I, as well as other scholars, have collected and lectured on, and all the information I used in the book was reported to me either orally or in writing through interim reports, lectures, and conferences in geology, geography, religion, history, and archaeology. I felt justified in presenting results of excavations that I either participated in (either directly or indirectly) and the work of others whose research I had read about or heard, but some of the information is presented here for the first time.

This volume follows a precedent that was started by Yigael Yadin in the 1960s (in Hebrew and later in English) and has been continued in the past few years with books such as Bruce Feiler's *Walking the Bible* and Israel Finkelstein and Neil Asher Silverman's *The Bible Unearthed*. These books have engaged the general public in thinking about the Bible and the archaeology that has been uncovered in the past half century in a serious and informed way. This book is different from the other books I have read because it includes a critical methodology of the Bible, covers all of the biblical periods and raises most of the major questions about which I have heard people asking. Unlike other works I have read, this book covers some three thousand years and does not end with the Bible but begins with the biblical traditions and then moves through the Hebrew Bible, New Testament, Quran, and Rabbinic and Christian texts and traditions and includes most of the archaeological periods from the Bronze Age through the premodern period. That is the main reason I called it *Digging through the Bible*. It goes beyond what the written Bible tells us and even beyond the traditional bounds of the biblical period to see what we can learn from other traditions that illuminate the biblical texts. Because for Jews, Christians, and Muslims, the Bible is much more than just the Hebrew Bible and the New Testament.

Over the past twenty years—since the excavations at Bethsaida began, I knew that I was engaged in an enterprise that was interesting to the general public. Thanks to television documentaries, many of our discoveries were directly brought to the public. UNO-TV, at the University of Nebraska at Omaha, made three documentaries, *The Lost City of Bethsaida, Return to the Cave of Letters,* and *The Road to Morocco* that slowly brought the results of our excavations to a larger and larger audience. This led to many other television documentaries including (among many others): *Kingdom of David, The Fifth Gospel,* Biblical Archaeology Society's *An Archaeolgoical Search for Jesus,* NOVA's *Ancient Refuge in the Holy Land,* and CNN's *After Jesus—The First Christians* and convinced me that we were engaged in an important enterprise that needed a written volume to tell the "rest of the story." It has been an education for all of us involved in the Bethsaida Excavations Project Consortium housed at the University of Nebraska at Omaha (UNO). While Rami has been my collaborator in the excavations at Bethsaida and at the Cave of Letters, I would like to acknowledge three colleagues who have accompanied me at Bethsaida and the Cave of Letters who over the past decade have helped us make important discoveries at Qumran, Nazareth, Burgos, Yavne, Har Karkom, and many other places. Paul Bauman of Worsley/ParsonsKomex, Harry Jol of the University of Wisconsin and Eau Claire, and Philip Reeder of the University of South Florida. The four of us have been joined in the past eight years by my University of Hartford colleagues, chief photographer Christine Dalenta, assistant archaeologist Maha Darawsha, and in many cases Dr. Carl Savage of Drew University. I want to thank Christine Dalenta in particular for her dedication to teaching students and faculty how to do scientific photography and archaeology. Many of her photographs together with student photographs were publicly displayed in exhibitions at the Sherman Museum and Silpe Gallery of the University of Hartford, and she has introduced a whole generation of students and community people to the aesthetic in archaeological photography work. The site maps that I have included in this volume are all of the work of Professor Phil Reeder of the University of South Florida. His maps have become the standard for archaeological work, and he has pioneered a new, scientific methodology for working in caves and land sites. Some of the early photography was provided from the Hazza Abu Rabia collection and has been published in our "Jerusalem in the Nineteenth Century" catalogue for our exhibition in 2007 at the George J. Sherman and Lottie K. Sherman Museum of Jewish Civilization at the University of Hartford. In addition, my colleagues from the Bethsaida Excavations Project Consortium, Professors H. W. Kuhn, Elizabeth McNamer, Mark Appold, and Nicolae Roddy helped me hone my ideas on many fronts as well as my colleagues and collaborators, John F. Shroder, Jr., Michael Bishop, Kevin Cornwell, Wendi Chiarbos, Stephen T. Reynolds, Moshe Inbar, Gloria London, Sandra Fortner, Fred Strickert, Chip Bouzard, John T. Greene, Gordon Brubacher, Arie Kindler, Hannah Cotton, Beno Rothenberg, David Harris, Jan Gunneweg, Joe Zias, Robert Eisenmen, Jeff Rubinstein, Lawrence Schiffman, Emmanuel Anati, Hanan Eshel, Magen Broshi, Yardena Alexandra, Danny Syon, Dan Bahat, Avner Goren, Elisabetta Boaretto, Menahem Mor, Adolfo Roitman, Gordon Moshman, Doug Andersen, Eric Stegmaier, Jen Bode, Rob Passow, Eric Pascal, Chris Morton, Danor Glazer, Rami Yatzkan, Uri Hofesh, Imanuel Goldstein, Chaggai Rosenbluh, Oded Danon, Noam Metzer, DreAnna Hadash, Charleen Green, Christine Nahas, Chris Pooley, Baruch Safrai, Pinchas Porat, Elias and Martina Shama-Sostar, the Kawar family of Nazareth, Daif Awwad, Santiago Enrique Arias, Director of ArchaeoSpain, Inc. together with our regional Spanish archaeologists,

Silvia Pascual, Gerardo Martinez, and Ana Maria Ortega Martinez. Working in Israel and Spain as a foreigner is not easy even for those of us who speak Hebrew, Spanish, and Arabic. In the case of Bethsaida, Yavne, Nazareth, Qumran, and the Cave of Letters to have a foreign university (especially one in Hartford) completely administrate, excavate, and publish the results of excavations in some of the most important locations of Israel is rare. We have done this by making most of the work results available to many scholars even in a "raw" state. From lectures at national and international conferences, articles in the popular and scholarly publications, to books, CDs, websites, documentaries, etc., the information has been available to other scholars to comment on. Four or five dissertations have utilized our results, and many books and articles by other scholars often use the information gathered by our teams without any citations. When I moved to the University of Hartford from the University of Nebraska at Omaha, the University of Hartford embraced the excavations projects as a natural extension of the Maurice Greenberg Center for Judaic Studies. The president, Walter Harrison, and the then Chair of the Regents, Arnold C. Greenberg, made sure that we had the funding and the administrative support we needed. The administrative assistant, Ms. Susan Gottlieb, made sure that the work of all of these excavations was properly administered. Susan and her husband, Phil deserve special honor in the creation of this book. Phil Gottlieb is one of the most informed and finest docents at our Sherman Museum of Jewish Civilization that houses the antiquities collection on loan to the university from the Antiquities Authority of Israel since 2003. Many of the talks that our docents give on the antiquities is formed around information on our different excavations. This museum collection has required me to create more general presentations about archaeology for the docents to use in their own presentations to school and community groups. Many of these talks have been incorporated into this book and I want to thank Phil and Susan Gottlieb who read the early drafts of the book to make sure they were meaningful for the public and corrected them.

In addition, I want to fully acknowledge the early editing of this book by Robin M. Romer, an excellent editor, who understands (much better than I do!) how the general public reads and understands religion and the Bible. Others have read parts of the text as well, but Robin helped me correct the original "academic" style into a more authentic voice. My editors, Brian Romer and Sarah Stanton at Rowman & Littlefield, have also helped shape the manuscript and the bibliographies, indices, and the reference guide. Catherine Forrest Getzie, the production editor at Rowman & Littlefield, also helped shape the "corrected" text.

This book is more than just a book. It is a book that accompanies filmed versions of all of our work. The director/producer of the NOVA *Ancient Refuge in the Holy Land*, Mr. Gary Hochman of Nebraska ETV, has filmed many of the excavations that are mentioned in the book, and he continues to work on documentaries that incorporate our work at Har Karkom, Qumran, and Nazareth stories for the television public. Filming in a foreign country is not easy. Filming an archaeological site and resolving difficult historical and archaeological questions in a fifty-six-minute production requires skill and a more than rudimentary grasp of multiple cultural and religious histories, textual traditions, and archaeology. Gary's great strength has been his ability to understand the story behind the texts and archaeology and make it intelligible to the public. Unfortunately, I never felt that all of the documentaries incorporated all of the elements that I felt were missing in the stories of the excavations and the layered biblical texts. This was another reason for me to write a book that did incorporate these other more complex histories and literary traditions in a way that I think tells "the rest of the story." Even this book is only a part of the rich details, and I included other books and articles in the bibliography for those who want to continue their search for answers. Much additional information on Qumran, Cave of Letters, Har Karkom, and Yavne is available on a variety of websites at links at the University of Hartford's Greenberg Center www.hartford.edu/greenberg. The sponsorship of most of our archaeological work at the university has been the Maurice Greenberg Center for Judaic Studies founded in 1985 by a substantial gift from Arnold C. and Beverly P. Greenberg of West Hartford, Connecticut. The Maurice Greenberg Center for Judaic Studies is an academic department in the College of Arts and Sciences at the University of Hartford (offering three different bachelor of arts and a joint masters program with the University of Connecticut) and is unique in recommending archaeology as part of the Judaic Studies curriculum. This began with my predecessor, Dr. Jonathan Rosenbaum, and thanks to three very supportive university presidents, Stephen Trachtenberg, Humphrey Tonkin, and now Walter Harrison, the excavations have continued almost from the beginning of the Center's work. The Greenberg Center is also an academic center of excellence at the university that together with the Sherman Museum of Jewish Civilization provides the students, staff, faculty, and general community of Greater Hartford ample opportunity for all types of cultural and academic events and exhibitions related to Jewish life and culture every year. Thanks to the generous donations of the founding donors of the Greenberg Center, one of the significant areas of research of the center has been biblical archaeology. The Greenberg Center is responsible for helping identify donors to underwrite some of the costs of these excavations through the donations of benefactors of the university. I would like to acknowledge the Development Office and Rachel Kimmelblatt, who has been instrumental in making our excavations a priority. I would like to personally acknowledge some of the donors and funding sources who made most of the excavations possible: John and Carol Merrill for funding the Cave of Letters and Qumran Excavations (thanks to the good offices of Hershel Shanks at *Biblical Archaeology Review*), Barnea Selevan and David Willner of Foundation Stone of Jerusalem for the development of a Tel Yavne Prototype Excavation Project, and especially William and Judith Freund for the funding of the Yavne Excavations Project at the University of Hartford, Joel and Sue Grae for the funding of our Har Karkom Excavations Project at the University of Hartford, Steven Konover and the Millie & Irving Bercowetz Fund at the University of Hartford for our Nazareth Excavations Project, the Same Seeds Different Winds Foundation Inc. for funding of parts of the Nazareth Excavations Project, Stanley and Sylvia Leven for the University of Hartford's Cave of Letter Excavations Project, and finally Stephen Weinstein for funding our Burgos Excavations Project. I also have to acknowledge our "fairy godmother" for our early work at the Bethsaida Project and indirectly for the original Cave of Letters and Qumran projects, Margie Scribante, who always found funds for us to use to continue our work. All of these people were not only interested in biblical archaeology but also in the funding of research. Many of them, like Stephen Weinstein, Margie Scribante, the Merrills, Barnea Selevan and David Willner, and Bill and Judy Freund, not only came to Israel to visit but often worked at the excavations. This type of dedication makes research a public event. In this regard, I need to acknowledge the thousands of volunteers who have participated in these excavations and who have contributed ideas to my own thinking in those long hours of excavating, pottery readings, and lectures. Another acknowledgment is necessary for the University of Nebraska at Omaha's International Studies and Programs and its dean, Thomas Gouttierre, who through thick and thin has helped the Bethsaida Project and the Cave of Letters Project and my own dean of the College of Arts and Sciences at the University of Hartford, Dr. Joseph Voelker, (and interim Dean Harry Workman) who also continued to support our efforts during difficult years in Israel. Mostly these last acknowledgments are for the people that do not receive mention in the course of the book. People like Amir Drori, former Director General of the Antiquities Authority of Israel who actually encouraged us to return to the Cave of Letters and Qumran. Drori, who had himself excavated in the

Cave of Letters with Yadin, intimately understood the importance of our work, and we are indebted to him for his consultations. The present Director General of the Israel Antiquities Authority, Shuka Dorfman, encouraged this work as well because he has the vision to realize that the technological advances that we used in the Cave of Letters could be used in many other archaeological contexts. I would also like to acknowledge the input of Uzi Dahari, Hava Katz, Gideon Avni, Baruch Brandl, David Amit, Orit Shamir, Peninah Shor, and Donald Ariel, all of the Israel Antiquity Authority for a variety of research, permits, insights, and consultations that they provided in the course of the excavations. These are the unsung "heroes" of Israeli archaeology because they toil daily to insure that the work is done well and systematically. I would like to thank the different officials of the Parks and Nature Reserves Authority of Israel and its Director of Science in 2000, Dr. Avi Pervolotsky, the head of Archaeology, Dr. Zvika Zuk, and the Parks and Nature Reserves officials who helped us in the field and who helped throughout our work. Mr. Uri Bonneh of the Jewish National Fund helped with the development of Bethsaida and gave us encouragement for our other work. The Jewish National Fund and the Parks and Nature Reserves of Israel protect and preserve enormous properties (and the flora and fauna inside of them) that stretch from one end of the country to the other and especially large desert reserves that often appear to people to be devoid of riches. These natural resources of the desert are so unique and fragile that they need our constant protection and deserve our admiration for the work they do. The longer we spent in these famous Judean and Negev deserts, the more I came to understand why my ancestors were drawn to the desert so often throughout our history, that I also came to respect the work of these agencies.

Over the years I have come to know personally a few people that have contributed to my own knowledge base and have passed away and deserve our thanks. John Rousseau, Father Bargil Pixner, Yizhar Hirschfield, Amir Drori, and staff members Phyllis Stetser and Pinchas Porat. Their presence at conferences and on-site, as well as their friendship, will be missed.

Our thanks to our neighbors and friends in our "Israel home" at Beit Yigal Allon Museum on Kibbutz Ginosar. Special thanks to Katy Bar-Noff, Bill Scheinmann, Shai and Judith Schwartz, and Nitza Kaplan, whose support for Bethsaida and all of our archaeological offerings over the past fifteen years has aided our work in innumerable ways. Maintaining an office and permanent laboratory space at Beit Allon has enabled most of our archaeological activities to continue uninterrupted. It is more than just storage, restoration, and research space. Over the years, Kibbutz Ginosar has made the pottery restorers and staff members who have stayed for extended periods feel like a part of the Kibbutz family and make our foreign visitors comfortable at the Nof Ginosar Hotel. Part of this book was written during my stays at Kibbutz Ginosar, and I have to thank Kati Bar Nof and the entire staff of the Ginosar Inn for their help. Kibbutz Ginosar is one of the reasons why so many of our volunteers keep coming back to work at Bethsaida each summer. Finally, special thanks goes to my wife Eliane, and my children Yoni, Eli, and Ethan, who had to hear about this book for so many years. They, like the doctors and nurses at Hartford Hospital and Dana Farber Cancer Institute, continued to listen to my ideas for excavations even as I recovered from leukemia. Special thanks to Dr. Robert Soiffer, my transplant physician, who continues to listen to my ideas on every single checkup at Dana Farber. I do not think that I could have completed writing up the experiences of the past twenty years of work if my family had not supported me during the good times and the bad times. The past three years since my bone marrow transplant have been the most physically challenging of my life and the most productive. Continuing to go to excavate after a transplant has made me appreciate just how dangerous and difficult the work we all do really is. I am thankful to have medical and family support that allowed me to do the work early in my career and continue now. And for those who are wondering who was the "one in a million" person that I dedicated the book to, it is Steve (Shlomo) Hackel, my bone marrow donor, who was the incredibly perfect match and which saved my life.

Richard A. Freund, University of Hartford
June 2008

Bibliography

Archaeology and the Ancient Near East

Dever, W. *Did God Have A Wife?* Grand Rapids, MI: Eerdmans, 2005.

———. "Is There Any Archaeological Evidence for the Exodus." In *Exodus: The Egyptian Evidence*, edited by Ernest Frerichs and Leonard Lesko, 71 (Winona Lake, IN: Eisenbrauns, 1997).

Freedman, D. N., and J. C. Greenfield, eds. *New Directions in Biblical Archaeology*. New York: Doubleday Anchor, 1971.

Hoffmeier, J. *Ancient Israel in Sinai: The Evidence for the Authenticity of the Wilderness Tradition*. New York: Oxford University Press, 2005.

———. *Israel in Egypt: Evidence for the Authenticity of the Exodus Tradition*. New York: Oxford University Press, 1997, 1999.

Kenyon, K. *Archaeology in the Holy Land*. New York: Praeger, 1960.

Noth, M. *The Old Testament World*. Philadelphia: Fortress, 1966.

Pritchard, J. B., ed. *The Ancient Near East: An Anthology of Texts and Pictures*. Princeton, NJ: Princeton University Press, 2 vols, 1965, 1976.

———. *The Ancient Near East in Pictures Relating to the Old Testament*. Princeton, NJ: Princeton University Press, 1969.

———. *Ancient Near Eastern Texts Relating to the Old Testament*. Princeton, NJ: Princeton University Press, 1969.

Sanders, J. A., ed. *Near Eastern Archaeology in the Twentieth Century*. [Glueck Volume]. New York: Doubleday, 1970.

Thomas, D. W. *Archaeology and Old Testament Study*. Oxford, UK: Clarendon, 1967.

Wright, G. E. *The Bible and the Ancient Near East: Essays in Honor of W. F. Albright*. New York: Doubleday, 1961; Doubleday Paperback edition, 1965.

———. *Biblical Archaeology*. Philadelphia: Westminster, 1962.

Bible

Aejmelaeus, A. "What Can We Know About the Hebrew." *Vorlage of the Septuagint Zeitschrift für die Alttestamentliche Wissenschaft* 99 (1987): 58–90.

Ap-Thomas, D. R. *A Primer of Old Testament Text Criticism*. Philadelphia: Fortress Press, 1966.

Barthélemy, D. *Les Devianciers d'Aquila*. Leiden: Brill, 1963.

Bickerman, E. *Studies in Jewish and Christian History,* Vol. I, Leiden: Brill, 1976.

Brown, J. W. *The Rise of Biblical Criticism in America, 1800–1870*. Middletown, CT: Wesleyan University Press, 1969.

Cross, F. M. *The Ancient Library of Qumran*. New York: Anchor Books, 1961.

Cross, F. M., and S. Talmon. *Qumran and the History of the Biblical Text*. London and Cambridge, MA: Harvard University Press, 1975. See esp. 1–41; 177–195; 278–305.

Engnell, I. *A Rigid Scrutiny: Critical Essays on the Old Testament*. Nashville, TN: Vanderbilt University Press, 1969.

Fishbane, Michael. "Biblical Colophons, Textual Criticism and Legal Analogies." *Catholic Biblical Quarterly* 42 (1980): 438–449.

———. *Biblical Interpretation in Ancient Israel*. Oxford, UK: Clarendon, 1985.

Frerichs, E. S. "The Torah Canon of Judaism and the Interpretation of Hebrew Scripture." 13 25 *Horizons in Biblical Theology* 9, 1987.

Friedman, R. E. *The Disappearance of God*. New York: Simon and Shuster, 1995.

———. *Who Wrote the Bible?* New York: Harper and Row, 1989.

Goshen-Gottstein, M. H. *The Bible in the Syro-Palestinian Version*. Jerusalem, 1973.

———. *The Book of Isaiah: Sample Edition with Introduction*. Jerusalem, 1965.

———. "The Textual Criticism of the Old Testament: Rise, Decline, Rebirth." *Journal of Biblical Literature* 102 (1983): 365–399.

Hayes, J. H., ed. *Old Testament Form Criticism*. San Antonio, TX: Trinity University Press, 1974.

Jellicoe, S. *The Septuagint and Modern Study*. Oxford, UK: Clarendon, 1968.

Klein, R. *Text Criticism of the Old Testament—The Septuagint after Qumran*. Philadelphia: Fortress, 1974.

Koch, K. *The Growth of the Biblical Tradition: The Form-Critical Method*. New York: Charles Scribner's Sons, 1969; paperback, 1971.

May, H. G., and B. M. Metzger, eds. *The New Oxford Annotated Bible with the Apocrypha*. New York: Oxford University Press, 1977.

Noth, M. *The Old Testament World,* chapter 4. Philadelphia: Fortress, 1966.

Orlinsky, H. M. "The Septuagint as Holy Writ and the Philosophy of the Translators." *Hebrew Union College Annual* 46 (1975): 74–93.

Oxford Annotated Bible, (Revised Standard Version) eds. Herbert G. May and Bruce M. Metzger. New York: Oxford University Press, 1962.

Patai, R. *The Hebrew Goddess*. New York: Avon, 1978.

Rosenberg, D. Interpreted by Harold Bloom. *The Book of J*. New York: Grove Weidenfeld, 1990.

Soulen, R. N. *Handbook of Biblical Criticis*. Atlanta: J. Knox Press, 1981.

Tigay, J. H. *Empirical Models for Bible Criticism*. Philadelphia: Fortress, 1985.

Tov, E. "Dimensions of Septuagint Words." *Revue Biblique* 83 (1976): 529–554.

———. "On 'Pseudo-Variants' in the Septuagint," *Journal of Semitic Studies* 20 (1975): 165–77.

Tucker, G. M. *Form-Criticism of the Old Testament*. Philadelphia: Fortress, 1971.

Wellhausen, J. *Prolegomena to the History of Ancient Israel*. Edinburgh, 1885. [also in paperback].

Wevers, J. M. "The Earliest Witness to the LXX Deuteronomy" *The Catholic Biblical Quarterly* 39 (1977): 240–244.

Jerusalem, Bethsaida, and Nazareth

Abu-Raya, R. "Jerusalem, Mount of Olives." *Excavations and Surveys in Israel* 16 (1997): 109–110.

Arav and Richard A. Freund, eds. *Bethsaida: A City by the North Sea of Galilee, Volume I.*

Kirksville, MO: Truman State University Press, 1995.

———. *Bethsaida: A City by the North Sea of Galilee, Volume II.* Kirksville, MO: Truman State University Press, 2000.

———. *Bethsaida: A City by the North Sea of Galilee, Volume III.* Kirksville, MO: Truman. State University Press, 2004.

———. *Bethsaida: A City by the North Sea of Galilee, Volume IV.* Kirksville MO: Truman State University Press, 2008.

Dalman, Gustaf. *Studies in the Topography of the Gospels.* New York: McMillan, 1935.

Eusebius. *The History of the Church*. New York: Dorset Press, 1965.

Freyne, Sean. *Galilee from Alexander the Great to Hadrian*. Notre Dame, IN: University of Notre Dame Press, 1980.

Gingres, George. *Egeria: Diary of a Pilgrimage.* New York: Newman Press, 1970.

Hunt, J. *Holy Land Pilgrimage in the Later Roman Empire, A.D. 312–460.* Oxford, UK: Clarendon Press, 1982.

Josephus, Flavius. *Works*, (English and Greek, 1958). Loeb Classical Library. 9 vols. Cambridge, MA: Harvard University Press; London: W. Heineman.

Murphy-O'Connor, Jerome. *The Holy Land, an Archaeological Guide from Earliest Times to 1700.* New York: Oxford University Press, 1980.

Pliny, *Natural History*, V. 15:15.

Rousseau, J. J., and Rami Arav. *Jesus and His World.* Minneapolis: Fortress Press, 1995.

Safrir, Y. *Eretz Israel from the Destruction of the Second Temple to the Muslim Conquest: Archaeology and Art.* Jerusalem: Yad Izhak Ben Zvi, 1984.

Small, D. "Late Hellenistic Baths in Palestine." *Bulletin of the American Schools of Oriental Research* 266 (1975): 59–74.

Smith, G. A. *The Historical Geography of the Holy Land*. New York: Harper and Row, 1966.

Stewart, Aubrey, trans. "Library of the Palestine Pilgrims' Text Society." Vols. 1–13. London: Palestine Pilgrims' Text Society, 24 Hanover Square, W., 1895. Reprinted ed., New York: AMS,1971.

———. *Theodoric, Guide to the Holy Land*. New York: Italica Press, 1986.

Wilkinson, John. *Jerusalem Pilgrimage 1099–1185*. Cambridge, UK: University Press, The Hakluyt Society, 1988.

Qumran

Allegro, J. M., *The Chosen People: A Study of Jewish History from the Time of the Exile until the Revolt of Bar Kocheba (Sixth Century B.C. to Second Century A.D.)*. London: Hodder and Stoughton, 1971. Garden City, NY: Doubleday, 1972.

———. *The Dead Sea Scrolls: A Reappraisal*, 2nd ed., Harmondsworth, Middlesex, UK: Penguin, 1964, repr. 1977.

———. *The Dead Sea Scrolls and the Christian Myth*. London: Westbridge Books, 1979.

———. *Search in the Desert*. London: W. H. Allen, 1965.

———. *The Treasury of the Copper Scroll*, 2nd rev. ed. New York: Doubleday, 1964.

———. *The Treasury of the Copper Scroll: The Opening and Decipherment of the Most Mysterious of the Dead Sea Scrolls, A Unique Inventory of Buried Treasure*. London: Routledge & Kegan Paul; Garden City, NY: Doubleday, 1960.

———. "An Unpublished Fragment of Essene Halakha (4Q Ordinances)," *JSS* 6 (1961): 71–73.

DeVaux, R. *Archaeology and the Dead Sea Scrolls*. London: Oxford University Press, 1973.

———. *Discoveries in the Judean Desert II*.

———. "Fouilles au Khirbet Qumrân." *Revue Biblique* 63, 1956.

———. "Preface" and "Introduction." *Discoveries in the Judean Desert III*, 200–202.

DeVaux, R, P. Benoit, G. M. Crowfoot, E. Crowfoot, and J. T. Milik. *Les Grottes de Murabba'at*. Oxford, UK: Clarendon, 1961.

DeVaux, R., M. Bailet, J. T. Milik with H. W. Baker. *Discoveries in the Judean Desert of Jordan III, Les 'Petites Grottes' de Qumran*. Oxford, UK: Clarendon, 1962.

Fitzmyer, J. A. "Bargil Pixner, Archaologische Beobachtungen zum Jerusalemer Essener-Viertel und zur Urgemeinde." *Christen*, 89–113, *Old Testament Abstracts* 16 (1993): 575.

———. "Dead Sea Scrolls." *NCE* 4, 676a–681a.

———. *The Dead Sea Scrolls: Major Publications and Tools for Study, With an Addendum*. Sources for Biblical Study 8, Missoula, MT: Society of Biblical Literature, Scholars Press, 1977. "(The Copper Plaque Mentioning Buried Treasure [3Qtreasure, 3Q15]"; 1st ed. 1975).

Fitzmyer, J. A., and D. J. Harrington. *A Manual of Palestinian Aramaic Text (Second Century B.C.–Second Century A.D.,* Biblica et Orientalia 34. Rome: Biblical Institute, 1978.

Flint, Peter W. "5/6HevNumbers" and "5/6HevPsalms." Pages 137–166, *Miscellaneous Texts from the Judaean Desert,* edited by James R. Charlesworth, et al. DJD 38, Oxford, UK: Clarendon Press.

Ganneau, C. Claremont. *Archaeological Researches in Palestine during the Years 1873–1874.*Vol. 2; London: Palestine Exploration Fund, 1896, 15–16.

Humbert J. B. and A. Chambon, Fouilles de Khirbet Qumrân et de Aïn Feshkha I. Novum Testamentum et Orbis Antiquus, Series Archaeologica 1. Göttingen: Vandenhoek & Ruprecht, 1994, 214.

Puech, E. "Essene Belief in Afterlife." *BASOR* 312 (1998): 21–25.

Steckoll, S. H. "Marginal Notes on the Qumran Excavations," *Revue de Qumran* 7 (1969): 37–38.

———. "Preliminary Excavation Report in the Qumran Cemetery," *Revue de Qumran* 6 (1968): 323–336.

Taylor, J. E. "The Cemeteries of Khirbet Qumran and Women's Presence at the Site." *DSD* 6, (1999): 285–336.

Dead Sea Scrolls and Cave of Letters

Aharoni, Y., "The Ancient Desert Agriculture of the Negev, III. Early Beginnings." See: Evenari, M., Aharoni, Y., Shanan, L. and Tadmor, N. H.

———. "The Archaeological Survey of Masada, 1955–1956." See: Avi-Yonah, M., Avigad, N, N., Aharoni, Y., Dunayevsky, I., and Gutman, S.

———. "The Expedition to the Judean Desert, 1960, Expedition B," 11:11–24, Pls. 4–11C;

———. "The Expedition to the Judean Desert, 1961, Expedition B–The Cave of Horror, 12:186–199, Pls. 23–34.

Albright, W. F. "On the Date of the Scrolls From 'Ain Feshka and the Nash Papryus." *BASOR* 115 (1950): 10–19.

Avigad, N. "The Palaeography of the Dead Sea Scrolls and Related Documents." In C. Rabin and Y. Yadin, *Aspects of the Dead Sea Scrolls,* Scripta Hierosolymitana IV (1957): 56–87.

Bar-Adon, P., "An Early Hebrew Inscription in a Judean Desert Cave." 25:226–232, Pl. 25.

———. The Expedition to the Judean Desert, 1960, Expedition C, 11:25–35, Pls. 11D–17A.

———. The Expedition to the Judean Desert, 1961, Expedition C, The Cave of the Treasure, 12:215–226, Pls. 35–42.

Cotton, H. M., "The Archive of Salome Komaise Daughter of Levi: Another Archive from the 'Cave of Letters.'" *Zeitschrift fur Papyrologie und Epigraphik* 105 (1995): 171–208.

———. "A Cancelled Marriage Contract from the Judaean Desert." *The Journal of Roman Studies* 84, (1994): 64–86.

———. "Courtyard(s) in Ein-Gedi: O, Tadub 11, 19, and 20 of the Babatha Archive." *ZEITSCHRIFT FUR PHILOSOPHIE UND KATHOLISCHE* 112 (1996a): 197–201.

———. "The Guardianship of Jesus Son of Babatha: Roman and Local Law in the Province of Arabia." *Journal of Roman Studies* 83 (1993): 94–108.

———. "The Impact of the Documentary Papyri from the Judean Desert on the Study of the Jewish History from 70 to 135 CE." Oppenheimer, A. (Ed.), *Judische Geschichte in hellenistisch-romischer Zeit,* Wege der Forschung: von alten zum neuen Schurer, Munchen (1999): 221–236.

———. "The Language of the Legal and Administrative Documents from the Judean Desert," *Zeitschrift fur Papyrologie und Epigraphik* 125–199, 219–231.

———. "The Rabbis and the Documents." Goodman, M., (ed.), *Jews in a Graeco-Roman Worlds,* Oxford (1998): 167–179.

———. "Some Aspects of the Roman Administration of Judaea/Syria-Palestine," Werner, E., ed., Lokale Autonomie und romische Ordnungsmacht in der Kaiserzeitlichen Provinzen von 1–3 Jahrhundert, Munchen (1999): 75–91.

Cross, F. M. *The Ancient Library of Qumran and Modern Biblical Studies: The Haskell Lecture,* 1956–1957, London: Geral Duckworth; Garden City, NY: Doubleday, 1958: rev. ed., Garden City, NY: Doubleday, 1961; 3rd ed., Minneapolis: Fortress, 1995.

———. "Excursus on the Palaeographical Dating of the Copper Document." *Discoveries in the Judean Desert III,* (1962): 217–221.

———. "The Manuscripts of the Dead Sea Caves." *Biblical Archaeoligist* 17i (1954): 2–21 (the first page has a photograph of the two copper rolls *in situ*).

———. "A New Qumran Biblical Fragment Related to the Original Hebrew Underlying the Septuagint." *BASOR* 132 (1955): 15–26.

Cross, F. M., Jr., and Freedman, D. N., *The Ancient Library of Qumran and Modern Biblical Studies.* Garden City, NY: Doubleday, 1961.

———. *Early Hebrew Orthography: A Study of the Epigraphic Evidence.* New Haven, CT: American Oriental Society, 1952.

———. "The Oldest Manuscripts from Qumran." *JBL* 74 (1958): 147–172.

Eck, W. "The Bar Kokhba Revolt: The Roman Point of View." *Journal of Roman Studies,* 89 (1999): 76–89.

Gaster, T. *The Dead Sea Scriptures.* New York: Doubleday Anchor, 1956.

Harkabi, Y. *The Bar Kokhba Syndrome,* Risk and Realism in International Politics. Chappagua, NY: 1983.

Isaac, B., "Cassius Dio on the Revolt of Bar Kokhba." Isaac B., *The Near East Under Roman Rule,* Selected Papers, Leiden 1998, 211–219 [*Scripta Classica Israelica* 7 (1983/1984): 68–76].

———. "Judaea After 70." Isaac, B., *The Near East Under Roman Rule,* Selected Papers, Leiden 1998: 112–121 [*Journal of Jewish Studies* 35 (1984): 44–50].

———. "Roman Colonis in Judaea, the Foundation of Aelia Capitolina." Isaac B., *The Near East Under Roman Rule,* Selected Papers, Leiden (1998): 87–108.

Isaac, B., and A. Oppenheimer. "The Revolt of Bar Kokhba: Ideology and Modern Scholarship." *The Near East Under Roman Rule,* Selected Papers, Leiden 1998, 200–256, *Journal of Jewish Studies* 36 (1985): 33–60.

Isaac, B., and I. Roll. "Judea in the Early Years of Hadrian's Reign." Issiac, B., *The Near East Under Roman Rule,* Selected Papers, Leiden (1998): 182–197[*Latomus* 28 (1979), 54–66].

Lehmann, M. "On My Mind," *Algemeiner Journal—A National Jewish Journal,* NY: Friday, April 30 (1993), B3 CC. 1–2, B4, c.1.

———. "Where the Temple Tax Was Buried: The Key to Understanding the Coper Scroll," *BAR,* 19 (1993): 38–43.

Levine, B. A. "Jews and Nabateans in the Nahal Hever Archive." In *The Dead Sea Scrolls: Fifty Years after their Discovery.* Lawrence H. Schiffman, Emanuel Tov, and James C. VanderKam, 836–851. Jerusalem: Israel Exploration Society, 2000.

Lewis, Naphtali. *The Documents from the Biblical Archaeology Review-Kokhba Period in the Cave of Letter-Gree Papyri.* Judean Desert Studies 2. Jerusalem: Israel Exploration Society, The Hebrew University of Jerusalem, The Shrine of the Book, 1989.

Lieberman, Saul. "The Importance of the Bar-Kokhba Letters for Jewish History and Literature." In *Texts and Studies,* 208–9. New York: Ktav, 1974.

Magness, J. *The Archaeology of Qumran and the Dead Sea Scrolls.* Grand Rapids, MI: Eerdmans, 2002.

Marks, R. G. "Dangerous Hero: Rabbinic Attitudes Toward Legendary Warriors." *Hebrew Union College Annual* 54 (1983): 181–194.

———. *The Image of Biblical Archaeology Review Kokhba I Traditional Jewish Literature.* False Messiah and National Hero: University Park, 1993.

McCarter, P. K., Jr. "Alterations of the 'Seqel' Standards during the Jewish War and the Bar Kokhba War" (Hebrew). In *Proceedings of the Fifth World Congress of Jewish Studies.* Edited by Pinchas Peli. Jerusalem: World Union of Jewish Studies, pp. 1:81–86. (Hebrew Section), 1971.

———. "The Copper Scroll Treasure as an Accumulation of Religious Offerings." *Methods of Investigation of the Dead Sea Scrolls and the Khirbet Qumran Site: present Realities and Future Prospects,* edited by Michael Owen Wise, Norman Golb, John J. Collins, and Dennis G. Pardee, *ANYAS* 722 (1994): 133–148.

———. "The Mystery of the Copper Scroll." *The Dead Sea Scrolls After Forty Years: Symposiumat the Smithsonian Institution, October 27, 1990,* ed., by Hershel Shanks, Washington, DC: Biblical Archaeology Society, (1991): 40–55.

———. "The Mystery of the Copper Scroll." *Understanding the Dead Sea Scrolls: A Reader from the Biblical Archaeology Review,* edited by Hershel Shanks, 227–241, 309. New York: Random, 1992.

———. "The Mysterious Copper Scroll: Clues to Hidden Temple Treasure?" *Biblical Research,* Chicago 8 (1992): 34–41, 63–64.

———. *Nabataean Coins,* Qedem 3. Jerusalem: Institute of Archeology, Hebrew University of Jerusalem; distributed by the Israel Exploration Society, 1975.

————. "One Hundred Ninety Years of Tyrian Shekels." In *Festschrift fur Leo Mildenberg: Numismatik, Kunstgeschichte, Archaologie = Studies in Honor of Leo Mildenberg: Numismatics, Art History, Archeology.* Edited by Arthur Houghton et al., 171–79. Wetterrren, Belgium: Editions NR, 1984.

Meshorer, Y. "A Coin Hoard of the Bar-Kokhba's Time." *Israel Museum News* 4 (1985): 43–50.

Mildenberg, L. "The Bar Kokhba War in the Light of the Coins and Documents Finds 1947–1982." *Israel Numismatic Journal* 8 (1984–85): 27–32.

————. *The Coinage of the Biblical Archaeology Review Kokhba War.* Typos 6. Aarau, Frankfurt a.M., Salzburg: Sauerlander, 1984.

————. "Rebel Coinage in the Roman Empire." Kasher, A., Rappaport, U.; Fuks, G., eds., *Greece and Rome in Eretz Israel, Collected Essays,* 62–74. Jerusalem: 1990.

Mor, M., "The Bar-Kokhba Revolt and Non-Jewish Participants." *Journal of Jewish Studies* 36 (1985), 200–209.

Pixner, B. (Virgil). "Das Essenquartier in Jerusalem und dessen Einfluss auf die Urkirche." *Das heilige Land* 113 (1981): 3–14.

————. "An Essene Quarter on Mount Zion?" *Studia Hierosolymitana,* Part 1: Archaelogical Studies, Collectio Maior 22, Studium Biblicum Franciscanum, 245–84. Jerusalem: Francisca Printing, 1976.

————. "Unravelling the Copper Scroll Code: A Study of the Topography of 3Q15." *Romische Quartalschrift Fur Christliche Alterumskunde Und Kirchengeschichte, Vatican City* 11 (1983): 323–361 plus plan I-iv.

Sperber, D. "Between Jerusalem and Rome: The History of the Base of the Menorah as Depicted on the Arch of Titus." in Israeli Y. (ed.), *In the Light of the Menorah, Story of a Symbol,* 50–53. The Israel Museum Catalogue, no. 425, Jerusalem: 1969.

————. *The Customs of Israel, Origin and History,* Vol. V., Jerusalem, 1994.

————. "The History of the Menorah." *JJS* 16 (1965): 135–139.

Talmon, S. *Masada VI. Yigael Yadin Excavations 1963–1965 Final Reports. Hebrew Fragments from Masada.* Jerusalem: Israel Exploration Society, 1999.

Wirgin, W. "The Menorah as Symbol of Judaism." *Israel Exploration Journal, Jerusalem 12:* 140–142, 1962.

————. "The Menorah as Symbol of Afterlife." *IEF* 14: 102–104.

————. Two Notes: 1. "On the Shape of the Foot of the Menorah." *Israel Exploration Journal, Jerusalem* 7: 151–153, 1961.

Wolters, Al (=Albert M.). *The Copper Scroll: Overview, Text and Translation.* Sheffield: Sheffield Academic Press, 1996.

Wright, G. E. "Qumran Excavations." *Biblical Archaeologist* 16 (1953): 7-8.

Yadin, Yigael. *Bar Kokhba: The Rediscovery of the Legendary Hero of the Last Jewish Revolt against Imperial Rome.* London: Weidenfeld and Nicolson, 1971.

————. *The Finds from the Bar Kokhba Period in the Cave of Letters.* Jerusalem: Israel Exploration Society, 1963.

———. *Masada: Herod's Fortress and the Zealot's Last Stand*. New York: Random House, 1966.

Yadin, Y., J. C. Greenfield, A. Yardeni, and B. Levine, ed., Contributions by H. M. Cotton and J. Naveh. *The Documents from the Bar Kokhba Period in the Cave of Letters.* Jerusalem: Israel Exploration Society, 2002.

Hellenistic/Greco-Roman/
Second Temple Period Judaism: Apocrypha

Avi-Yonah, M., ed., *The Herodian Period* (*World History of the Jewish People,* Vol. 7). New Brunswick, NJ: Rutgers University Press, 1975.

Baron, S. W. *A Social and Religious History of the Jews*, Vol. 1 and 2. New York: Columbia University Press, 1952.

Charles, R. H. et al., ed. and trans. *The Apocrypha and Pseudepigrapha of the Old Testament*, 2 volumes. Oxford, UK: Clarendon, 1913.

Charlesworth, J. H. *The Pseudepigrapha and Modern Research*. Missoula, MT: Scholars Press, 1976.

Cross, F. M. *The Ancient Library of Qumran and Modern Biblical Studies*. New York: Doubleday, 1961.

Driver, G. R. *The Judean Scrolls: The Problem and a Solution*. Oxford, UK: Blackwell, 1965.

Dodd, C. H. *The Bible and the Greeks*. London: Hodder and Stoughton, 1935.

Feldman, L. H., ed. *Scholarship on Philo and Josephus: 1937–62.* New York: Yeshiva University, 1963.

Flavius, Josephus. The complete translation of Josephus's works in the Loeb Classical Library, 9 vols., is by H. St. J. Thackeray, Ralph Marcus, and Louis H. Feldman, (London and New York: Heinemann and G. P. Putnam's Sons, 1926–1965).

Freund, R., "Alexander Macedon and Antoninus: Two Greco-Roman Heroes of the Rabbis." In *Jewish Heroes,* edited by M. Mor, 60–100. Omaha: Creighton University Press, 1995.

———. "The Apocalypse of Rabbi Aqiva." Studies in Jewish Civilization Volume 12. In *Millennialism From the Hebrew Bible to the Present*, edited by Leonard J. Greenspoon and Ronald A. Simkins, 150–165. Omaha: Creighton University Press, 2002.

———. "The Decalogue in Early Judaism and Christianity." In *The Function of Scripture in Early Jewish and Christian Tradition,* edited by Craig A. Evans and James A. Sanders, 60–100. Sheffield: Sheffield Academic Press, 1998.

———. "Jewish-Christian Sects and The Jewish-Christian Debate in the First Four Centuries of the Common Era." In *Jewish Sects, Religious Movements and Political Parties*, edited by M. Mor, 53–100. Omaha: Creighton University Press, 1993.

———. "The Mystery of the Menorah and the Star." In *Nationalism, Zionism and Ethnic Mobilization of the Jews in 1900 and Beyond,* edited by M. Berkowitz, 125–147. Leiden: Brill, 2004.

————. "The Myth of Jesus in Rabbinic Literature." In *The Seductiveness of Jewish Myth: Challenge or Response,* edited by D. Breslauer, 185–209. Albany: State University of New York Press, 1997.

————. "A New Interpretation of the Incense Shovels of the Cave of the Letters." In *The Dead Sea Scrolls: Fifty Years After their Discovery,* of the Jerusalem Congress, July 20–25, 17. Jerusalem: Israel Exploration Society in Cooperation with the Shrine of the Book, Israel Museum, 2000.

————. "Pope Receives Bethsaida Key." *Biblical Archaeology Review,* vol. 26, no. 3. (May/June 2000): 60ff.

————. "Recovering Antiquity: The Convergence of Ancient Literatures and Archaeology in the Search for the Lost City of Bethsaida." In *The Solomon Goldman Lectures, Vol. VII,* edited by D. P. Bell, 1–46. Chicago: The Spertus Institute of Jewish Studies Press, 1999.

————. *Secrets of the Cave of Letters: A Dead Sea Mystery.* Amherst, NY: Prometheus, 2004.

Freund, R., H. M. Jol, J. F. Shroder, Jr., and P. Reeder. "A GPR Archaeological Expedition at the Cave of Letters, Israel." In Eighth International Conference on Ground Penetrating Radar, edited by D. A. Noon, G. F. Stickley, and D. Longstaff, 882–886. SPIE. 4084, 2001.

Freund, R., J. F. Schroder, and R. Arav. "Bethsaida Rediscovered!" *Biblical Archaeology Review,* vol. 26, no. 1. (January/February 2000): 44ff.

————. "Individual vs. Collective Responsibilty: From the Ancient Near East and the Bible to the Greco-Roman World." In *Scandinavian Journal of the Old Testament,* vol. 11, no. 2, Fall 1997.

————. "And the Land Bled Forth its Produce: Biblical Criticism and Exilic Biblical Images." Pp. in *Scandinavian Journal of the Old Testament,* vol. 13, no. 2, (Fall, 1999): 284–297.

Freund, R., and R. Arav. "The Bethsaida Stele and City Gate Altar." *Biblical Archaeology Review,* vol. 24, no. 1, (January/February, 1998): 34.

————. "Bethsaida: The City of the Geshurites." *Le Monde de Bible,* (French), vol. 139, (November/December, 2001): 59.

————. "The Ethics of Abortion in Jewish Hellenism." *Helios,* New Series. vol. 10, no. 2, Fall (1983): 125–138.

————. "From Kings to Archons." *Scandinavian Journal of the Old Testament,* Summer, (1990): 58–72.

————. "An Incense Shovel from Bethsaida." *Biblical Archaeology Review,* vol. 23, no. 1, January/February (1997): 32.

————. "Jewish Sexual Ethics and Hellenism." *Journal of Reform Judaism,* vol. 36, no. 4., Fall (1989).

————. "*Kata Phusi* –According to Nature": The Hellenistic Jewish Bio-Medical Ethics Argument." *Shofar,* vol. 7, no. 1, Fall (1988): 36–48.

————. "Murder, Adultery, and Theft?" *Scandinavian Journal of Old Testament,* Summer (1989): 72–80.

———. "Naming Names: Some Observations on Anonymous Women Traditions in the Masoretic Text, the Septuagint and Hellenistic Literature." *Scandinavian Journal of the Old Testament,* Fall, (1992): 213–232.

———. *National Geographic,* (Hebrew) contributor on our excavation, "The Cave of Letters Excavations." Israel, (2001): 52–59.

———. "Return to the Cave of Letters." *Biblical Archaeology Review,* vol. 27, no. 1. (2001): 54 ff.

———. "Thou Shalt Not Go Thither: The Punishments of Moses and Aaron in the Masoretic Text, Septuagint and Jewish Hellenistic Literature and Evidence for Varying Theodicies in the Pentateuch. "*Scandinavian Journal of the Old Testament,* Spring (1994): 105–125.

———. "Universal Human Rights in Biblical and Classical Judaism?" *Shofar,* vol. 12, no. 2, Winter (1994): 50–66.

———. "The Varying Ethical Perspectives on Lying and Deception in Genesis as Reflected in the Masoretic Text and the Its Hellenistic Interpreters." *Scandinavian Journal of the Old Testament,* Fall, 1991: 45–61.

———. "What Happened to the 'Milk and Honey': The Disappearance of 'The Land of Milk and Honey' from Post-biblical Jewish Literature. *Proceedings of the Klutznick Symposium at Creighton University, 1998.*

———. "Which Christians, Pagans and Jews?: Varying Responses to Julian's Attempt to Rebuild the Temple in Jerusalem in the Fourth Century CE." *Journal of Religious Studies,* vol. 18, no. 2 (1992): 65–68.

Frey, J. *Corpus Inscriptionum Judaicarum,* Vol. 1 reprint. New York: Ktav, 1975.

Freyne, S. *Galilee From Alexander the Great to Hadrian: 323 BCE to 135 CE.* Notre Dame, IN: Michael Glazier and University of Notre Dame Press, 1980.

Goodenough, E. R. "An Early Christian Bread Stamp." *HRT* 57:133–137, 1964b.

———. *Jewish Symbols in the Greco-Roman Period,* I–III, New York, 1953.

———. *Jewish Symbols in the Greco-Roman Period,* IV, New York, 1954.

———. *Jewish Symbols in the Greco-Roman Period,* V–VI, New York, 1956.

———. *Jewish Symbols in the Greco-Roman Period,* VII–VIII, New York, 1958.

———. *Jewish Symbols in the Greco-Roman Period,* XI–XI, New York, 1964a.

———. *Jewish Symbols in the Greco-Roman Period,* XII, New York, 1965.

———. *Jewish Symbols in the Greco-Roman Period,* XIII, New York, 1968.

———. *Jewish Symbols in the Greco-Roman Period.* 12 vol. New York: Pantheon Books, Inc., 1953–1965.

———. "The Menorah among Jews of the Roman World," *HUGA* 23 (1950–1951): 449–492.

———. *The Politics of Philo Judaeus.* New Haven: Yale University Press, 1938.

Goodman, M. "Babatha's Story." *Journal of Roman Studies* 81 (1991).

Hachlili, R. *Ancient Jewish Art and Archaeology in the Land of Israel.* Leiden, New York, Kobenhaven, Koln, 1988.

———. "The Conch Motif in Ancient Jewish Art." *Assaph, Studies in Art History I.,* Tel Aviv (1979): 57–65.

———. "An Iron Candelabrum of the 8th century BCE." *Michmanim* 2 (1985): 29–42.

———. *Jewish Art in the Golan,* Catalogue no. 3. The Reuben and Edith Hecht Museum, University of Haifa, 1987.

———. "The Niche and Ark in Ancient Synagogues." *BASOR* 223 (1976): 45–53.

———. "The Zodiac in Ancient Jewish Art: Representation and Significance." *BASOR* 228 (1977): 61–77.

Hachlili, R., ed. *Ancient Synagogues in Israel. Third–Seventh Centuri CR.* BAR International Series 499. Oxford, 1989.

Hadas, M. *Hellenistic Culture: Fusion and Diffusion.* New York: Columbia University Press, 1959.

Hengel, M. *Judaism and Hellenism: Studies in their Encounter in Palestine during the Early Hellenistic Period,* 2 vol. trans., J. Bowden. Philadelphia: Fortress, 1974.

Jewish Apocryphal Literature, 7 vol. editor-in chief, S. Zeitlin. Philadelphia: Dropsie University, Harper and Brothers and E. J. Brill, 1950–1972.

Kadushin, M. "Aspects of the Rabbinic Concept of Israel in the Mekhilta." *Hebrew Union College Annual* 19d (1943–46): 57–96.

———. *A Conceptual Commentary on Midrash Leviticus Rabbah: Value Concepts in Jewish Thought.* Atlanta: Scholars Press, 1987.

———. *Organic Thinking: A Study in Rabbinic Thought.* New York: Jewish Theological Seminary of America, 1938.

———. *The Rabbinic Mind.* New York: JTSA, 1952.

———. *The Theology of Seder Eliahu: A Study in Organic Thinking.* New York: Bloch, 1932.

———. *Worship and Ethics: A Study in Rabbinic Judaism.* Evanston, IL: Northwestern University Press, 1964.

Leon, H. J. *The Jews of Ancient Rome.* Philadelphia: Jewish Publication Society of America, 1960.

Mantel, H. *Studies in the History of the Sanhedrin.* Cambridge, MA: Harvard University Press, 1965.

Meshorer, Y. *Jewish Coins of the Second Temple Period.* Tel Aviv: Am Hassefer, 1967.

Pagels, E. *The Gnostic Gospel.* New York: Random House, 1979.

Philo. The complete translation of Philo's work in the Loeb Classical Library, 10 vols. and 2 supplementary vols., is by F. H. Colson, G. H. Whitaker, and Ralph Marcus, (Cambridge, MA and London: Harvard University Press and William Heinemann, 1929–1962).

Pomeroy, S. *Goddesses, Whores, Wives and Slaves.* New York: Schocken Press, 1976.

Rabin, C. *Qumran Studies.* New York: Schocken, 1975. First published in 1957.

Rhoads, D. M. *Israel in Revolution, 6–74 CE: A Political History Based on the Writings of Josephus.* Philadelphia: Fortress Press, 1976.

Rostovtzeff, Michael. *The Social and Economic History of the Hellenistic World.* Oxford, UK: Clarendon Press, 1941.

————. *The Social and Economic History of the Roman Empire*. Revised by P. M. Fraser. Oxford, UK: Clarendon: 1957.

Russell, D. S. *The Method and Message of Jewish Apocalyptic, 200 BC–AD 100*. Philadelphia: Westminster Press, 1964.

Safrai, S., and M. Stern. *The Jewish People in the First Century: Historical Geography, Political History, Social, Cultural, and Religious Life and Institutions*, 2 vol. Philadelphia: Fortress Press, 1974–1976.

Sandmel, S. *Judaism and Christian Beginnings*. New York: Oxford University Press, 1978.

Schürer, E. *The History of the Jewish People in the Age of Jesus Christ (175 BC–AD 135)*. A new English edition revised and edited by Geza Vermes and Fergus Millar. Edinburgh: T. and T. Clark, 1973.

Smallwood, E. M. *The Jews under Roman Rule, from Pompey to Diocletian* (Studies in Judaism in Late Antiquity, XX). Leiden: E. J. Brill, 1981.

Stern, M., ed. and trans. *Greek and Latin Authors on Jews and Judaism*, 3 vol. Jerusalem: Israel Academy of Sciences and Humanities, 1974–1984.

Tcherikover, V. *Hellenistic Civilization and the Jews*, Translated from the Hebrew by S. Appelbaum. Philadelphia: Jewish Publication Society of America, 1959.

Tcherikover, V., A. Fuks, and M. Stern, editors. *Corpus Papyrorum Judaicarum*, 3 vol. Cambridge, MA: Harvard University Press, 1957–64.

Vermes, G., ed. and trans. *The Dead Sea Scrolls in English*, 2nd Edition. Baltimore, MD: Penguin Books, 1975.

————. *The Dead Sea Scrolls: Qumran in Perspective*. London: Collins, 1977.

Wolfson, H. A. *Philo: Foundations of Religious Philosophy in Judaism, Christianity, and Islam*, 2 vol. Cambridge, MA: Harvard University Press, 1947.

Yadin, Yigael. *Masada: Herod's Fortress and the Zealots' Last Stand*, New York: Random House, 1966.

Zeitlin, Solomon. *The Dead Sea Scrolls and Modern Scholarship*, Philadelphia: Dropsie College, 1956.

————. *The Rise and Fall of the Judean State*, vol. 1: 332–37 BCE. vol. 2: 37 BCE–66 CE. vol. 3: 66 CE–120 CE. Philadelphia: Jewish Publication Society of America, 1962–1978.

Rabbinic Judaism

Alon, G. *The Jews in Their Land in the Talmudic Age*. Cambridge, MA: Harvard University Press, 1989.

Avi-Yonah, M. *The Jews of Palestine: A Political History from the Bar Kokhba War to the Arab Conquest*. Jerusalem: Magnes Press, 1984.

Babylonian Talmud, 35 vol. ed. I. Epstein. London: Soncino Press, 1935–48.

Baron, S. W. *A Social and Religious History of the Jews*, vols. 2–5. New York: Columbia University Press, 1952.

Cohen, B. *Jewish and Roman Law*, 2 Volumes. New York: United Synagogue Books, 1966.

Finkelstein, L. *Akiba: Scholar, Saint, and Martyr*. Cleveland, OH: William Collins & World Publishing, 1962.

Ginzberg, L. *On Jewish Law and Lore*. New York: Meridian Books, 1962.

———. *The Legends of the Jews*, 7 vol. Philadelphia: Jewish Publication Society of America, 1909–1938.

Guttmann, A. *Rabbinic Judaism in the Making: The Halakhah from Ezra to Judah I*. Detroit: Wayne State University Press, 1970.

Halivni, D. Weiss. *Midrash, Mishnah and Gemara*. Cambridge, MA: Harvard University, 1986.

Herford, R. T. *Christianity in Talmud and Midrash, 1903*. Originally published by Loudon, Williams & Norgate, 1903. Republished by Ktav Publishing House, New York, 1975.

Levine, L. *The Rabbinic Class of Roman Palestine in Late Antiquity*. Jerusalem: Yad Ben Zvi Press, 1989.

———. *The Synagogue in Late Antiquity*. Philadelphia: The American Schools of Oriental Research, 1987.

Lieberman, S. *Greek in Jewish Palestine*. New York: Feldheim, 1956.

———. *Hellenism in Jewish Palestine*. New York: Ktav, 1962.

Maimonides, M. *Moreh Nevuchim (Guide to the Perplexed)*. Translated by M. Friedlander, Hebrew Publishing Company, New York, 1904.

Mechilta on Exodus (translation). ed. J. Neusner. Atlanta: Scholars Press, 1988.

Midrash Rabbah, translated into English with Notes, Glossary and Indices, 10 vol. ed. by H. Freedman and M. Simon. London: Soncino Press, 1939. *The Mishnah*, ed. and trans. by H. Danby. Oxford, UK: Clarendon, 1933.

Neusner, J. *Development of a Legend: Studies on the Traditions Concerning Yohanan ben Zakkai*. Leiden: Brill, 1970.

———. *Early Rabbinic Judaism: Historical Studies in Religion, Literature, and Art* (Studies in Judaism in Late Antiquity, XIII). Leiden: Brill, 1975.

———. *First-Century Judaism in Crisis: Yohanan ben Zakkai and the Renaissance of Torah*. Nashville, TN: Abingdon Press, 1975.

———. *From Politics to Piety: The Emergence of Pharisaic Judaism*. Englewood Cliffs, NJ: Prentice Hall, 1973.

———. *In Search of Talmudic Biography*. Chico, CA: Scholars Press, 1984.

———. *Invitation to the Talmud: A Teaching Book*. New York: Harper and Row, 1973.

———. *A Life of Yohanan ben Zakkai*. Leiden: Brill, 1962.

———. *Talmudic Judaism in Sassanian Babylonia: Essays and Studies*, (Studies in Judaism in Late Antiquity, XIV). Leiden: Brill, 1976.

———. *There We Sat Down: Talmudic Judaism in the Making*. Nashville, TN: Abingdon Press, 1972.

———. *Understanding Seeking Faith*. Vol. 2. Atlanta: Scholars Press, 1987.

———. "Miqvaot of the Second Temple Period at Jericho." *Qadmoniot* 11 (1978): 54–59 [Hebrew].

Netzer, E. "The Winter Palaces of the Hasmonean Kings and of the Herodian Dynasty at Jericho." *Qadmoniot* 7 (1974): 27–36 [Hebrew].

———. "The Winter Palaces of the Judean Kings at Jericho at the End of the Second Temple Period." *BASOR* 228 (1977): 1–13.

Rivkin, E. *A Hidden Revolution: The Pharisees' Search for the Kingdom Within*. Nashville, TN: Abingdon Press, 1978.

Safrai, S. "The Era of the Mishna and the Talmud (70–640)." In *In A History of the Jewish People,* edited H. Ben-Sasson, 307–382. London: Weidenfeld and Nicolson,1976.

Sifra on Leviticus (translation). Edited by J. Neusner. Atlanta: Scholars Press, 1988.

Sifrei on Deuteronomy (translation). Edited by J. Neusner. Atlanta: Scholars Press, 1987.

Sifrei on Numbers (translation). Edited by J. Neusner. Altanta: Scholars Press, 1986.

Strack, H. L. *Introduction to the Talmud and Midrash*, trans. from the 5th German Edition. Philadelphia: Jewish Publication Society of America, 1931.

Swidler, L. *Women in Judaism: The Status of Women in Formative Judaism*. Metuchen, NJ: Scarecrow Press, 1976.

Talmud, Palestine. *The Talmud of the Land of Israel*, ed. J. Neusner, 35 vol. projected. Chicago: University of Chicago, 1982.

Tosefta. *The Tosefta Translated From the Hebrew*, ed. J. Neusner, 5 vol. New York: Ktav, 1977–80.

Tosefta and Tosefta Ki-fshutah [Hebrew] 13 vol. critical edition ed. S. Lieberman. New York: Jewish Theological Seminary, 1955–1973.

Urbach, E. E. *The Sages: Their Concepts and Beliefs*, 2 Vol. trans. from the Hebrew by Israel Abrahams. Jerusalem: Magnes Press, 1975.

Urman, D. "The House of Assembly and the House of Study: Are They One and the Same." *Journal of Jewish Studies* 44, no. 2 (1993): 257.

White, L. *Building God's House in the Roman World*. Balitimore: J. Hopkins University Press, 1990.

Early Christianity and Post-Biblical Judaism

Brandon, S. G. F. *Jesus and the Zealots: A Study of the Political Factor in Primitive Christianity.* New York: Charles Scribner's Sons, 1967.

Charlesworth, J. H. *Jesus and the Dead Sea Scroll*. Anchor Bible Reference Library, New York: Doubleday, 1992.

———. "Reinterpreting John. How the Dead Sea Scrolls Revolutionized Our Understanding of the Gospel of John." *Biblical Research,* Chicago 9 (1993): 19–25, 54.

Frend, W. H. C. *The Rise of Christianity.* London: Darton, Longman and Todd, 1984.

Sanders, E. P. *Paul and Palestinian Judaism: A Comparison of Patterns of Religion,* Philadelphia: Fortress Press, 1977.

Sandmel, S. *A Jewish Understanding of the New Testament.* New York: Ktav, 1974.

———. *We Jews and Jesus.* New York: Oxford University Press, 1965.

Stendahl, K. *Paul Among Jews and Gentiles.* Philadelphia: Fortress Press, 1976.

Vermes, G. *Jesus the Jew: A Historian's Reading of the Gospels.* London: Collins, 1973.

Index

Aaron, 12, 21, 23, 58–59; Moses and, 55, 61–65; River Nile to blood and, 66; staff of, 61

Aaronid priesthood, 9, 121; cemetery and, 268; leadership of, 13; on Moses, 60; P writers on, 61; in Tabernacle, 61–62

Abel, 11, 12, 57

Abraham (Abram), 12, 23, 70, 142; collapsed traditions of, 18, 21; Isaac story and, 19–20; land of departure of, 16

Abram. *See* Abraham

Absalom, 109, 110, 116

"accidental tourist" object, 30–31

Acre excavation site, 248

Acts of the Apostles, 207

Adoni-Tzedek (king), 132–33

Aegyptiaca (Hecataeus), 82

Aelius Hadrianus, Jerusalem as, 140

Against Apion (Josephus), 83–84

Against Helvidius (Jerome), 162

Agrippa I (king), 202, 205

Agrippa II (king), 206

Ahab (king), 187–88

Ahaziah (king), 117

Ai, city of, 88, 132

Akhenaton (pharaoh), 97, 99

Al Aqsa Mosque, 125

Alexander the Great, 62, 124, 172–73

American Palestine Exploration Society, 128

Amoraic-Geonic period, 243–44

Anati, Emmanuel, 49–50, 93–94

Ancient History of the Jews (Antiquities) (Josephus), 83, 85, 165, 170–72, 195, 206, 249

Ancient Israel in Sinai: The Evidence for the Authenticity of the Wilderness Tradition (Hoffmeier), 99

"Ancient Refuge in the Holy Land" (NOVA), 184, 327

Angel of the Lord, 20

angels, 12; J writer and, 20

Antiochus Epiphanes (king), 45, 119, 124

Antiochus III, 204

Antiquities. See Ancient History of the Jews

Antiquities Authority of Israel. *See* Israel Antiquities Authority

Apocrypha, 44, 307

The Apostle (Asch), 167

Al Aqsa Mosque, 139–40, 143

Arav, Rami, 149

Archaeological Researches in Palestine, 1873-1874 (Clermont-Ganneau), 129

archaeology, roles of: background, 39–41; direct correlation, 41–46; illumination, 38–39

Aristobulus (king), 204, 282

"Ark in the Land of the Philistines" mural, 239–40

Ark of Covenant, 117, 226, 262

artifacts: biological science analysis of, 31; carbon-14 dating for analysis of, 31, 274, 279; CT scan for analysis of, 30–31; monumental from Exodus, 79–87; religious text truths and, 24; Temple of Solomon pomegranate, 29; women's household, 185

Artzy, Michal, 298

Asch, Scholom, 167

"The Assumption of Moses," 45

Assyria: defeat of, 41–42; as Iraq, 10; Sennacherib of, 41–42

Assyrian Conquest, 31

Assyrian Empire, Northern Kingdom destruction by, 10

Assyrian Exile, of Ten Tribes of Israel, 10–11

Augusta Caesar, 195–96, 199, 200, 205, 249

Avdat, bathhouse at, 306

Babatha, 189; at Cave of Letters, 184, 208–14; documents of, 208, 212–13; husbands of, 211; life of, 210–14; property of, 211–12

Babylon, 138, 269

Babylonian Exile, 12, 13, 62, 101, 124, 137, 187, 228

Babylonian Talmud (BT), 64, 154, 165, 180, 215–16, 314; on bathhouse, 303, 306; Beruriah in, 216–17, 219–22; on cemetery building, 270–71; collapsing in, 220–21; five disciples in, 177–78; on incense burning, 237; Jesus in,

173–74, 176, 182; virgin birth in, 317

Barak, 79, 193

Bar Kokhba coins, 323, 329–30; Kindler on, 332–33

Bar Kokhba Revolt, 72, 122, 140–41, 151, 202, 213, 214, 226, 278; Maximalist-Minimalist controversy and, 329–31; Roman Empire and, 330; Yavne and, 249–50. See also Cave of Letters, Second Revolt against Rome (132-135 CE)

Bar Kokhba, Simon, 33–34, 41, 72, 173, 209, 326; letters of, 328–29; as Son of the Star, 327–29

Bar Yohai, Shimon (rabbi), 44, 152

bathhouse: at Avdat, 306; Babylonian Talmud on, 303, 306; Beth Shean, 305, 316; Beth Zur, 303; Hammat Gader, 304; Hammat-Tiberias, 305; in Hasmonean period, 308; in Hellenistic period, 306; of Herod the Great, 305; in Maccabean period, 308; at Mary's Well, 300–301; Mikveh on ritual bathing in, 306–11; in Negev, 305; in Ptolemian/Selucid Greek periods, 308; return to, 309–11; Roman, 316–20; in Roman period, 302–6

Bathsheba, 113, 116, 191

Bauman, Paul, 48, 145, 251, 266

Beer Sheva, 100, 138

Ben Ezra Synagogue, 284

Beni Hassan tomb paintings, 77

Ben Sira, 317–18

Berenice, 189, 202–8, 249; coin of, 205; Josephus on, 206; as judge, 207; as King Agrippa I's daughter, 202; on synagogue, 229; Titus and, 207–8

Beruriah, 189; in Babylonian Talmud, 216–17, 219–22; Hananiyah and, 214–23

Bet David. See House of David inscription

Bethlehem, 32, 112, 121, 126

Bethsaida: anchor cross at, *164;* climate/terrain of, 110; Cross of, *162,* 162–63; excavations at, 39–40, 49, 108, 129, 248–50; geographical presentation on, 40–41; Greco-Roman period, 108; incense shovel from, *225,* 233–36, *235,* 240, 242; in Iron Age, 108; Josephus on, 194; Key of Peter at, *147,* 148–50, 163; Livia Julia statuette from, *183;* pilgrimage and, 150; renaming of, 195–201. *See also* Bethsaida Excavations Project

Bethsaida, A City by the North Shore of the Sea of Galilee (Freund), 163

Bethsaida Excavations Project, 130, 189, 198–99, 231

Beth Shean: bathhouse, 305, 316; mosaic, 242; Roman bath at, 316

Beth Zur bathhouse, 303

Bible. *See* Hebrew Bible

Bible Commentary of the Anchor Bible Series (Speiser), 17

Biblical Writing: Fifth/Final Period of, 13; First Period of, 8; Fourth Period of, 12–13; Second Period of, 8–10; Third Period of, 10–12

biological sciences, artifact analysis by, 31

Bloom, Harold, 186

Bomberg, Daniel, 174

bone box tradition, Jesus and, 158–59

"Bones of Contention," 272–73

The Book of J (Rosenberg/Bloom), 186

Book of Splendor. *See Zohar*

Bronze Age, 39, 45, 49, 76–77; camels, lack of, in, 77; donkeys as transports in, 77–78, 104; Exodus from Egypt and, 54; infant burial devices in, 58;

Mount Karkom in, 95; slave camps in, 88

BT. *See* Babylonian Talmud

Bulletin of the American Schools of Oriental Research (Small), 308

Byzantine monks: Mount Sinai and, 101; Noah's ark and, 26; oral traditions of, 90

Byzantine period, 62, 151, 203, 301; incense burners in, 242; literary texts of, 72, 171; Mount Karkom at, 95

Byzantine Period Synagogue, *Teacher of Righteousness* evidence in, 291–92

Caesarea excavation site, 248

Cain, 11, 12, 57

Cairo Museum, 69; bulrush basket in, 39, 58; Tempest/Israel Stele at, 80–82

Cairo Synagogue Geniza, 285

camels, 77, 93, 104

carbon-14 dating, for artifact analysis, 31, 274, 279

Cave of Letters, 30, 72, 326; Babatha and, 184, 208–14; Bar Kokhba and, 34; documents, 328; excavation of, 184, 209, 248, 251; incense shovels in, 234, *235,* 240; Maximalist-Minimalist debate on, 330–31. *See also* John and Carol Merrill Cave of Letters Project

censorship, 174, 179–80

chemistry, artifact analysis by, 31

Christianity: relics/relic sites and, 27; religion of, 22; traditions within, 32

Christianity in Talmud and Midrash (Herford), 169

Christian literature: Mary's Well in, 311–14; *Teacher of Righteousness in,* 290–91

Christians: Abraham/Isaac story of, 19–20; David's Tomb pilgrimage

by, 121; Exodus and, 51; incense ritual of, 233, 243; Jerusalem as pilgrimage site by, 125; Jesus/Mary physical manifestation and, 14; Jesus view by, 167, 179–80
1 Chronicles, 115–16
2 Chronicles, 42, 100, 118, 137
Church of the Holy Sepulchre, in Jerusalem, 125, 130, 139, 159–60
City of David, 111, 144
Clement, of Alexandria, 83, 282
Clermont-Ganneau, Charles, 129, 258
Commentary on Habbakuk (Pesher Habbakuk), 284, 286
Commentary on Micah (Pesher Micah), 284
Commentary on Psalms (Psalms Pesher), 284, 286
"Consecration of the Tabernacle and its Priests" mural, 240
Constantine the Great, 125, 173
Copper Scroll, 251–52
Cotton, Hannah, 184, 189, 208
Crimean War, 127, 131
cross, symbol of, anchor, 164; of Bethsaida, 162, 162–63
CT scan, for artifact analysis, 30–31

Damascus, 109, 140
Damascus Document, on Teacher of Righteousness, 285, 289
Darawsha, Maha, 49, 297–98
Darwin, Charles, 59
David (king), 23, 36, 108, 142, 144, 226; adultery and, 115; background of, 112–13; Geshurite connection with, 109; Goliath victory by, 115; Jerusalem burial site of, 119, 121; Josephus on burial of, 119, 122; Maachah and, 109, 194; palace of, 111; peace treaties and, 109; Psalms, 44; relic tomb of, 118–23; of United Kingdom of Israel, 8, 112

Day of Atonement. See Yom Kippur
Dead Sea, 36, 133, 209; Lynch's map of, 126–27; refuge caves at, 213; sects on Teacher, 288; surveying of, 127
Dead Sea Scrolls, 1, 72, 167, 250–52, 264, 269, 326, 328; as "accidental tourist" object, 30; carbon 14 dating of, 279; Cave 4 and, 278; chronology of discoveries of, 278; discovery/provenance of, 278–81, 281; of Hebrew Bible manuscripts, 279; hygiene/purity issues and, 258–59; Qumran and, 275–81. See also Copper Scroll; "Project Scrolls"; Temple Scroll; War Scroll
The Dead Sea Scrolls: Fifty Years After Their Discovery (Schiffman/Tov/VanderKam), 259
Deborah (judge), 79, 188, 192–93
Deuteronomistic Tradition: on Exodus from Egypt, 100–102; Mount Horeb as Mount Sinai in, 100
Deuteronomy, 6, 30, 109, 115, 134, 178, 260, 278; D writing and, 12–13; Exodus from Egypt in, 54, 100–102; forgery of, 30; Moses as prophet in, 59–60; Mount Horeb in, 91, 100
Development of a Legend: Studies on the Traditions Concerning Yohana ben Zakkai (Neusner), 156
Dever, William, 15, 86, 187, 309
Diaspora, 22, 124, 152, 155, 205, 226, 244, 329
Did God Have A Wife? (Dever), 187
Documentary hypothesis, 134; Moses and, 59–60; as scientific theory for Bible reading, 59–60; on traditions, 62
The Documents from the Bar Kokhba Period in the Cave of Letters (Yadin/Greenfield/Yardeni/Levine), 208
Dome of Rock, 127, 139–40, 141

Dura-Europos synagogue, 239, 240
D writing, 12–13

E, as Northern Kingdom writer,
10–11; on Exodus, from Egypt, 66,
103–4; Isaac sacrifice by, 19
Ecclesiastes, 44
Egypt, 14, 33, 39; Hebrew enslavement
and, 55–56, 96–98; Highway of
Horus exit route and, 98; history
editing by, 96–98; Hyksos Exodus
from, 85; Manetho on Israelites in,
55; synagogues in, 226
Egypt (Roberts), 129
Egypt: plagues in, 25, 55, 81
Ein Gedi, 36, 210–11, 253
El Borg excavation site, 99
Elijah, Mount Horeb and, 100
Elohim, 10, 12, 19
End of Days, Qumran and, 256
Enlightenment, 24–25, 33
Eshel, Hanan, 213, 254, 332
Essenes: Latrines of, 258–65; at
Qumran, 275–76, 308
Esther, 13, 279
Eusebius, 162, 300
excavation site: Acre, 248; Berenice
Hill, 202–3; at Bethsaida, 39–40,
49, 108, 129–30, 189, 198–99, 231,
248–50; Caesarea, 248; at Cave
of Letters, 184, 209, 248, 251; at
City of David, 144; El Borg, 99;
exploration of, 337–40; at Jericho,
248; at Jerusalem, 111, 246; Jezreel,
187–88; at Masada, 34; Megiddo,
248; Qumran, 248–50, 278, 284–88;
of Qumran Cemetery, 251–53,
256–57; Yavne, 249
Exodus, 2, 25, 43, 51, 54, 57, 60, 67,
69–70, 81–82, 84, 95, 98, 101, 135,
191–92, 262, 314; Aaron at center
of, 61; illumination and, 39; Mount
Horeb in, 100; P writing on, 66,
103; Redactor account in, 86–87;
scientific reading of, 62
Exodus, from Egypt, 9; Anati's
background theory of, 94–96;
background of, 53; Bronze Age
and, 54; direction of, 66–67, 88, 91,
99–100, 103; in Exodus/Numbers/
Deuteronomy, 54, 100–102; as
foundational epic, 74; J/E accounts
of, 66, 103–4; Josephus on, 54–55,
84–85; literary argument for,
71; mistakes on, 68–100; mixed
multitude in, 55, 103; monumental
artifacts of, 79–87; Mount Sinai/
Passover and, 48; P writer on, 66,
78, 85, 103; questions about, 51–52;
Rameses II and, 68–73, 81; Redactor
account of, 54, 86, 103; refugee
numbers in, 53, 78–79, 89; scientific
method and, 70–73; story of, 54–56;
three time periods for, 67–68, 91,
102–3; time period of, 53, 89. *See
also* Hyksos Exodus
Exodus: The Egyptian Evidence (Dever),
86
Ezekiel, synagogues in, 228
Ezra the Priest (Scribe), 13, 284

Fifth/Final Period of Biblical Writing:
536-519 BCE - Fifth Century
BCE, 13
The Fifth Gospel (Pixner), 148, 153
First Revolt against Rome (66-73 CE),
7, 34–35, 150, 206, *207,* 217, 230,
249, 303, 327
forgeries, 29–35; of coins, 31;
Deuteronomy and, 30; in
inscriptions, 29; "James" ossuary
box as, 29; pomegranate artifact
in Temple of Solomon as, 29; of
Temple Mount Al Aqsa Mosque, 29
Fourth Period of Biblical Writing: 640
BCE-586 BCE, 12–13

Freund, Richard A., 163, 208
Friedman, Richard E., 6, 8
Frith, Francis, 130–31
From the Ground Down (Ussishkin), 187
Fundamentalist Maximalists, 14

Gabriel, 141–42, 311
Galilee, 148; importance of, 150–52;
    Miriam's Well at, 315–16; Rabbinic
    life in, 150–51
Gamla, synagogue at, 230
ben Gamliel, Shimon (rabbi), 152,
    237–38, 249, 288
Gaon, Saadiah (rabbi), 244–45
Gaza Strip, Samson's burial site in,
    27–28
Geiger, Abraham, 166, 233
Genesis, 6, 19–21, 69, 75, 78, 103, 137,
    138–39, 190–91, 238, 278; Abraham
    image in, 17–18; discrepancies in,
    16; Exodus from Egypt and, 54; on
    Israelites in Egypt, 55; Maachah in,
    109; Noah in, 39
German Society for the Exploration of
    Palestine, 128
Gnostic Gospels, 5, 161, 177–79
Goddesses, Whores, Wives and Slaves:
    Women in Classical Antiquity
    (Pomeroy), 189–90
Golden Calf, 66, 85
Goodenough, Edwin R., 239, 245–46
Gospel According to Nicodemus, 177, 179
Gospel of Philip, 179
Gospel of Pseudo-Matthew, 311
Gospel of Thomas, 178
Gospels: on Jesus, 175, 200. *See also*
    John, Gospel of; Luke, Gospel of;
    Mark, Gospel of; Matthew, Gospel of
Great Schism: 922 BCE-722 BCE, as
    Second Period of Biblical Writing,
    8–10
Greco-Roman period, 44, 83, 108,
    151, 166, 172

Greenfield, J. C., 208

Hadith, 5, 23, 25, 143, 165
Hadrian: Bar Kokhba coins of, 332–33;
    Jerusalem/Judea name change by,
    124, 332
Hammat Gader bathhouse, 304
Hammat-Tiberias bathhouse, 305
Hananiyah (rabbi), 214–17, 218
HaNasi, Yehudah (rabbi), 7–8, 304
Hanukkah, 155, 181, 236
Har Karkom. *See* Mount Karkom
Hasmonean period, bathhouse in, 308
Hazael (king), 36, 117
Hebrew Bible, 5–6, 154, 242, 263, 279;
    anachronisms in, 70; archaeology
    v., 37; Babylonian Rabbinic
    interpretation of, 22; collapsing
    of, 63; critical study of, 6–13;
    David in, 112; discrepancies in,
    16; on Exodus, 51; Isaac sacrifice
    in, 19; J/E combination of,
    11; Jerome translation of, 162;
    Jerusalem in, 135–36; on Mount
    Horeb geographical forces, 101;
    Nazareth absence in, 299; Rabbinic
    interpretation of, 22; on rebellion
    against Moses, 63–64; Redactor of,
    62, 86; ritual bathing in, 259, 306;
    ritual sacrifices in, 11–12; scientific
    study of, 14; Solomon's Temple
    in, 113; synagogue, absence of, in,
    226; *Teacher of Righteousness* in, 291;
    women in, 190–93; Zion in, 136–
    37. *See also* Biblical Writing
Hebrew University of Jerusalem, 132,
    184
Hebron burial tombs, 28, 316
Hecataeus, 82
Hellenistic period, 45, 117, 152, 203,
    240, 281–82, 303; bathhouse in,
    306; incense shovel in, 233, 242;
    Josephus on Exodus in, 96; Qumran

and, 276, 284–88; ritual bathing in, 306
Hellenistic-Roman period, 5
Herford, Robert Travers, 169
Herod (king), 113, 122, 230
Herodium, synagogue at, 230
Herod the Great, 124, 194, 197–98, 202, 204, 210, 249, 305, 324
Hezekiah (king), of Judah, 41–42, 118, 126
Highway of Horus, Egypt exit route of, 98
Hirschfeld, Yizhar, 189, 304; Berenice Hill excavation by, 202–3
historical argument, 71; for Exodus, from Egypt, 76–78
Hoffmeier, James, 99
Holy Bible (Frith), 131
The Holy Land (Roberts), 129
Holy of Holies, 12; Foundation Stone of, 139
Horeb. *See* Mount Horeb
House of David *(Bet David)* inscription, 117–18; Maximalist-Minimalist debate on, 36; Minimalists on, 36, 118
Hyksos Exodus, 53, 83–85, 97–98, 99, 103

IAA. *See* Israel Antiquities Authority
illumination, Moses/Exodus and, 38–39
Imperial Cult of Rome, 196–97, 201, 239, 242
incense: aromatic use of, 232; Bethsaida and, 231; BT on, 237; burning in Iron Age, 232–33; burning ritual, 227; conical burner of, 239–40, 242; Gaon on, 244–45; Jewish ceremonies and use of, 236–40; Midrash on burning of, 238; ritual in synagogue, evidence for, 240–46; Roddy on, 231; shovel

at Bethsaida, *225*, 233–36, *235*, 240, 242
In Search of Talmudic Biography (Neusner), 156
Ipuwer Papyrus, Tempest Stele and, 80–82
Iraq, 10, 143
Irenaeus, 161–62, 242
Iron Age, 45, 54, 76, 91, 93, 111–12, 122, 144, 152, 278; altars in, 226–27; Bethsaida in, 108; incense burning places in, 232–33; woman statuette from, *185*; women in, 186
Iron Age II, Mount Karkom in, 95
Isaac, 12, 19–20, 95
Isaiah, 6, 37, 42, 278
Islam: Abraham/Isaac in, 19; archaeologists and, 25; archaeology and, 25; Jesus and, 165; religion of, 22–23; religious council of, 139
Islamic period, 139
Israel, 14, 33; Joshua conquest of, 32; as Northern Kingdom, 9. *See also* Land of Israel
Israel Antiquities Authority (IAA), 251, 297, 301; on forged inscriptions, 29; "Project Scroll" of, 251
Israel in Egypt: Evidence for the Authenticity of the Exodus Tradition (Hoffmeier), 99
Israeli War of Independence (1948), 131
"Is There Any Archaeological Evidence for the Exodus" (Dever), 86

Jacob (patriarch), 12, 21, 69; collapsed traditions of, 18; in Egypt, 55; heavenly ladder of, 138, 142; Shechem acquisition by, 18–19
Jacob's Well, 319
James, brother of Jesus, 320
James ossuary, 161; inscription as forgery on, 29; Josephus and, 171; Maximalists-Minimalists on, 37–38

J, as Southern Kingdom writer, 10–11, 20; anonymity of women by, 190–92; on Exodus, from Egypt, 66, 103–4; on women, 190–91

Jebel Musa, 90–91

Jehoash (king), 29; inscription, 144

Jehoram (king), of Israel, 36, 117

Jehosaphat (king), of Judah, 36

Jephthah (judge), 102, 193

Jeremiah, 6, 100

Jericho: excavations at, 248; Kenyon on, 88; as relic site, 31–32

Jerome, 312; Hebrew Bible translation by, 162; on Nazareth, 300

Jerusalem, 9, 11, 32, 108; ancient history/archaeology of, 126–33; Antiochus Epiphanes conquest of, 45; climate/terrain of, 110; Davidic refounding of, 132; David's tomb outside of, 119, 121; destruction of, 13, 34; excavation of, 111, 246; Hadrian renaming of, 124, 332; history of, 123–26; Jesus' bone boxes in, 158–59; Jewish names for, 133–37; Josiah rule of, 12; Mandelbaum Gate in, 125, 132; Muslim names of, 140–43; Nebuchadnezzar conquest of, 45; photographers/illustrators of, 129–30; as pilgrimage site, 95, 125; politics, 143–45; scientific mapping of, 126; Sennacherib water tunnel in, 41; Torah and, 134; underground tunnels of, 145; UN/WWI/WWII and, 125; Wilson/Warren on, 127; Zion as, 136–37, 290. *See also* Church of the Holy Sepulchre; Peace Treaty of Jerusalem; Temple of Jerusalem

Jerusalem Day, 123–24, 142

Jerusalem Mosque, 140

Jesus, 3, 23, 32, 127, 142, 160, 167; at Bethsaida, 157; Bethsaida renaming and, 200; bone boxes of, 158–59; in BT, 173–74, 176, 182; Christian view of, 167, 179–80; crucifixion of, 21; David as ancestor of, 112; in Galilee, 148; Gospels on, 175, 200; healing of blind man by, 75, 200; inscription of, 157; Isaac's sacrifice and, 20; James ossuary and, 37–38; Jews view of, 167; Josephus on, 165–66, 181–82; ministry timing of, 197–201; Mishnah/Tosefta absence of, 181; name of, 157–58; *Pantera* story and, 176–77; in PT, absence of, 175, 181, 182; of Rabbinic literature, 165, 167, 174–77, 180; resurrection of, 169, 170; Sermon on the Mount of, 119; in Tannaitic literature, absence of, 170, 174–77, 181; as teacher, 288; transfiguration of, 101; virgin birth of, 317; walking on water story of, 40–41, 201.

Jewish Queens, 204; Berenice as, 202–3

Jewish Symbols (Goodenough), 239

The Jewish War (Josephus), 34

Jews: dispersion of, 7, 22; God's lack of physical manifestation and, 24; incense ceremonies of, 236–40; Jerusalem as pilgrimage site for, 125; Jerusalem names by, 133–37; Jesus view by, 167; Josephus writings on, 170; relic sites and, 120

Jezebel (queen), 187–88

Jezreel excavations, of Jezebel, 187–88

Job, 283, 317

John and Carol Merrill Cave of Letters Project, 251

John and Carol Merrill Excavations at Qumran, 284–88

John, Gospel of, 7, 20, 62–63, 75, 200, 288, 319

John Paul II (pope), 298; Key of Peter and, 148–49

John the Baptist, 4, 28, 127, 142, 198, 275, 277, 284

Jol, Harry, 48, 145, 251

Joseph, father of Jesus, 158–59, 191

Joseph the Patriarch, 16, 69, 142; burial tomb of, 27–29; Muslim veneration of, 28

Josephus, Flavius, 5, 34, 85, 155, 170–72, 195, 206, 226, 249, 283; on Alexander the Great, 172–73; on Bethsaida, 194; on David/Solomon burial, 119, 122; on Exodus from Egypt, 54–55, 84–85; on hygiene, 264–65; on Jesus, 165–66, 181–82; Nazareth absence by, 172, 299

Joshua, 9, 14, 16, 28, 100, 101, 132, 133; Assyrian Conquest/Babylonian Conquest and, 31; Land of Israel conquest by, 32

Josiah (king), 115; Deuteronomistic Tradition and, 100; rule of, 12

Judah: Hezekiah of, 41–42, 118, 126; Jehosaphat of, 36; as Southern Kingdom, 9

Judaism: Abraham/Isaac story in, 19; relic sites and, 72, 120; religion of, 22; traditions within, 32

Judas Gospel, 3, 174–75

Judea, 7, 19

Judges, 13–14, 78–79, 100–102, 133, 192–94

Judith, 45

Julius Caesar, 195

Karaites, temple rituals of, 244–45

Karo, Joseph (rabbi), 151

Kenyon, Kathleen, 32, 88

Key of Peter, *147,* 148–50, 163

Khirbet Qumran, 258, 267, 278

Kibbutz Ginosar, 50, 149

Kindler, Arieh, 332–33

1 Kings, 100–101, 116, 136

2 Kings, 36–37, 41–42, 100, 101

Klauzner, Joseph, 167

Koran, 5, 23, 25, 121; on Exodus, 51–52; Hebrew Bible *v.,* 23; Jesus in, 165; Joseph the Patriarch in, 28

Kufa Mosque, 143

Land of Israel, 73, 81, 114, 180–81, 226; Ai/Jericho in, 88; Israelites in, 54

Last Supper of the Apostles, 121

"Late Hellenistic Baths in Palestine" (Small), 308

Latrines of Essenes, 258–65

Law of Mount Sinai, 51, 53, 100

Levine, Baruch, 208

Leviticus, 232, 236

A Life of Yohanan ben Zakkai (Neusner), 156

Livia Julia, 189, 194–201, 249; as Augusta Caesar's wife, 196; coin of, 197–99; deification of, 198–99; as Julius Caesar's daughter, 195; scribal error on, 195–96; statuette, from Bethsaida, *183*

Livia Julia Temple, 146

Louvre Museum: Mesha/Moabite Stele at, 129; Moabite Stone in, 36

Luke, Gospel of, 7, 62–63, 159, 169, 179, 200, 288

Lynch, William F., 126–27

Maachah, 109, 194

Maccabean period, 155, 181; bathhouses in, 308; families in, 152

Maccabean revolt, 124

I Maccabees, 309

II Maccabees, 282

Magdalene, Mary, 3, 158

Magness, Jodie, 259

Maimonides, 161, 237

ben Maimon, Moses. *See* Maimonides

Manasseh, 28, 79

Mandelbaum Gate, in Jerusalem, 125, 132

Manetho: collapsing of Jewish history by, 84; on Exodus, from Egypt, 83, 85; on Israelites in Egypt, 55

Manual of Discipline, 285, 287

Mark, Gospel of, 7, 40, 62–63, 75, 169, 200, 288

Martyrology, as collapsed version of Rabbinic martyrdom, 64–65

Mary (Asch), 167

Mary, mother of Jesus, 5, 23, 319–20; annunciation of, 311–12; apparitions of, 320; Jesus' birth announcement to, 311

Mary's House, in Loreto, Italy, relic site of, 296

Mary's Well, *295*, 297–302, 311–16, *321*; bathhouse at, 300–301; healing powers of, 315, 320; Minimalists on, 302; Ottoman period and, 301–2; pilgrimages to, 298

Masada, 34, 41, 306, 309; Ben Sira, 318; excavation of, 34; Roman bath and, 316; synagogue at, 230

Masada (Yadin), 229

Matriarchs, 19, 188

Matthew, Gospel of, 7, 41, 62–63, 148, 159, 169, 179, 288, 327

Maximalist-Minimalist debate, 13–15; Bar Kokhba Revolt and, 329–31; on Cave of Letters, 330–31; on House of David, 36; on Moabite Stone, 37

Maximalists, 35, 324, 326; on House of David, 36; on James ossuary, 37–38; Yadin as, 330. *See also* Fundamentalist Maximalists; Non-Fundamentalist Maximalists

McNamer, Elizabeth, 189, 199

Mecca, 25; Kaaba in, 141; Mosque, 140; as Muslim pilgrimage site, 125

Medina, 25, 300; Mosque, 140; as Muslim pilgrimage site, 125

Megiddo excavation site, 248

Meir (rabbi), 120, 216–17, 222, 304, 316

Merneptah Stele, 80, 88

Merrill, Carol, 251, 253, 284–88

Merrill, John, 251, 253, 254, 284–88

Mesha/Moabite Stele, 129

Mesopotamia, 33, 39, 70

The Messiah, Bar Kokhba and, 33–34

Middle Ages, 62, 112; Shabbat in, 236–37; virgin birth in, 319

Middle Bronze Age, 102, 311; Exodus, from Egypt and, 88; Mount Karkom at, 93, 95

Middle East, 53, 72, 98, 126; camel domestication in, 77; Gnostic traditions of, 179

Midrash, 5, 21, 136, 191, 314; on incense burning, 238; on Psalms, 289–90; on Samson, 27–28

Midrashim, 180; Halakhic, 175; Mose's name in, 58

Migdal, synagogue at, 230

Migdol, 103; tower fortress of, 92

Mikveh, bathhouse ritual bathing in, 306–11

Minimalists, 14, 34–36, 118, 324–26; on James ossuary, 37–38; on Mary's Well, 302

Miriam, 186, 192

Miriam's Well, 314–16; healing powers of, 315, 320; miracle of, 315

Mishnah, 5, 7–8, 120, 215, 222, 288; on graves, 268; Jesus, absence of, in, 181; redaction of, 181; Seventh Order of, 152–53; Six Orders of, 153

MiYeshu ad Paulus (Klauzner), 167

Moabite Stone, 36

monumental artifactual argument, 73; Israel Stele as, 80–81; Tempest Stele as, 80–82

Moreh HaTzedeq. See Teacher of Righteousness

Moreh Nevuchim (Guide to the Perplexed) (Maimonides), 237

Moses, 16, 21, 23, 191–92; Aaron and, 55, 61–65; bulrush basket of, 39, 55, 58; burning bush and, 61, 65, 192; disfigurement of, 60; Documentary Hypothesis and, 59–60; Hebrew Bible on rebellion against, 63–64; illumination and, 39; in Midrashim, 58; Mount Sinai and, 65; name meaning of, 57, 58; as prophet, 58–59; Redactor on, 65–67; River Nile to blood and, 66; search for historical, 56–57; staff of, 61; twelve spies and, 114

Mosque: Al Aqsa, 125, 139–40, 143; Dome of Rock, 140; at Jebel Musa, 90; Jerusalem/Mecca/Medina, 140; Kufa, 143; of Omar, 125; Temple Mount Al Aksa, 29

Mosque of Omar, 125

The Mountain of God: Har Karkom (Anati), 49

Mount Ararat, Noah's ark and, 26

Mount Berenice, anchor church at, 202–3

Mount Catherine, 91

Mount Horeb, 91, 100–101

Mount Karkom: abandonment of, 93–95; altars/cult sites at, 93; Anati's archaeological site of, 49–50, 93–94; biblical descriptions of, 96; J/E writer on, 94

Mount Moriah, Isaac near sacrifice at, 95

Mount of Olives, 129, 268

Mount of the Beatitudes, 119

Mount Scopus, 125, 129

Mount Sinai, 47; Byzantine monks and, 101; distance from Egypt, 92; location of, 89–92; Moses and, 65; Mount Karkom location of, 92–94; Negev location of, 48, 92; Passover and, 48; P writer account of, 91; Saint Catherine's Monastery at,

89–90; tradition site of, 89–90. *See also* Law of Mount Sinai

Mount Tabor, 188

Mount Vesuvius, volcanic eruption of, 82, 85

Mount Zion, 111, 121, 137, 139

Muhammad, 141–42

Muslims, 33, 121; Exodus and, 51–52; Jerusalem as pilgrimage site by, 125; Jerusalem names by, 140–43; Joseph the Patriarch veneration by, 28; physical manifestation and, 24

Nablus, Joseph's tomb in, 27–28

Nag Hammadi, 3, 167, 174–75, 177

Native American Graves Protection and Repatriation Act (1990), 256–57

The Nazarene (Asch), 167

Nazareth, 32, 296–97; Josephus, absence of, 172, 299

Nebuchadnezzar (king), 289; Jerusalem conquest by, 45

Negev, 99, 103–5; bathhouse in, 305; Mount Sinai at, 48, 92

Nehemiah, 118, 279

Neusner, Jacob, 155, 156, 307

New Archaeology, of 1960/1970s, 14–15

New Testament, 90, 154, 209, 283; oral traditions and, 20; Philo and, 173; *Teacher of Righteousness* in, 290–91; well in, 319

The New Testament (Greek/Christian Bible), 5

New York Times, 144, 324

Nile River. *See* River Nile

Noah, 11, 12, 39

Noah's Ark, 26, 142; relic site of, 296–97

Non-Fundamentalist Maximalists, 14

Northern Kingdom: Assyrian Empire destruction of, 10; Israel as, 9; Shechem as capitol of, 18; tribes of, 7, 10, 133, 152. *See also* E, as Northern Kingdom writer

NOVA, 184, 327

Numbers, 54, 61, 63, 78, 86, 114, 192, 262

numismatics: coin evaluation by, 31; Jesus and, 32

Obadas III, 305

Old Testament, of Christians, 5

Onias III, 284, 287

oral traditions, 153; collapsing of, 19–20; documentary hypothesis and, 59–60

Origin of the Species (Darwin), 59

Oslo Accords, Qumran and, 250–51

ossuary, of Jesus, 160

Ottoman Empire, 33, 131

Ottoman period, Mary's Well and, 301–2

paleography, inscription/manuscript analysis by, 31

Palestine, 128, 131, 141

Palestine Exploration Fund (P.E.F.), 128

Palestinian Talmud (PT), 64, 154, 174–77, 314, 328; on incense burning, 238–39; Jesus, absence of, in, 175, 181, 182

Pantera, Julius Abdes, 177

Pantera story, Jesus and, 176–77

Papyrus Anastasi V, 99–100

parallel writing, Gospels as, 62–63

P, as Priestly writer: anonymity of women by, 192; J/E writers *v.,* 11–12; on ritual sacrifices, 11–12; YHVH and, 12

Passover, 51; Mount Sinai and, 48; Seder, 49–50, 121, 123

Patriarch, 11, 23, 75; Jacob, 12, 18–19, 21, 55, 69, 138, 142; Joseph, 16, 27–29, 69, 142; Sophronius, 139–40

Patriarchal period, 66

Peace Treaty of Jerusalem, 127

P.E.F. *See* Palestine Exploration Fund

Pentateuch, 9, 136

period: Amoraic-Geonic, 243–44; Byzantine, 62, 72, 95, 151, 171, 203, 242, 301; Greco-Roman, 44, 83, 108, 151, 166, 172; Hasmonean, 308; Hellenistic, 45, 96, 117, 152, 203, 233, 240, 242, 276, 281–82, 284–88, 303, 306; Hellenistic-Roman, 5; Islamic, 139; Maccabean, 152, 155, 181, 308; Ottoman, 301–2; Patriarchal, 66; Persian, 6, 54, 90, 91, 117, 118; Persian-Hellenistic, 15; Pseudo-Philo, 193; Ptolemian/ Selucid Greek, 308; Roman, 240, 262–63, 276, 281, 284–88, 301, 302–6, 308; Second Temple, 151, 226–27, 229, 256, 260–61, 270

Persian-Hellenistic period, 15

Persian period, 6, 54, 90, 91, 117, 118

Peter, 41. *See also* Key of Peter

2 Peter, 291

pharaoh: Akhenaton, 97, 99; Hebrew enslavement by, 55; Rameses II, 68–73, 81, 99, 104; Rameses II/Exodus and, 69; Seti II, 99; Sheshonk, 102; Tuthmosis I/II/III, 97

Philip Herod, 194, 197, 204

Philo Judaeus, 5, 170, 205, 228; Jesus, absence of, by, 182; New Testament figures, absence of, by, 173

Photo-Pictures from the Lands of the Bible, Illustrated by Scripture Words (Frith), 131

pilgrimage sites, 32–33; Bethsaida, 150; of Christians/Jews to Jerusalem, 125; David's Tomb, 121; Mary's Well, 298; Mecca/Medina, 125; for women, 186, 188

Pithom, 70; Hebrews building of, 55

Pixner, Bargil (priest), 73, 148, 153

plagues, in Egypt, 25, 55, 81
Pomeroy, Sarah, 189–90
Priestly writer. *See* P, as Priestly writer
"Project Scrolls," 251
Promised Land, 54; Moses/Aaron not allowed in, 61
Prophets, 12, 13
Proverbs, 44, 283
Psalms, 44, 278, 283; on Jerusalem, 123; Midrash on, 289–90; Zion in, 136
Pseudo-Philo period, 193
PT. *See* Palestinian Talmud
Ptolemian families, 152, 204
Ptolemian/Selucid Greek periods, 308
Ptolemy (king), 229, 282

Qumran, 72; bathing process at, 309; burial caves at, 265, 269; cave at, *247*; chronology of excavation of, 278; Dead Sea Scrolls and, 275–81; developing theory of, 275–78; earthquake damage at, 267; End of Days and, 256; excavation of, 248–50, 278, 284–88; geography/climate of, 255–56; during Hellenistic period, 276, 284–88; Latrines of Essenes and, 258–65, *261*; map of, *261*; mystery of, 250–55; Oslo Accords and, 250–51; resident identity, theories for, in, 280–81; secrets of, 257–65; Tomb #1000 at, 271–75; unexpected findings at, 267–71. *See also* John and Carol Merrill Excavations at Qumran; Khirbet Qumran; *Teacher of Righteousness*
Qumran Cemetery, *263*; Bedouin burials at, 274–75, 284; excavation of, 251–53, 256–57; reconstruction of, *293*
Qumran Excavations Project, 253
Rabbinic archaeology, 151
Rabbinic Bible, 5; interpretation of, 22

Rabbinic Judaism movement, 152
Rabbinic literature, 209; on Alexander the Great, 172–73; ancient sources for Jesus in, 169–74; Beruriah in, 214–23; collapsing in, 180; critical study of, 155–56; criticisms of information in, 168–69; destruction of, 168; Jesus of, 165, 167, 174–77, 180; on Jewish incense ceremonies, 236–40; Josephus of, 180; Mishnah and, 153; resurrection of Jesus in, 169, 170; on synagogues, 229; Tannaitic, 170, 174–77
Rabbis, oral traditions writing and, 7
Rameses, city of, 84, 87; Hebrew building of, 55; name meaning of, 57–58
Rameses II (pharaoh), 99, 104; Exodus from Egypt and, 68–73, 81
Rashi: on Beruriah, 222; on incense shovel, 237
"A Reassessment of the Excavations at Qumran" (Magness), 259
Redactor/Editor: collapsing use by, 62, 86; on Exodus from Egypt, 54, 86, 103; Ezra as, 13; of Hebrew Bible, 62; on Moses, 65–67
Red Sea: crossing location of, 98–100; parting of, 55
reductionism, 52
Reeder, Philip, 48, 258, 261
Reed Sea, 79, 87, 98–100, 103, 186
Rehoboam (king), 110, 113; as Solomon's father, 10; succession of, 9
relics, 26–35; Noah's Ark, 26–27; revelation and, 26
relic sites: Christianity and, 27; Jericho as, 31–32; of Jews, 72, 120; Judaism burial sites as, 27; Mary's House, in Loreto, Italy as, 296; of Noah's Ark, 296–97; of Solomon's tomb, 118–23
religious texts, skepticism of, 24–25
revelation, relics and, 26

Revisionist Debate, 35–38, 321
ritual bathing: in Hebrew Bible, 259, 306; in Hellenistic period, 306; in Mikveh bathhouse, 306–11; in Roman period, 306, 308
ritual purity, of Rabbis, 214–15, 260–62, 270
rituals: of incense burning, 227, 233, 240–46; in Karaite temple, 244–45; sacrifices as, 11–12; in synagogue, 241, 243–44; from Temple of Jerusalem, 245
River Nile, Aaron and, 66
Roberts, David, 130
Roddy, Nicolae, 231
Roman bathhouse, 316–20
Roman Catholic Church, 9, 148
Roman Imperial Cult. See Imperial Cult of Rome
Roman Jewish Temple, 33
Roman period, 240, 281; bathhouses in Israel in, 302–6; Mary's Well and, 301; plumbing/sewage systems in, 262–63; Qumran and, 276, 284–88; ritual bathing in, 306, 308
Rosh Hashanah, 19, 236, 243
R writer, Ezra as, 13

sacrifice, 134–35; child, 19; of Isaac, 19–20; ritual, 11–12
Safed, 28, 151
Saint Catherine's Monastery, 89–90
Salome, 197, 204–5
Samson: Midrash on, 27–28; Tomb of, 28
1 Samuel, 14, 100, 101, 111, 113, 115, 194
2 Samuel, 14, 100, 101, 109–10, 111, 112, 137, 194
Santorini, volcanic eruption in, 82, 85
Sarah, 16, 18, 23
Sargon of Akkad, 39; bulrush basket of, 58

Saul (king), 16, 115
Schiffman, Lawrence, 251, 259, 275, 287
scientific method, 14, 24; archaeological argument and, 71–72; archaeology v., 52; geographical argument, 73–74; historical argument and, 71; literary argument and, 71; monumental artifactual argument, 73; scientific reductionism and, 52
scientific theory, for Bible reading, 59–60
Scribe. See Ezra the Priest
Sea of Galilee, 40, 49, 73, 108, 120, 151, 155, 197, 200, 202
Second Revolt against Rome (132-135 CE), 7, 122, 150, 217, 230, 326, 327; Babatha documents and, 209; chronology of, 333–35
Second Temple period, 151, 256, 270; purity rituals in, 260–61; synagogues in, 226–27, 229
Secrets of the Cave of Letters: A Dead Sea Mystery (Freund), 208, 327
Sennacherib (king), of Assyria, 41–42
Septuagint, 113, 283, 307
Sermon on the Mount, of Jesus, 119
Seti II (pharaoh), 99
Seventh Order of the Mishnah, 152–55
Shabbat, incense use at, 236
Sheba (queen), 117
Shechem, 18–19, 28
Sherman Museum, 30; Jewish exhibition at, 126; Siloam inscription copy at, 41
Sheshonk (pharaoh), 102
Shulchan Aruch (Karo), 151
Siloam inscription, 41–42
Sinai Desert, 2, 105; Mount Sinai in, 89
Six Day War, 125, 248
Small, David, 308
Solomon (king), 8, 16, 108, 110, 142, 144; background of, 113; death of,

9, 133; excesses of, 116; Josephus on burial of, 119, 122; Queen of Sheba and, 117; Rehoboam, son of, 10; reign of, 102; relic tomb of, 118–23; Song of Songs/Proverbs/ Ecclesiastes of, 44. *See also* Temple of Solomon

Song of Songs, 44

Son of the Star, Bar Kokhba as, 327–29

Sons of Light (Merrill, J.), 254

Sophronius (patriarch), 139–40

Southern Kingdom, 7; J as writer of, 10; Judah as, 9; tribes of, 10. *See also* J, as Southern Kingdom writer

Speiser, E. A., 17

Steckoll, Salomon, 257, 266

Steles: as commemorative stones, 79–80; Israel, 80–81; Mesha/Moabite, 129

Stratonice, 204

Strickert, Fred, 189, 198, 199–200

synagogue(s): Ben Ezra, 284; Berenice on, 229; Cairo Geniza, 285; Dura-Europos, 239, 240; in Egypt, 226; in Ezekiel, 228; First Revolt against Rome (66-73 CE) and, 230; at Gamla/Herodium/Masada/Migdal, 230; iconography of, 233–36; incense ritual, evidence for, 240–46; Rabbinic literature on, 229; rituals, *241, 243*–44; *Teacher of Righteousness* evidence in Byzantine period, 291–92

Tabernacle, 2, 61–62, 226, 262

Tabor, James, 264

Talmud, 8, 33–34; on ben Abuya, 220; Bomberg edition of, 174; censorship of, 174; Mose's name in, 58. *See also* Babylonian Talmud; Palestinian Talmud

Talmudim, 5, 166; collapsing of parallels in, 64

Tannaitic literature: Jesus, absence of, in, 170, 174–77, 181; Mary/ Miriam's Well in, 314

Teacher of Righteousness, at Qumran, 271, 275, 281–82; identification of, 284–88; in Jewish/Rabbinic tradition, 289–90; literary evidence for *Moreh HaTzedeq* title, 282–84; *Man of Lies* group and, 286–87; in New Testament, 290–91; Schiffman on, 287; as Thanksgiving Hymns/ War Scroll/Temple Scroll author, 281; *Wicked Priest* and, 285–87

Tel Dan Inscription, 36, 117

Tell el-Dab'a, 86; excavations of, 84

Tempest Stele, 80; Ipuwer Papyrus and, 80–82

Temple for Aphrodite, 125

Temple of Dagon, 239; Samson and, 27–28

Temple of Jerusalem, 124–25, 139, 140, 215, 253, 327; destruction of, 7, 11, 21, 22, 102, 150, 219, 226, 236, 308; rituals from, 245; Yavne for refugees from, 249

Temple of Karnak, 69

Temple Mount, 33, 118–19, 127, 136, 138, 140, 141, 143, 332

Temple Mount Al Aqsa Mosque, forged enlargements in, 29

Temple of Solomon, 29, 113, 140, 239; pomegranate artifact as forgery in, 29

Temple of the Tabernacle, 136

Temple Scroll, 264, 278

Ten Commandments. *See* Law of Mount Sinai

Ten Tribes of Israel, Assyrian Exile of, 10–11

Tertullian literature, 176; on incense, 242

tetragrammaton: of J writer, 20; YHVH name of God, 12

Thebes, kings of, 83–84
Third Period of Biblical Writing: 722
    BCE-586 BCE, 10–12
Tiberias, 154, 202; Roman bath in,
    316; tomb of Matriarchs at, 188
Tiberius Alexander, 206, 249
Tiberius Caesar, 196, 198, 199, 205
1 Timothy, 291
Titus, 249, 291; Berenice as mistress to,
    207–8
Tomb #1000, 292; at Qumran, 271–75
Torah, 9; assault on, 14; Jerusalem,
    absence of, in, 134; P writing of, 66
Tosefta, 178–79, 215, 228; on graves,
    268; Jesus, absence of, in, 181
Tosephta. See Tosefta
Tov, Emanuel, 259, 276
Tuthmosis I/II/III (pharaoh), 97
HaTzedeq, Moreh, literary evidence for
    Teacher of Righteousness title, 282–84

UN. See United Nations, on Jerusalem
Understanding Seeking Faith (Neusner),
    156
United Kingdom: 1000 BCE-922
    BCE: as First Period of Biblical
    Writing, 8; Northern Tribes split
    from, 9; wealth/optimism in, 8
United Kingdom of David, 112, 133
United Kingdom in Jerusalem, 132
United Nations (UN), on Jerusalem,
    125
University of Hartford, 49;
    Geophysical Survey Project of,
    93; Jerusalem exhibition at, 126;
    Sherman Museum at, 30, 41
Ur of Chaldeans, 16, 70
Ussishkin, David, 187

VanderKam, James, 259
Vatican, Key of Peter and, 148
de Vaux, Roland, 72, 250, 258, 265–66,
    274, 278

Vestal Virgins, 318–19
Via Maris highway, 110, 133
Virgin Birth, 316–20

Wailing Wall, 107. See also Western
    Wall
Walker, Dennis, 272
Warren, Charles, 127, 153
War Scroll, 264
Washington, George, 33, 56, 69
West Bank/Gaza, Samson/Joseph
    burial tombs and, 28–29
Western Wall, 33, 123, 127, 131, 145;
    CPR data collection at, 130
Who Wrote the Bible? (Friedman), 6, 8
"Wilderness Encampment and the
    Miraculous Well of Be'er" mural,
    240
Wilson, Charles, 127
Wissenschaft des Judentums literature,
    153, 166, 168
women: Babatha, 184, 189, 208–14;
    Bathsheba, 113, 116, 191; Bathshua,
    191; Berenice, 189, 202–8, 229,
    249; Beruriah, 189, 214–23; Bible
    and, 184–89; Deborah (judge),
    79, 188, 192–93; in Egypt, 187;
    goddess and, 187; in Hebrew
    Bible, 190–93; household artifacts
    of, 185; in Iron Age, 185, 186;
    Jezebel excavation, 187–88; J/P on,
    190–92; Livia Julia, 183, 189, 194–
    201, 249; Livia Julia Temple, 146;
    Maachah, 109, 194; Mary, 5, 23,
    311–12, 319–20; Mary Magdalene,
    3, 158; Mary's House, 296; Mary's
    Well, 295, 297–302, 311–16, 321;
    Miriam, 186, 192; Miriam's Well,
    314–16, 320; pilgrimage sites
    for, 188; relic tombs/pilgrimage
    sites of, 186; religion of, 185–86;
    Salome, 197, 204–5; Stratonice,
    204; in Tomb #1000, at Qumran,

271, 273. *See also* Matriarchs; Vestal Virgins; Virgin Birth

World War I (WWI), 71; Jerusalem and, 125

World War II (WWII), 115; historical Jesus after, 167; Jerusalem and, 125; theology/archeology and, 35

WWI. *See* World War I

WWII. *See* World War II

Yadin, Yigael, 72, 208, 229, 234, 241, 309; Cave of Letters excavation by, 184, 209, 248, 251; as Maximalist, 330

Yardeni, A., 208

Yavne, 248–50

Yavne Excavations Project, 249

Yeshu HaNotzri (Klauzner), 167

YHVH, P writer and, 12

Yom Kippur, 12, 64, 215, 232–33, 236, 243

ben Zadok, Eleazar (rabbi), 238

ben Zakkai, Yohanan (rabbi), 152, 207–8, 249

Zealots, 230

Zeitlin, Solomon, 166

Zeus Aelia Capitalina, 141

Zias, Joe, 274

Zion, 136–37, 290. *See also* Mount Zion

Zionism, 125, 131

Zohar (Book of Splendor), 43–44, 166